SOLDIERING FOR PEACE

by
Major General Carl von Horn

DAVID McKAY COMPANY, INC.
New York

SOLDIERING FOR PEACE

First American Edition 1967

Library of Congress Catalog Card Number: 67-17116

MANUFACTURED IN THE UNITED STATES OF AMERICA

VAN REES PRESS • NEW YORK

CONTENTS

ajor General Carl von Horn

Soldiering for Peace

e stirring personal history
a dedicated Commander of
e United Nations peace-
eping forces in Pal-
tine, the Congo,
d Yemen, and his
uggles against
litical intrigue,
reaucratic fum-
ng, and lack of
oney and men

and I wish to give food for thought, hoping to spare future commanders of international peacekeeping missions unnecessary frustrations. If any soldiers so employed can be spared hardships not entirely due to a "Commander without (or even with) field experience," this book has achieved its aim.

I have not submitted my manuscript to the Secretary General of the United Nations because it would be too much to expect his official approval and also embarrassing to ask for censorship. In the long run, however, the book could perhaps win for him indirectly wider support for any proposals for improving the means of UN peacekeeping.

An original draft chapter with "Conclusions" was deleted when I read several recently published books in which better pens than mine suggest improvements warranted by my own experience but which probably are easier to accept if not directly suggested by me. Many of my views will be criticized. To those who, for some reason or other, challenge my veracity I stress the point of my relating only my impressions and I simply ask: Would I ever have been retained in UN employment beyond the initial term of two years if these impressions always had been wrong?

I should like to acknowledge the literary and editorial advice of Mr. James Kinross.

March 1966

Carl von Horn

PREFACE

INNATE taciturnity makes me loath to comment in public. Disappointed journalists in Sweden used to say that "In comparison with C.v.H. the oyster is a garrulous creature." Their colleagues of the world press found reason to subscribe to this opinion on many occasions in later years. I have always consistently turned down numerous calls to write about my experiences of international service. This book, being a reconsideration of a previously irrevocable decision, therefore requires an explanation as it mainly deals with my service with the United Nations.

I was a firm believer in the United Nations—and I still am, though nowadays painfully aware of the need, long overdue, of an agonized reappraisal of the whole sector of Peacekeeping Operations, where many hard-won lessons seem forgotten. This need applies both to the political taskmasters of its member states and the executive secretariat. There seems to have developed a somewhat superstitious belief in the magic of a mere "UN presence." Soldiers and their political masters seldom see eye to eye on the aims and tasks, and definitely not on the means and methods in the field, where soldiering and politics meet on more or less ill-defined and impossible missions. The political decisions easily become tantamount to self-deception, and the soldiers are left in the lurch even before financing the operation becomes the nightmare of the Organization.

Every Commander has dual loyalties to his superior master and to the troops for whom he is responsible. Where these loyalties contravene the natural priority of the superior one has a limit that cannot be passed without betraying the troops. I was facing that limit at last and resigned accordingly. This is the story of "Why and How" with no intention of vindicating myself. I strongly feel a lasting obligation to those who served under me,

Photograph by Esselte Foto

Major General Carl von Horn greets Dag Hammarskjöld at Léopoldville Airport, August 1960. Behind author is Captain Bent S. Fredriksen of the Danish Army, his A.D.C., and behind Bent S. Fredriksen stands Paul Berthoud of Switzerland, legal adviser to O.N.U.C. (Operation des Nations Unis au Congo).

$6.95

SOLDIERING FOR PEACE

by Major General Carl von Horn

16 Pages of Photographs

General Carl von Horn's outspoken narrative of his experiences as a commander of United Nations peace-keeping forces has made headlines throughout the world since its publication in Sweden last fall.

News stories carried on the front pages of newspapers in Europe and America cited von Horn's accusation that the UN was "riddled with espionage and corruption," and that UN administrators had "foggy ideas about reality" and "became like a swarm of angry bees when their hive was threatened with criticism."

His first duty tour with the UN was as Chief of Staff to the United Nations Truce Supervisory Organization in Palestine, where all his diplomacy and generalship were required to meet the crises of Israeli-Arab border clashes, espionage, and threats on his life.

From Israel, von Horn was shifted to the Congo, where he was charged with the responsibility of bringing order out of the military and political chaos involving the warring factions of Lumumba, Tshombe, Mobutu, and Kasavubu.

Later U Thant sent von Horn to Yemen to cope with the problem of keeping the Saudi Arabians and the Egyptians from each other's throats, as these arch rivals supported opposing factions in the battle for control of the country.

In this volume von Horn assesses the role of the UN in world affairs and its strengths and weaknesses as an international peace-keeping organization. He also provides vivid profiles of top officials in the UN with whom he worked—men like Dag Hammarskjöld, Ralph Bunche, Andrew Cordier, David Vaughan, U Thant, and many others.

Beyond the general's personal experiences—which are always colorful—is the sense of vision and dedication that shines through this book. It is an essential spirituality of feeling and belief that he shared with Dag Hammarskjöld, who was his good friend.

In the final analysis, though *Soldiering for Peace* will undoubtedly be one of the most controversial books on world affairs to be published in this decade, it is also a living legacy of a man who gave the best years of his life to the cause of international peace.

Chapter One

A MILITARY CAREER

I HARDLY recommend international soldiering as a tranquil occupation. Often during the frustrating days in Jerusalem and Sanaa or in steamy heat of Léopoldville, I used to find myself thinking nostalgically of the quiet and unbroken calm of the rich fields and wooded country of the Swedish province of Scania where I was born.

Not that Scania, now the granary of Sweden, has not been racked with troubles. But that was in 1658 when its dour, obstinate, slow and self-conscious people bitterly resented being wrenched away from Denmark, and made their reaction plain in so redoubtable a fashion that the King of Sweden was driven to consider deporting the whole population to Holland.

Oddly enough, a Dutchman had settled in Sweden only fifty years before. His name was Paridon van Hoorn, and his privileges as the result of heavy financial contributions to the armies of Gustavus Adolphus during the Thirty Years' War were considerable when he arrived from Amsterdam to make his home in this country of lakes and forests.

Since Paridon was my ancestor, I can claim international stock as his family had come originally from a long established line in Germany. Once settled in Sweden, however, the financial talent that had always distinguished the van Hoorns seemed to grow weaker as thrifty Dutch blood became diluted through marriage after marriage into Swedish families. Before long there were few men of affairs, but an ever-increasing number of devoted but impecunious sailors, soldiers, and civil servants.

Consequently, it was natural almost exactly a hundred years ago that my grandfather—Henning—should enroll as a cadet at the Royal Swedish Military College. What was a little out of the ordinary was that he somehow or other contrived to stay there no less than eight years before suddenly disappearing from this august establishment.

On inquiry, it was discovered he had made his way to join the Danish Army, then engaged in a desperate struggle. The fighting raged in the old Danish Duchy of Slesvig, at the base of the Jutland Peninsula, which had long been a bone of contention between the Danes and the Prussians under the headstrong and determined influence of Bismarck. Since mere Danish gallantry was not proof against the Prussian war machine, the outcome was a foregone conclusion, and before long my grandfather was taken prisoner at the Battle of Dybbol; a precarious position since it was rumored that all non-Danish prisoners were destined for a firing squad.

Fortunately the fate of prisoners in those days was still determined by a chivalrous outlook which was not then lacking among the Prussians. So Grandfather emerged from captivity to discover himself in trouble on his belated return to his homeland. Whatever explanation he put up must have sounded convincing; King Charles XV took a personal interest in him and granted him a commission as a second lieutenant in the Second (Goeta) Footguards.

This was his only taste of war. Not long afterward, he married Baroness Florence Bonde, the daughter of a Swedish nobleman, retired from the army, and settled down to a life of doing absolutely nothing. Whether he could afford this idyllic existence amid horses, dogs, and guns is debatable. What rapidly became apparent was that he had acquired a remarkable mother-in-law, whose character was to exert a profound effect on succeeding generations of von Horns, as we were now known. For Baroness Florence Bonde was Irish, the daughter of Sir Richard Robinson of Rokeby and the granddaughter of the Earl of Mountcashel. Whether this Irish blood has contributed to my proverbially hasty temper (as some of my more critical friends hasten to claim) I rather doubt; but I do suspect it has left me with an innate tendency to be a bit of a rebel.

My father, the second son of this marriage, became rather a worry to his parents. As he grew older it was slowly and reluctantly borne in on them that whatever other family gifts he might have inherited, brainpower was not notably apparent. As he developed into a tall and good-looking young fellow (whose photograph today reminds one of the Victorian ideal of a dashing guardsman), his total lack of interest in anything unconnected with shooting and horses and his carefree disregard for the future are said to have elicited a heartfelt sigh beneath the parental roof: "Poor Carl is so stupid there is nothing for it but the Church or the Horse Guards."

Possibly in fairness to Our Lord, he chose the latter. But once settled down, his extremely expensive tastes soon dictated an early marriage on a sound financial basis. His choice (or rather I strongly suspect it was hers) was a beautiful and patrician-looking lady called Martha Stjernsward, the only sister amid a brood of six brothers in an old and landed Scanian family. Since the Stjernswards had strong linear connections in France, Courland (which was later to become Latvia), and Germany, our family tree blossomed with more international foliage. A more marked inheritance was a family characteristic which my mother passed on to me: a deep-rooted talent for making one's own decisions and sticking to them in the teeth of the fiercest family opposition.

I was born on July 15, 1903, and have often wondered whether my love of travel developed as a result of my first journey abroad a month later, when cocooned in shawls and blankets, I arrived to join my family in Hanover where my father had been seconded as a student at the German Imperial School of Equitation.

I believe his horsemanship left a lasting impression on the Germans, just as Germany left a lasting impression on me because it was at this tender age I began my career as a linguist. Although I can remember nothing about the two years we spent there, German has always been my "first" language although there was little call for it during the years following our return, which we spent happily in a house appropriately called Horn close to the

Swedish Equitation School at Stroemsholm in Vaestmanland. Although I was brought up within trumpet call of the stables, I never shared my father's consuming passion for horses. Somehow the family obsession seemed to pass me by. Fortunately I was blissfully unaware of the fate in store for me.

I developed into a rather shy and sensitive boy, more inclined to the intellectual than the athletic. At school, during four miserably hungry years caused by the food shortages of the First World War raging outside Sweden, I became an avid reader. Geography was my first great interest. But I had always been good at languages, and soon was devouring English novels, histories, and biographies, until I discovered my real passion. After that when we were not out quartering the surrounding forest in search of something to supplement our frugal rations, there was seldom a moment when I was not reading British military history.

There was soon little I did not know about the British Army, its customs, traditions, and record of hard-fought campaigns in every climate and quarter of the globe. This was considered highly unusual at school, perhaps even a little unnatural. Sweden had looked to Germany and France for centuries as the fount of cultural and military inspiration; my teachers and schoolmates were puzzled and sometimes sarcastic over my knowledge of British military history and my increasing vocabulary of English slang.

This early passion has subsequently stood me in excellent stead. Since those days, I have never missed a chance of adding unusual and often lurid slang in a dozen other languages to my original English stock. In the middle of tricky negotiations with Germans, Russians, Britons, and the polyglot nationalities within a United Nations command, I have been delighted to discover that an apparently hopeless stalemate can be resolved by recourse to a little down-to-earth language in one's opposite number's coarser vernacular. Nothing amuses me more than the look of blank astonishment a few pungent words can produce. Properly timed, I have found this method has a remarkable tendency to get things moving.

In a way it was almost inevitable I should go into the army. I sometimes wonder whether I made the right choice, but at that time there seemed a highly valid reason: my mother had set her mind firmly against the idea. Perhaps this sounds ridiculous, but so strongly ingrained is this family trait of flying in the face of parental opposition that her strong disapproval left me no possible alternative. Of course, there were other factors; a financial crisis had ended my dreams of a freer life at a university. Subconsciously, too, I must have been impelled by a desire to prove myself, to escape from the world of books into the hard, challenging atmosphere I expected the army to provide.

And then, too, the atmosphere at home kept me in a constantly simmering state of rebellion. At seventeen I may have been oversensitive, but it hardly struck me that my father's attitude was conducive to inculcating the self-confidence I knew I was lacking. I can still recall with a shudder one of his less pleasing forms of entertainment. Regularly after dinner when the guests had withdrawn to his smoking room, I used to be dispatched round these "horsy" gentlemen, bearing a box of cigars, accompanied by a running commentary in the best horse-coping tradition on my unusually heavy knees, fleshy calves, and ample behind.

Forewarned, I must have displayed an astonishing lack of judgment when in June, 1921, I followed Father into his own regiment. It was the biggest mistake of my life; and once I had joined this crack regiment of Horse Guards, and wore its dashing uniform of blue and sliver, topped by burnished silver helmet, we both had plenty of time for regrets.

Not that life was without its compensations. Although discipline and etiquette were extremely strict, we were a free and easy lot, and if, when I joined in the twenties, the Troop Commander failed to turn out at the appointed time on early morning parade, his Troop Sergeant (aware the poor fellow was probably sleeping off a night's celebrations) simply put the men through their drill secure in the knowledge that the Squadron Commander was most unlikely to put in an appearance until either the culprit had made a belated return or the parade was over. One of my brother officers was so consistently late that our senior subaltern, who kept an eagle eye on any outré behavior, actually hired a servant at the offender's expense to shake him awake each morning and insure he turned up at the right moment.

Life in a Household Regiment has its drawbacks and disadvantages. On the one hand there is the real pride of serving in a crack unit where routine runs almost on oiled wheels. There is, too, a sense of "belonging," of being a member of a unique family inside which officers and men are probably more distant from each other and yet more closely knit in regimental *esprit de corps* than in any other unit in the army. If one has a taste for ceremony, there is enough to keep the most ardent traditionalist happy for a lifetime; standing guard in polished top boots and burnished helmet and riding at the head of one's troop in front of visiting state coaches while a troop of the Life Dragoons bring up the rear. But inevitably, once the trumpet calls are muted, the fluttering standards returned to their racks, the horses led away to be rubbed down and fed, there comes a sense of boredom and frustration.

Although I was still too young to suspect that this was not real soldiering, and was very happy with my troop, which I found an ideal command, I was soon plunged into family ramifications within the regiment and became the innocent target for an explosion of spleen between two dominating personalities: my father and his brother-in-law, Count Reinhold von Rosen, a highly strung, intolerant, hasty-tempered individual, short in stature but possessed of ample means. The relationhip between these two reminded me of the love-hate between Cardigan and Lucan. Inevitably, I suffered from their vendetta. For by the time I had been commissioned into my uncle's old troop, he had become Inspector General of Cavalry, where normal regimental drill soon took a poor second to his own fads and fancies. One spring, in the course of an inspection lasting three days, he descended on my troop in stables.

I was delighted with my men's smart turnout, their meticulous stable drill, the intelligent way they answered questions.

Not so the old man. His cheeks purpled, his bantam chest swelled.

"Who is responsible for this?" he roared.

There was dead silence; not an officer in his entourage dared explain that "this" was first-rate stable drill in scrupulous accord with the cavalry manual, even though it did not happen to fit in with the general's private fads.

Since no one else volunteered a word, I snapped crisply: "I am, sir."

"You!" Beneath its outsize cap, the face became more purple. And now his half-pint frame almost exploded in rage, doubtless ignited by the indignity of having to look *up* to his erring nephew in order to dress him down. It was a tirade to remember, ending with choking fury: "And this has to happen not only in my own old regiment, but in my former squadron and my own old troop!"

I bore this stoically. I needed to. At the end of the three-day inspection my colonel was informed that his regiment was deteriorating sharply, thanks to the shortcomings of young Mr. von Horn.

Uncle and I were to collide again the following year (it was only when the old man retired that he and my father became the best of friends). Meantime, I trod warily, listening with a degree of skepticism to my senior's glowing accounts of the next stage in my military career; one which, I was assured, would be "the happiest year of my life." There was no escape; every cavalry subaltern had to spend the second year of his service at the School of Equitation. So before long I became a reluctant pupil at this former Royal Palace, set in the most attractive surroundings of lush meadows, downs, and forest-fringed lakes.

One could see immediately on arrival that Stromsholm was a horseman's idea of Heaven; there was even a renowned royal stud attached to the establishment. Within a few hours of arriving, I discovered with gloomy foreboding that the Commandant and most of his instructors were all former pupils or colleagues of Father's; even the stable staff had been there in his time, and to a man were anticipating an elegant, accomplished equestrian chip off the old block.

Unfortunately, I was no centaur. I can still remember the look on the face of Harald, my personal groom, when this horrible truth dawned upon him. It was a pained expression (restrained at first in deference to my father), with which I was to become progressively familiar during the massive endurance test ahead—month after month of rigorous training when we rode five or six different mounts a day: charges, remounts, race horses, and stallions, the latter so well versed in the intricacies of advanced dressage that they virtually instructed the pupils on their backs.

Every day brought some new penance; constant sessions in the covered riding school, gallops across the downs, endless successions of fences looming up as I approached with no stirrups. The tempo never relaxed; dressage, mounted sword drill, night cross-country rides and drag hunts twice a week when we rode without stirrups for the first three months left us so weary that the occasional lecture on tactics found most of us aleep within the first five minutes.

Our "recreations" followed the normal pattern of those times: drinking, cards, and the occasional amorous adventure. Although I was fond of the grape and began my apprenticeship in the art of holding one's drink like a gentleman, I had absolutely no card sense and very seldom played.

It was not surprising, therefore, that a spring evening should find me abandoning my friends to their cards after dinner. Outside the mess, I borrowed my roommate's car and set off to spend my time to better purpose in the company of a charming young lady.

It was almost dawn by the time that I returned. Song birds were heralding a glow in the east as I parked the car and walked toward my quarters.

The first sight that met my eye was my favorite armchair (vital for resting weary limbs) smashed on the ground outside my window.

Indoors, there were more signs of trouble. Although from his conspicuous snores my roommate appeared to be asleep, there were sounds indicating the presence of interested watchers. Looking cautiously around, I discovered a king-size windowpane had been inserted ready to receive me as I leaped between the sheets.

I took position, poised for a mighty spring into bed. My ruse worked. At the last minute, my roommate sat up, a warning cry on his lips.

I regret to say the whole business riled me so acutely that I drew my revolver, put a couple of shots close beside his feet and emptied the remainder of the magazine in a neat row of bullet holes in the wall above his head.

Fortunately there were no casualties. Since that day I've firmly discouraged young officers from fooling about with loaded weapons in their quarters.

The year I spent in this equestrian "paradise" left such a lasting impression that even now I can recall my aching thigh muscles, the smell of horse sweat and saddle soap, the acrid tang of the stables, the relentless zeal with which my instructors made me aware that I was not the brightest star in the establishment. No pains were spared to make it crystal-clear that I would never make a "horseman" in the sense that noble word was understood there.

All this must have been a bitter disappointment for my poor father. For the stories that came back through his old cronies must have been scathing: a poor seat, rubber legs, an iron hand and even, it was hinted, a poor heart. Occasionally I had to admit this latter failing myself, although I gradually learned to master it through sheer will power despite frequent periods laid up with injured knees and spells of concussion. On one occasion—when I was on "the limping squad"—Uncle crossed my path again. Although I was excused from riding lessons, I was not allowed off the premises in duty hours. But being madly in love, I ignored this rule, got a lift in a friend's car, and disappeared to Stockholm to spend an enchanting time with an equally enchanting girl.

Returning by train, I was unlucky enough to be spotted by the Commandant's wife and shortly found myself under eight days' open arrest, confined to my room every moment I was off duty.

Uncle chose this moment to descend on the school. The behavior of my steed on parade (like me, it distrusted *all* senior officers by now) aroused his ire, and I was delighted that my punishment gave me a cast-iron excuse for not turning up at the formal dinner which concluded his inspection.

Unfortunately my absence was noted. The mess steward arrived to fetch me. Climbing hastily into my mess kit, I reported to Uncle, who, in the place of honor at a long and beautifully laid table, glared at me in a far from friendly manner.

I clicked my heels. "Mr. von Horn under open arrest but present, sir."

This announcement was greeted with gales of malicious hilarity by the assembled company, who were all "well away."

Except Uncle, who was quite sufficiently under control to bombard me with a string of embarrassing personal questions laced with nasty remarks.

More laughter. At last I was permitted to retire ignominiously back to my open arrest, fuming with rage. It was, I felt, unfair that propriety had not allowed me to remind Uncle that he too had once abandoned his post. As a young subaltern and a picket officer of the Horse Guards *he* had absconded to the Riviera with a beautiful actress, the wife of an officer in a rival regiment.

As the weeks went on in this small enclosed world, horsemanship seemed to have become an end in itself. The fact that I did very well in strictly military training, such as day and night scouting and swimming in full field kit with my long-suffering mount, cut no ice with my dedicated, bandy-legged instructors. As up till now I had never succeeded in winning a local steeplechase, I began to doubt whether I would ever be allowed to pass out. Finally my gallant little charger "Dixie" and I just made it, but I still suspect the only reason I was passed was because the staff could not bring themselves to face enduring me for another year.

Needless to say, my reputation had preceded me back to the regiment. Probably as a result, I was appointed signals officer on my return. But when I demanded technical training to make me suitable for this "newfangled" job, I was told it was out of the question; all my spare time would be spent riding and training remounts.

During the next few years I began to grow increasingly irked because my seniors seemed unable to comprehend that a "good seat" was not the sole requisite to a military career. The good moments, maneuvers, training recruits under hard conditions (what I suppose would be called Adventure Training these days), country life, good friends, only temporarily disguised the realization that I was thoroughly restless.

At this time, I was six feet tall, dark-haired, weighing about 170 pounds, and hiding an unhappy soul behind a mask of artificial sternness.

Why I should have been unhappy, I am not quite sure, for in 1925 I had married the charming Maud von Otter and had every reason for contentment. Maud was a beautiful creature, blond, slender, and very gay. She was a passionate horsewoman, a very good sport, and a delightful companion. I was very much in love. And perhaps because I sensed my parents would object for no other reason than that this was something I really wanted to do, I married her without their consent. Unwisely, too, I further neglected to ask my colonel's permission. Although he took this well enough, I was soon in hot water again for failing to recommend for commissions several young gentlemen cadets who had been attached to us. I knew I was right. Not one of them had the caliber for officer material.

Unfortunately they were all related to high court officials, and I was summoned to the colonel, who seemed pained. I can still see the look on that charming and kindly face as he murmured: "My dear von Horn. I must admit to doubting whether the future holds a Grand Cross in store for you."

Perhaps this was the deciding factor. I had had enough of this stifling world. I was weary of ceremonial drill, of mounting guards and sitting all day with nothing to do while my guardsmen stood like statues in the palace courtyard, ears cocked for the welcome sound of top boots tramping to their relief. Even the glamor of state occasions had lost its charm. And then in the mess there was always the unending chatter: jumping seats, Italian hunting, points of breeding; only actual soldiering was seldom mentioned.

Sheer frustration drove me to take the entrance examination for the Staff College, and it was undoubtedly this powerful drive that got me through this highly competitive test at such an early age. When I arrived there in 1928, I discovered an atmosphere totally different from the regiment, a tough and dedicated existence which reminded me of some sort of semimonastic community.

I discovered that Swedish staff training, which had been modeled on that of the Imperial German Army, was extremely thorough and efficient. From time to time the curriculum was interrupted by short secondments to artillery or engineer units, but before long we were back in our lecture rooms working at a pace on problems and set exercises that left us in no doubt that the final passing examination would test our abilities to the limit.

For two years I enjoyed this hard work; it seemed to be a

challenge where I could show that, though I had been an abject failure as a horseman, I could at least achieve success through using my brains. And when I emerged succesfully in 1930 and became an apprentice general staff officer, I discovered that I was now on the verge of being admitted to a small selective corps.

One did not qualify for the honor of wearing broad yellow staff stripes down the sides of one's uniform trousers right away. For two years, I was to remain learning my apprenticeship first in the Military Science Section, then in the Movements and later in the Operations directorates, and it was not until 1934 that I emerged as a fully fledged captain in the general staff corps.

A year later, I was seconded for technical training to the Defense Directorate of the State Railway Board. And here, I rediscovered a world that had fascinated me ever since I had been allowed to drive the train on the private light railway on my grandmother's estate. From boyhood I had been a fervent model railway fan, and now I was plunged into the real thing, starting off with a full year learning the business the hard way.

I began as an assistant porter and worked my way up through a number of jobs to the elevated rank of sleeping car attendant. From here, I progressed toward the real aristocracy of the rail fraternity, being allowed to board the footplate as a stoker, and eventually (after a tough apprenticeship shoveling coal) achieved the peak of my ambition and took over the controls.

Certain vivid memories stand out: firing an engine up a steep gradient in the depths of winter with the heat from the boiler roasting one's face while an icy wind blowing into the cab turned one's ears into what certainly felt like pillars of ice; long nights amid the reverberating clang of buffers in a lonely marshaling yard when one often had to run like a deer to escape being cut in two by rogue freight cars rolling silently down from the hump. Here, occasionally pondering on the recent fate of the shunter whose job I had taken over after he had been killed on the rails, I came to respect the judgment that goes to making up freight trains. I also learned a great deal about the highly individual tastes of towns from the loading bills on the cars.

One remote branch-line station, which served a lumber camp and a mining town, especially caught my imagination; the only freight I saw loaded into cars destined there was kegs of snuff and opulent-looking radios. I came to have visions of those miners and lumberjacks taking great fistfuls of snuff while they listened to the latest radio programs from Stockholm, London, or New York.

In 1936 I returned to a world of plans, charts, and graphs in my new job as Staff Captain in the Movements Directorate. I brought with me a lasting affection for railwaymen, who struck me as the salt of the earth, and they had taught me a lesson I have never forgotten: that timetables have about as much value as toilet paper unless the planner realizes he is dealing with men and machines whose limits and capacities must be understood and assessed from hard experience. It is no good asking for the impossible if it *is* impossible; the only result is likely to be chaos.

As a rail-movement specialist I was soon plunged into incessant work on plans to move our mobilized forces into defensive positions in the event of an outbreak of war. Even when I first arrived, the international situation had become so ominous that often we would work straight through the night after a hard day. Time was running out.

We were aware that German rearmament would reach its peak in September 1939. Night after night the German radio was broadcasting an increasingly raucous chorus of hysterical *"Sieg Heils"* and reiterating demands for the return of the Danzig Free State *"ins Reich,"* which made the fate of Poland appear to hang dangerously in the balance.

The Civil War in Spain did not seem to have opened the eyes of the European democracies, whose labor parties took refuge behind an excessive trust in the "system of collective security" which gave them an excuse for openly rejecting any proposals to improve or build up national defense.

In France the fifty Communist members of the Chamber and the strong, Communist-dominated trade unions openly fought every effort to speed up defense preparations, thus paving the way for the coming defeat. In England it seemed that the administrators were playing into the hands of the enemy, and anniversaries (such as King George V's jubilee) were celebrated with organized displays of Britain's weakness at sea and on land, notwithstanding the fact that the RAF bomb stock was mainly Great War vintage.

The predominant attitude of Americans was "Let Europe settle its own problems," though the able and far-seeing Ambassador Bullitt had reported his conviction that a European conflict would threaten the United States.

My first staff training had coincided with the rise of Nazism in Germany, and the *Machtübernahme* of January 1933 and the July purges, which had followed in 1934, had filled us with a deep distaste and apprehension. From this time onward, each succeeding year had seemed to bring war closer. From afar, we had seen the reoccupation of the Rhineland, the occupation of Austria and Czechoslovakia, and the planes, tanks, and artillery "exercising" in the Civil War in Spain. Now we were forced to watch the final touches being put to the German war machine, which impelled our reluctant professional respect, but filled us with foreboding.

Sweden had a long-established tradition of neutrality, but we felt certain that, were this to hinder the Nazis schemes for *Lebensraum,* it would count for less than the traditional scrap of paper. Nor were we in any great shape to defend ourselves. Ever since 1926, heavy cuts in establishment had reduced our armed forces to a nadir of defensive strength. Even now there was still no attempt to build up our forces. A succession of Labor governments remained deaf to all warnings. And although the armed services were determined to fight should we find ourselves attacked, the haunting question was invariably "With what?"

This uncomfortable knowledge made it all the more vital to finalize the railway war plans on which the strategic backbone of the country's defense would rest. Our army might be under strength, our equipment hopelessly outdated, but at least we could insure that both were in the right places should the worst come to the worst.

In this atmosphere of growing tension, which heightened in 1938 and reached an ever-increasing tempo as the fateful year of 1939 wore on, I virtually lived, ate, but seldom slept amid mountains of files and intricate railway graphs, charts, and reports in the Directorate. We were a small, dedicated band of railway planners, fortunate in being under the direction of a succession of senior officers whose foresight was to stand the nation in excellent stead. Our plans were designed to meet two eventualities: attacks from the south (where the Germans might come) and the east (Finland was to show how right we were to look on the Soviet Union as a potential aggressor). These two major schemes meant month after month of complicated planning to insure a flexible system of switching the Swedish rail network onto a war footing without bringing civilian and industrial traffic to a grinding halt.

Throughout those last months of peace in 1939, this demanding and unceasing task never let up or allowed me a moment in which I could be with my family. Ironically, the vigor and determination with which I threw myself into this exacting work were destined to contribute to the break-up of my first marriage. It was, in truth, to be a wartime story without an actual war—long periods away from home, long months which Maud spent staying with her parents or relatives, feeling more and more neglected. It was to be a drifting rather than a parting, sad, but familiar to so many others who look back on those years.

But at that time it seemed only the present which mattered; over all our work inside the Directorate loomed two dominant forebodings: the knowledge that time was fast running out, and a suspicion that when war came, political factors might prevent us from putting our carefully worked-out war plan into operation.

Chapter Two

THE SWEDISH STATE RAILWAY BOARD

On a September morning in 1939, soon after the news of Germany's attack on Poland had come through, six of us sat around the radio in our office at the Movements Directorate in GHQ in Stockholm, listening to our Prime Minister—Per Albin Hansson—broadcasting to the nation.

We were too well placed not to know the true state of affairs behind his trenchant assurances that the Swedish armed forces were adequately prepared to withstand a similar onslaught from Germany or Russia; the complicated plans we had just completed left us in no doubt that the units we were now ready to move into defensive positions on our extensive and exposed frontiers were totally inadequate to withstand an attack on the German "blitz-kreig" pattern, which at this very minute was sending the Polish armies reeling hundreds of miles back from strong frontier positions.

Were Sweden ever to be attacked, we knew how futile it would be to look to the West for support. The French were sitting passively behind their Maginot Line. The British Army was only now mobilizing. And both would have to face German superiority in training, equipment, perhaps most of all in leadership. As for ourselves, we were so unprepared that the Prime Minister's assurances sounded ludicrous. We had always had to rely on a cadre army, with a core of regulars to train conscripts and provide a framework on which divisions could be built up in times of emergency, but even so our requirements had been invariably cut to the bone.

After Munich, our Chief of the Defense Staff had urged the Government to put Swedish armaments factories on a wartime footing, but his advice had been disregarded and only a trickle of light tanks and new field and antiaircraft artillery had been reaching our understrength units from the Bofors factories while a tightfisted Treasury had limited the state factory at Eskilstuna to turning out pathetically small quantities of small arms and light machine guns.

Our army had been cut down to five divisions backed by a number of ancillary units, and grouped into two army corps. Its total strength was 372,000 men, of whom only 217,000 were fighting troops, much of whose training had been done with dummy guns and flags. Even these were paper figures until the reserves were fully mobilized. Our Air Force, whose planes had had to be imported from Germany and England, consisted of five wings of fighters and bombers; a total of 106 planes incapable of providing air cover for the army, let alone our cities, against the sort of aerial bombardments battering the Poles to destruction only a few flying hours away. Our only saving grace was the Navy, which, although short of oil, gasoline, and ammunition, was still a force to be reckoned with in the Baltic.

There was no miraculous wand to be waved, no political formula that would transform our armed forces overnight. If we were ever to be in a position to stand on our own feet, a long, hard period of rearmament lay before us. And in the days that followed the Polish collapse we scarcely had a chance to begin to come to grips with the problem before desperate appeals for arms, ammunition, and supplies began to pour in from the Finns, who were staggering under an unprovoked Soviet attack.

Just when our armament factories were beginning to turn over to full war production and our depots were turning conscripts and reservists into trained soldiers, a great surge of national sympathy for the hard-pressed Finns left us no alternative but to send them all the arms and equipment we could spare while the Government gave its tacit blessing to the departure of large numbers of privately raised troops whose adventurous spirit and initiative we could have put to good use in our own units.

At the Directorate we soon became aware of secret liaison visits heralding the transit of French and British arms and equipment. We knew, too, that these had been preceded by Allied requests to allow them to send an expeditionary force across Sweden to help the Finns.

A firm refusal in line with Sweden's traditional policy of neutrality had been badly received, and the negotiations now going on over arms and equipment gave us the inescapable impression the Western Allies had little conception of the times and distances involved. We ourselves were only too aware of them and alive to the fact that the gallant stand the Finns were putting up could not be prolonged indefinitely.

We recommended the quickest rail route, which lay north between Narvik and the Finnish town of Tornio at the head of the Gulf of Bothnia. But despite our advice, the Allies chose to ship supplies to Oslo and Trondheim in Norway, whence they were slowly shuttled on a long and involved route across the Norwegian, Swedish, and Finnish railway networks. Inevitably, they began arriving just when the Finns were compelled to sign an armistice.

I saw the result of this tragic delay in March 1940 when I

received unexpected orders to take two motor transport companies over the ice route across the frozen Gulf of Bothnia to help the Finns evacuate the population of Karelia, which the terms of the armistice had ceded to the Soviet Union.

I don't know whether I was more astonished at the sight of this gigantic frozen stretch of water (the Gulf freezes only once in a hundred years) or the mounds of equipment that I found piled on the quays at Umeaa. But even had this reached the Finns in time, I doubt whether it would have had much effect on the outcome of the war; most of the British equipment appeared to date back to the Boer War, while the French contribution looked as though it must have been resurrected from depots where it had moldered since the Franco-Prussian battles.

The reason for my visit was that I had been posted to the Army Service Corps in January in line with the Staff Corps' custom of rotating its personnel in different arms of the service. The transport companies I commanded were part of a great rescue operation; a sort of Dunkirk on wheels across ice. In addition to the men and vehicles sent by the army, hundreds of private lorry owners had responded to the Government's appeal so that roads leading toward the Gulf were jammed with long convoys of civilian and military vehicles.

The Gulf itself, a glittering expanse of frozen water stretching as far as the eye could reach toward the east, was an amazing sight. Snowplows working from either end of the hundred-mile crossing were managing to keep an ice road open, and the whole route had been marked out with juniper boughs to enable the drivers to keep direction in the blinding snow. Across this Arctic route moved a continuous procession of lorries on their way to help the Finns in their evacuation of Karelia. But by the time we arrived, the blizzards had become so bad that I was told to send my companies on the land route round the head of the Gulf. Much to my mortification, I was ordered not to accompany them into Finland.

The very morning I sent the lorries off on their journey the blizzard stopped. Determined not to miss the chance of traveling over the ice route, I drove across in bright sunshine. Since I had strict orders not to enter Finland, I was forced to turn round in the outskirts of Vaasa on the farther shore, and drove back between high walls of ice and snow, following the juniper boughs along this icy route until I had recrossed the Gulf. Here, at Solleftea, I was forced to await the return of my transport companies, which were busily employed on the other side of the Gulf along the roads from Karelia, their lorries heavily loaded with all the worldly possessions of the inhabitants of the small hamlets and villages who had decided to abandon their homes and move deeper into Finland, rather than stay behind under the Russians.

I was glad to be back in Sweden; the stories my drivers had told me on their return of long columns of villagers and Finnish troops tramping doggedly along, their belongings heaped under a white curtain of driving snow on convoys of makeshift carts and lorries, had made a saddening impression on my mind. It was my first experience with the disturbing upheavals of war. And now as I settled down amid a peaceful Swedish winter countryside to train drivers and run an NCO's cadre course, I became increasingly restive; I could sense in my bones that when the spring came there would be trouble.

It came one morning in April. All day we listened to the radio as reports came flooding in: Copenhagen occupied, Denmark overrun by German troops. Soon we heard that German merchant ships in Norwegian ports were disgorging soldiers, who swarmed up from holds the unsuspecting port authorities had presumed to be stowed with less lethal cargo. Next, it was parachutists descending on Oslo airfield, and then the crack and boom of coastal defense guns as German warships came steaming into the fiords with turrets belching orange-colored pillars of smoke.

I could imagine the reaction in my old office. This was *not* the moment we had foreseen. Until that morning danger had always seemed to threaten from the south or the east. There would be frantic activity. For with Denmark gone and Norway under attack our mobilized field forces would have to be switched along the railway tracks toward new defensive positions. For years, I had been trained for such work. Yet here I was marooned in the depths of the country with nothing better to do than train army drivers. Picking up the telephone, I told the local operator to put me through to GHQ in Stockholm.

For once my tactful suggestion met with complete approval. I actually learned that I had been recalled four days earlier by GHQ (eventually, I discovered that this order had progressed no farther than the next floor down). I hung up, and summoned my second-in-command, handed over the sacred office accounts, and boarded the next train for Stockholm. On arrival at the central station, I deposited my baggage at the check-room; I was not to collect it until a week later.

I went straight to the GHQ building. Gazing up with red-rimmed eyes from my old desk was Captain Eimar Kjebom, the slim blond open-faced officer I had trained to replace me. Normally, he was always smiling. But not now. I could see he was on the point of collapse from overwork and strain, but before I sent him away for a good night's sleep, he was able to give me a rough briefing.

The immediate situation threatened to resemble a strategic planner's nightmare. For years our plans had been based on the assumption we could expect to be attacked by Russians from the east or Germans from the south. Although there were plans in existence for moving troops up to the Norwegian frontier, these had never been kept up to date because the West had always been considered a "safe" area. Now we had been caught with one army corps on the Finnish frontier. Its units (which were being slowly run down) were still equipped with Arctic clothing and field equipment, making them quite unsuitable for redeployment on the Norwegian frontier.

The only solution was to rush up other units from garrisons throughout the country while the troops on the Finnish borders were brought back to their depots for reorganization and re-equipment. But no plan was in existence for such a complicated maneuver, and the railways were already jammed with reservists on their way to report to their mobilization depots. Other units in the far north were standing by under orders to start entraining for positions on the Baltic coast. Unless something was done rapidly, the situation showed every likelihood of developing into a vast and uncontrolled military migratory movement that would completely clog our already heavily burdened railway system.

Seldom had there been a clearer case for immediate military

control of the railways. But as the briefing continued, I learned that the Government (which had contributed to the chaos by postponing mobilization until the last possible moment) had forbidden us to disrupt normal passenger and freight traffic, in case it might cause the people unnecessary alarm.

There was nothing for it but improvisation; a completely new plan would have to be devised within days. I sent my colleague home, sat down at his desk, and ordered the beautiful plans on which we had spent too many of the best days and nights of our youth laid aside and earmarked for destruction. I ordered up a large stock of blank graph paper to supplement the supply my poor colleague had been working on. I knew roughly what I was going to do because, subconsciously, I must have been preparing myself for just this moment; what I did not know was whether there was still enough time.

I began work on a Sunday; I remember the sun was shining brightly outside. After that, I have no recollection of the weather. I seemed to exist among graphs, roll after roll of minutely lined paper pinned to boards, great virgin areas on which the movements of the trains must be programmed. Gradually, the colored lines crept across the sheets, red, blue, yellow, and green all snaking closer together until the sheet was nearly full and the bottlenecks bulged dangerously. As one was finished, another blank sheet was pinned on the board.

For seven days I lived on coffee and an occasional sandwich; the work was too detailed and complex to risk a drink even when I felt I had reached the physical point of no return. For I *had* to go on; the work was vital and I had been trained to do it. For years I had lived with the blueprint of the Swedish railway complex in my head, had talked and argued about the sort of unforeseeable situation I was having to cope with now. And as the plans were improvised, the graphs finished and taken away, the orders sent out, I began to feel a glimmer of hope. I had a reassuring feeling, too, that my civilian railway friends on whom a mass of hastily typed orders was descending, at central, regional, and even local level, would be capable of rising heroically to the occasion.

The first forty-eight hours were the worst. On that Sunday I had only two days' grace before our first major troop movements were due to start. Yet somehow it was done, thanks to the flexibility of our troop movements system, which—as I found out later—was superior to that of all other armies.

On Tuesday the involved concentration movements began miraculously on schedule. For a time we waited anxiously for the first major snarl-up, but before long it was clear the plan was working. Over the next few days the whole complex operation went off without a hitch and all movements were completed on the scheduled target. Only one unit (not a fighting one) arrived at the wrong destination. I waited until I was *quite* certain before I literally staggered off to bed.

It was not until some days later that a remark reported back from the German Military Attaché in Stockholm restored me to a shadow of my normal form: "We know you have mobilized," he had said. "We are quite aware you have concentrated your troops along the borders. But how the hell did you do it?"

Now that our troops were in position along the Norwegian frontier and had to be supplied on a war basis, it became apparent just how white we had bled ourselves in our determination to help the Finns. There was a shortage of everything from grenades to small-arms ammunition; mines did not exist; the bulk of our antiaircraft shells had long ago gone hurtling through Finnish barrels at Russian aircraft so that our entire general reserve of ack-ack shells had shrunk until it could be accommodated in *four* ten-ton trucks (about enough to sustain all the guns through less than one minute's hard firing) and had to be rushed at breakneck speed from one end of the country to another whenever a tense situation developed.

From our ill-defended positions along the frontier we were able to observe how the fighting was going in Norway. Abortive Allied landings at Aandalsnes, Steinkjaer, and Bodo collapsed one after another, the troops were evacuated, and more and more Norwegian soldiers sought refuge in Sweden.

Only at Narvik were the Allies successful in hammering General Dietl's Alpine troops back into the mountains. And with their troops in trouble here, we knew there would soon be German pressure on Stockholm to allow the transit of troops and arms across Swedish territory. Unknown to us, this had already begun, and although the Government stood firm (just as they had turned down British and French requests for troop transits to Finland), we had little doubt there would come a time when Sweden would be unable to withstand the mounting pressure.

On this occasion the only German trains allowed to pass through our territory to and from Narvik contained food and medical supplies, homebound wounded German soldiers and merchant sailors. Field Marshal Goering's suggestion that some of the trains should include specially sealed trucks which need not be examined was firmly turned down. So was a proposal that Germany supply Sweden with four batteries of heavy guns, in return for which Sweden would sell Germany three of her own heavy batteries, to be delivered at a northern transit point—which not unexpectedly turned out to be Narvik.

The fighting there, however, soon came to an end when the Allied force was withdrawn. On June 10 Norway capitulated and Sweden was now isolated and in an increasingly difficult position. On June 15 Ribbentrop saw our Ambassador in Berlin and demanded free passage for German troops and equipment through Sweden. A glance at any map will explain this insistence. The new German garrisons, which stretched along the broken and indented Norwegian coastline, had to be maintained by land or sea, and although there was always a large number of vessels en route for Norwegian ports, the land route was infinitely safer, shorter, and more practicable. The garrison at Narvik was a particular example; here the rail journey saved an inordinate amount of time by the direct land route and could be carried out with no danger from the mines and torpedoes in Norwegian waters.

I was grateful never to be involved in the technical negotiations that accompanied the distressing concessions which Sweden was now about to be forced to make. But since we have all too often been accused of giving way to the Germans, it is pertinent to inquire whether we were expected to commit national suicide in order to resist this pressure.

There was no blinking the fact that Germany *could* have overrun us had she decided to, and had we been attacked in 1940, we would have fought and would have destroyed our strategic installations as we fell back into the interior. But our appallingly weak forces would have merely delayed collapse against a superbly armed enemy. Nor was there any point in looking to the West for help; France was in her last death throes. In fact, had we resisted, we should not only have been committing suicide, but would have destroyed our chances of being able to help the unfortunate Danes and Norwegians, whose soldiers and civilians were crossing our frontiers in thousands and were being given refuge on Swedish soil. There was no alternative but to play for time and build up our forces to a state of readiness and efficiency.

Understanding of our position dawned slowly in London, reluctantly on the exiled French, but least and last of all in Washington. Meantime the tension between Stockholm and Berlin became more severe and was increasingly backed with threats of force. I was in no position to know much about the struggle that raged far above our heads, but I gathered that German negotiations in Stockholm were being handled by a Dr. Schnurre, a supercilious man whose manners grated on Swedish susceptibilities. Our own able Ambassador in Berlin, Arvid Richert, undoubtedly had to pass on an increasingly tough series of demands. But in the end all decisions had to be made by our cabinet. And I shall never forget my reactions when we learned on July 5 that, since hostilities in Norway had ceased, our Government had agreed to German transit traffic.

From now on German trains were to be allowed through Sweden carrying nonmilitary supplies, leave personnel, arms, ammunition, and military equipment (the latter, however, only to be licensed after advance notice). The whole decision reeked of Nazi blackmail. I could guess the pressures that had been applied, the threat to cut off all raw materials for our own armament industry, the direct warning that it might be necessary to occupy Swedish territory *unless* cooperation was forthcoming. But that made it no easier to swallow one's sense of outrage.

Like most professional soldiers, I had found it difficult not to feel admiration for the superb professional performance and technique of the Wehrmacht. But it was difficult not to feel it was being used by the Nazis and too often defiled in the process. We had seen what had happened to German generals who disagreed with the Fuehrer, and had been disturbed at the underhand methods used to get rid of them, which had been tolerated by the "old guard" and welcomed by a new race of army party supporters. It seemed to us that a once magnificent professional army had been bent and twisted. And now it was threatening to trample our neutrality and crush us.

That morning I was depressed and bitterly angry, wondering whether I would ever be able to go on working at the Directorate, where I was bound to come into contact with representatives of the "Master Race" whose hated trains would be passing through our country. I felt it a slur on the honor of the Swedish Army, and took a vow never to visit Germany or her occupied territories until we had become strong enough to tell these arrogant, blackmailing Nazis what they could do with their trains and their demands.

We were doomed to suffer this indignity for another thirty-seven months, a long, heartbreaking period of waiting during which determined measures gradually brought our armed forces back to a strength which once more enabled them to stand firm on the principles of peace and freedom. Although during this period we had the sympathy and good will of that stout and amiable bachelor, Hershel Johnson, the American Ambassador, and a considerable degree of understanding with his British confrere, Sir Victor Mallet, we were entirely on our own when it came to helping ourselves. It was not easy, but gradually popular opinion, which earlier had reflected a mood almost of indifference, became increasingly anti-German, strengthened ironically by the constant irritations and hardships which life on a war footing brought home to every family. Before long "those damned Germans" were blamed for everything.

By August 1942, after holding several posts, I had been promoted to military director of the State Railway Board. In an interview with the Deputy Chief of the Defense Staff, Colonel Count Ehrensvard, I now found it necessary to reconsider my vow not to visit German-occupied territory. This brilliant man, who combines imagination, foresight, and drive with outstanding personal integrity, is a remarkable character. Ehrensvard, who looks like and is a natural aristocrat, proved a beak-nosed ball of fire whose patent contempt and loathing for the Nazis hardly endeared him to some of our more timorous politicians. He spoke with an inimitable nasal burr and never spared scathing criticism when he believed it necessary. On occasion I have often felt like cursing him, but I have seldom trusted or admired a senior officer more.

I had been invited to celebrate my takeover of duties by accompanying my predecessor on a tour arranged by the German Army Command in Norway. I was loath to accept, but Ehrensvard not only told me not to be a fool but *ordered* me to go, and pointed out that there might be certain advantages in taking a long, cool look at how the Germans were using the Norwegian railways to supply their garrisons.

Occupied Norway was an unhappy and haunted place. I did not enjoy our tour of control points, rail installations, and depots since we had no choice but to travel everywhere accompanied by the top brass of the German occupation command.

Their "Master Race" attitude toward the unfortunate Norwegians became apparent during a dinner party at Narvik where the main course consisted of thick whale steaks smothered in gravy. With horror, I watched a nervous Norwegian mess waiter bend low over the shoulder of a German colonel. From the tilted plate a juicy whale steak shot out like an avalanche and landed square in the colonel's lap. A generous portion of gravy followed, cascading down an immaculate gray tunic. With an outraged roar, the colonel leaped to his feet and drew his revolver.

"Schweinehund!" His face was convulsed with fury.

The wretched waiter quailed, trying to sink into the ground.

Other horrible curses followed. And then a sinister "Come with me."

I could sense what was likely to happen.

"Colonel," I said, interposing my by no means insubstantial form between the would-be executioner and his victim. "Please calm yourself. The whole thing was a genuine mistake."

He glared at me.

"Mistakes can occur in the best families," I said, and began talking hard and fast. Even so I was almost sweating by the time I got him to see reason. During this long and ticklish exchange the unlucky waiter wisely vanished into the night.

As we toured through the mountains in cars or special coaches,

I came to dislike the company of the German Chief of Staff. General Bamler, a capable and efficient officer, had all the arrogance of a full-blown Nazi, and described the Norwegian Resistance Movement as *"Banditen."* In striking contrast was the Director of Movements at German HQ in Oslo, Lieutenant Colonel Dr. Steltzer, a cultured, soft-spoken, and highly civilized officer who I discovered held very different opinions, which sprang from deep Christian views fundamentally opposed to Nazi policy.

Later we were able to invite him to Stockholm, where we discovered he was a member of the Christian wing of the German Resistance Movement. Fortunately, he survived the wave of executions that followed the attempt on Hilter's life and was appointed to an important administrative post in Holstein by the British soon after the German collapse. Poor Dr. Steltzer had, however, been badly knocked about and was still suffering from long months in Gestapo prisons. We brought him to Sweden for a holiday and medical care, which gradually helped to restore his health.

Having made a careful examination of the transit traffic passing into Norway, I came home, feeling certain there was room for tightening up our system of controls. I suspected that the Germans were taking advantage of our rather casual inspections at staging points and on the frontier to evade our system of allowing only specially licensed freight cars to carry arms and ammunition. But when I suggested discreet but effective improvements to the Foreign Office, these were promptly turned down. I then appealed to the Deputy Chief of the Defense Staff. Count Ehrensvard's reaction was both different and typical; he told me to take whatever measures I wished and assured me I would have his personal backing should any trouble arise.

Our Swedish rolling stock was becoming run down through poor maintenance and shortage of supplies. I discovered an excellent pretext for a close inspection, thanks to a marked increase of hot-box trouble on certain lines.

Now hot-box trouble (which means that bearings seize up through overheating) demands immediate attention. So once we "suspected" a German train of this malady, we had an immediate excuse for diverting it to a preselected marshaling yard, where a discreet check of the loads could be carried out as the noise of "repairs" floated up from below. Much to my chagrin, however, we never made a catch; even a train we believed loaded with poison gas turned out to have nothing more harmful on board than a consignment of insecticides.

As 1943 wore on we knew it to be only a matter of months before our Government felt strong enough to cancel the transit traffic. Plans were already afoot, and my official position enabled me to make several visits to Norway and Denmark, where I made useful contacts with elements of the Danish resistance; they were organizing a highly efficient network that was harrying the German occupational force, undermining its civil administration, and making long-term plans to take over the country once the moment of liberation came. With D day (the longed-for moment when the Government would take a firm stand against the Germans) coming closer, this stood me in excellent stead.

In the middle of July 1943 there was a sudden outburst against the traffic, brought on by the discovery of detailed maps of Sweden in a German freight car near one of the northern transit points. Although it was not unreasonable for any troops stationed in Norway or North Finland to have maps of adjacent Sweden, this find brought on a sort of national hysteria. The clamor in the press became tremendous; warnings of a German rape of Sweden were splashed across the headlines. Just as it seemed the uproar was in danger of dying down, a message reached me through the grapevine from Denmark: I was told to expect a present the following day.

It arrived on time; a new set of marked maps was discovered in a freight car at Hälsingborg, a southern transit point from Denmark. A member of our customs brought them to light, the papers seized on the story, and the whole controversy flared up more fiercely again. It seemed the Government was about to act. But it preferred to keep its own commander-in-chief in the dark. The Cabinet seemed unable to realize that certain precautionary military measures would have to be taken in case there was a violent German reaction.

General Ehrensvard has described in his own autobiography the unreal situation, explained personally to him by Erik Boheman, the Under Secretary of State for Foreign Affairs and a close friend. Ehrensvard's reaction was firm. He stated categorically that unobtrusive military preparations would have to be put in hand two weeks before the political message was delivered in Berlin. His insistence on this action made some of the Cabinet members livid with rage, because they feared the news might leak out. It had been their intention originally to present the High Command with a *fait accompli* because of simultaneous complicated negotiations for a British trade agreement, in which the import of essential items was subject to cancellation of the transit traffic.

On August 5 I was rung up by the Swedish Foreign Minister. He told me: "We have canceled the transit traffic today. You must go to Berlin and make the necessary arrangements."

I have seldom felt so relieved and delighted; it was as though a personal humiliation had been lifted from my shoulders. I immediately telephoned the office of the German Movements Liaison Officer in Stockholm and demanded clearance for a seat on the plane to Berlin next morning.

Tempelhof airfield showed no signs of British bombing when I arrived the following day. On the way to the Swedish Embassy, I peered out of the car windows for signs of war damage. There were tragic queues of refugees who looked in poor physical shape, and numerous trucks loading salvaged files and office equipment from the gaunt, blasted skeletons of tall buildings; a heavy, almost melancholy atmosphere hung over the doomed city despite the hot August sunshine.

The meeting at German Army Transport Headquarters at Bendlerstrasse 4 that afternoon was a memorable occasion. I entered a room in the middle of which was a huge table covered with green baize. This was the temple of German railway control, and here were gathered some thirty soldiers, Foreign Office officials, and members of the Reichsbahn, SS and SD (the Gestapo). Rather to my surprise, my hosts seemed anxious to be cooperative, even resigned to making the best of a bad business, and masked their chagrin with a cloak of affability. I was offered Dutch cigars and French cognac. Obstinately sticking to my own cigarette case, I refused; I have no taste for loot unless I happen to have "liberated" it myself.

I shall never forget that conference. Anticipating a highly unfavorable reception, I had memorized an introductory speech. I did not even have to use it. From his chair at the head of the table, a general (the *Transportchef im Oberkommando der Wehrmacht*) welcomed me in a not unfriendly fashion, stressed the limited time at our disposal, and went straight to the point: when, where, and how?

"Can we agree, Major"—he was obviously playing for time—"that we start unwinding the traffic in ten days' time? Of course, we could not complete it until our personnel on leave in Germany have returned to Narvik. Let's say about the end of September?"

"No," I said firmly. "The cancellation must apply immediately. Our only obligation is to allow leave trains through which are already en route and loaded cars that have already arrived at Swedish transit points."

He boggled a little.

"I intend to issue orders along these lines the day after I return to Sweden," I told him. "I also want a reservation on the plane back to Sweden tomorrow afternoon."

The General shrugged, and during the technical discussions that followed I became more and more conscious that my presence here was not just highly satisfactory to me personally, but represented the feelings of my brother officers. I knew I was only a very small cog in the machine, but I was wearing the uniform of the Swedish Army, and in a position to be able to say "No" at last. In doing so, I knew I represented the thoughts of the overpowering majority of all ranks in our army who shared my hatred for the Nazi regime.

Chapter Three

OFFICER OF THE INTERNATIONAL RED CROSS

IN September 1943, a few days afer we had toasted the departure of the last German train from Swedish territory, I was asked by Count Folke Bernadotte to come to see him at his office in the Swedish Red Cross where he was deputizing for the President, Prince Carl, King Gustaf's brother.

At this time, while the war in Europe still dragged on, he had not yet acquired an international reputation, but his concern for lightening the human tragedy soon became apparent as he explained in his quiet and friendly voice that he wanted me to act as his executive and make all rail arrangements for a repatriation of German and Allied prisoners of war, which was about to take place through Sweden.

Folke Bernadotte was a very pleasant, soft-spoken man. Tall and slim, his natural good looks were somehow enhanced by a radiance of genuine nobility of mind and humanity. It was no wonder that he and Ralph Bunche were later to take so naturally to each other. Both shared the same qualities, and as I listened with growing enthusiasm, the job he was offering me began to seem enormously worthwhile.

The plan was complicated; Allied ships would bring one thousand German repatriates from England to Göteborg, wait until four thousand Allied sick and wounded had crossed Sweden, and then transport them back to British and overseas ports. Stretcher cases would be brought straight to Göteborg in German hospital ships, but the main Allied parties would be brought over on the train ferries from Sassnitz in Germany to the Swedish port of Trelleborg. Here they would transfer into Swedish trains while the ferries returned to Germany loaded with German repatriates who had come overland by train from Göteborg.

Since heads had to be counted at Sassnitz and Trelleborg before the exchange was made, rigid adherence to timetables would be vital, not an easy business now that the German rail network was suffering serious disruption from Allied bombing. Nor, I felt, were the exchanges likely to pass off without argument; my experience with the Germans had taught me that humanity took a very poor second to the Teutonic passion for exact figures.

Folke, however, struck me as the ideal man for the job. I had known him since my cavalry days, and remembered his tact as adjutant when drastic reductions in the army establishment necessitated a forced merger between the 1st Royal Horse Guards and the 2d Life Dragoons. And as he stressed the importance of the operation going off without a hitch, so there should be no chance of a recurrence of the crushing disappointment that had overtaken an earlier party of wounded Allied prisoners who had been turned back almost in sight of their ship two years before, at Saint Nazaire in France, it was obvious just how wholeheartedly he had thrown himself into this job.

Despite some intricate last-minute planning, the exchange turned out a great success. As the first batches of Allied prisoners began to board the train ferries at Sassnitz, we were struck by their cautious expressions. It was not until the ships came within sight of the neutral Swedish port of Trelleborg that they appeared to realize their long captivity was over. Drifting across the water from the train ferry dock came the martial sounds of a Swedish band putting its soul into a succession of welcoming British tunes. From this moment the pale faces began to light up, the strained lines relaxed, and the hard-learned prison camp philosophy, "Never believe anything good until you see it happen," collapsed as it dawned upon them that this was *real*.

No doubt each had his own private reaction. And what a strange mixture they were as they clambered down from their trains onto Swedish territory; sick and wounded from the British units who had fought at Calais, Dunkirk, and Saint Valery, New Zealanders and Australians from the ill-fated expeditions to Greece and Crete, emaciated but immaculately turned-out men from the Indian regiments, Americans captured in Tunisia, Africans in Pioneer Corps uniform, a stray Norwegian in the British Air Force, a few Frenchmen and even an occasional Pole.

Then there were the civilians: internees from the Channel Islands, First World War veterans wrenched from their jobs as caretakers in British war cemeteries, even a few specimens of that indomitable breed, the English governess who had been teaching in Continental households until the Germans arrived and carried her off to internment camp. Here and there was the odd stowaway who had smuggled himself on board and now hastened to mingle happily with the throng. All were festooned with Red Cross parcels, issued by the Germans at the last minute to show how well and faithfully they were observing the Geneva Convention.

When they boarded our trains, there was a spontaneous outburst that has stayed vividly in my mind. For in these beautifully clean coaches the final realization that it was true burst over them, and they threw their arms round the necks of our Lottas from the Women's Army Corps and the Red Cross nurses who were there to serve tea, food, and fruit.

Two incidents stand out in my mind. One of our Lottas, determined that a bearded and emaciated Indian soldier in an immaculately wound turban should be fed back to health and strength without a moment's delay, pursued him along the platform with a bowl of our traditional army dish of split pea soup and slices of fat pork. I can still see her dismay at his horrified expression. Next a rumor spread along the crowded platform that Sweden was experiencing a serious cigarette shortage. After a quick whip around, two soldiers approached me with a couple of laundry baskets piled high with cigarettes, dumped them at my feet, and with two quivering Guards' salutes requested *me* to accept them as a token of their gratitude. Not daring to hurt their feelings, I asked them to bring the baskets along to the stationmaster's office, where the Swedish Customs fell upon them immediately these two generous souls had departed to board their train. On subsequent visits to Trelleborg, I was to become accustomed to a flagrant aroma of Players and Woodbines coming from the direction of the Customs offices.

Train after train pulled out full of men who, despite shrunken faces, missing legs, empty sleeves, bandages and plaster casts, were clearly experiencing a tremendous resurgence of spirit. Often it was difficult to get them away on time since the trains arriving at the German ferry dock on the other side of the Baltic were running consistently late. One morning toward the end of the exchange, I was waiting impatiently on the German side for one of the final sections that would make up the last train to run north. At last it steamed in, and a youngish, slim RAMC officer with a neatly trimmed mustache stepped down.

"Captain X [I cannot recall his name] reporting, sir. I've fifty-eight mental cases with me. Can your medical staff take over?"

My jaw must have dropped. "I've only two Red Cross orderlies. All our doctors are in Sweden." I was upset by his horrified expression. "We've had no notice you and your poor charges would be arriving."

"I see, sir." His face was eloquent.

"Look here, Captain. I suggest you accompany them through to Göteborg and on to England."

"No such luck, sir." He had a charmingly rueful smile. "I'm not due for repatriation. In fact, I'm going straight back to a prison camp. I'm a psychiatrist, you see. I've been looking after these poor fellows for two years, and if I abandon them now, with no one to look after them—well, anything could happen, suicide attempts . . ."

I must admit I felt a cold shiver down my spine. "We'll manage," I said. "I'll have to improvise. For God's sake don't look so worried. I promise you I'll do my best."

"Thank you, sir," he said doubtfully.

"And the best of luck. I don't envy you going back, but by God I admire your sense of duty."

Fortunately the final section of the train came in at that moment. I leaped on board and made a rapid tour down the corridors in search of assistance. But the only doctor I could discover was a red-bearded lieutenant in the RNVR fondling a mongrel dog and already in an advanced state of intoxication. Since there was literally no one else, I shook him out of his stupor.

He must have been a good-natured fellow since he followed me gamely until I made my next catch, a British sergeant major. I went on down the coaches, selecting six of the fittest-looking men

I could find. God knows what their reaction must have been when a Swedish officer burst in on them with the startling news: "You. Medical orderly." Whatever their private thoughts, they followed me willingly enough to the two coaches where some of the more enterprising among my fifty-eight poor demented charges were performing antics at the windows.

Before my new "medical team" had a chance to ponder on their enforced role. I told them that the quicker they got in and started looking after their new patients, the better. All they had to do was make sure that no one came to any harm before they got to the hospital ship at Göteborg. Meantime, I had no choice but to lock the doors. All of them responded splendidly; though one of the patients had to be put into a strait jacket, my amateur medical team was to bring them all safely through to Göteborg; even the mongrel dog came through with flying colors. But even now I can remember their faces as they climbed aboard: to lighten their burden, I had a couple of cases of drink handed up before the doors were locked.

I traveled north on this train myself. At dawn the sun rose to reveal an almost breathtaking view of autumnal woods as our train topped a high ridge and began the long descent toward a vista of peaceful valleys. Touring the coaches amid a sustained noise of excited chatter and nostalgic songs, I opened a door and found myself in a long coach where in contrast there was almost profound silence. Only a low murmur of voices rose from the tightly packed seats, and gradually I realized that I had entered a world of the blind where lines of eager, sightless faces stared through the plate-glass windows while more fortunate "chums" beside them described the Swedish scenery in low voices.

The coach seemed somehow redolent of calm, almost a gentle serenity, as though these men's sufferings had been so great that at last they had discovered peace of mind. Rather humbly, I started chatting to one pair, a guide and his charge who three years ago must have been a tall, strapping Guardsman. Now his face was covered with a cloth to obscure the features that had been half shot away. As he stood up, I could see that his big frame had been shrunk and twisted so that now he was bent half double. His "chum" told me that he, too, had once been temporarily blind, and assured me: "So I know how it feels, Sir. And I know what Bill here wants."

I went on to chat to other little groups of these splendid men. But before long I found it increasingly difficult. And I had to retire to the privacy of my own compartment and sit there until my eyes had stopped smarting; I had never known what it was to feel so humble nor to have to struggle with such a choking lump in my throat.

Just short of Göteborg, we had arranged a staging point at a junction where the trains were to be split up before being shunted down to the quays. Here the late Queen of Sweden (then the British-born Crown Princess Louise) was to inspect the repatriation, and no effort had been spared to insure that every man was on the right coach for the right ship.

Unfortunately we had not been able to distribute the large numbers of artificial limbs that the Germans had thrust on us at the last moment. Each was neatly labeled with its potential owner's name and rank and had presumably been lying in some German depot ever since it had arrived from Geneva. Naturally the owners, who for years had had to make do with empty sleeves and peg legs, showed a keen interest in laying hold of this highly personal property. But we had simply not had time to do anything more than load the entire shipment into a freight car at Trelleborg, which was then attached to the train.

This car had been loaded in a fashion that would have done credit to a Guards quartermaster; row after row of artificial limbs had been stacked in neat piles of rights and lefts. It traveled safely across Sweden, and all went well until the Crown Princess' inspection was over, when a contingent of porters was discovered on the point of reloading all the lefts into a local luggage wagon instead of the truck that was to carry them to the ships. At this moment, the situation became even further complicated. A British soldier, suspecting there was some monkey business afoot, decided personally to retrieve his missing limb. Failing to locate it, his search became a frenzy that disintegrated all the neat piles into chaotic confusion.

Once the ships had sailed, I returned to my duties as Military Director of the State Railway Board with the warm feeling that few jobs I had done had been more worthwhile. The memory of those men we had been so glad to help stayed with me, so that in September 1944 I was delighted to find myself back at the German ferry dock at Sassnitz on the next big repatriation. The numbers * were much the same as the year before, but this time there was a high percentage of civilians.

All went well for the first few days until one morning I was watching a long line of freight cars loaded with goods draw in. A line of German guards sprang down as the train clanked to a halt, and took up position around the cars. As the sliding doors were pushed back, great choking clouds of dust streamed out, and soon the platform was crowded with an eager stream of civilians who rapidly formed up into single file for their last check through the control points before the train ferries.

At this moment I became aware of shouting from a coach at the rear end of the train. As I walked up the platform to investigate, the noise grew louder until soon I could see a German sentry jabbing his rifle menacingly upward toward a crowd of agitated men, standing in the open doorway of a box car. It all looked thoroughly sinister; the cries of protest, the guttural curses in furious German, and the rifle muzzle barring the gateway to freedom.

From the truck a heartrending shout went up: "For Christ's sake help us, we are only spares."

"Was ist denn los hier?" I asked the sentry.

"Diese Dürfen nicht aussteigen ohne Genehmigung." (These men can't detrain without special orders.)

"Blödsinn," I said.

More yells for help from the box car.

"What the hell is this?" I shouted. "Get them all out quick."

"Unmöglich," the sentry snapped sourly.

"Ich spreche nur mit Offizieren. Holen sie Ihren Vorgesetzten sofort hierher, aber schnell." (I only deal with officers. Get your superior here immediately. At the double.)

"Laufschritt," I yelled as he shambled off before he could change his mind.

* Actual numbers were: 1943, Allies 3503, Germans 1781 (by rail)
1944, " 2691, " 2143

Grateful faces stared down on me while a torrent of excited voices made it difficult to understand what was wrong. But before long I discovered that these wretched men had been brought all the way from internment camps starting in Greece as what was known as "spares," to take the places of any official repatriates who died on the journey. Since no one had succumbed, their services were not required and they had just been told they were to be returned to internment. This news had been broken in full view of two beautiful white ships flying a free flag, waiting to carry a thousand of their more fortunate comrades home.

I told them they had my heartfelt sympathy, and that I would do everything I could to help. Catching sight of a party of German officials approaching, I decided on rapid action.

"Jump out of the other side of the car," I told them, "and sneak along under cover of the train until you can join the queue. Once you get there push straight on board. And don't dare to breathe until the ship casts off."

It was like the flight out of Egypt. I was still talking as they took my advice and I have seldom seen men move quite so fast. There must have been a good forty men in that box car and they disappeared down the track at such a pace that by the time the ship's barrier finally came down there were only seventeen panting figures who had failed to elbow their way on board.

The resultant exchange of views with an outraged but rather out-of-breath German officer began politely enough.

"Aber Herr Major, was ist denn dieses? Dieses Leute sind . . ."

"Dieses Leute" was the unhappy party still marooned on the dock.

"Get them on board quickly," I snapped, seeing them so close to freedom. I strode down the gangway toward another German who was barring their path.

"Wer macht Radau hier?" I barked. (Who is making a row here?)

"Far too many men have come on board already," said the German stiffly.

"Too many! What about these?" I pointed to the dejected file. Come on. Let them through."

"Meine Zahlen und die Meines Schwedischen Kollegen stimmen nicht, deshalb können die Leute nicht an Bord Gehen."

His tone was *very* unfriendly. I knew the game was up.

The crisis came when a sinsister-looking Gestapo official told me that he was coming on board. "Strictly forbidden," I snapped.

A bitter discussion followed in which they insisted on checking suspected discrepancies before we were allowed to sail. It was pointed out that I had no authority on German soil.

"Do we have to use force?" the Gestapo man inquired.

"Force!" I thundered. "Understand this. I am responsible for running the complicated transport system between Sassnitz and Trelleborg, which has already been sufficiently disrupted by confusion on German railways. I *have* to sail at once. What if there is a discrepancy? Your figures may be right, so may be ours. In any case both are probably wrong. A countercheck on board now would jeopardize the whole repatriation program. Any discrepancies must be settled in Göteborg by the joint Swedish-Allied-German board. I guarantee that *if* we have any surplus individuals on board, they will be taken off and interned in Sweden. This seems fair enough to me. Or do you (pointing at the Gestapo fellow) want to take the blame for a recurrence of the Saint Nazaire scandal? I doubt it. I shall sail now. I shall use my wireless the moment I have cast off. And don't try to stop me! Any monkey business will release a prearranged W/T signal and then you (pointing) will be in trouble. Good day, *meine Herren."*

From the hesitant expression on his tight-lipped face, I gathered that this had shaken him. At least my "spares" already on board were safe. After more argument, I managed to persuade him to hold the disputed "Englanders" at Sassnitz until I returned next morning with a large number of Germans.

We sailed several hours late. Once at sea I signaled Bernadotte over the W/T, and as soon as we reached Trelleborg, I had a long conversation with him on the telephone. Folke behaved exactly as I had expected. When I asked for official authorization to bring the remaining seventeen Englishmen back to Sweden the following day, I was delighted to hear him assuring me that I had his official backing even though we were both in no doubt about the extremely tricky international complications.

Next morning at Trelleborg we embarked a full trainload of German civilians who showed no marked enthusiasm at returning to the Fatherland. Long before we came into sight of Sassnitz with its welcoming display of flags and bunting, I had the feeling that, after years of comparative comfort in their internment camps on the Isle of Man, they were in terror of being pitchforked back into the last convulsions of the Third Reich.

Although more than one of them had discreetly visited my cabin to inquire whether there was some way of avoiding disembarkation on German soil, the homecomers put a good face on it as we neared the German ferry dock. Every schoolchild and patient from the local hospitals had been mobilized with flowers and flags while brass bands belched out a hearty welcome. Down on the quay, however, I noticed an ominous increase in the numbers of officers and officials, which made it obvious that *I* was not included in the general welcome. But I had already issued orders that no Germans were to be allowed ashore until we had recovered the seventeen stranded "Englanders." As we came into the dock, I posted double sentries on the gangway.

First up the gangway came a German warrant officer whose blitzkrieg suggestion that "we get things moving right away" collapsed on my insistence he hand over the "Englanders" first. He was succeeded by a junior officer whose arguments produced even less result. Before he left, however, I was aware that the affair had become a top-level issue. I had caught sight of an irate and bulky figure striding up and down the quayside, escorted by three aides who, taking strict seniority from the right, all changed places like so many gray automatons whenever their angry superior commenced an abrupt about turn.

From my next visitor, an elderly senior Naval Commander, I learned the bulky one's identity. And gathered that everyone on shore was in a furore of apprehension lest the Gauleiter of Pomerania became seriously incensed over my stubborn behavior. The naval officer explained that this high-ranking Nazi was far too overburdened with official duties to have his time wasted on a trivial issue. Surely, he suggested, the whole business of the "Englanders" could be happily cleared up later?

When I assured him that I was not going to budge without

them, the Commander grew quite pale. A runner was dispatched to bear the news ashore. Before long, I realized that the report of my attitude must have reached the Gauleiter because his pace quickened significantly. In any other circumstances the sight of his aides, who were now in real difficulties following his abrupt about turns, might have been funny. But I knew just how seriously Gauleiters were taken in this country, and when I was asked to step ashore "so that we can go into the matter more thoroughly," I told Captain Yngue Ekberg as I went down the gangplank that no Germans were to be allowed ashore until I returned. Should I fail to return, he was to advise Göteborg immediately.

I never met the Gauleiter. I almost forgot about him during the two hours of furious argument that followed in a draughty transit shed where I found myself surrounded by angry Germans who ranged from senior naval and military officers to the inevitable Gestapo officials.

Every trick in the book was produced to intimidate me or make me change my mind. When I flatly refused, produced my cable of authorization, and told them they were holding up the disembarkation of their own nationals, they became so angry and menacing that I was relieved to see Captain Ekberg appear. Ekberg, the Commodore of the State Railways ferry service, was a stout fellow and a welcome reinforcement. While he had been maintaining vigil from his deck, I had been stubbornly insisting that the seventeen should be handed over. I had given the Germans my word of honor that they would be interned in Sweden should the joint board discover there had been a discrepancy. So far, we had made no progress, but now I felt we had reached a crisis. Singling out the senior Gestapo official in the hostile crowd, I described his less attractive characteristics to the Captain in Swedish. Although the choicer epithets were lost on him, there was no mistaking his reaction when, pointing an accusing finger at him, I switched to his own language. "I can't make out what this —— has done with those seventeen men. But I do know I won't let a damn German on shore until they are on board. *That* fellow—the one with the ugly mug—is holding the whole repatriation up. I've had enough. If my 'Englanders' are not delivered on board within fifteen minutes, nip back and send the code word. And *that* gentleman (I pointed to ugly mug) can take the full consequences."

These tactics worked. Within five minutes the "Englanders" had been released from their uncomfortable quarters in a nearby shed, and were hustled aboard over the rail ramp aft out of sight of the restive crowds ashore. I told them to get down out of sight below decks until we had sailed, and then returned to disembark our Germans. Once on deck again, I noticed the Gauleiter and his aides had disappeared, no doubt to draft the official report about my "most unusual conduct" which was to reach us a few days later.

Out at sea, I sat down to an enormous meal with seventeen happy and relaxed guests surrounding me at the table.

Chapter Four

POSTWAR NEGOTIATIONS

IN April 1945, I became Director of Movements and Transportation at GHQ. The German collapse could now be only a matter of weeks away and I was plunged into plans for moving home a Danish Brigade Group, which we had raised, trained, and equipped in Southern Sweden. It had been recruited from among the many Danes who had taken refuge with us during the war and we had camouflaged it as a police force. Now it was about to be urgently needed for internal security duties once the underground Danish Government took over from the Germans.

I was attending its field maneuvers in southern Sweden when an order arrived for me to accompany a party of Swedish officials to Copenhagen. This visit was to turn out to be a mixture of official and secret liaison meetings. I found it a strange experience. On the one hand there were official visits to the Swedish Legation, which still maintained normal relations with the German occupational authorities; there were visits, too, to Folke Bernadotte to learn the latest aspects of his tortuous negotiations with Himmler for freeing the Scandinavian inmates of the concentration camps. Then in contrast there were highly unofficial discussions with the Danish shadow cabinet over the quickest means of moving their Brigade back to Denmark to maintain public order in what promised to be a very hectic time.

Having flown back to Sweden to report progress, I returned again the next day. I heard the news of Hitler's suicide in clandestine company. We were in Davidsen's Vinstue, a famous Copenhagen drinking house with low oak beams and an immense and generous profusion of open sandwiches. Seated at the table around me was the whole Danish shadow cabinet, whose dangerous role was within days of being exchanged for real power. I well remember their faces as they listened with profound and unconcealed satisfaction to Admiral Doenitz's sonorous voice announcing the Fuehrer's death over the radio. Their confidence about the future was understandable; our intelligence reports indicated that the Germans were likely to put up a fight. It all tied in with the keen interest shown by Dr. Werner Best, the Reichsminister for Denmark, when in an interview at the Swedish Legation during my previous visit he had spoken in an almost dreamy voice of the longing he had always felt to see something of our beautiful country of lakes and forests.

In Copenhagen the atmosphere was electric with rumors; British armored spearheads were reported fanning out across the North German plains, a last-minute hitch had developed in Folke's negotiations with Himmler, the Danish resistance was becoming so bold that fighting had broken out at a dozen different spots, and an entire German unit stationed in a town was reported to have surrendered to the nearest "authority" in the comforting guise of a postman's scarlet uniform. We crossed back to Sweden by steam ferry the next morning.

The ferry was crowded with emaciated victims whom Folke's Red Cross units had succeeded in rescuing from the concentration camps. From the deck, too, we saw the first signs of another tragic exodus: a number of ships filled with German refugees who had escaped the advancing Russian armies in East Prussia.

Sweden's future still looked dangerously complex, because we were uncertain whether we might even at this late stage become involved in the war. For months the Norwegian Government in Exile in London had been exerting the utmost pressure to persuade Sweden to agree to full-scale intervention. Preparations were actually afoot for our units on the frontier to move into Norway before the collapse, and a special volunteer battalion was being privately raised.

There were, too, some fifteen thousand Norwegians whom we had raised and trained from the refugees and soldiers who had escaped in such large numbers over the past five years. Still disguised as police forces (eight crack mobile police companies and about twelve battalions of reserve police), they were actually infantry units well armed and trained, and eager now to help liberate their homeland. At Kirkenes in northern Norway too (where the Germans had abandoned territory above the Arctic Circle during their retreat from Finland) there was a token force of Norwegians flown in from Scotland and built up by American planes operating from a Swedish air base at Kallax.

We were confident that the German troops in Denmark would surrender as soon as the final collapse came, but it was impossible to foresee what would happen in Norway where well over three hundred thousand Germans were still under arms. Despite the fact that the Army Commander, General Boehme, had been casting round for a suitable pretext which would enable him to surrender, resolute orders from the German Reichskommissar to his SS troops to fight on after the collapse might swing the reluctant Wehrmacht alongside them.

The last week seemed to pass unnervingly slowly. Sweden refused to declare war on Germany and send her armed forces across the Norwegian frontier. This made her extremely unpopular with the Government in Exile, but was greeted with relief by the Swedish people, the armed forces, and the Norwegians in their own country who were only too well aware that no act could have been better calculated to provoke the Germans into a last-ditch stand.

As it turned out, this was a wise move and when the moment came there was no resistance. The German collapse in Denmark came swiftly, and the Brigade arrived at exactly the right time. In Norway, too, the transition took place without any fighting. General Boehme had no trouble with the SS units, and accepted the surrender terms signed in Germany on May 7, so that the huge garrison scattered over the mountainous length of the country was already quietly surrendering to the Norwegian Resistance as the "Free" battalions (which had been held back by orders from SHAEF until May 10) were beginning to cross the frontier.

A combined Allied Headquarters was set up in Oslo. One of its tasks was the repatriation of vast numbers of liberated prisoners besides the three hundred thousand soldiers of the German garrisons. As this involved considerable transport problems, the Allies requested my secondment there as Swedish liaison officer.

On arrival I was allotted quarters in the Bristol Hotel amid a host of polyglot Allied officers, and the extremely efficient young woman who supervised the car pool soon provided me with a driver. Something about his face struck me as vaguely familiar. He was not inclined to be communicative, so it was not until some time after he had been driving me on my missions that he unbent sufficiently to enlighten me. With a deadpan expression he told me that, during my tour through the country with the German movement control authorities three years earlier, the Norwegian Resistance had detailed him to shadow me. Having reminded me of some of those trips, his face relaxed into a smile as he assured me there was nothing in their security files against me. I was delighted to hear this from "the horse's mouth." And not a little flattered when, a week or so later, I had a chance to study a report that the Allies had unearthed from the captured German Security Archives, couched in very different terms.

Unfortunately the intoxicating atmosphere of liberated Norway was marred for me by the knowledge that an unpleasant job lay ahead. Despite the wild excitement, the flags, the hope and enthusiasm that seemed constantly in the air, there was no escaping the realization that before long I would be tackling the repatriation of the Russians.

Only a few days before, I had watched an improvised company of these former prisoners of war bring up the rear of the first big Allied parade in front of the Royal Palace. Lavish applause had greeted the smartly turned-out British and American units as they marched past the saluting base where General Sir Alfred Thorne and his American deputy, Colonel Charles Wilson, were taking the salute. There was a vast roar of enthusiasm as one of our Swedish-trained Norwegian battalions swung past after them. But the really deafening clamor was reserved for the Russian company which hove into sight at the tail of the column, a well-drilled body of emaciated men who marched smartly although they carried no arms.

There were the best part of one hundred thousand Russians scattered throughout Norway; a remnant of the vast horde the Germans had transported for forced labor into the frozen territory beyond the Arctic Circle. The Norwegian people had taken them to their hearts during those years when overwork, starvation, and inadequate clothing had taken a terrible toll, and had always shown them great compassion, which combined a spontaneous sympathy with a desire to demonstrate their open contempt and defiance for the Germans.

Almost a year before, the Swedish Government had offered the Soviet Union assistance in repatriating the survivors once the war was over. And in April, I had been informed that I was to have the responsibility for moving them across Sweden to embarkation ports for their journey home. The more I saw of them now, the more I wondered how many harbored some well-founded disinclination to exchange the easygoing life of a free country for their own war-wrecked homeland where, we gathered, returning prisoners of war were viewed with the deepest suspicion.

I felt certain there were bound to be "marching losses" during the operation, and this thought was much in my mind when I returned to Stockholm for discussions with a Soviet delegation, which had arrived to work out details for the repatriation. My spirits were not raised by arguments that immediately developed with its leader, Major General Ratov, a squat bulky Russian whose head seemed to have been screwed straight down between his shoulders as though his Maker had forgotten to provide him with a neck.

This conference was an interesting if disquieting experience. The actual plan was straightforward: the Russians were to be collected by Swedish trains at various selected Norwegian entraining points, and brought overland with Swedish escorts to three ports on the East coast of Sweden whence Finnish ships would take them across the Baltic. Since making up full shiploads is a complicated business, it would be necessary for the Russians on every second train to spend a night en route in a Swedish transit camp. At first this seemed to raise no complications. We guaranteed food and medical care throughout the journey to the ports, and in addition were to provide the Russians with four days' extra rations for their subsequent journey home.

But soon it became apparent the delegation had its own views as to what was to happen in the transit camps. General Ratov insisted flatly that Russian officials must be stationed in each one, empowered with full authority to decide jointly with the Swedish authorities on any question that might arise. I could see what he had in mind, but this demand struck me as tantamount to allowing the Soviet Union jurisdiction on Swedish territory. And the squat General, ably supported by a buxom girl interpreter who never missed a linguistic trick, had by no means finished.

He produced another "vital" condition. Plainly, he shared my apprehensions about "marching losses" during the journey, because now he insisted that any of his countrymen who disappeared from the trains en route must be hunted down by the Swedish authorities who, once they had laid hands on them, were to hand them over, if necessary by force, to the Soviet officials on the waiting ships.

I was accustomed to negotiating with intractable Teutonic characters. But these cold-faced and implacable Russians were something new. Even when the head of our political department of the Foreign Office, who was chairing the meeting, pointed out that were we to accept these conditions we would be directly contravening traditional Swedish sanctuary for political refugees, and suggested that any Russians who were picked up by the police should be treated according to Swedish law, his proposals were greeted with a blank wall of refusal. Finally, to break the deadlock, I suggested a compromise; were the Russians to refrain from insisting on their first point, we would accept the distasteful task of ensuring that there should be no discrepancy in the numbers boarding the ships.

With a massive scraping of chairs, both sides withdrew for private consultation. Although I disliked the whole business, I felt convinced it was better to agree to rounding up the Russians who escaped off the trains rather than accede to Ratov's demand for authority inside our own transit camps. Were we once to agree to this sort of authority, we would be in danger of establishing a precedent that could give the Soviet Union an excuse for making similar and perhaps more dangerous requests.

I was not impressed by General Ratov. His attitude struck me as highly indicative of the type of Soviet approach the Swedish Government might expect from now on. This was not an encouraging prospect but, as I pointed out to my diplomatic chiefs, these demands probably seemed reasonable enough to the Soviet Mission since the original Swedish offer had been unconditional.

Doubtless it had originated through a mixture of political and humanitarian motives, and illusions were now about to be rudely shattered. But if, as I suspected, the former motive had been dominant, then once our Government had taken a political decision, we were hardly in a position to quibble over its technical implementation; our immediate task was to ensure the Russian interpretation was not allowed to endanger our own national security.

When we reassembled, the buxom interpreter informed us that General Ratov had accepted our proposal. And now another bout of intensive haggling ensued during which the fate of the Russian ex-prisoners seemed almost forgotten in a fierce argument about transport costs.

This was my first experience with the Russian talent for tight-fisted business dealing, although I doubt whether they—even less than I—suspected that their tough insistence that we quote them an immediate figure per head for the journey was to lead to my making a substantial profit for the Swedish Government.

It seemed impossible to arrive at any realistic or near-accurate estimate around a green baize conference table; transport costing is an involved business hardly suited to lightning calculation. But the Russians were adamant; they insisted separate figures be quoted for the railway journey, the stop in transit camps, the rations, even the cost per head per Russian for the Swedish escorts and the staff of the camps whose demobilization we had had to defer until the operation had been carried out. There was no alternative but to estimate right away; before the conference was much older, I produced a sheaf of figures which, despite a renewed bout of argument, were eventually accepted.

The repatriation commenced in June. Whether it earned the Swedish Government the faintest flicker of good will is open to considerable doubt. Fortunately, however, it passed off without political repercussions. All of us who were entrusted with handling the operation had the distasteful task of carrying it out to the letter.

I remember that, just before it started, I had a bet with General Thorne as to which of us would have the highest "marching losses": he in Norway where the Russians were due to be entrained, or I in Sweden throughout the subsequent rail journey toward the waiting ships. I do not know whether General Thorne grows roses in retirement somewhere in England; had I his address, I might still be tempted to go and collect my "fiver." Immediately after the repatriation was over, however, I was in no mood to collect my winnings.

The experience had been most distressing. First of all it had been delayed because the Russian ships failed to arrive when expected. Then there had been a rumor that the Allies were holding the ex-prisoners back to "fatten them up" a little. At last, however, it got under way and for weeks afterward I found it hard to forget those lines of docile men filing aboard the ships. Here they were immediately divested of their brand-new bicycles, clocks, and watches, and stripped of the fruits of their humble shopping sprees and the gifts showered on them by Norwegian families, before being unceremoniously battened below decks.

Getting them to the ports had been depressing. This had been no exultant joyride of happy men going home. Though the majority raised no fuss, there had been some nasty incidents when would-be escapers had had to be manhandled aboard trains and ships.

There had been many suicides, too. The most horrible scene

that lingered in my memory was the sight of a Russian racing up the shrouds of the ship he had boarded peaceably and quietly only a moment before. Scrambling upward, he reached a precarious perch high on one of the masts. For a second, he paused there looking wildly round, then flung himself downward, his arms and legs flailing until he hit the deck below with a sickening bursting sound.

After this disturbing episode, I was relieved to return to GHQ where the situation in Norway soon demanded most of my attention. Although the British were shipping home as many Wehrmacht and refugees as they could, the astonishing human flotsam the Germans had left stranded there was going to need the assistance of the Swedish railways for many months to come. So many and so varied were the contingents waiting to be repatriated across Sweden that I had to make constant visits to Oslo to confer with the Allied authorities.

I discovered a tower of strength in the Allied officer in Oslo in charge of sorting out this odd blend of humanity. John Macdonald was a major in the Black Watch whose ebullient spirits had been in no way diminished by the loss of a leg in 1940. His ability to dance Highland reels with or without his "tin leg" aroused my heartfelt admiration on the few occasions when we were able to relax from our mounting problems.

The task facing the Allies was staggering. Every day revealed some new group of stranded nationals, usually in bad physical shape but desperate to get home with the minimum delay. Typical of the groups we had to move across Sweden was the sadly depleted remains of a once large transport of Yugoslav Partisans who had been rapidly dying off in slave labor camps north and south of the Arctic Circle under inhuman conditions. These liberated remnants, just under two thousand emaciated and half-frozen skeletons, were only too eager to board the trains. They never gave us a moment's trouble on the journey until they filed aboard the train ferries at Trelleborg where, however, having recovered a trace of their normal exuberance, our Master had the greatest difficulty in preventing them from hoisting the Red flag.

Another headache were the Tibetans whom we discovered dressed in Wehrmacht uniforms in a remote and frozen corner of the Far North. For now the German Army was being repatriated, it was apparent that the three hundred eight thousand men who had surrendered on VE day were by no means an ethnic Aryan group or tightly knit military fraternity. Every race under the sun seemed to be concealed under the uniform Wehrmacht gray, and the most exotic "recruits" were being brought to light.

The Tibetans, over whose bewildered heads an inter-Allied wrangle was to develop, had had the misfortune to be overtaken by the outbreak of war while visiting Bavaria on a world tour. For a time, they had been allowed to exist unmolested, but then there came a day when these gentle creatures were thrust into an internment camp.

As the German drive for manpower became desperate, an even worse fate befell them. Drafted into the Wehrmacht and rigged out in the ubiquitous field gray, they found themselves en route to a frozen garrison post beyond the Arctic Circle where they had presumably sat ever since, watching their prayer wheels revolve and comparing the North Cape with their distant Himalayas.

Now, rescued from their long exile, they discovered to their horror the Russians had laid claim to them. And such was the political honeymoon of those days that under Soviet pressure the Allies handed them over, to be classified as Uzbeks or Kalmyks and last seen departing in an easterly direction.

As the great exodus came gradually to an end, my work decreased and I returned to HQ little suspecting that a very different and bitterly unpleasant repatriation lay before me. It was only on my return from a visit to Germany that I discovered I had orders to take part in an episode that was to arouse a political storm.

During the last days of the war when Russian armies were advancing deep into Germany, a small number of German troops had escaped with their Baltic allies from the pockets in Courland and at Danzig in leaky or half-sinking boats. Just managing to make landfall on the Swedish coast, they had given themselves up in the belief they would be interned or allowed to travel on to Germany. Once behind the wire of their camps, however, they discovered they had become a target for an outburst of anti-German feeling. The full horrors of the concentration camps had just become public knowledge, and local sentiment was so outraged that the new refugees were only too delighted to remain behind the wire while violent demonstrations raged outside.

Before long, however, there was a complete reversal in the public attitude. On June 2 the relentless arm of Russian retribution appeared in the form of a *démarche* requesting the return of all German personnel who had taken refuge on Swedish territory.

The Swedish reply when it eventually came amazed and horrified our people. Not only had our Coalition Government agreed to the demand but the Labor administration, which had succeeded them, was prepared to implement it. Six days passed before this news was officially made known to the "Alien" section of the Defense Staff. It came in the guise of instructions to contact the Russian Legation to discuss the necessary arrangements. By this time, it was apparent that despite a smoke screen of words, both Governments under Soviet pressure had abandoned the long-established Swedish tradition of sanctuary for political refugees.

Our reaction at GHQ was one of horror and disbelief; horror since we had no illusions that this was tantamount to a death sentence to the wretched Balts and probably the Germans too; disbelief because in the heat of indignation we could hardly bring ourselves to face the realization that *we* would sooner or later be called on to implement this revolting political gesture.

I doubt whether the preliminary negotiations that followed with Commander Slepenkov, the Russian Naval Attaché, would have found us discussing the technical details had it not been for the wise and statesmanlike advice of our Chief of Staff, General Ehrensvard. Never before had I been through such a grueling test of conflicting loyalties. And I lost no opportunity to make Slepenkov aware that I found the necessity for our meeting highly distasteful.

At first the negotiations had been kept secret. But by the time Slepenkov arrived to see me, the information had leaked out. Despite the fact that the country was horrified and shocked and that petitions were descending on King, Government, and Parliament as though from a conveyor belt, this amiable Russian professed himself unable to understand why the Balts and Germans should feel apprehensive. The generous expanse of steel dentures that had earned him the nickname of "Silvertooth" positively gleamed as he brushed aside my warnings about heavy "marching losses" with the bland assurance: "But why? Why should they have any fear?"

With visions of some three thousand desperate men, we asked him what would happen were a train to arrive with a seriously depleted passenger list through violent resistance, suicides, and deaths on the way. The Russians were sticklers for exactitude in numbers. Undoubtedly they would accuse us of having deliberately sabotaged the operation. What proof of our integrity would they require? Perhaps Commander Slepenkov would like the bodies delivered at the Russian Legation? Or would just noses and ears be sufficient?

Never at any stage was I able to detect in Slepenkov the slightest concern over the fate of the unlucky victims. All my warnings were brushed aside. Nor was there any change in his bland exterior when on November 30 strong units of soldiers and police descended on the internment camps to drag the wretched repatriates onto the waiting trains.

I hated this distressing and macabre episode, which I thought the most disgraceful moment in modern Swedish history. Far from all being German nationals, the victims included Austrians, Czechs, Alsatians, Frenchmen, Finns, and Poles. There was even a fourteen-year-old Russian boy who had been picked up somewhere in the fighting line like a stray dog and had faithfully refused to leave the soldiers who had befriended him. And then there were one hundred sixty Balts (mostly Latvians but including some Letts and a few Lithuanians) whose Wehrmacht and Forestry Official uniforms were bound to seal their fate and whose plight aroused the especial compassion of the Swedish public.

Amid hysterical scenes of attempted suicide and self-mutilation, these terrified men were dragged onto the trains where they settled down for the journey in a sort of numbed apathy. At Trelleborg, where a Russian ship was waiting, there was comparatively little trouble. But the betrayed, haunted faces, the stumbling gait as though every step brought them closer toward a living death that we had unjustly brought down on their heads, exerted such an overpowering sense of shame and degradation that we could hardly bear to watch.

At the control point they were permitted one last flicker of hope. Moored some distance away was a Swedish ship chartered to take a small number of them to Travemunde and on to the haven of the British zone in Germany. Here the lucky few learned their destination, and I shall never forget their faces. But for the others . . . We had to watch them going up the gangway where, as soon as they reached the deck, their personal possessions were immediately taken away. It was horrible as man after man reluctantly left the quay and climbed that narrow gangway to vanish below decks.

There was only one good moment. Unexpectedly the escort officer on the Swedish ship came up to me and remarked in an undertone: "There seem to be more people aboard than I was expecting. Shall I sail or check, sir?"

"Sail at once and don't dare to check until you reach British-controlled waters," I told him.

For several hours, I waited anxiously in case his ship had been stopped and searched by a Russian vessel. But mercifully there was no distraught radio message, and I had only to deal with Commander Slepenkov as he came hurrying angry and disturbed along the quay.

From the reproaches that issued from between his steel dentures, I discovered what I already knew: the number of victims embarked on the Russian vessel had fallen far short of the expected total. Despite our constant warnings over the past months, the Russians had failed to anticipate the high numbers of "marching losses" that had occurred between the camps and the ships.

My feelings, already badly strained, were not improved when "Silvertooth" drew himself up to his full height and announced: "The number of repatriates is considerably short of the future given to the Soviet Government on June 16. Until this discrepancy has been satisfactorily explained, the *Kuban* will remain here in port."

Those gleaming dentures were the final straw. I completely lost my temper. But even through my blazing though excusable rage

All photographs by Esselte Foto

Major General Carl von Horn

With Dag Hammarskjöld and Ralph Bunche (on the left) at Leopoldville Airport, August 1960. Behind author is Captain Bent S. Fredriksen of the Danish Army, his A.D.C., and behind Bent stands Paul Berthoud of Switzerland, legal adviser to O.N.U.C.

The German Emperor Wilhelm II (on the left) and King Gustaf V (next to the Emperor) inspecting the Royal Horse Guards at Stockholm during the former's State Visit to Sweden in 1908. The tall officer in foreground is author's father, Lieutenant Carl von Horn

Author's mother, Martha Stjernawärd

ABOVE: Exchange of prisoners-of-war in September 1944. Allied soldiers disembarking from German hospital train at Gothenburg, September 1944

ABOVE: Swedish ferry-boat *Queen Victoria* arriving from Germany at the Swedish town of Trelleborg with British prisoners-of-war for repatriation

AT LEFT: Scene during the repatriation through Sweden in June 1945 of Russian soldiers captured in Norway by the Germans

Author's wife, Scarlett

At Basman Palace, Amman, July 1958, with (from right to left) King Hussein of Jordan, Dag Hammarskjöld, and Prime Minister Samir Rifai

ABOVE: The garden and author's view of Jerusalem from Government House

AT LEFT: Henri Vigier and author awaiting Dag Hammarskjöld's arrival at Jerusalem in July 1958

Jordan refugee delegate petitioning Dag Hammarskjöld at Jericho main camp, August 1958

Dinner given by 2nd Maratha Light Infantry (Kali Panshwin), celebrating Keren Day at Gaza. Author is seated on the left of Lieutenant-Colonel J. D. Stanley, the C.O., and at his left are Mr. Neville Kanakaratne, the Sinhalese adviser to the commander, U.N.E.F., Major Kalkat and Captain S. K. Shrinagesh, the Adjutant

Corporal Singh of Indian Army, Corps of Military Police, bodyguard, Congo, 1960

With author are his two A.D.C.s, Bob Dontoh (Ghana) and Bent Fredriksen (Denmark) at 'Flagstaff House,' Leopoldville, November 1960

Courtesy visit to President Nasser, Cairo, September 1958

Main Square, Sanaa, Yemen

I was aware I held a trump card that seldom failed with the Russians. I played it now, down there on the quay with the wretched Germans battened below decks only a stone's throw away.

I reminded Slepenkov that he had consistently disregarded our warnings that losses on his filthy operation were bound to be unusually high. Now when our hospitals were living proof of this truth, *he* had the nerve to reproach the Swedish Government. I was not authorized, I told him, to hold back one single Swedish soldier, let alone a train, now that we had carried out our side of the agreement. Unless I had telegraphic confirmation from the Soviet Embassy in Stockholm within an hour accepting full financial responsibility for costs incurred through the delayed departure of the *Kuban,* Slepenkov must make himself personally responsible.

When I had finished the Foreign Office representative beside me stepped in and fired an additional salvo in fluent Russian, which wrought a profound change in the Russian's normally bland expression. We watched him hurry off down the quay in search of the nearest telephone.

He was back within the hour. Once more the dentures gleamed as he informed us that the Soviet Government had been made aware of the serious discrepancy in numbers, and had taken note of Colonel von Horn's explanation. Pending thorough investigations, the *Kuban* would sail at once.

To our profound relief the final repatriation of the sick and wounded whom our hospitals had nursed back to health, only to see them handed over to the Russians, was entrusted to the civilian authorities. And so, for dubious political motives, this pitiful procession was gradually but forcibly shipped back across the Baltic amid scenes of violent public protest, which left an indelible stamp on anyone taking part in it.

Whether the Government derived any subsequent benefit from improved relations between Sweden and the Soviet Union is highly unlikely. Certainly the politicians who deluded themselves that a theoretical improvement was worth so great a cost in human misery and national shame would never have been able to comply with the demand had the civilian and military authorities not reluctantly stood by them in a crisis that put a terrible strain on their loyalties.

I doubt whether many of us would have been able to go through with it, had General Ehrensvard not reminded us of our duty to the State, and made our tasks a little easier by his personal appearance at some of the most difficult moments. For months afterward we were unable to forget those haunted faces. Without realizing it, I had been undergoing a liberal education in the fields where soldiering and politics meet.

Chapter Five

DAG HAMMARSKJÖLD CALLS

DURING the bitterly cold January of 1958, while in bed at my home in Malmö, racked with Asian flu, I received a letter from my old classmate, the Army Chief of Staff, to say that Dag Hammarskjöld, the Secretary General of the United Nations, had asked for a Swedish officer to go to New York. A Chief of Staff to the United Nations Truce Supervision Organization (UNTSO) was required in Palestine, and General Akerman had nominated me. From the letter I gathered that there would be a screening period and that I was to meet the Arab and Israeli permanent delegates in New York. The Secretary General would then decide whether I was suitable for the post.

Lying back on the pillows, I felt delightful. Not only was it a remarkable opportunity, but I was honored to have the chance of serving the United Nations in whose ideals I firmly believed. During the Suez crisis of 1956, I had even put my name down for the post of Chief of Staff to the Emergency Force in the Gaza area since it struck me as exactly the sort of opportunity I had often longed for.

Unfortunately, my dreams of international military experience, the chance to put my languages to some real use, had withered under the cold reaction displayed by GHQ. Discreet inquiry revealed the reasons: I was considered too old; so old, it appeared, that six months in a warmer climate were likely to finish me off. And then there was that little matter of my Irish streak, which was rated so difficult and short-tempered that, after that rumor of having once outspokenly advocated Sweden abandon her neutrality and join NATO * I probably was considered a natural for head-on clashes with Colonel Nasser.

That had been only two years before and it was unlikely the Personnel Branch had since become converted to the belief that I had grown wiser or more silver-tongued with the encroaching years. Could it be, I wondered, that their changed attitude was a precautionary measure to avoid my creating more trouble in Sweden as I grow older and more crusty, whereas in Palestine a little heated altercation would pass unnoticed in a theater renowned for bickering and discord? The tone of the letter, however, made it clear that I had been the Chief of Staff's personal nomination.

Whatever the reasons, I was determined to seize the chance. Picking up the telephone, I summoned my doctor. When he arrived, I told him briskly that I must go to New York at the earliest possible moment.

"Quite out of the question." Doctor Enbom looked startled.

"I have to get to Stockholm, and then on to New York," I told him firmly, brushing his thermometer aside. "How long do you need to get me mobile?"

"A week," he said reluctantly. "But you'll be taking a risk."

"Leave that to me," I assured him. "Just do your best. Pills, injections, whatever you like—so long as I'm on that plane a week from today."

Once his black bag and disapproving expression were round the door, I rang up General Akerman and asked him to confirm my acceptance. And then, belatedly, I broached the news to my poor wife.

I had married Scarlett in 1945, after my divorce. When I had

* The rumor arose out of a private conversation I had had while military attaché in Norway in 1948. Probably expanded by wishful thinking, it had been reported back in Washington, from whence it boomeranged back on my head.

first met her, she had had no less than three Christian names, but her wonderful auburn hair must have struck a hidden chord in my mind. I don't think I have ever been so instantly infatuated. She was a beautiful creature, gay, witty, and quite outstandingly good-looking, and after a four-hour session of "Gone with the Wind" I had already made up my mind that that auburn hair could only possibly make her "Scarlett" to me.

And so it was that I fell in love and married again. Me, who distrusted publicity, madly in love with a girl whose job up to now had been handling the public relations interests of a film company. How odd that I, of all people, should have married a journalist. For that roughly was Scarlett's real talent, and her ability for depicting people and scenes, even now she has gone, is still with me in writing this book.

Since our marriage this unusual and charming creature, whose temperament and literary gifts were so in contrast with the normal dull routine of Army life, had stood by me without complaint through a succession of military posts. As I had expected she took the news remarkably well now, despite the fact that she had been looking forward to a settled existence in our delightful new house with its idyllic view over pastoral country.

I had only just been posted to Malmö as Defense District Commander after a long spell of command in Southern Sweden. And now with her son too young to be wrenched away from the new school where he had just settled down, her soldier husband was coughing waves of Asian flu germs over the bedclothes and enthusiastically prattling about a new command, which was going to tear this settled life apart.

I think that what made it bearable must have been my patent enthusiasm. Just like me, she realized that this chance opened wider vistas than I had dared allow myself to believe possible. Until now, it had seemed my life as a soldier was destined to follow a set pattern inside the limited framework which is all a small European army has to offer. Both of us felt the letter had come as an undreamed order of release.

So the following Tuesday found me on my first transatlantic flight, settling thankfully into my seat, for my knees were still wobbly. I was the sole passenger in the first-class section, and was able to make special efforts to further the instruction of a trainee steward. As my spirits rose and a succession of cheering libations battled with the depressive drugs still combating the remnants of my Asian flu, I began to feel certain that I had made a wise decision.

Since the end of the war, I had traveled extensively on the Continent, spent two years in Oslo as Military Attaché, and had commanded a Brigade Group (the Swedish equivalent of a Regimental Combat Team) and a Field Division in Sweden. I was now within six years of retirement, and never in the whole course of my thirty-six years' service had there been a stimulating opportunity like this. Despite the unknown difficulties and complications that might lie ahead, in spite of the stories of frustration that had filtered back to us, I felt myself lucky to be joining an international force where my specialized knowledge and training would have wider scope. Although hard experience had taught me to be skeptical of high-faluting words such as "ideals," and I was already familiar with unrewarding service, I was confident that in becoming an "international soldier" I was entering a new and very worthwhile period of my life.

At Idlewild airport, where snow was driving hard across the runways, I was met by a member of the permanent Swedish delegation to the UN. The early morning sky was dark and cloudy as we drove into New York toward the great glass building on the East River, so that the impact of the city's skyline was almost lost as we plunged into the canyons between lines of skyscrapers, and entered a world of steel and concrete that seemed to envelop us until, in my still shaky state, I had the impression it was difficult to breathe.

Straight from the bitter cold, we entered the almost tropical heat of the glass palace. My first impression was of some giant hothouse whose endless corridors stretched away into infinity from the central lobby where a plethora of lifts poised like body snatchers, impatient to abduct the visitor and whisk him in high-velocity silence to one of the countless floors above.

In due course we were snatched up and carried to the thirty-eighth floor, where the Secretary General and his top executives had their offices and council rooms. Floor 38 was the powerhouse of the whole Secretariat building. The offices of principal and undersecretaries spread down to the next floor, but it was here the inner councils were held and decisions taken.

I had hardly stepped out of the lift when I was warmly welcomed by a Canadian, Leo Malania, who was Georgian by birth and whose father had held a high post in Czarist Russia. He turned out to be an exceptionally charming man, and as he showed me the office I had been assigned during my stay, and began the first of many briefings on the way in which the UN Secretariat functioned, I was much impressed by his patent honesty and sincerity, and imagined in my innocence he must be typical of the high standard of international civil servant who worked in this polyglot beehive.

I was glad to have his help in the days that followed because, without his guidance and ironic humor, I would have been quite bewildered. Not only had I to acclimatize myself to the vibrant atmosphere of the thirty-eighth floor, but there was a mass of documents and reports heaped high on my desk, waiting to be read. There were many other things too on which I had to inform myself. Basic facts that anyone about to enter UN service had to grasp: the charter itself, the staff rules, and the actual machinery through which the decisions of the Security Council and the General Assembly were carried out.

My first visit was to Leo's chief, a man whom rumor credited with being the flywheel of the whole secretariat. Andrew Cordier was the Secretary General's Chief Executive Assistant and undoubtedly one of his closest and most trusted advisers, a key member of the small group who would help Hammarskjöld decide whether I was suitable to command a UN Field Mission.

Cordier—"Uncle Andy" to this intimate circle on the thirty-eighth floor and far beyond—was a big man with a genial, rather fleshy face. His hand, which gripped mine in a welcoming clasp, was like a big ham and was just as capable, as I was to learn later, of thumping the table violently in my support. I was impressed by his face, the eyes a curious mixture of lucid hardness and twinkling humor which left one in no doubt that this was a man who knew his own mind. But I had no conception then of his fund of good stories, tremendous sense of fun, and the love of good food that he had inherited from Alsatian ancestors.

Our conversation was limited to some direct and searching questions and a very brief résumé of the difficulties I might be facing. There was not the slightest attempt to disguise the fact that the job of Chief of Staff of UNTSO had a wealth of disturbing features about it, and I was aware I was being shrewdly summed up by a man who had become something of a master at assessing human nature.

A couple of days were to elapse before we paid our next visit to another of the Secretary General's trusted executives. As Ralph Bunche rose from behind his desk with outstretchd hand, I was aware that never in my life had I met a man with such kind eyes. No one could have made me more welcome or done more to reinforce the feeling already implanted by Cordier, that I had come into an organization dedicated to preserving world peace and the service of mankind. Our personal relationship was destined to become strained, but I liked Ralph instinctively, and became extremely fond of him. When later on we clashed and I criticized him it was inevitable I should be hurt and upset at his bitter resentment. For I was to discover that beneath that gentle exterior Ralph combines a touchy soul with a highly individual working pattern likely to create unnecessary complications in times of emergency.

Perhaps through an instinctive desire to maintain security, he seems reluctant to delegate a single detail. Even in a crisis, the most minute issues demand his personal attention with the inevitable result that action is held up, no decisions are taken, and subordinates are driven to frenzy while the conscientious Ralph works himself into the ground.

But on that cold January day there was a real warmth between us as he told me about his own experiences in Palestine, where he had taken over as Mediator after my old friend Folke Bernadotte had been murdered by Jewish terrorists in Jerusalem. Everything he said coincided with and reinforced the impressions I had gained in the meantime from my predecessor's reports.

The situation there, according to all their reports, was so unsatisfactory as to make the UN's role virtually impossible. Clichés may seem unwarranted but Palestine was a cliché in itself—"a running sore," "a bone of contention," "an insuperable problem," and as far as I could see any Chief of Staff was in for a permanent "hot seat."

To do him justice, Ralph was very frank and made no attempt to gloss over the realities of the situation in Jerusalem. Consequently, when I was summoned to see the Secretary General next day, I was in a slightly skeptical frame of mind which was at odds with the mood of high optimism in which I had arrived.

I had met Dag Hammarskjöld several times, both as a young man and during the war years when he had been working for the Swedish Government. But since the moment when he had moved out into the international stage, our paths had never crossed.

But he was just as I remembered him, of medium stature, fair haired, brisk and alert in an outwardly rather cool impersonal way that hid a capacity for spontaneous feeling which was seldom manifest except to his close friends and trusted colleagues. There was something dedicated about him, perhaps some powerful inner ambition closely intermingled with idealism.

I was to come to know him well, but on that morning, greeted with a disarming smile and a casual reference to an earlier meeting, my first instinctive impression was of two complex characteristics. On the one hand, an iron will. On the other, beneath that protective cloak of faint aloofness, a very warm heart, which radiated great charm.

I felt completely relaxed with him; there was never a moment when Dag tried to create an impression of superiority. Although his position as Secretary General, his crystal-clear brain, and natural authority would have made this easy with a soldier like me unversed in international politics, he talked to me as an equal: so fast that sometimes the words lagged far behind his thoughts.

At first, I found it difficult to keep pace with the ideas, impressions, and advice that flowed so rapidly. His lightning thumbnail sketch of Palestine was masterly, but studded with so many allusions, names, and places with which the short time I had had to study the reports had left me unfamiliar, that I was often left miles behind him, still struggling to comprehend some especially tangled point while he was already discussing another—or even one beyond that! Nonetheless, out of this rather one-sided conversation came a growing certainty that were I to take up the post, I should never lack his support, and always be able to rely on him for guidance. Instinctively, I sensed him to be a man who would stand by one in times of trial, who would always listen, and whose judgment and advice would be frank and honest.

What a man he was: seemingly ambiguous and ambivalent outside his inner circle of executives and field commanders, because without these qualities he would never have survived the crucible of power alignments that shaped the growing United Nations. With his spring-steel resilience, he was able to bend to the winds of the Great Powers, even anticipate the gusts as they came from a dozen different directions, yet invariably he came upright, singleminded in his main purpose of preserving the power of the Secretariat.

In the days that followed, I became increasingly aware of the real power held by the Secretary General and the small group of permanent staff he had gathered around him in the top echelon of the Secretariat. Some of these he had inherited, others he had chosen himself. But the more I saw of this exclusive inner circle that seldom numbered more than half a dozen, the more I had the impression that it had formed itself into a sort of club under the presidency of the Secretary General who directed, served, and inspired the fount of UN policy.

This group and the greater structure of the Secretariat around it provided the only element of stability and continuity in the international Phoenix which had risen (and was still fast growing) from the ashes of the last war. At this time its preponderance of Americans was a reflection of the early days at Burnt Oaks and San Francisco when the infant UN had been almost entirely dependent for its existence on the United States. The United States was still the largest single contributor to the United Nations, paid most of its bills, provided its major transport and ancillary facilities, and bore the greatest share of the costs of its field missions. Recently, however, the Secretary General had been under heavy fire from the Soviet Union and its satellites because of the number of his American advisers. At this time Dag was still strong enough to disagree. He defended himself vigorously, claiming that he had created a new race of supranational civil servants whose loyalty was solely to the UN. Whatever the rights and wrongs, he leaned heavily on this outstandingly able and devoted American element, and I was to discover that they repaid his trust with unswerving loyalty.

Over the next few days, I became increasingly immersed in the mass of reports. One of the obvious things that stood out from the confusing day-to-day details of the harassed activities of the UNO mission in Palestine was that neither Israel, Egypt, Jordan, Syria, or Lebanon (the states which had signed the Armistice) showed any enthusiasm for observing it. All seemed to have their own conflicting interpretations.

I was, therefore, intrigued to meet some of their permanent delegates. Mr. Kidron, the Israeli Ambassador, small, dark, and neat with a high, sloping forehead, left me with the impression that the Government would soon "put me right" once I got out there. In contrast, Omar Loutfi, the Ambassador for the United Arab Republic, was a jovial man who radiated great charm and went out of his way to be friendly. But I was left in little doubt that these courtesy visits within the rarefied air of the glass building bore little relation to the experiences that lay before me once New York was exchanged for the heat and dust of the frontiers.

Not that I would not have welcomed a little warmth in the temperature in New York. Outside the great building, the city was freezing. And perhaps because I was still feeling far from well, I have never since come to like it; the only emotion New York has ever succeeded in arousing in my heart has been a lasting dread of colds and gastric flu.

The glass palace, however, was fascinating. Each day saw fresh doors opened to me, doors whose knobs were likely to give one a nasty shock because of the vast amount of static electricity that seemed to live a life of its own in the building. Despite this hazard, the huge rabbit warren never ceased to intrigue me, as a vast sort of international meld where competition for votes never seemed to flag.

As each new nation arrived, it was wooed and feted by the power blocs or any country with a case to make. Never have I seen such a bargaining place, although most of this went on out of sight in this natural hive of intrigue and speculation. Even top-brass offices were equipped with doors opening into different corridors, discreetly to obviate collisions between parties with differing interests.

I toured its political lobbies, its delegates' dining rooms and lounges vibrant with rumor and speculation. Every time one ate there the operative question always seemed to be, "Who is lunching with whom . . . and *why?*" Nor could I guess how much this barrel-rolling was to be intensified over the next few years as delegates from thirty emergent nations arrived in exotic national garb or black coats and striped trousers to add their votes and voices and a new power bloc to this international changing house on the East River.

For the next few days I was totally absorbed in Palestine. Here the United Nations had inherited the shredded remnants of a legacy that stretched back to 1917 and the Sykes-Picot Agreement (named after the British and French negotiators who, in May 1916, had carved up the old Ottoman Empire in anticipation of its collapse once the war came to an end). This had soon been followed by a solemn promise to establish a national home for the Jews in Palestine. Its terms, agreed upon by Mr. A. J. Balfour, were, however, ambiguous. But in 1918 this hardly seemed to matter.

The British had captured Palestine and were to continue to administer it under mandate from the League of Nations. At first all went well, but as the war clouds gathered over Europe, the increased tempo of Jewish immigration began to raise such problems that the Holy Land gradually developed all the characteristics of a great armed camp in which murders, skirmishes, and minor rebellions became rehearsals for a full-scale Arab-Jewish clash rendered inevitable once the growing pressures and stresses engendered by the Second World War began to be felt.

There is no time here to give a detailed picture of the devoted efforts to avert this clash. There are few more tragic tales than the history of round-table conferences, discussions, and lines of tentative division sketched across a dozen successive maps, while in the background the toll of murder mounted and arms and ammunition were smuggled across the frontiers or stolen from a British garrison which had become an unhappy target for both sides.

Toward the end of 1947, the British informed the United Nations that they were relinquishing the Mandate and would withdraw their troops from the country. This they proceeded to do and it soon became plain that with their going there was bound to be war between the new State of Israel and the Arab countries.

The tension became so great that on April 11, 1948 the Security Council called for a truce between the two sides and twelve days later established a Truce Commission (the forerunner of UNTSO) in Jerusalem. On May 14, as the last of the British troops were leaving, the General Assembly decided to appoint a mediator. But on May 15—with the British gone—the new State of Israel was proclaimed and its troops, who had long been training in secret, rapidly occupied considerable sectors of the country. Simultaneously, the Arab states declared war and Egyptian, Syrian, Jordanian, and Iraqi troops moved over the frontiers.

Fighting was fierce and the UN was not slow to act. On May 21 the post of mediator was filled by Folke Bernadotte, who was instructed eight days later by the Security Council to act in concert with the Truce Commission and set up teams of military observers.

After the Security Council had made a second unsuccessful appeal for a truce, Bernadotte eventually succeeded in arranging a cease fire. But this lasted only from June 11 until July 9, when fighting began again.

On July 15 the Security Council *ordered* both sides to cease hostilities and Bernadotte was able to arrange a truce, which came into effect in Jerusalem on July 16 and two days later elsewhere. It was an uneasy peace because, during the recent "ten days' war," Israel had had considerable military success and had occupied 50 per cent more territory than any international plan had previously allotted her, and the best part of a million Palestine Arabs were in flight. There were frequent breaches of the truce and Egypt remained at war with Israel.

On September 17 came the tragic news that Folke Bernadotte had been murdered in the streets of Jerusalem by the Stern gang. All Swedish officers who had been serving with him were withdrawn, and Ralph Bunche, who had been acting as the Secretary

General's personal representative, was given full authority over the Palestine Mission as Acting Mediator while Brigadier General W. E. Riley, USMC, was appointed Chief of Staff UNTSO (United Nations Truce Supervisory Organization).

On October 22 continual breaches of the truce made it necessary for the Security Council to renew proposals for a cease fire. This was accepted by both sides except on the Egyptian-Israeli border, where fighting was only brought to a halt on December 29 after the British Government had threatened to intervene against the Egyptians.

In mid-January 1949, Armistice negotiations were commenced between Israel and her neighbors. One after another the States reached agreement until, with Syria's signature on July 20, the Armistice Agreement covered all the territory.

On August 11, UNTSO, no longer subordinated to the Mediator, became a subsidiary mission of the United Nations. It faced a difficult task. The cease fire had brought large-scale hostilities to an end, but it had left ill-defined armistice demarcation lines like deep fissures across the old map with neutralized areas stretching eight to ten miles back on either side.

Unfortunately these lines had never been properly marked out on the ground and the exact locations, where heavy guns, tanks, and troop concentrations were forbidden, were hotly disputed by both sides, who based their claims on totally differing sets of maps. These zones, which engulfed small villages, fields, hills, rivers, and lakes, were supposed to contain only a minimum of troops and border police, forbidden under the terms of the Armistice, "to commit any hostile or warlike act against each other."

In addition, a number of completely demilitarized zones had been created, designed to lower the tension at particularly sensitive spots. Here the idea was to ban any military force whatsoever. But the troubles that promptly sprang up over land ownership and cultivation, in an area whose sovereignty was not likely to be decided until a final peace was signed, led to such contention that each of these areas had developed into a potential flash point.

The UN blueprint for peace looked viable enough on a map. UNTSO had a strong base in Jerusalem, and each frontier had a separate Mixed Armistice Commission composed of Arabs and

Israelis under the chairmanship of a United Nations officer whose observers were stationed at observation and control points along the border.

The machinery was in existence to make the Armistice work effectively, but from the beginning there had been incessant trouble ranging from random firing and sporadic raids to a full-scale war between Israel and Egypt, which had carried the Israelis to the Suez Canal and had drained off many of UNTSO's best officers when a United Nations Emergency Force had had to be rushed into the Gaza area.

In the political field, too, there had been incessant trouble. Although UNTSO's first Chief of Staff, the American General Riley, had been regarded as taking too favorable a view of the Israelis, his successor, the Danish General Bennike, had been declared *persona non grata* by the Israeli Government. In turn *his* successor, the Canadian General Burns (who left UNTSO to take over the Emergency Force) had been accused of favoring the Arabs.

This was the uneasy "hot seat" I was being offered. As I read through the files that had accumulated during the previous years, I could understand why Colonel Leary, the American Marine who was temporarily holding the fort, was anxious to get away to less troubled fields. It seemed the observers there had been saddled with an impossible dual role. Not only were they supposed to check frontier violations, but to *prevent* them. Nor, when trying to insure no military or political advantage was gained after incidents *had* taken place, was their work made easier through their enforced reliance on Arab and Israeli liaison officers who accompanied them to interpret evidence on the spot.

Worst of all was the realization that transgressors on either side were confident UN observers could expect no strong backing from their parent organization; the shadowy threat of sanctions over so small an issue as a border incident evoked nothing more than hollow laughter. As far as I could see, the observer endeavoring to resolve some border conflict where men, and all too often women and children, were being killed, had little more than his own personality to fall back on.

I was concerned, too, about the logistic support. The prime

necessity for an efficient observer force is first-rate communications, helicopters for observation, transport planes and vehicles, and the air crew, radio operators, and maintenance staff to keep them functioning on a round-the-clock basis. As far as I could make out, these were nonexistent or in short supply. The air force consisted of exactly *one* Dakota, and reading through the memoranda on supply, I sensed a lack of *rapport* between the commanders of the Mission and the administrative services in New York.

I had met the head of these administrative services, David Vaughan, and one of his assistants in Andrew Cordier's office. Vaughan, a small, voluble, bald-headed American with a round face had explained the ramifications of his General Services Branch, which coordinated supplies, personnel, and administrative support for UN missions.

I had been delighted to meet the man on whose cooperation so much would depend. But after listening for a while, I had had the rather disturbing suspicion that in New York the quartermasters dictated to the generals. This struck me as strange. I had imagined this principle had been settled for all time in the post-mortem that had followed the Crimean war. But once I had a chance to discuss it with more knowledgeable people on the thirty-eighth floor, I found that a state of friction existed between the top executives around the Secretary General and many of the administrative people seventeen floors below.

There, on the twenty-first floor, were the teeming offices of another large and powerful club, which had created an existence for itself, holding the purse strings, administering the building, controlling the recruitment and employment of personnel, handling the purchasing of stores and supplies from blotting paper and computers to tons of wheat or rice and exercising an extraordinary degree of control over the missions in the field.

I had heard that there was some controversy about its activities and that complaints from the field about the "21 Club's" * tend-

* My nickname for a group of administrative big-wigs on the twenty-first floor. There is, of course, no connection with any club or business establishment that may have the same name.

ency to take a hand in policy matters had resulted in summonses from the Secretary General's executive staff.

For the moment I was more preoccupied with making up my own mind. On the face of it, the job I was being offered seemed impossible. But a command is always what one makes it, and the rebel in me sensed a challenge. I had always responded to challenges, and Dag and his executives on the thirty-eighth floor had fired me with something of their own enthusiasm and sense of purpose. After a great deal of thought, I decided to grasp the nettle, totally unsuspecting its deep and tenacious roots.

When I met him again and he asked me how I felt about tackling the job, I told Dag that provided the United Nations wanted me, I would take the post. At that time it seemed to offer two distinct possibilities; I might succeed, I might fail—in either case, I was determined to survive for a couple of years.

Once I had arrived at my decision to accept that post, Dag *really* began to talk about Palestine. I have never forgotten that highly objective summary. Some of it he promised to confirm in writing. The more confidential parts he merely asked me to remember. There was little likelihood I would forget since every word had a direct bearing on the situation in Jerusalem.

He concluded, "When you get there you will find a weak Mission, which has become depressed because of a number of setbacks. Just now the Acting Chief of Staff is in disfavor with the Arabs, but I imagine you have already discovered how easy it is to incur the antagonism of the Israelis. Take your time. Study the Mission and your staff and take an especially close look at the Administration. Remember that personal integrity is vitally important. Clean your own stables if you find it necessary. And once you've done that, make sure they stay reasonably clean."

I was not quite certain then what he meant by "reasonably" but had no time to ask as he went on, "Do everything to gain the confidence of the Arabs, but remember that whatever you do, you will never have the wholehearted confidence and cooperation of the Israelis. When you come to me with suggstions, rest assured you will have all the support you need."

Had he added: "But not the wholehearted support and cooperation of some of our administrative people," the picture might have been complete.

Chapter Six

MISSION IN JERUSALEM

On March 20, 1958 my car with its UN escort came slowly up the winding road toward El Mukkabir hill and I caught my first glimpse of the white building with its flagstaff and little cupolas that was to be my home. An imperial remnant, there was still a flavor of the old colonial dream about its square white walls set amid beautiful flower gardens; the British flair for selecting imposing sites had not deserted them when they chose this dominant spot on "The Hill of Evil Counsel" with its breathtaking views over the Old City and its surrounding hills.

Since the departure of the last High Commissioner in 1948, Government House had stood isolated in a no man's land between two hostile states. Folke Bernadotte had selected it as a UN Headquarters only a few hours before his death. Throughout the next ten years, its square white tower had flown the UN flag, its lofty rooms and arcades had echoed to the clatter of typewriters and the shrill ring of telephones, and its flat roofs had sprouted antennae from the powerful short-wave sets that linked this outpost in the Judean hills with a UN network between New York, Geneva, Bangkok, and Korea.

Later that evening, gazing out over the Old City from my balcony and watching the interplay of light and shadow across the distant hills that appeared deceptively tranquil, I knew I had been right to make Government House my home. Looking toward the Mount of Olives and away northeast across Bethany toward the ridges marking the descent into the Jordan Valley, I knew there could be no doubt about it. In the distance rose the purple outline of the distant Mountains of Moab. It was quiet here, the only

PALESTINE
0
20
40
60
Miles
N
LEBANON
R. Hasbani
Damascus
SYRIA
Naqoura
Queneitra
Lake Huleh
Moussadiye
Kafr Aequeb
ISRAEL
Jordan
Lake Tiberias
Koursi
Nuqeib
Ein Gev
Tawafic
Haifa
Tiberias
Porya
R. Yarmouk
Hadera
MEDITERRANEAN SEA
Nablus
R. Jordan
JORDAN
Tel Aviv
Latrun 'No-man's-land'
Ramallah
Amman
Jericho
Latrun
Issawyia
Buffer area between the lines
JERUSALEM
Bethany
Bethlehem
Gaza
GAZA STRIP
Hebron
Dead Sea
Bersheba
ISRAEL
NEGEV
EGYPT
Armistice line
International boundary
1 2 3 4 Observation posts in ISRAEL controlled territory
A observation post ALPHA
B observation post BRAVO
C observation post CHARLIE
D observation post DELTA
E observation post ECHO
F observation post FOX
in SYRIA

spot where I would find freedom from the tensions on either side of the coils of barbed wire that cut Jerusalem into two hostile camps. In this unhappy city, the only breath of genuine neutrality was beneath the UN flag that hung limply in the evening air.

It had been a long and tiring day. At Beirut airport I had noted the lined and exhausted face of my Acting Chief of Staff, Colonel Byron V. Leary. Leary was visibly relieved to see me, and introduced me to the sole Dakota that constituted our one-plane UN air force. After obtaining clearance for our flight route over Lebanon, Israel, and Jordan we had left Beirut and our white plane with its distinctive UN markings (which I was later to discover did not always protect us from the attentions of Israeli fighters) soon had Tel Aviv to port as we flew across Israel to Kalandia, the Jordanian airport for Jerusalem.

Here I had been received by the military and civic authorities with flowery but time-consuming speeches in impeccable English. Finally, our car had brought us along the Nablus Road skirting the Old City, and I had had my first sight of its medieval walls, glittering white against a background of tawny hills and gray-green olive groves.

The faces that greeted me in Government House had been encumbered with that half cautious, half quizzical expression that the arrival of a new Chief invariably evokes. There had been Colonel Nelson, my American Chief of Operations, a thin, stoop-shouldered man with a permanently worried expression. Next I had been introduced to Henri Vigier, a Frenchman who had seen more chiefs come and go than he cared to remember since he had started his service with the League of Nations in Geneva.

"The Old Fox," as I was to come to know him, was a remarkable character. He had joined the UN when already past pensionable age and had been in Jerusalem since 1947, serving Bernadotte and Bunche and a succession of other masters. His experience was formidable and I was glad to have him as my special political adviser. He had drafted and virtually negotiated the Armistice Agreement, and owing to his long and unbroken service had become the anchor pin in a Mission whose efficiency had been weakened through a high turnover of staff. I sensed that here was a man of exceptional caliber, astute to a degree and motivated by a high sense of duty. I was right. Once I had gained his confidence, the Old Fox proved a wonderfully loyal collaborator and I came to lean heavily on his experience and political judgment.

It seemed I was to be surrounded by French-speaking executives. I had met Paul Berthaud, my tall, stooping and bespectacled legal adviser, whose extrovert Swiss personality struck me as being flavored with a shrewd sense of humor. I had taken a liking, too, to Albert Grand, my Press Officer, a chunky, well-built fellow of Norman extraction with blue eyes, a ruddy complexion, and a ginger crew cut, who was to give me help and cooperation in the days ahead far beyond the official line of duty.

From the first I had the strongest feeling that the presence at HQ of these three gentlemen, whose mutual morning cry of "Bonjour" was to become a familiar and welcome greeting and who, I gathered, were already collectively known as "The Fifth Republic," * augured well for the future. As yet, I had hardly had time to have a word with my chief administrative officer.

I was almost in danger of allowing myself to become optimistic. Perhaps it was the effect of the clear light, the olive trees, the patterns of light and of shade across the hills. Possibly even, the dark blue haze across the distant Mountains of Moab, and the scent of the flowers from the gardens beneath my balcony. For the moment, I seemed to have laid aside forebodings.

I was brought sharply back to reality next morning. Colonel Leary's drawn face and obvious fatigue as he took me round headquarters were eloquent of the pressures in store. Leary, a devout Catholic, was in high disfavor with the Arabs, who accused him of Israeli sympathies.

The manner in which this had come about was ludicrous but typical of the climate of suspicion that surrounded us. It was his custom to attend early Mass at a convenient neighboring convent, after which he would come straight on to headquarters, entering the building promptly at seven o'clock each morning. His arrival was noted by our local Jordanian staff. And since he invariably entered through the gate facing the Israeli lines (the nearest entrance to the convent) it was presumed by Jordanian Intelligence

* A jocular reference to their natural habit of talking French together and forming a little enclave within a Mission whose operational speech was mainly English.

(who knew that his family had been evacuated from Jerusalem) he had come straight from the arms of an Israeli mistress in the Jewish sector. Nothing could shake them from this belief and I congratulated myself on my decision to make my own home *inside* Headquarters.

It was not an auspicious morning. As I went around the W/T room, the operations center, the executive and administrative offices which were the framework for our observer groups hundreds of miles away on four different frontiers, I began to realize that sharp lines of division were separating my new command.

Netted in to those high-powered sets in the W/T room were the headquarters of the four Mixed Armistice Commissions (MAC), which controlled the activities of one hundred and nine observers. Almost all these observers were officers loaned from the armed forces of twelve Member States. There were Americans, Australians, Belgians, Canadians, Danes, Frenchmen, Irishmen, Italians, Dutchman, New Zealanders, Norwegians, and Swedes. Each had an unusually difficult task to carry out, observing and reporting with the simple tools of the peacekeeper's trade: maps, binoculars, compass, radio hand set, a radio-equipped jeep, and most important of all, his own personality and authority.

All these observers would have been totally immobilized without the other element in my command—the one hundred fifty-one civilians who were career employees of the United Nations. It was they who manned the radios, drove the staff cars and supply trucks, maintained vehicles and equipment, acted as guards, and provided the key personnel who kept headquarters functioning in Jerusalem.

Each different element, I gathered, soldiers and civilians, had very definite views about where their loyalties lay. From a military point of view this was an extraordinary situation that would have been considered suicidal in any national force. But it seemed this was the established pattern of a UN Field Mission that other commanders before me had accepted. To me, however, it seemed an amorphous arrangement that invited internal dissension.

A glance at the maps in the operations room made one aware how disastrous this could be. Each MAC was faced with a formidable task. Apart from her stretch of coastline, Israel was surrounded by five hundred and forty-five miles of hostile Arab territory. From north to south Lebanon, Syria, Jordan, and Egypt hemmed her in along a continual frontier which on the map resembled a cartographic game of snakes and ladders. On first sight, it appeared incredible, on a second, incomprehensible.

The old international boundaries were still there, but the Armistice Demarcation Line, based on the military lines held at the time when the fighting had been stopped, had turned them into a nightmare of bulges and enclaves. The bulges on either side of the international boundaries had been declared demilitarized zones, with areas stretching back on either side where armored troops and heavy artillery were excluded. But, although there were maps galore, no survey teams had yet delineated the armistice lines on the ground. And as both sides worked from their own maps and vehemently denied the validity of either the other side's or the UN's serious trouble was always in the air.

Each of the four frontiers had highly individual characteristics. In the north, along the Lebanon-Israeli border where the Chairman of the MAC was the French Colonel Le Petit, the situation was almost idyllically quiet. Relations were as near excellent as they can be in the Middle East, and mutual problems were settled in a surprisingly cooperative manner. So gentle was the tempo here that the MAC needed only three observers. Its headquarters were in Beirut with an outpost station on the coast at Naqoura.

A very different picture emerged along the Israeli-Syrian border where fierce outbreaks of shooting and shelling invariably coincided with ploughing, sowing, and harvesting. It was a fruitful if disputed zone where the wheat and barley fields sometimes yielded two crops a year, and the ploughing time, when the Israelis tended to encroach on Arab-owned land, was regarded by both sides as the beginning of the shooting season. Every mile of ground in and on either side of the demilitarized areas here was a source of potential trouble.

We had fifty-three observers under the Canadian Lieutenant Colonel Bertrand manning four observation posts on the Israeli side and five on the Syrian side of the Armistice Line, which stretched for forty-five miles up to the Lakes of Tiberias and Huleh and on to the headwaters of the Jordan. Each post was occupied by two observers on a twenty-four-hours-a-day basis and there was such implacable hatred on either side of this border world of dusty stone villages, wheat fields, and banana groves that Colonel Bertrand and his observers always had their hands full.

Headquarters operated from Damascus with control points on either side of the frontier at Tiberias and Queneitra, and its work was a peacekeeper's nightmare because the Israeli members refused to attend meetings at which Syrians were present. And this despite their obstructionist tactics having been roundly condemned by the Security Council in New York.

South again . . . and stretching back toward the Judean hills was my second largest MAC, under Colonel Flint, a Canadian, whose observers watched the whole length of the Israeli-Jordan border with headquarters in Jerusalem in no man's land near the small square known as the Mandelbaum Gate.

Thirty-one observers kept a round-the-clock watch from a line of outpost stations along the border, and maintained jeep patrols along the west bank of the Jordan (always a sensitive spot since —as can be seen from the map—heavy guns rushed up here could shell Tel Aviv across the thirteen-mile waist of the new State). In addition, they had the tricky task of supervising twice weekly convoys that supplied Mount Scopus, whence, amid the buildings of the Hebrew Hospital and University, a Jewish "Police" garrison gazed down at Jerusalem and their homeland while their compatriots below gazed up with a fervor that led to constant disputes over the supplies carried by the convoys.

Lastly, there was the Israeli-Egyptian frontier where our MAC was commanded by a New Zealander, Lieutenant Colonel Maurice Brown. Normally the scene of constant forays and border incidents, this area had become potentially less explosive owing to the presence of UNEF, the Canadian General Burns's Emergency Force with its headquarters in Gaza.

An extraordinary situation existed here. The Israelis (who claimed that the Sinai campaign had invalidated the Armistice Agreement) professed themselves unable to deal with our MAC but only with General Burns in the event of trouble arising from border incidents. Yet it was the observers from our own MAC in Gaza who were subsequently employed in investigating complaints because the UN would not accept this unilateral Israeli concept of invalidating the Armistice Agreement.

UNTSO in Jerusalem controlled all the MAC's, was in constant W/T contact with their headquarters, and over the net could hear the reports of their observers on the spot. By listening over the W/T I soon discovered what a hard and unrewarding job they had. It was a hot and dusty life on those frontiers. They were frequently in the middle of the fighting, and never failed to make the most strenuous efforts to impose a cease fire lest a skirmish trigger off a more serious clash. As though this were not enough, they were often forced into assuming a quasi judicial role in the villages where trouble flared; exchanging peasants who had become "prisoners," securing the return of strayed or stolen livestock, even the more peaceful role of advising on rabies, malaria, or child delivery; or assisting in the battle against the locusts, which knew no frontiers and descended on the fields of friend and foe in huge impartial clouds.

What depressed me was the feeling that I lacked the ultimate strength to back them up in a crucial emergency. I was, of course, experiencing the "moment of truth" that overtakes every soldier up against the reality of a peacekeeper's role. Possibly the few remaining British may have felt the same way during the more dreadful times of the Indian partition. Certainly more and more UN officers were destined to experience it in the Congo and Cyprus. It was an uncomfortable feeling. Instead of combat troops, tanks, and artillery or even the threat of sanctions, all I had was my own determination and Dag's moral support.

The more I talked to my staff and delved into the files (which were in a sad state owing to a hopelessly inept filing system, and the Old Fox's habit of secreting his memoranda in some private cache) the more it became clear that immediate trouble could be expected from two spots.

First, there was Mount Scopus on our doorstep where the Jewish enclave tactically commanded the greater part of the Old City and the main road to Ramallah and Nablus. Second, there was the Syrian frontier, that seemed certain to erupt. Every factor pointed toward it: the Syrians' professed intention to hurl the Jews back into the sea, Jewish plans for diverting the headwaters

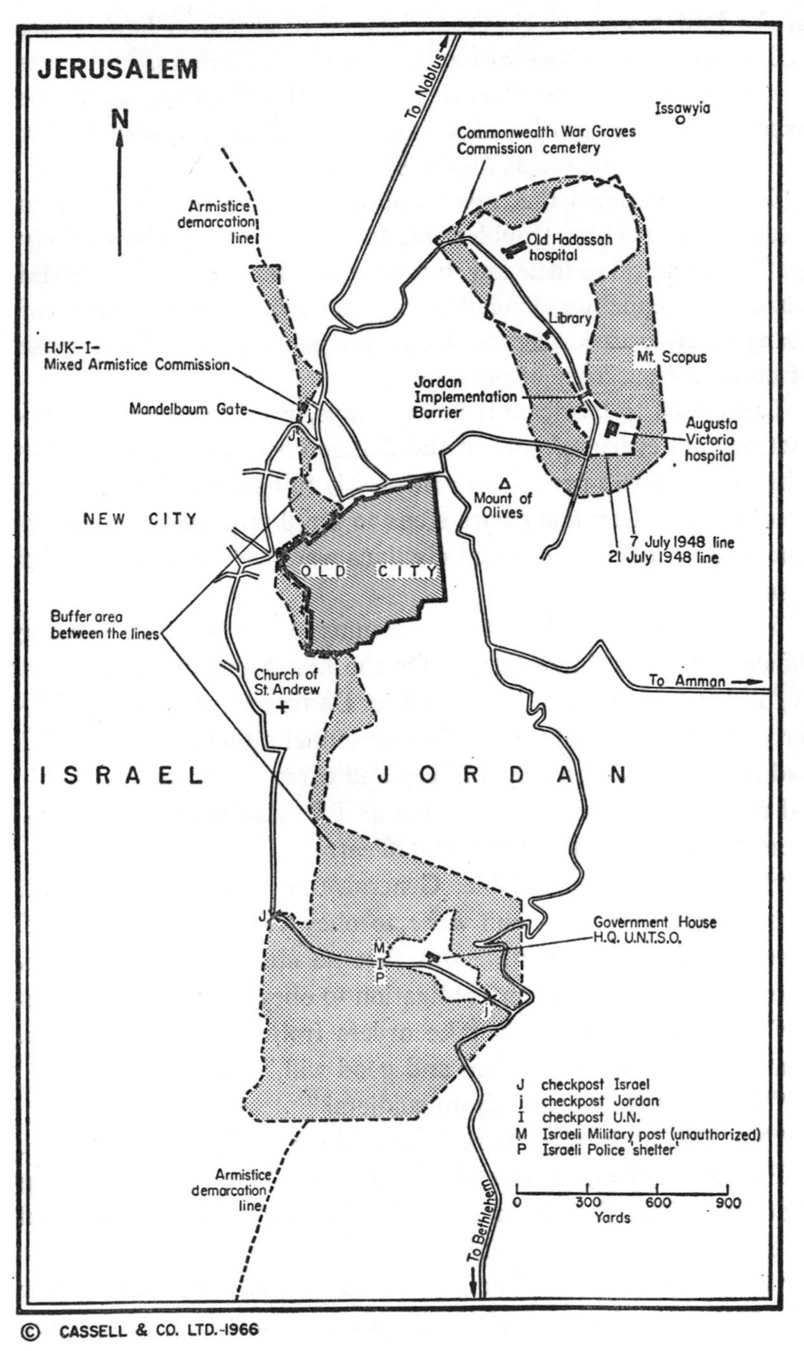
JERUSALEM
N
To Nablus
Issawyia
Commonwealth War Graves
Commission cemetery
Armistice
demarcation
line
Old Hadassah
hospital
Library
HJK-I-
Mixed Armistice Commission
Mt. Scopus
Jordan
Implementation
Barrier
Mandelbaum Gate
Augusta
Victoria
hospital
Mount of
Olives
NEW CITY
7 July 1948 line
21 July 1948 line
OLD CITY
Buffer area
between the lines
Church of
St. Andrew
To Amman
ISRAEL
JORDAN
Government House
H.Q. U.N.T.S.O.
J checkpost Israel
j checkpost Jordan
I checkpost U.N.
M Israeli Military post (unauthorized)
P Israeli Police 'shelter'
Armistice
demarcation
line
0 300 600 900
Yards
To Bethlehem

of the Jordan, and the claims and counterclaims over land tenure and agricultural activity within the demilitarized zones. There was a tense and bitter confrontation along this frontier; even the fishermen on the Sea of Galilee (now Lake Tiberias) were subject to fusillades of rifle fire as they cast their nets.

I was determined that my mission should be in a fit state to meet a crisis at either trouble spot. Its authority might be severely limited, its morale a little low, but our observers had done splendid work under appalling difficulties before now, and were capable of rising to the occasion again. What was needed was a fresh sense of unity, a resurgence of purpose.

I proposed to inculcate it in two ways. First, by personal contact, so that every member of the Mission became aware the new Chief of Staff was prepared to throw his full support behind their efforts. Second, by immediate steps to build up a fully integrated command so that soldiers and civilians were welded into one solid team.

My intention to integrate my command ran into illuminating difficulties almost immediately. On the first Monday I received a W/T call from Colonel Bertrand in Damascus complaining bitterly that members of the civilian personnel attached to his MAC had refused orders to stay on duty and carry out urgent mechanical repairs to some jeeps. As soon as I had switched off, I summoned my Chief Administrative Officer.

"It's quite understandable, General," he said earnestly, "you must realize our men don't *have* to obey Colonel Bertrand. I'd take the liberty of pointing out that no staff member who has taken the oath is under any obligation to obey military orders. As UN civilians, when we *do* take orders from soldiers, it's just a demonstration of cooperation and good will."

"You don't take orders from soldiers?"

"No. Not from soldiers, *sir,*" he told me firmly.

For a moment, I was flabbergasted. Then an interesting thought: "Does that include me?" I inquired. "Are you allowed to take orders from a general?"

"Of course, sir." His face broke into a reassuring smile. "After all, that's *quite* different. Although you happen to be a soldier, you rank as an Under Secretary, and that makes you an international civil servant."

It was evident that this attitude could only have its origin in one source. It was an example of the "administrative prerogative" mentality that the 21 Club in New York inculcated in its staff.

As we continued our talk, I learned that when a chief administrative officer was appointed to UNTSO, it was made quite clear to him that he was going there as the Number Two of the Mission, and on coming to Jerusalem he had naturally expected to have this state of affairs emphasized by a large figure 2 affixed to his UN number plates. Only on arrival did he discover that Henri Vigier, who had been with the Mission ever since its conception, already held this coveted number. His concern had been great and it had had to be explained from New York (who had overlooked this fact) that this was merely a concession to Vigier's age and long service.

Although there was absolutely no doubt about his status and position, he would have to settle for a mere figure 3 on his plates. Unfortunately this numerical demotion had evoked a bitter complaint from the colonel in charge of operations, who had to surrender his 3 for a 4.

It seemed I had much to learn. But my immediate concern was to put an end to a system that allowed young civilians to ignore or refuse orders from officers. Since the efficiency of the Mission depended on their technical skill, this state of affairs was courting open disaster. I put this right at once. And my Chief Administrative Officer, to do him justice, raised no objections when I ordered that from now on his civilians *would* take orders from my officers, and that *everyone* in the Mission would most certainly take orders from me.

An hour or two later, I called a meeting of all my senior civilian and military staff from Headquarters and the neighboring Jordanian MAC. I can still remember their faces, a remarkable mélange of expressive reaction, as I laid down my first laws. During the whole of their service out here, the peculiar system I had just abolished had been tolerated by a succession of chiefs of staff. And now here was a new chief who had hardly had time to "get his knees brown," brandishing an uncouth Swedish broom. My ukase, however, got home—subsequent information made me aware the wires had been red hot that night.

Had I suspected the contents of the Pandora's box waiting to be opened in Jerusalem, I might have been a little more blunt when I told them that the United Nations' reputation in the Middle East was already sufficiently tarnished without being further weakened by internal dissension. All soldiers here already knew where they stood when it came to discipline. But from this moment onward, I wanted the civilians to understand their new position, too.

Starting today, any civilian member of the Mission who refused to obey orders would be sent home immediately, and if New York failed to support my action, then I myself would resign. If anybody had any complaints about my methods, I wanted them made direct to me, and *not* through their own channels to New York. I was aware of these channels. And because I was aware of them, I wanted an assurance of complete cooperation and loyalty from all my staff.

The assurances were immediately forthcoming. But I was not finished. I told them that I regretted finding it necessary to remind soldiers and civilians alike that during their present tour of duty, their *only* loyalty was to the United Nations. For this reason the practice of reporting to their own diplomatic missions in Jerusalem would cease at once, whatever instructions individuals might have received before coming here.

My observers (at whom this was aimed) took it very well despite the fact that they were such a mixed group. I felt we had come some way toward putting our house in order. Though I was to have trouble with a few problem children over the next two years, the more I got to know the rest, the more I found that, on the whole and as far as their actual *work* was concerned, I could hardly have inherited a more loyal, devoted, and hard-working team, who, knowing their actions must invariably bring them into disfavor with one side or other, almost invariably displayed a scrupulous impartiality.

Although I was particularly impressed with the young officers seconded from the Royal Netherlands Marine Corps, it was difficult to single out any one nation whose observers stood head and shoulders above the others. Inevitably the poor Swedes must have suffered from my determination not to show partiality for my own countrymen. I hope they forgave me because they were as good as any in this mixed command that seemed to attract three main types of very dissimilar characters. The first was the best: officers of unusual ability driven by a pioneer spirit to seek an unusual type of service. Next came those who may well have had a share of these characteristics, but basically preferred service abroad for financial or domestic reasons. Finally there was the inevitable leavening of unfortunates whose departure for Palestine had probably been greeted with sighs of relief from subordinates and superiors alike.

During that first hectic week struggling with the complexities and difficulties within my own command, the Old Fox had been continuing my political education. I had a great deal to learn and time was short because I had a round of courtesy calls before me.

As Chief of Staff, UNTSO, it was necessary to visit President Nasser of Egypt, President Ben Zwi of Israel, King Hussein of Jordan, President Chamoun of the Lebanon, and President Shukri Kuwatli of Syria: in fact, all the heads of states and prime ministers whose countries were signatories to the Armistice Agreement. And then, of course, there was Mr. Ben Gurion, the Prime Minister of Israel.

My first visit was not to him but to the Israeli Foreign Office. Although I had been briefed in New York on the Israeli "attitude," I had had no practical experience with the climate that surrounded our negotiations with them, most of which took place through this channel, the only Israeli Government Office functioning in Jerusalem at that time.

I listened carefully to the sage advice of the Old Fox before making my first official visit. Owing to the absence abroad of the Foreign Minister, Mrs. Golda Meir, I was received by Mr. Walter Eytan, its Director General, a high-browed, dart-eyed man of rather short stature. I found it a curious experience, listening to this Bavarian-born Oxford Don with his impeccable but overstressed English.

Eytan did all the talking on this occasion. With him in the room was Yosef Tekoah, the Siberian-born Director of Armistice Affairs with whom I was destined to have many tortuous dealings. I regret to say that even at this first meeting Tekoah's look and manner reminded me forcibly of the reptilian order Ophidia, and although the atmosphere was affable, almost genial, Mr. Eytan's discourse sounded almost like a repetition of the wealth of guidance with which the Israeli Press had greeted my arrival in Jerusalem.

I was soon left in no doubt that the United Nations had failed regrettably to cooperate with Israel's sincere desire for a peaceful settlement, had entirely neglected, in fact, to show the understanding and sympathetic tolerance for a small, oppressed state that would have been in keeping with its role as a world force dedicated to peace. His was a torrent of eloquence that never missed a chance to stress the Israeli case, their sincere desire and unstinted efforts to work toward a peaceful settlement that somehow—it was not always delicately phrased—had been frustrated through the lack of cooperation and understanding of my predecessors.

Obviously, Eytan was now hoping for something better. And the gist of his advice to assist me in my task was that I should refrain from sticking to the rules of the Armistice Agreement. Behind the cultivated Oxford accent, the gracious manners, I sensed an arrogant personal hint that, although the Israelis had no alternative but to put up with me, it was unthinkable that a brutal and licentious soldier from the unknown wastes of the frozen North was likely to be able to negotiate from the same intellectual level as men of culture and political experience within the Israeli Foreign Office.

Once out of his office, I was almost glad to discover myself in the charge of Yosef Tekoah, who had so far spoken very little. But as soon as we were settled in his own room, I discovered that I had stepped from the frying pan into the fire. Once again, I was subjected to the same moralizing, as he half wooed, half reproached me.

It was a remarkable performance. But Yosef, with whom I was later to strike up quite a happy relationship, despite our frequent clashes, was a curious mixture of snake and charmer. Despite the distrust I felt for him, it was not difficult to understand the root cause of his attitude toward us that made him echo Mr. Eytan's advice that I should no longer stick to the rules. Having got rid of the British, the Israeli mind plainly found it hard to accept another parcel of foreigners who, in their view, were constantly carping, criticizing, and actively obstructing their struggle for national survival.

I sensed the same latent resentment in the Foreign Minister, Mrs. Golda Meir, some weeks later, when she returned from an extensive tour in Africa. She is a heavily built lady who seems to exist on a diet of cigarettes and coffee and radiates an aura of what I can only describe as more guts than charm. At the end of our first meeting I took the opportunity of asking a favor. Might I, whatever differences arose between us in the future, always feel at liberty to be entirely frank with her? In an accent that reminded me more of Brooklyn than her native Ukraine, she assured me that this was something she would welcome; in return, she proposed to be equally frank with me.

Chapter Seven

CRISIS

ALTHOUGH I had arrived in Jerusalem during a period of seeming quiet, I was rapidly to discover that we were destined to live from one crisis to another. Before I even had the chance to commence my round of courtesy calls or visit my observers, I was flung headlong into my first shooting incident on the Syrian frontier—which my staff had expected to remain quiet long enough to give us a chance to deal with an ugly situation that was threatening to boil up in the City.

I had been warned about this impending trouble in New York, where Dag had been gravely concerned about the Israelis' declared intention to stage a military parade on April 24 to celebrate the tenth anniversary of the new State. I had raised this subject at the Israeli Foreign Office without success, the only result being a wealth of advice not to stick by the rules of the Armistice Agreement. After that I had consulted the Old Fox, and it was quite clear that in staging their parade the Israelis had no intention of observing the Agreement. It was equally clear that once they moved their guns and tanks into the forbidden zone in Jerusalem, the Jordanians were bound to mobilize in retaliation, the Arab crowds in the Old City would become dangerously stirred up, and we would have a major crisis on our hands.

But on March 24 the Syrian frontier diverted our attention from Jerusalem. Reports coming in from our observation posts in the Lake Huleh sector on the Israeli-Syrian border informed us that heavy firing had broken out and that Syrian shells were pitching among the earth-moving equipment with which the Israelis were digging a new canal.

The swamps around this lake on the northern sector of the border had always been a bone of contention. Even while the British had still been administering the country, the Jews had been busy draining tracts of swampland that they had purchased from Arab proprietors and were turning the fertile marsh earth into rich arable land.

But then the Arab-Israeli war had come, and the Armistice that followed had left a disputed and ill-defined demilitarized zone across this half-touched swampy stretch of country. Inside this zone, however, life went on and property changed hands, invariably in one direction, so that before long the Jews were claiming the right to exploit all the land they had bought whether its eventual nationality had been settled or not. Unfortunately, too, they developed a habit of irrigating and ploughing in stretches of Arab-owned land nearby. For the ground was so fertile that every square foot was a gold mine in grain.

Gradually, beneath the glowering eyes of the Syrians, who held the high ground overlooking the zone, the area had become a network of Israeli canals and irrigation channels edging up against and always encroaching on Arab-owned property. This deliberate poaching was bitterly resented by the Syrians who, shortly after a new canal had been started on March 24, opened fire on the Israeli irrigation teams.

To our observers, they complained that the Israelis had been breaking the Armistice Agreement. Not unreasonably, they also claimed that the canal would prejudice the future ownership of the land whose sovereignty was still to be decided, when and if ever a lasting peace was signed.

The firing was heavy and sustained. Although I could hear from the crowded radio network my observers doing all they could to impose a cease fire, I could imagine, and this was soon substantiated from our control points on either side, the tank and artillery support that must be moving into the forbidden zone.

It was vital to avert a major clash. But my efforts ran into an almost classical pattern of obstruction. On the night of March 26, after receiving an official Syrian complaint, I tried repeatedly to contact Yosef Tekoah, the Israeli Director of Armistice Affairs. The Syrians who had always acknowledged UN authority in the area were already showing signs of listening to reason. But in Jerusalem I was fobbed off by a succession of petty officials (with whose evasions I was to become only too familiar) who informed me that Mr. Tekoah was not in his office and that they were unable to contact him or give any indication of his movements during the next few days.

There was no alternative but to draft a strongly worded letter, suggesting that the Israelis suspend all work on the canal until a United Nations survey team had investigated whether the Syrian complaint was justified. It was almost dawn by the time that I had finished, and I insisted on a reply that day. While I was waiting, I alerted a Canadian survey team and dispatched it at top speed to the Lake Huleh area.

I heard nothing from the Israelis until the afternoon, when Mr. Eytan summoned me to the Foreign Office and informed me coldly that although my approach, indeed my whole attitude, was resented, the Israeli Government was prepared to accept my suggestions. It struck me as remarkable that they had given in so easily since the Old Fox told me that hitherto they had always interpreted the Armistice Agreement to suit their own purpose. During the next few days the Canadians carried out their survey, and I duly communicated their long and complicated report to both governments. I then sat down to study it again myself, aware that the final decision must lie with me.

A close scrutiny soon showed me that the Israelis had been basing their claims in this area on the waterline of a small lake whose level had been steadily sinking for years since the last maps had been made. As its waters had receded, so the Israelis had advanced the "frontier" to their own advantage, a state of affairs not corroborated by the survey that had clearly marked the old level as the real boundary.

Even the Book of Revelation could not have foreseen a situation in the Holy Land in which disputes over the level of a lake fringed with reeds and echoing to the call of flying ducks and the ugly rumble of bulldozers was to fill the air between Jerusalem and New York. But this was what happened once I had decreed that the botanical evidence of the upper level line—in survey parlance, "the vegetation transition line"—should decide the issue in favor of the Syrians.

It was a simple enough decision to take. But Albert Grand had the thankless task of producing six drafts before we could formulate a suitable press release. I requested the Israelis to stop digging their canal and to suspend all work until a seventy-five meter stretch already dug had been rerouted. I anticipated a violent reaction, but much to my surprise they agreed. It was not until the frontier had returned to its normal smoldering state that their newspapers belatedly informed their readers that United Nations surveys were not accurate or binding.

There were other items we gleaned from this face-saving operation in the press. Mr. Ben Gurion, who earlier had vigorously quoted the Bible at me but had hardly impressed me as a religious man, had announced that only American pressure had made him accept my decision. And taking their cue from him the papers put up a wail that Israel had accepted my decision only because otherwise the USA had threatened to invalidate the passports of eighty-five thousand American tourists who were expected to visit the new State that year.

Even Mrs. Meir was later to deny this mythical American pressure. The real explanation was that the Israelis had been caught off guard at a moment when they were especially anxious to push forward their irrigation work. The rapid rerouting of a canal was a pawn they could afford to discard in their unremitting chess game with the United Nations but their cries of foul play at this minor setback were typical of a national phobia, an inherited capacity for translating every event into terms of persecution. Inevitably this state of mind bred vindictiveness, and I was left in no doubt that although I might have won the first round, it was more than likely that there would soon be active measures to insure this never happened again.

I felt the weight of this almost immediately in Jerusalem as April 24 came closer. And after I had come back from a visit to Samir Rifai,* the Jordanian Deputy Prime Minister, whom Dag Hammarskjöld regarded as one of the few real statesmen in the Middle East, I could visualize the reaction there was going to be in Amman once Israeli guns and tanks started moving into Jerusalem.

I raised the issue again with Mrs. Meir but her attitude merely confirmed my fears that the Armistice terms were about to be deliberately broken. There was, therefore, nothing for it but to request details of the number of guns and tanks taking part in the Anniversary parade. It was essential that I knew what to expect. But though well aware that the parade contravened the terms of the Armistice, the Foreign Office professed an entire lack of knowledge, merely assuring me the Chief of the Defense Staff would give me all the information I needed.

It was an impossible situation, made all the more infuriating as days went by without a word from General Haim Laskov. I knew him quite well. He was a heavily built, able officer and was normally an exception to the rule of national self-assertion. In relaxed moments he would even openly admit how proud he was to have learned his soldiering under the British. But now he remained totally unforthcoming and I was forced to try again.

On April 14 I made a formal application for an interview in three days' time. I was forced to submit this through the Foreign Office because protocol forbade a UN Commander to contact the Israeli Chief of Staff direct. This was annoying because I knew relations between the Foreign Office and the Defense Ministry were strained owing to internal rivalries. Had I been able to con-

* Samir Rifai died in November 1965.

tact Laskov direct, I might have been spared a three-day wait without even the courtesy of a reply. It was only on the afternoon of the day on which I had demanded to meet him that I was informed that Laskov would see me at 6 p.m. in three days' time; the delay, the Foreign Office informed me, *was due to their difficulties in contacting the Chief of Staff!*

No excuse could have sounded more ridiculous. One ministry not being able to contact another in a tiny country where communications were remarkably efficient! Weary of this deliberate evasion, I stated flatly that I *would* see the General not later than noon the following day.

We met even earlier. At five o'clock that afternoon, I was told that he would see me in four hours' time. And when nine o'clock came I found myself facing his heavily built figure as he rose reluctantly from behind his desk. Under less exacting circumstances, Laskov was amiable enough. But this evening he was in a rage. His voice sounded constricted and his myopic eyes smoldered as, almost before I could get a word in, he snapped: "We can have a parade when and where we choose in our own country. This is a great day for us. The nearer it gets, the more enthusiastic I become."

I warned him that the parade would mean mobilization in Jordan. My anger at the stupidity of the whole business must have struck home because when I demanded exact figures of the parade strengths he reluctantly peered down at some handwritten notes, and told me there would be eighty tanks, twelve self-propelled guns, some twelve field guns, and six 3.7-inch antiaircraft guns. Before he could continue, I asked whether he had informed the Jordanians.

"No," he replied. "We have told them that there is going to be a parade." Then: "And I don't for the life of me understand what all this fuss is about."

I left him in no doubt. Strong Scotches and sandwiches appeared, the tension gradually eased, Laskov even mellowed a little. But when I tried to persuade him to remove the powder keg that threatened to blow our Armistice sky high, I might just as well have wasted my breath on one of the self-propelled guns he was bent on bringing up from Tel Aviv. Every argument was countered with the perpetual Israeli refrain: "You expect too much. What are we supposed to do . . . stop breathing?"

I had troubled dreams that night, but these could hardly be laid at Laskov's door. Next morning I was prostrated by an attack of gastric flu which proved so violent that it was two days before I was able to stumble out of bed and drive to Amman.

Samir Rifai's reaction was exactly what I had anticipated and feared. This remarkable man was entirely calm; there were no protestations of a Jordanian necessity to "breathe." He was a gray-haired man of medium height whose oval, slightly wrinkled face was usually irradiated by a charming smile.

I had found him a man of wisdom and culture. And now his attitude was typical of the Arab style when dealing with the United Nations. Often just as intransigeant and opportunist as the Israelis, they invariably preserved the formalities that denote breeding and good manners. His voice was regretful, almost as though weary from holding back the tide, as he told me: "Of course, you realize it is quite impossible for us to accept this flagrant violation of the General Armistice Agreement. We have no alternative but to mobilize."

I returned to Jerusalem and reported to Dag in New York that we now had two breaches on our hands. After this there was literally nothing I could do but sit tight and wait. I knew that Dag would be busy pulling whatever political strings were available, but that was his business. I expected active trouble, and told Colonel Flint of the Jordanian MAC to liaise closely with Colonel Nelson in our operations room.

We pulled in every observer who could be spared, and I got my staff busy drafting notes that informed both sides that we were establishing UN observation posts overlooking the route of the parade. At one point this threatened to run dangerously close to the walls of the Old City where crowds of angry Arabs were bound to be peering down. It was from the troublemakers among them, rather than the excitable but disciplined sentries of the Jordan Arab Army, that danger was likely to come.

During the nights before the parade I could hear the rumble of Israeli tanks moving up to their assembly area from the railway station. Each dawn, I had only to look eastward to see the road from Amman blocked with a column of tanks, guns, and trucks as the Jordanians brought in their mixed but potentially lethal armored division. Soon they started digging gun positions in the shadows of the walls of the Old City. No doubt I was still depressed by the aftermath of my gastric flu, yet all of us began to feel the mounting tension. But for once we had underestimated the moral impact of the United Nations presence.

On the eve of the parade, I received two messages that helped to raise our spirits. Each was typical: the Jordanian merchants of Jerusalem assured me that all political troublemakers in the City had been under surveillance for the last two days. "The General," their message read, "can rest assured no trouble will start from here." Then, almost dead on midnight, Laskov came on the telephone: "Look here, General. I want to make something quite clear. I blame you entirely for the tense situation here tonight. If there is trouble it will be you who have started it. There was no tension at all until you began interfering."

I knew he must be rattled and replied: "I take note of what you say. Not a word of that is true, and nobody knows it better than you."

For the first time in days, I slept well. Before dawn on April 24 I was up, visiting our small groups of blue-bereted observers. We could hear through the clear air the distant sound of tank engines starting up. From where I stood on the walls amid the crowds already beginning to thicken, I could imagine the drivers and gunners climbing up into their tanks and self-propelled guns.

Yet the result was anticlimax. When the columns had rolled past the flag-bedecked saluting base, passed through cheering crowds of Israelis, and eventually came rumbling and clattering along the road in full view of the Old City, they were greeted by nothing stronger than an angry growl from the crowd. On they went beneath the gun pits manned by the Jordan Army, until finally the line of tanks and guns vanished out of sight in a haze of exhaust fumes.

In Government House we heaved a sigh of relief. Our harassed mission had achieved its purpose. But the strain had been considerable, so much so that I was glad to slip away to Gaza for a few days to visit my predecessor, General Burns. On my return, I found myself envying him his command in the desert. I had hardly been back two days before another crisis was upon us.

It blew up around Mount Scopus this time, where the activities of the Jewish "police" garrison operating from behind a wire fence around the grounds and buildings of the Old Hadassah Hospital and the Hebrew University were arousing grave concern. Although the whole of the disputed area on these pine-covered slopes was officially under the supervision of the United Nations, the Israelis had always prevented us from carrying out our task. Now the garrison had taken to sending out armed patrols to harry their Arab neighbors in the dusty little village of Issawaiya, insulting them and virtually sealing them off behind road blocks as soon as darkness fell. They were penetrating, too, into another area, known as Solomon's Gardens, which they claimed was Israeli territory.

At the root of the trouble was the old problem of conflicting maps. But it could only be a matter of time before the Jordanian troops, who were forced to watch their brother villagers being harried, would take vigorous counteraction. When I pointed this out to the Israelis they showed not the slightest interest. Some time before, Dag's special representative, Dr. Urrutia, had come out especially to try to settle the Scopus issue, but had been turned back by Israeli troops while visiting the area in full view of hundreds of watching Arabs. It struck me as unlikely I was going to be able to do much better.

However, the daily reports of worsening tension from Colonel Flint (the Chairman of our Jordan-Israel MAC), made it imperative I should try. I therefore advised the Israeli Foreign Office that I intended to make a visit to Mount Scopus—and was a trifle amused when they asked for several days' notice so that they could prepare a suitable guard of honor. Since this seemed superfluous, I decided to go straight ahead, and drove up to the entrance gate of the Jewish enclave in my green staff car. The commandant of the "police" received me politely enough, and conducted me on a tour of the whole area inside the wire fence. Before I left, I told him that I would come back the following day, using the route that led from the Arab side. It was essential to do this since otherwise one was unable to get a clear impression of the disputed area.

Next day, I drove up to the Arab village of Issawaiya, following exactly the same route Dr. Urrutia had taken. I reached the village and talked to the Mukhtar, who expressed himself strongly on the indignities his villagers were being made to suffer. And then, still following Dr. Urrutia's trail, I left my car and walked up the steep winding road toward the wire of the Jewish enclave.

Behind the wire, I noticed a flurry of activity. I continued on and was having a look at a couple of houses on the slope, which had been the subject of particularly bitter dispute, when a panting and heavily armed "police" squad under the command of an officer appeared, formed a line across the path, and refused to let me go any farther.

Although the Armistice Agreement had put me in *direct* control of this area, there was little I could do in face of such a determined show of force. I had taken the precaution of bringing a walkie-talkie set with me, so I advised my headquarters what had happened, and with the best grace I could muster, walked back down the hill, got into my staff car, and drove to Government House.

Clearly the discomfiture Dr. Urrutia had suffered had been reenacted for my special benefit. I have no doubt it was staged deliberately, since the sight of the UN Chief of Staff being turned back in an area where he had every right to be was hardly likely to raise the prestige of the UN with the Arabs. But when I protested officially to Mrs. Meir, her only explanation was the rather inappropriate rejoinder: "We Jews do not like to be pushed around."

Consequently, I had to leave investigations to Colonel Flint and his team of observers. Flint was a fine soldier (a DSO), who had already been badly wounded by a mine in this area some time before. He reported increasingly strong patrol activity and I had every reason to rely on his considered opinion that unless steps were taken to check the Israeli patrols immediately, there was bound to be fighting.

By May 23, the situation had become so acute that I paid another visit to Mrs. Meir and told her that in my opinion unless the patrols were stopped there would be bloodshed within the next week. "Frank" as ever, Mrs Meir was still plainly determined not to be "pushed around," and despite explicit warnings, pooh-poohed the whole issue.

Three days later, an Israeli patrol in Solomon's Gardens was heavily fired on. Two of its soldiers were killed immediately, and the subsequent exchange of fire was both fierce and prolonged. Colonel Flint rushed up in an effort to intervene and rescue the survivors who had gone to ground.

In the confused shooting that ensued, two more Israelis were killed, and Colonel Flint was shot dead. It was a senseless, stupid, unnecessary skirmish that could so easily have been prevented.

The investigation that followed was little more than a farce. Our observers (at long last allowed inside the wire fence) soon discovered while cross-examining the Israeli police commandant that every inconvenient question was followed by his withdrawal to another room to receive guidance and instruction over his radio. Feelings in Israel ran high. There was great bitterness about their dead and, as we might have anticipated, it was now the United Nations who were painted in the blackest colors. Our warnings, all our efforts, were conveniently forgotten, and we were now accused of having precipitated the incident.

Mourning poor Flint (although his body had been returned, we were prevented from visiting the spot where he had been killed) we were amazed at the ingenuity of the falsehoods that distorted the true picture. The highly skilled Israeli Information Service and the entire press combined to manufacture a warped, distorted version that was disseminated with professional expertise through every available channel to their own people and their sympathizers and supporters in America and the rest of the world. Never in all my life had I believed the truth could be so cynically, expertly bent.

There was a British cemetery in no man's land. It was a beautiful spot where the headstones, cut with names from the British regiments which forty years earlier had taken Jerusalem from the Turks, had become sadly stained and overgrown through neglect. Repeated efforts had failed to tidy up this little colony of gray headstones that still kept watch across the hills.* I should have liked to have had Flint buried there, and I think he would have approved. But it was not to be. All the Commonwealth war cemeteries in Palestine were officially closed. So we buried him in Egypt, far from the troubled Holy Land for which he had given his life.

Chapter Eight

SECURITY PROBLEMS

A FEW weeks after this episode, I was strolling in the gardens of Government House. These gardens, the pride of many a former British High Commissioner, were especially attractive at this time of year when their green lawns, roses, carnations, marigolds, and asters were a wonderful contrast in freshness and color to the tawny Judean hills with their brittle gray-green patches of olive groves. The old head gardener (who had been there twenty years) and his staff tended the place with meticulous care. There were wild cyclamen and huge black lilies, seed nurseries, a sunken garden with a large rockery, even two tombstones marking the graves of a former High Commissioner's pet dogs.

It was a place I liked, a green and tranquil retreat heavy with the scent of flowers and the drowsy hum of bees. Strolling along the neatly kept paths this afternoon, I felt at peace with the world, and at first hardly noticed the sheets of paper nestling against the stems of some tall carnations. Absentmindedly, I bent down to pick them up and found myself grasping three or four copies of cables to New York which I realized immediately could only have come from the coding room.

I stuffed them into my pocket, went straight to the coding room

* Sadly this was the only one of the Commonwealth War Graves Commission's nearly twenty-four thousand war cemeteries where politics had denied the dead a fittingly kept resting place. To this day the Scopus cemetery remains shamefully neglected, the resting place of so many who gave their lives to pave the way for a Jewish national home.

whose windows overlooked the gardens, but discovered it locked and not in operation. I felt certain I had stumbled on a clue to a problem that had been causing me grave concern.

The classified cables in my pocket were like telltale scum on top of a pool. Conceivably they might be put down to administrative carelessness; if so, this was something we could not afford. There might, however, be a more sinister aspect; recently the gist of coded messages resulting from policy meetings at which only I and two of my most trusted executives had been present had within twenty-four hours been discussed in the Israeli newspapers.

Next morning, I went to Headquarters and questioned the staff at work. I discovered that, though the code room was always kept locked, there was no strict security drill over access to offices on the operational floor. I gathered that the copies I had found the previous afternoon must have come from filing trays in the secretaries' offices on this floor where my own office, Vigier's, and the operations room were situated. The doors of these offices had not been locked and the windows were sometimes left open because of the heat.

Down in the coding room, I learned that five copies were made of every cable coded or decoded, but that there was no routine system of filing them, or standing orders on how to destroy carbons. Nor was this key office permanently staffed. Code work was done by whichever of the girl typists happened to be duty secretary. Since there was a difference of six or seven hours between Jerusalem and New York time, code traffic was almost invariably at night. This created a problem because only a small number of the girls on our staff had been trained for this type of work. Consequently, a period of real tension when code traffic was heavy reduced them to a state of exhaustion, besides disrupting the ordinary office routine. During the Scopus incident, the flow had been so heavy that the whole routine work of headquarters had been seriously affected.

I summoned my principal assistants to a hastily convened meeting and told them the result of my investigations. All agreed with my suspicion that there had been a continuous leakage of information, and the members of my "Fifth Republic" were highly critical of the Administration whose lack of security and inefficient office organization they blamed for this dangerous state of affairs.

It was now that I began to understand the Old Fox's habit of caching away so much confidential material. I told them that from now on I intended to create special security areas in headquarters where access would be strictly limited. We would set up a special "green room" for coding that would be permanently manned by an exclusively assigned all-male staff of code clerks. By the time I had explained what I had in mind, I felt there was a definite resurgence of confidence. Only my Chief Administrative Officer appeared worried at the reaction in New York over the costs of structural alterations that a redistribution of offices would make necessary.

Obviously, it was going to take time before we were able to set up a restricted security area and obtained the right personnel we needed for the code room. Meanwhile, it was vital to start to try to trace and eliminate the leakage of information. At this time, I still had no real suspicion of how deeply the Israeli Intelligence Service had penetrated my command. But I was in no doubt as to its efficiency. I knew its personnel were drawn from individuals with experience in every intelligence service in the world, while its inspiration and direction came mainly from Polish-born leaders whose standards were highly professional, reinforced by a natural ruthlessness and a determination that no means should be neglected provided the ends were achieved satisfactorily.

With first-rate backing from my staff, our early investigations pointed within a matter of days to a person whose activities appeared to be such as would lay him open to blackmail. Whether he was the culprit and whether this or some other motive was at the root of the leakage of information we now had reason to suspect was never certain, because the evidence we were able to collect was so circumstantial that we had to proceed with extreme restraint. Lacking real proof my hands were tied, and it was not until Andrew Cordier came out a little later that I was able to discuss the case with him and ask him to get the suspect removed.

"Uncle Andy" promised to ease him out as soon as possible and was as good as his word. Not long afterward our suspect was recalled to New York where in due course he obtained promotion in the glass building.

In June 1958 any chance of a farther-reaching investigation was temporarily set back by a crisis in the Lebanon where the pro-Western president Chamoun's personal hold on the country had roused growing opposition among the predominantly Muslim populations in sectors of Beirut and in the southern and northwestern areas of Lebanon.

This country's one and a half million population consists of a delicate balance between one half Christian (Roman Catholics and Maronites) and one half Muslim inhabitants, and for some time past Chamoun had been stubbornly resisting conciliatory advice to strengthen the constitutional coalition that provided for a balanced distribution of governmental posts.

Outside the country, Syria had merged with Egypt earlier that year to form the United Arab Republic. Now Cairo (in order to counter American influence, which bore heavily with Chamoun) was suspected of encouraging the Lebanese Muslims to revolt. In May and early June armed clashes had broken out, which signaled the possibility of civil war. Support for the Muslim faction was reported to be coming across the Syrian border in the form of gold, arms, and agents. This led President Chamoun to appeal to the United Nations, complaining that the United Arab Republic was interfering in Lebanon's internal affairs.

In reply the Security Council decided to send an Observation Group to observe and report whether there was any infiltration of men and arms across the Syrian border, and generally make efforts at mediation and conciliation.

Once again a UN nomenclature was created overnight, and UNOGIL (The United Nations Observer Group in the Lebanon) came into being. Its personnel were eventually to come from states all over the world whom the Secretary General persuaded to participate, but in the meantime there was no one on the ground. At midnight on June 10, I received a cable from Dag ordering me to dispatch six observers to cross over into Lebanon to join the infant UN Mission forming in Beirut.

Our information about the situation in the Lebanon was sketchy, although we gathered the whole frontier area was in opposition hands. Between two and four in the morning, I had to select and brief a hastily improvised team drawn from Gaza, Jerusalem, and Damascus. Our operational staff acted swiftly and the six observers were able to cross the Lebanese frontier at three o'clock in the afternoon, three hours ahead of Dag's target, but with few more tangible instructions than to "show the flag" and establish the areas where fighting was going on or likely to break out.

The next few days found me constantly traveling between Jerusalem and Beirut in our one-plane Air Force, to liaise with the heads of the new Mission whose observers were now flying into Beirut, followed by a chaotic tail of stores, supplies, and administrative personnel.

This was my first experience in how the United Nations threw a field mission together. Although I knew that New York had no permanent military planning staff, no standing force on which to draw, no stockpiles of material or even the beginnings of a logistical structure designed to function swiftly in times of crisis, I found the marked evidence of lack of planning most disturbing. The chaotic state of UN planning that became evident as the buildup continued went against the basic principles every staff officer has instilled into him early in his training.

As I watched this heterogeneous collection of men and material swell into a polyglot mission stuck together with United Nations glue, I wondered whether officers who left their own armies for command rank with the UN were not inevitably doomed to operate under nightmare conditions, where the lack of central planning—without which no modern army can survive—might not endanger the lives of men who looked to them for leadership.

UNOGIL grew with startling speed. Within a month its numbers had risen to two hundred, and at Dag's instigation was to go on expanding until by November there would be nearly six hundred observers including an air section of ninety officers and a massive administrative organization in Beirut. Meanwhile, the buildup in those frenetic early days resembled a sort of mad hatter's tea party, and once the observers took to their jeeps and drove toward the frontier, they discovered a Gilbertian comic opera situation.

Their task was border control along the Lebanese-Syrian frontier where they were to set up fixed posts and send out roving patrols (later they made heavy use of air reconnaissance). They had orders to observe strict impartiality where there was civil strife over the internal, constitutional issue. But on their way to the frontier they saw few signs of bloodshed. Indeed, they discovered that near harmony characterized all "strife" between the armed bands of Muslims and Christians, while the Government's own Security Forces showed a marked reluctance to discharge their weapons at rebel Muslims for the very good reason that an unlucky shot might involve them in the ramifications of the blood feuds which enlivened many parts of the country.

There was never any difficulty in moving about in Government-controlled territory, but penetrating into "rebel" country was a different and often dangerous matter. The experiences of Colonel Stig Mollersward, one of my own six officers, were typical. Mollersward, a Swedish cavalry officer, an altogether splendid fellow with an allergy for the more extreme exaggerations of democracy and a passionate love of horseflesh that led to remarkably erratic performances behind the wheel of a jeep, had seen UN service in Korea and Kashmir. He had served, too, with the Finnish army in both their wars against the Russians.

One morning he had just managed to negotiate, rather to his own surprise, a particularly nasty bend on a mountainside, when he came face to face with a road block manned by a dozen or so heavily armed Lebanese Muslims in picturesque attire. Each brandished a highly lethal modern weapon while Mollersward, an elderly, slightly paunchy veteran, possessed no armament heavier than his monocle.

Descending slowly from his jeep, the colonel screwed the monocle more firmly into his eye, peered haughtily at the least scruffy among his ambushers, and inquired whether he was their commander.

The surprised warrior fingered his automatic, but did not deny it. And then surprisingly, in reply to Mollersward's jocular inquiry: *"Est-ce que vous êtes un rebel, monsieur?"* snapped to attention and roared: *"Oui, Excellence. Un peu."*

Before very much longer, the road block had been enthusiastically opened up and the old veteran was conducted with full honors to the Muslim Area commander with whom he struck up such cordial relations that his Swedish name (soon pronounced in the local vernacular) became a password throughout this part of the Lebanon. Eventually, he set up his headquarters in a beautiful villa in a fertile valley from which he supervised a hundred other observers while keeping house in a style that was a mixture of feudal Swedish and opulent Oriental.

Nonetheless, the situation remained tense and the observers were kept busy patroling the frontier and sending their reports back to Beirut where the mission was swelling in the finest Parkinsonian tradition so that its headquarters and administrative services had been able to take over the whole of the Riviera Hotel. Here, in contrast to the observers constantly on the move in their jeeps or flying observation missions along a rugged frontier, an inflated number of senior officers and administrative personnel were soon engaged in a battle of paper warfare waged across the narrow corridors of the hotel.

I had an excellent opportunity to observe this new Mission. Its three leading members (to whom the observers' reports were funneled through an operational headquarters) did an excellent job and had come to a happy arrangement over the distribution of their duties. Galo Plaza, an ex-President of Ecuador, dealt with the Lebanese Government; Rajeshwar Dayal of India coped with the Opposition; Major General Odd Bull from Norway battled to get some administrative and logistic order into the inflated Mission, which now boasted a Principal Secretary. It was also saddled with a less desirable minority from some of the more recently emergent states whose talents were less suited to the field than to the bars and casinos of Beirut.

Other new arrivals were a number of officers from Latin America who became virtually grounded through an inability to speak more than a few words in anything other than Spanish or Portuguese. It was not until some remote villages populated with returned Lebanese emigrants from South America were discovered deep in Opposition territory that they had a chance to come into their own.

The situation in the interior remained somewhat unreal. Whole Muslim areas had gone over to the Opposition (the civilized Lebanese on both sides dislike the uncouth appellation of "rebel") and were sealed off behind barbed wire barricades on the main roads. On the other side sat the government troops and police whom General Chehab, the Commander of the Security Forces, had no intention of committing to offensive operations. His men discreetly held their fire while the gas, electricity, telephone, and postal services continued to function smoothly with full cooperation between both sides.

The crisis, if such it could be called, brought out a number of leading figures from New York. I was glad to welcome Andrew Cordier when he came on to Jerusalem. Here the Scopus incident, instead of acting as a deterrent, had merely been the signal for increasingly provoking forays by the Israeli police garrison. Week after week had been wasted in an endeavor to make them see sense, but Mrs. Meir seemed unwilling to offer the slightest cooperation or to put a brake on the garrison's activities. Since my own authority as UN commander was being constantly flouted and the Jerusalem MAC's task made virtually impossible through a policy based on the necessity for Israel to "breathe" (or as I now privately termed it, "the Laskov Respiratory Theory"), I was delighted to receive reinforcements in the shape of Uncle Andy's telling weight.

Cordier (as Bunche had once done before him) came fresh to negotiations with the Israelis, but even he, a very tough negotiator, was unable to achieve any improvement. Inevitably his efforts were frustrated by a vicious circle of Mrs. Meir hiding behind "our military" or "our military" sheltering behind that bulky lady. Before long negotiations ground to a halt.

Cordier did, however, succeed in obtaining her reluctant permission to visit Solomon's Gardens where Colonel Flint had been killed. His tactics here were a joy to watch. Blithely, he informed her that he would feel perfectly safe in my hands because although I had been prevented from exercising my responsibility in the area, I was *actually* responsible for it. He was quite certain, too, that the Jordanians would not fire on us *provided* no Jewish police escorted us beyond their own wire.

At last she gave way, and beneath the brooding gaze of the Israeli garrison—who appeared remarkably well behaved now that the whole population of Issawaiya and its neighboring villages were out manning their hills—we were able to walk out in full view of both sides. At the place where poor Flint had fallen, I discovered his white truce flag still lying on the ground. As I picked it up, I knew what a long way I had come toward understanding what peacekeeping entailed. And because I felt so strongly, I sent the flag with an inscribed silver plate to his Regiment, Princess Patricia's Light Infantry of Canada, the Member State he had served so well.

If Cordier's reception could hardly be described as warm, the Israeli "welcome" that greeted the Secretary General as he flew across their country a few weeks later was little short of amazing. I was with Dag when we took off from Beirut airport to fly to Amman for discussions with King Hussein of Jordan.

Our flight had been cleared through all the official channels, and our white UN plane was flying on its prescribed route when, approaching the Israeli coast, we were intercepted and deliberately buzzed by two Israeli jet fighters. Dag was immersed in the contents of his heavy briefcase and appeared unconscious of what was going on. But his comments when we told him would not have pleased the Israeli Prime Minister.

In the early days of July, the bloody revolution in Iraq coincided with a changed situation in the Lebanon, where American intervention had been requested by the Chamoun Government when General Chehab (who was later to replace Chamoun) had refused to commit his troops to all-out operations to suppress the rebels.

The entire Middle East was going through a difficult stage. Nasser's conception of Pan Arabism had led to a fusion of Egypt and Syria into a United Arab Republic on January 14, 1958. Thoroughly disgruntled, Iraq and Jordan had followed suit with an "Arab Union" dominated by that grand old statesman Nuri Said.

The latter movement displeased President Nasser whose machinations doubtless provided the spark that exploded into a bloody *coup d'état* in Baghdad. Both King Feisal and Nuri Said were murdered and it was soon obvious that Pan Arabist schemes were threatening the stability of the Middle East. The Western Powers were swift to take effective action. Although this produced results, it did little to enhance the United Nations prestige with the Arab States.

On July 15 American Marines landed on the beaches South of Beirut under the air and surface cover of a special task force from the American 6th Fleet. The invaders were plainly expecting heavy opposition as they deployed from their landing craft and must have been surprised at the reception given them. On the beach were gathered the top brass of the American Embassy accompanied by the leaders of the Lebanese Government and its Security Forces, who escorted the marines inland amid throngs of bikini-clad beauties and ice cream and Coca Cola vans rushed to the scene by the enterprising locals. Next day, we heard that the 16th British Parachute Brigade had arrived in Amman, where it was followed shortly afterward by an infantry battalion.

Although UNOGIL had still a great deal of useful work to do, this Anglo-American deterrent to Cairo-inspired trouble had a stabilizing effect. This was noticeable in the Lebanon, where much of the Lebanese Security Forces work around Beirut had been taken over by gum-chewing Marines whose main complaint was that the fleshpots of the city were permanently out of bounds.

Much to our amusement, a story was soon current of a truce certainly not carried out under United Nations supervision. It was rumored to have originated in a near riot in a certain professional quarter of Beirut, once it became known that "the saviors of civilization" were forbidden the delights of the city. The outcry met with sympathetic consideration from both sides and was followed by a local truce during which civil strife was suspended until the Marine Fleet Force had had the chance to make full and proper use of a three-day spell during which Beirut was declared an open city. When the truce expired, they staggered back to their mosquito-infested olive groves, civil war was resumed, and the banks in Beirut stayed open several extra hours the following day.

Some time before the British paratroops arrived in Amman, Hammarskjöld had told me to increase quietly our observers along the West bank of the Jordan in case a Cairo inspired *coup d'état* against King Hussein in Amman gave the Israelis a chance in the resulting confusion to move across the demarcation line and seize the whole stretch of Jordanian territory up to the river.

Here was another exercise in United Nations tactics. Normally the observers should have been increased in both Israeli and Jordanian territory, and I was under no obligation to ask the Israelis for permission. However, I could imagine the howls of protest that would arise, and to save time simply asked the Jordanians, who raised no objections to our establishing a number of new outposts in their territory.

We had hardly got our patrols operating from these new posts than the Israelis objected on the grounds that they had not been consulted. Well aware of our reasons, however, they obviously did not intend to press the issue. In fact, in more normal times our activities would have suited them well enough since they were constantly pressing us to put a stop to "infiltration and murderous attacks" from this strip. But when I now suggested that the trouble would soon end were we to increase our observers' activities in their territory, the response confirmed our opinion that it was Israeli policy to maintain a situation pregnant with threats of Arab attacks.

It seemed to all of us in UNTSO that there were two reasons why this suited them. First, it insured a high state of readiness and efficiency within their own army, which showed a marked tendency toward internal disputes immediately tension relaxed. Second, it enabled them to make sure that their plight received the maximum amount of attention in foreign and particularly in American newspapers, with the natural corollary that sympathy, aid, and money continued to flow into Israel in substantial quantities.

The setting up of these new posts in Jordan placed a heavy strain on our manpower, and I was anxious to obtain reinforcements. But although UNOGIL was now deploying the best part of six hundred observers along *one* frontier compared to our own under-strength mission which had to cope with *four,* I was told that no more observers could be spared. I realized that there was no possibility of increasing our strength until the time came for UNOGIL to be disbanded, when there should be an excellent chance of our being able to take over some of its observers who had been doing outstanding work, and might welcome a chance to transfer to UNTSO.

In October, the American forces in the Lebanon were withdrawn, and the situation became comparatively stable, the bloodless civil strife being replaced by a succession of lethal but minor blood feuds. It seemed only a question of time before UNOGIL was run down.

During my visits I met many of its observers and discovered that a number of them would like to transfer to UNTSO once their work in the Lebanon was over. I drew up lists of the officers I considered most suitable and submitted these to Hammarskjöld in New York. He assured me that I could have as many as I needed once UNOGIL was wound up. Unfortunately, I had neglected to take into consideration the reactions of the Administrative Services, which had been entrusted with unwinding the unwieldly organization they had built up in Beirut.

In November, UNOGIL reported to New York that its mission had been accomplished. But it was not until December, when the Security Council (acting on an earlier Lebanese notification that it was now withdrawing its complaint) decided to disband the Mission, that I discovered the Administrative Services were not implementing the assurances Dag had given me. No doubt I had incurred the enmity of some of the administrative bigwigs by insisting on a first-rate replacement for my Chief Administrative Officer whose time in Jerusalem was now at an end, and to do it had bypassed them to deal directly with the Secretary General.

I sent them a signal, drawing attention to the lists of officers I had submitted for transfer to UNTSO: each was keen to come to Jerusalem and would have been eminently suitable for the work. I waited for a time, feeling that I could hardly run to the Secretary General whenever there were difficulties with the Administrative Services. But when at last my signal was acknowledged, I wished I had. The reply from the glass building merely informed me it was regretted that the vast majority of the officers I had selected for transfer to UNTSO had already left for home and could not be recalled.

Chapter Nine

INTRIGUE AND INFILTRATION

As the situation in the Middle East became more stable, I was able to take a hard, deferred look at the internal health of my own command. Had I been serving in an ordinary army, the procedure would have been simple. All that would have been necessary was to hand over the distasteful business of investigation to the Special Intelligence Branch and await their report. But in Jerusalem the structure of the UN Field Mission left me no alternative but to tackle the job myself.

I had, in fact, been provided with a chief security officer, but I did not wish to use him for the particular task I had in mind. A UN field commander really needs to have the ability to turn himself into a jack of all trades—especially since his very role as a peacekeeper disallows the employment of an intelligence service—else he will find himself virtually on a war footing with both sides.

Although Dag was later privately to bemoan the lack of such a service in the Congo under different conditions, the innate nature of a peacekeeping force precludes the employment of an efficient intelligence service. In Jerusalem, UNTSO was able to carry out its task only with the consent of the States that had signed the Armistice. We were not a military force in the strict sense, but rather a collection of military personnel whose host countries (to use UN phraseology) would have taken the gravest exception and undoubtedly action also had they discovered we were operating an intelligence service to obtain information about their political and military affairs. Any work of this kind (if only to defend ourselves) had to be carried out on the most strictly unofficial basis.

Our immediate problem called for counterintelligence. Our

under-strength, harassed, but in the main devoted force was being penetrated to a dangerous degree. Although I was determined to put an end to it, I did not rate the survival chances of an amateur counterintelligence service high in a country that had espionage in its bones and understood the twin elements of corruption and blackmail to a degree that was probably the envy of any country in the world.

Counterintelligence is a sordid and distasteful business, more so in an international force whose purpose is normally equated with high ideals and the service of mankind. Shortly after taking up office as Secretary General, Dag Hammaskjöld had appointed a committee under the chairmanship of Professor Thalassis Aghnides, which had laid down a code of conduct for international civil servants. Its standards had been clear enough but in Jerusalem, at any rate, it had foundered on the rock of human frailty.

This was not surprising because my command consisted of a most diverse collection of human beings drawn from a variety of nations whose standards of probity and integrity were not all the same. In taking over UNTSO, I had become responsible for four hundred and ninety-two people drawn from twenty-four different countries including Greece, Honduras, India, Italy, Ireland, Japan, China, Mexico, the Philippines, Spain, and Vietnam.

One of the factors that contributed to the breakdown of standards, in many cases, and made our task such a formidable one, was Jerusalem itself, which was a natural breeding ground for corruption and subversion. Cut into two hostile camps, the city's only neutral area was our headquarters in Government House. It must have looked like a beacon to the intelligence services of both sides.

Every morning our staff members reported for work and every evening they left for home, carrying the white card that took them through one of the three control points to their houses or apartments in the Arab or Jewish sector. Once in the privacy of their homes (whence most of their families had been evacuated during an earlier scare) they became a natural target for the most friendly advances from Arab or Israeli neighbors who seemed only too well informed about their individual tastes, habits, and failings, and engagingly eager to help in indulging them.

Of course, the same sort of advances were being made to our personnel in every town and city between Damascus and Tel Aviv. But here in Jerusalem they invariably followed a standard pattern. First there were the heartbreaking stories of how the division of the city had disrupted family life, coupled with a plea to take one, just one, letter through the control points to a despairing relative on the opposite side of the wire. Even an oral message would do; a very human request to which it was natural to accede under the circumstances.

It worked exceptionally well with new arrivals; only a monster —or a well-briefed employee—could have declined. And the men who were being asked these favors were most often civilian career employees whose natural sympathies had not been hardened by long service in ambiguous political climates. Before long the seed had been planted and letters began to be accompanied by little packets of razor blades, cigarettes, or chocolate, sometimes supplied by the sender and at others bought by the carrier at UN stores. Gradually, during the ensuing months, this role of postman entwined the unsuspecting victim like an ivy tendril until it burgeoned into films, transistor radios, tape recorders, and sooner or later gold, diamonds, even drugs, the most profitable traffic of all.

By the time these latter stages had been reached, the "friendly little service" had been put on a sound financial basis, so that the UN smuggler with his white pass and identity card had become so involved that he was drawing a regular salary or getting a substantial cut on goods he bought at our bonded stores and resold to his friends.

At this stage, he might well set up in business on his own, but whatever the method of dealing in genuine "U.N. stuff," the path was now clear to ask selected individuals to supply the information that fetched even higher prices, while his services once secured could be guaranteed on a virtually permanent basis through cleverly applied blackmail.

This was the standard pattern and it says much for individual integrity that so many resisted it. Fear, too, prevented a proportion of the frailer characters from taking the final step of selling UN information. But once involved in corruption, they, too, automatically became security risks while the men who had gone the whole way were now a very real danger to the Mission. The pressure on staff was unremitting; often a man would be offered a regular salary for doing no work at all for quite a time, then once on the hook, hear of "special commission" for services rendered.

Even I was not neglected as a potential target. One morning a worried executive who had recently joined the staff requested a personal interview. I hardly knew the man by sight, yet he told me he had been approached by an Israeli who had offered him a regular salary in any currency paid into any bank he liked to name in return for simple duties. The first was the completion of a questionnaire on my more personal and intimate habits. I was grateful that he actually had this document to show me.

As I read it, it became evident that the fact that my wife was still in Sweden was giving somebody food for thought. There appeared much eagerness to know whether, for instance, I preferred Arab or Israeli mistresses; information on any other little quirks of human nature or idiosyncrasies—the possibilities were listed—would be welcome, too.

This had its amusing side, but the second condition for insuring the very generous salary offered was a regular supply of copies of all code cables that passed between the Secretary General and myself. I was glad to learn in this backhanded fashion that my activities had blocked their previous source of information.

I kept the questionnaire and instructed my informant to decline the salary offered him on the grounds that the work was much too dangerous. I felt quite certain, however, that it would not be long before he was approached again, and I told him to come to me immediately this happened.

He promised that he would, but when the inevitable approaches commenced once more, he must either have been too frightened or too tempted to keep his word and was very soon on the Israeli payroll. Even so, they must have regarded him as suspect after his visit to me because before long he was caught red-handed in a minor black market transaction that had all the hallmarks of a frameup with him as the fall guy.

I had no more offers of "home comforts" from either side though I suspect that this interest in the Chief of Staff's welfare had its genesis in some sort of precedent. I regretted that none of my predecessors had managed to clean up the situation in Jerusalem, but it was plain the exhausting demands of day-to-day peacekeeping had never given them the time. I knew I was up against great difficulties. Even were I successful in stirring up this antheap of corruption, one of the factors hampering sweeping changes would be my inability to dismiss UN career personnel.

But on the civilian side, I would have to operate through the people in our Administrative Services, many of whom would be loath to admit such a state of affairs could exist, would bitterly resent my "interference," and would be bound to insist that each case be referred to their own courts of appeal. With corruption known and acknowledged to exist by those of us on the scene, it was ridiculous that one should have to battle with some of the very people upon whom one should be able to rely.

Although I was acting on Dag's instructions, the structure of the organization and the anomalies in its chain of command made me aware that in order to obtain the authority vital to do any real good, I would have to provide a memorandum revealing sufficient data to strengthen Dag's hand and enable him to override his own administrative service. From the almost superficial knowledge I already had, there was no doubt such a memorandum would make distressing reading set against the Aghnides Report.

This remarkable little booklet had been printed and circulated to all UN personnel and had been my service Bible since I had joined the organization. Now ironically the need to enforce its exalted code of integrity was going to make it necessary for me to proceed without the knowledge of the United Nations' own Administrative Services.

However, I had no hesitation in going ahead and appointing a special investigator charged with drawing up a full report on the situation. I installed the tall, gray-haired and distinguished Major Ragnar Hansen (one of the few officers I had been successful in securing from UNOGIL on its disbandment) in his own office in Government House, and I could hardly have made a sounder choice.

Well versed in the intricacies of security work, discreet, clear-headed, and wonderfully methodical, this Swedish officer had within a surprisingly short time unearthed a fruitful number of contacts in both camps. An endlessly patient listener in an atmosphere permeated with rivalries, hostility, and personal jealousies, his own integrity and technique of evaluation never faltered. Slowly at first but gathering momentum, the information that was to result in a whole series of case histories began to come in.

Soon it was apparent that in some of the worst cases no action could be taken because the individuals concerned had been posted back to New York where they were presumably enjoying an honored, promoted career in the glass building or had left UN service. On the other hand, there was disturbing evidence of espionage and leakage that had to be stamped out immediately. Fresh evidence came to light in increasing quantities. Often there were long interviews during which suspects sometimes broke down and confessed but more often, taking a truculent stand on their supposed "diplomatic rights," had to be grilled, confronted with each other, sometimes left alone together for hours in a room which the methodical Hansen had had appropriately equipped.

Gradually the complete picture evolved. On the one hand there were the straightforward cases of espionage and selling information. On the other, the less immediately harmful but widespread corruption that made every man involved a potential risk. Amid the evidence the talent of the Israeli Intelligence Service shone like a clear light through an opaque haze of muddled personal motives. It was clear the Arabs had endeavored to employ similiar methods, but their success had been negligible in comparison with such Western professional competence.

As Hansen's investigations went on, the one saving grace in all the information he collected was evidence that the core of the Mission remained sound. It seemed to me, too, that many of these activities that were a menace to the successful operations of the higher echelons of a loyal staff at both MAC and Headquarters level were capable of being brought under control, if not stamped out, once I had the necessary authority by swift and drastic examples, increased security precautions, and constant watchfulness.

The thought that saddened me, however, was the suspicion that whatever I did and however successful I might be, it would only need my replacement to set the whole process off once more unless the new chief of staff was also alive enough to the danger to take the same risks of antagonizing the Administration. The political climate in Jerusalem, the rebuffs and frustrations, the endless temptations, mitigated against lasting success unless some agonizing reappraisal in New York awakened them to the vulnerability of the Field Mission.

It was almost pathetic: an Intelligence Service unsurpassed in the Middle East for gathering information and mounting special operations pitted against our amorphous force. Unhampered by any regard for sovereignty other than its own and completely uninhibited in its actions, Israeli Intelligence was aided by an almost total security blackout in its own country and the knowledge that it enjoyed not only the support of every Israeli citizen from the Prime Minister downward, but the benefits accruing from its penetration of almost every other important intelligence agency in the world.

It had, however, one Achilles heel (and still has to this day). Perhaps in 1958 and the years that followed, we were more fortunate in it than we knew. No country so outwardly united in appearances as Israel was more riddled with internal dissension and personal jealousies springing from the national immigrant blocs that had made it.

Each Ministry was honeycombed with personal and factional rivalries and each was divided against the others: every service was plagued with those fierce, jealous antagonisms that seem endemic in the Jewish character. Knowing this, I found it hard to believe that any objective, agreed evaluation would ever be chosen from the data supplied by its brilliant Intelligence Service.

But this provided little consolation now that we knew what a remarkable degree of success the Israelis had achieved with the frailer members of my staff in Jerusalem and the MAC's. For the first time we were able to understand why the Arabs (it had seemed unfair at the time) had declared certain individuals in the MAC *persona non grata;* Hansen's investigations revealed that many of these men had been rendering useful service to the Israelis. And whether facing actual espionage or mere corruption, what disturbed me most was the long-established nature and extent of these activities.

Often it seemed to me that the blame lay less with the culprits than the Organization itself in Jerusalem and New York. A peculiar lopsidedness seemed to have characterized too many UN administrators over the past ten years, so that they had concentrated too much on accounts and office detail, almost totally neglecting the basic necessities of man management. None of them ever seemed to have issued a warning on what they must have realized very clearly was going on under their noses. One staff member, we discovered, had actually noted down a host of transgressions in a little black book, and after leaving UNTSO to return to New York had used it to punish those who were in his personal disfavor—but not a word had ever been said to the individuals on the spot when he had been their chief, and those in his favor had been allowed to continue their activities.

Altogether, the standard had fallen to a remarkably low level and too many individuals who had got away with it were still in UN employment. Some of the means of temptation were obvious, even amusing; others stand out in any language.

For example, there was a junior official in a Ministry we knew well who kept open house for United Nations personnel in a lavish style quite inconsistent with his salary. Since we had been able to establish that this was his only admitted income, we decided that we ought to learn more about him and the attractive Israeli girls who embellished his household and assisted in entertaining UN visitors. With a little perseverance, we discovered that some of these alluring creatures had been released from their National Service for "special duties." So special that we nicknamed them "the Commandos" (with no slur intended on that fine body of men), as we unearthed other members of this sisterhood in Tel Aviv and Tiberias.

It was a diverting investigation. But unguarded tongues and "pillow talk" conversion to the Israeli cause took second place to highly organized corruption. We soon grew well informed on the nature and contents of Israeli payrolls and the staggeringly high incomes earned by smuggling that led to more sinister employment. The temptation was always there.

Jerusalem was naturally a post of opportunity for corruption and intrigue. But there were other avenues, too. Personnel with access to Syrian or Lebanese ports who were prepared to smuggle goods in their UN jeeps could, undetected over the years, build up the sort of capital sum that would take care of every problem when they retired from national or United Nations service.

Unfortunately I found it very difficult not to come to the conclusion that United Nations personnel would always be vulnerable to this sort of temptation because, though it is easy enough to join the international staff, the Organization invariably shows the greatest reluctance to dispense with its misfits. The lamentable shortcomings of this system were to become even more manifest some years later when for political reasons the geographical basis of recruitment was broadened with the automatic result that a balanced proportion of numbers became more important than the quality and standards of recruits. From that moment on, discharges or transfers were to lead to totally unfounded charges of racial discrimination.

No nation is without a corruptible element and it is invidious to make comparisons. But in Jerusalem I was to discover that certain nationalities tend to be a great deal more susceptible to corruption than others. Perhaps religion and tradition lie at the root of the problem. In the course of the investigations we were forced to make, I found that the countries with the fewest offenders were Catholic Eire and the Protestant states of North and Northwest Europe.

There were in Jerusalem none of the normal restraints that mitigate against corruption in a national force, and in the UN it seemed a tragedy that neither Dag's ideals nor the Aghnides Rules had been proof against an "overseas mentality" among the international staff. Long before they had been posted to the Holy Land, a knowledgeable and infectious minority had sized up foreign service in terms of financial return, so that each year abroad became worth so much in duty-free cars, foreign allowances, special pay, and other fruitful perquisites.

For this type of character a mental pattern had already become set before the undreamed riches of the Middle East had been skilfully maneuvered into their avaricious but nevertheless gullible hands. And once the Arab or Israeli hooks were in, they did not find it difficult to bury their heads (and consciences) like ostriches in an aura of self-delusion fostered by assurances from New York that personnel abroad were entitled to enjoy a degree of "diplomatic privilege."

I felt that this ingrained attitude of mind could only be checked by stern examples. A typical instance was the abuse of the United States Army Postal Service, that had lingered on from the days when a high proportion of U.S. Army enlisted men had served with UNTSO.

My attention was first drawn to this racket by the arrival of a number of Israelis at Government House to collect their "stuff" (parcels which they had ordered and paid for, and which were now awaiting them addressed to UN staff members who had left the Mission).

It was easy to put a stop to this, but the investigation that followed was depressingly illuminating. Each spring and autumn some two hundred sixty Sears and Roebuck, and an equal number of John Plain of Chicago, catalogues were airlifted into Jerusalem for UNTSO staff. These thick volumes made such fascinating reading and produced such a flood of outgoing orders that the efficiency of the Mission dropped by about 25 per cent until the first fine flush of the shopping spree had exhausted itself. All sorts of friends' and neighbors' orders must have gone in under their names, to an extent that explained why so many shops and bars were in the happy position of being able to provide their clients with "genuine UN goods."

A more startling demonstration of laxity occurred late one January night in 1959 in the Government House compound, which had two gates on the roadway leading through its neutral ground from Jordanian to Israeli territory. An alert guard on the Jerusalem gate spotted a UN jeep that had already managed to pass the guard on the Jordan gate, and was now approaching at top speed in an attempt to get through into the city without being checked.

He stopped it at gunpoint, and made the occupants get out. It was discovered that they were Israelis, one of whom held an American passport. The white jeep yielded a rich store of equipment and a set of maps covering most of Jordan.

Unfortunately, my Chief Security Officer immediately handed

the men over to the Israeli authorities. Not unexpectedly, this was the last we saw of them, although the authorities were quick to assure me this exploit had been a purely private foray into Jordan, the pair having stolen the jeep and set off on a sightseeing tour of Jordan, completely unaware of the vehicle's contents!

Alarmed lest this incident might lead the Jordanians to suspect every genuine white UN jeep entering their territory, I informed Amman exactly what had happened, and expressed my regret. While vague rumors were leaked to us of the trial of the culprits, I set about my own investigations, discovering that the jeep had been stolen more than a month ago from a parking line near Government House where vehicles from the defunct UNOGIL Mission had been stored. Unfortunately, the story proved a little more complicated. We had to dismiss a UN guard on a charge of colusion in the theft of the jeep.

I decided it was time to have a talk with my Chief Security Officer. Shortly after I spoke to him, he submitted his resignation, which I immediately accepted.

Since Hansen had joined me, I had been in the habit of keeping Dag and Cordier fully informed of his investigations whenever they visited me in Jerusalem. Both were fully alive to the serious implications of the activities we had uncovered, and in January 1959, when I made a trip to New York, I had a very full and free discussion with them both and told them that I wanted Hansen as my new Chief Security Officer once his finalized report was in their hands.

Dag seemed saddened but not surprised by what must have made uncomfortable listening. While I was talking to him, I recalled a happier moment when, looking out from my balcony over Jerusalem, he had said with a sigh of content that it was one of the most beautiful views he had ever seen, and that there, at least, he felt able to relax.

There was little relaxation for Dag on the East River, however, and I warned him that my personal dealings with him and Cordier would be bitterly resented by the Administrative Services. I told him, too, that in my opinion any career employee who served me loyally in the future would be prejudicing his chances for advancement or promotion. Dag smiled and nodded sympathetically. He then told me that *he* would deal with the Administration, and that he never wanted to hear the word "prerogative" again.

I returned to Jerusalem. Within a month, I was lucky to receive a replacement for my Chief Administrative Officer whose tour of duty was at an end. This man proved to be the best Chief Administrative Officer I have ever known. Jan van Wijk, a Dutchman, was one of the shining exceptions to my UN experience with administrators. Seconded from the Dutch Foreign Office, he was fortyish, enthusiastic and dedicated. From the day he took up his duties, all conflict of loyalties ceased, and the foundations were swiftly and efficiently laid for a thoroughly integrated Mission. Unfortunately urgent family reasons prevented him from staying with me for more than a year.

In April, Hansen completed his report, and I forwarded it to Cordier with a strong official recommendation that Hansen should be appointed to the upgraded post of Chief Security Officer, with direct responsibility to me. Within a matter of days this recommendation was accepted, Hansen was appointed, and I knew I had incurred bitter resentment from the Administration, which would seek a suitable moment to make itself felt. I had gone over the heads of the "right people" and had ignored the "right channels." Sooner or later, I would be made to feel the consequences.

Meantime I had Hansen and we could get to work. As a start, we reorganized our whole security arrangements on a sound and nearly watertight basis. Our "green room" was a new creation—a permanently manned code room staffed by specially trained security officers permanently assigned to code work. Leading off it, through a locked and permanently guarded door, was our operational room, which had been turned into a special restricted area. Security was tightened throughout headquarters. And down the line, the same procedure was applied to the Headquarters of each MAC, whose offices had always been a target for skilfully installed listening devices.

Having taken these steps to seal off leakages, we now had to get rid of a number of individuals. A few case histories will show the sort of thing we were up against. There were many different types of individuals and situations. For instance A.* was a very

* Fictitious name.

able security officer, seconded from his police job in a European capital. To begin with he made an excellent impression—on duty. Off duty he traveled a lot, in an expensive car bought surprisingly soon after his arrival (he was later discovered to own two cars). He was an extrovert and in no time seemed to know everybody in Tiberias and later in Damascus. Although he had his family with him at these stations, he was often seen in Jerusalem without them, having volunteered to take mail runs there when it was not his turn. Discreet surveillance revealed him to be in constant touch with shady customers on both sides.

One day a Syrian complaint revealed the news that A. had been apprehended *in flagranti* taking photographs and making sketches of a Syrian military airfield. Although alleged to have confessed that he was collecting information for the Israelis, he had been released from custody and merely declared *persona non grata*. This sounded dubious to me because the Syrian *deuxième bureau* was noted for hanging onto anyone who fell into its clutches. I suspected some illegal business transactions.

Extensive investigations revealed A. as a very hard-boiled customer. Even after continuous grillings he never confessed in full but readily agreed to resign from the United Nations, not immediately, but "in three days' time." Five days later we had evidence enough to be able to piece together what appeared to be the true picture of why and how A. needed and spent those three days of grace.

From the information available to us, the following appeared to be the sequence of events: He had gone straight from Government House to Beirut, collected a consignment of gold, driven through Syria, Jordan and Jerusalem to the south coast of Tel Aviv, where he met two operators from Israeli Jerusalem. The gold was buried on the beach. A. (having taken his cut) went off on his own without incident. But his confreres were not so lucky. Returning to Jerusalem, their car was stopped and searched by police four times. Everything, however, was in order, and next day they returned to the beach, ostensibly for a swim, dug up the gold, and drove unmolested to Jerusalem, where they spent a long time in a synagogue, thanking and praising the Lord for his protection.

When last heard of A. was back in his own national police service, had been promoted, and was enjoying a fat bank account in Switzerland.

B.* was a luscious, raven-haired Sabra girl, adept at making new acquaintances among recently arrived UN personnel. C.,* a sex-starved young grass widower, fell for her at once and was only too delighted to accept her invitation after the D.'s * "regular" party to escort her home. And he had no reason to regret it—until he left the house, and found himself being offered a lift home by a friendly fellow who was just starting his car parked outside the door.

"You seem to be a new arrival here. Why not let me show you around a bit? It is such a lovely morning."

"That's very nice of you. It *is* a lovely morning. Spring is in the air."

"Isn't it?" (after a while) "By the way, I understand that you are expecting your young wife to join you soon?"

"Yes, thank God, at last."

"You love her?"

"Of course."

"Wouldn't she feel, hmhmmm . . . disappointed, if she knew about B.?"

"Look! What the hell is all this?"

"Don't worry, she'll never find out—if you are sensible."

"What do you mean?"

"Even reckoning keeps long friends—I promise not to give you away to your wife, E." *

"Hell. How do you know her name?"

"Listen, Buster. We know everything about you. So you had better play ball, and do as we tell you—"

"But, but . . . then I shall be in trouble with my boss. The General is hard as hell on that sort of thing."

"That silly old b . . . . . d! Trying to outwit US!—You'll be safe as houses if you use your brains and collect odd bits of information we shall need from time to time. It pays substantially too. Just tell me where you want a new bank account."

* Fictitious name.

Fortunately, C. did *not* play. He went straight to the silly old b . . . . . d.

Another case was a staff member whom I shall call F.*—a reserve officer whose native language was neither English nor American. For a long time he carried out his duties so efficiently that I was impressed, seriously considered him for, and even tried him in a special administrative task (I was willing to overlook his massive monthly purchases of gin because I knew "his wife's" fondness for it as an astringent). This special trust shown to F. made him overventuresome. Before long, instead of approving his application for permanent UN employment I found it necessary to investigate an increasing number of rumors. Our researches paid off: he was caught red-handed as an established smuggler.

It was not easy for a mere soldier to interrogate a man with legal training and court experience before he had been expelled from the bar. But we broke him in spite of repeated assurances "on his word of honor." I was not at all surprised when F. subsequently surfaced as a mercenary in the Congo and was later discovered conducting Pilgrim tours to the Holy Land. Spotted in the street by a former colleague, he quickly donned dark glasses, which in that area are also worn by some honest people.

Then there was G.*—a member of the Mission who was due for transfer from Gaza. Shortly before leaving, a local acquaintance offered him Israeli currency at a favorable rate of exchange. G. ordered 10,000 pounds, Israeli, before devaluation, which was handed over in unopened packets of brand new banknotes. On arrival at his next station he paid one year's rent for his house in advance. The following morning he had a visitor from the Israeli Police.

"Where did you get that money?"

"In Gaza."

"From the Finance Office UNEF headquarters?"

"No. From a money-changer. Is anything wrong?"

"Only this: first the transaction and the transfer are illegal. Secondly your banknotes are fakes."

When I informed the Israel authorities that this individual was

* Fictitious name.

precipitately leaving the Mission, I was surprised that their attitude was merely "Too bad to get caught, isn't it?"

Nothing succeeds like examples and soon there was a trickle of personnel back to New York or to the armies of Member States. On a lower level, too, Hansen began to turn his attention to the bonded stores where the monthly accounts of certain staff members made enlightening reading. At the beginning, each investigation resulted in a similar reaction: outraged dignity on the part of the suspect, a defiant attitude that it had been impressed on them in New York that they enjoyed diplomatic status overseas, and what they did with bonded goods they bought was their own damned business.

But as we sent them home or "persuaded" them to ask for their release from UN service, urgent warnings must have gone out over the grapevine. I had a distinct impression that on a very wide front business had virtually come to a halt. We had made a real start, and I was grateful for Hansen's natural flair for unearthing information and patiently piecing it together until we began to feel that we were getting a grip on the ground roots of corruption.

It was information from a local contact that sent Hansen out on his last mission. He had discovered that a grocer in Chtoura in the Lebanon had been complaining that certain UN officers had not been settling their accounts. Although this grocer was known to be a double agent for the Syrians and Israelis, his instincts as an outraged shopkeeper must have triumphed over his discretion as an agent. Subsequent investigation proved that the accounts were pretty large; some bills revealed the purchase of three Frigidaires that had doubtless been whisked off into Syrian territory (where they were very expensive) to be resold.

Once on this trail, more exhaustive inquiries pinpointed one of our observers whose activities were then carefully watched. More information coming in established that he was endeavoring to reopen a regular "mail run" from Tel Aviv via Tiberias and Damascus to Beirut; a run which had been successfully operated for a long time by another observer, and had closed down only because he had left the Mission. From his contacts Hansen had become convinced that the reopening of this mail run was motivated by a plan to smuggle information rather than goods. Perhaps a few harmless items might be carried in the white jeep for cover, but he left me in no doubt as to what country he thought was backing the operation. Hansen had discovered the date of the first run and told me he was going to trail the officer along the whole length of the route. I can remember that moment vividly. He seemed so very confident and capable of looking after himself.

I wished him luck. I had to fly to Cairo that night to report to Dag, who was stopping over there for discussions with President Nasser on his way back from Laos. And in the plane, I must admit, I hardly thought of Hansen because I was preoccupied with a report from the Chairman of our Jordan-Israel MAC; a report which the Israelis were turning Heaven and Earth to have altered.

It was January now, but the trouble had begun in October with a Jordanian complaint that the Israelis had expelled a number of Bedouins of the Azazme tribe from the Negev into Jordan where they were now miserably encamped with their tents and flocks, forcibly ejected from the grazing lands they had roamed for centuries because the land was about to become part of Ben Gurion's plan "to make the desert bloom."

I had ordered an immediate inquiry, but so many difficulties were put in our way that it was a little time before we were able to dispatch a team of two Italian observers, one of whom (unknown to the Israelis) spoke fluent Bedoui-Arabic. A special radio jeep had been attached to this team so that any attempts at interference or double-crossing could be immediately reported to Jerusalem. In no time this had started.

There were protestations that it would be wilfully dangerous to enter the area, which was an old artillery training range, and which the Israelis claimed was heavily mined from the earlier fighting. Our observers promptly requested that they be accompanied by a mine detection team, which the Israelis refused, so our observers then asked permission to proceed at their own risk, and eventually this was grudgingly granted (after I had informed Dr. Biran, Yosef Tekoah's successor, what I thought and what the world would think about these silly attempts to stop a perfectly correct investigation).

The two Italians drove into the territory with a skeptical but eagle eye for mines and unexploded shells. They saw none, but they did discover a large sign in newly painted bold letters: 'This Way to the Antiquities' and on investigating a little closer, observed that the entrance fee, too, was clearly marked for American tourists at 50 Piasters.

Our observers reported that there was no doubt the Bedouis had been wrongly expelled. The frantic Israeli efforts to have this report changed, even down to adding a clause accusing me of having treacherously smuggled in a Bedoui-speaking observer without their consent, were something I felt Dag with his keen sense of humor would enjoy. But on arrival at Cairo, I found that the brief period available for his discussions with the Egyptian dictator left us little time for relaxed conversation. Nor did Egyptian catering rise to providing any dinner late on the final night we spent together. Our sole sustenance consisted of four double whiskies. Dag was to leave early the next morning, and during the short time we had together, our discussions were mainly concerned with trouble that seemed imminent on the Syrian front.

When later that night a coded message arrived from Jerusalem, I suspected that fighting must have broken out. I was sure that I was being summoned back, and waited impatiently for the cable to be decoded. But when it had been translated into clear it told a very different story.

I read the message with dismay: Hansen had met with a serious motor accident and was critically ill in a hospital at Haifa. As I crumpled it up and stuffed it into my pocket, I recalled our conversation such a short time before. I felt quite certain then, as I do now, that this was no ordinary accident. But I knew, too, that I should never be in a position to be able to prove it.

It was an unhappy homecoming to Jerusalem. Hansen was critically ill as a result of his injuries. It was impossible to have him moved from his hospital bed in Haifa where he was in a state of delirium, cared for most attentively by the nursing staff—and watched over by an Israeli from the Intelligence Service who never stirred from his bedside.

I hated to think of him there, and tried to close my mind to thoughts of that alert listener, noting down anything Hansen said, awake or asleep, any questions he asked, any message he tried to pass to his Headquarters. Instead, I concentrated on setting up a thorough investigation into the "accident."

As I had anticipated, there was no shred of evidence to substantiate what I was certain had taken place. Hansen's car had crashed in broad daylight at a sharp S bend on the road from Tiberias to Hadera. Trucks loaded with barrels of raw olive oil had been passing there recently on their way from the groves and the crude oil had leaked onto the road, leaving a surface more lethal than ice. But this in itself was nothing unusual at this time of year when the olive harvest was in full swing. We were all used to avoiding these dangerous patches, and Hansen would have been no exception since he was a careful driver.

A meticulous examination of the road and the trees along both sides yielded nothing to give a clue to our investigations. Nor when I had the wrecked car virtually taken to pieces was there the slightest indication it had been tampered with. Everything was in order as I had expected; even the kingpins were firmly in place. On the face of it, it had been a perfectly ordinary accident.

But hardly ordinary for Hansen, who was never to recover properly. From Haifa he was brought to Jerusalem where we installed him in the French hospital on the Jordan side. All his personal effects were subsequently returned—with the exception of his pocket diary, which "had not been found." Eventually poor Hansen was sent back to Sweden for a long period in hospital, and though he returned to Jerusalem just before I left for the Congo, it was distressing to discover that he was only a shadow of his former self.

It was a sad day for the United Nations when this loyal and talented officer was put out of action. He had been on top of his job, a brilliant security officer on the verge of breaking right through the mesh of corruption and espionage that Dag had ordered me to clear up. Now he was already out of the fight. Unlike his fellow Swede, Folke Bernadotte, he was fortunate to survive with his life. But to my mind, his name should stand on the casualty roll in the same selfless tradition.

Chapter Ten

ISRAELI-SYRIAN BORDER CLASHES

WITH Hansen out of the fight there was a long spell during which I had to be my own Security Chief aided by an exceptionally able British secretary—Miss Coral Kent—whom Dag loaned me, but although we had a number of successes in tracing and stamping out unorthodox activities, it was never a satisfactory solution and proved a constant distraction from the day-to-day work of the Mission.

I had hardly settled down in Jerusalem when on February 1 heavy fighting broke out in the demilitarized zone between the Israeli and Syrian borders. Since an Israeli attack was to be launched here against the Arab village of Lower Tawafiq, the action came to be known as the Tawafiq incident. The events leading up to this episode, the actual fighting, and the subsequent investigation are an illuminating example of the sort of situation we were constantly being called on to deal with.

In 1950, the Israelis had established a new kibbutz at Beit Katzir in the demilitarized zone. Like most of their kibbutzim in troubled areas, it was fortified with trenches and a double-apron barbed wire fence from behind which its settlers sallied out to cultivate the surrounding land, digging irrigation canals to channel the water from Lake Tiberias with such vigor that before long no Arab farmer in the area was allowed into the stretch of land between the kibbutz and the lake. From here they soon extended their activities so that the inhabitants of two neighboring Arab villages, Lower and Upper Tawafiq, observed the kibbutznik tractor drivers with alarm as they speeded up on each turn at the eastern boundaries of their fields, making the ploughs swerve out, thus slowly but surely extending their "previous" cultivation eastward into Arab land. This was, of course, part of a premeditated

Israeli policy to edge east through the demilitarized zone toward the old Palestine border (as shown on their maps) and to get all Arabs out of the way by fair means or foul.

The Arab villagers in the two Tawafiqs, which were on high ground thirteen hundred meters east of the kibbutz, resented this gradual encroachment; the land below them was intricately apportioned into narrow parallel strips which were either Arab- or Jewish-owned or mixed property predominantly Arab or Jewish. This intricate apportionment had never been respected by the Israelis, who cultivated where they pleased. In fact, the Israelis had never observed the rules of the Armistice Agreement which allowed only limited numbers of locally recruited civilian police in this demilitarized zone. Instead a patrol from the border police of the State of Israel would arrive, usually in an armored vehicle. These police, too, had established three vantage points to protect the kibbutznik activities and prevent the villagers of the twin Tawafiqs from using land to the east of the kibbutz. It was hardly surprising the Arab farmers should feel themselves and their fields threatened.

As early as September 1957 an Israeli survey team had been fired on from Lower Tawafiq, and during the tense situation that followed the villagers abandoned their homes and moved up into Upper Tawafiq where they felt safer. Two months later the Israelis announced their intention to dig an irrigation ditch right through the lower village. But when three of their workers escorted by border police arrived and began cutting the wire with which the villagers had protected their homes, firing broke out. One Israeli was killed and another wounded. From this time on, the Arab village became virtually deserted; only from time to time would a few of the inhabitants venture down to resume their normal lives.

Throughout this trouble the work of the Mixed Armistice Commission, where Lieutenant Colonel Bertrand of Canada had succeeded Lieutenant Colonel Moe of Norway, had been rendered extremely difficult because of the Israelis' refusal to attend any of its meetings. Although the Security Council had made it clear that it called upon both parties to be represented, the Israelis continued their boycott, and had questioned the right of the Chief of Staff to make findings as Chairman of the Commission without actually going so far as to reject them out of hand. Informal conversations with the Israeli Delegation had got us nowhere. After the shooting, however, they apparently thought the situation sufficiently serious to warrant their attendance. A meeting was held in November 1957 at which both Israeli and Syrian delegations were present, our observers' reports were examined, and both sides agreed to the rather overoptimistic formula that legitimate work in the area should not be interfered with and that differences of opinion should be solved by a peaceful means.

Plans for the irrigation ditch through Lower Tawafiq were abandoned. But within twelve months, the Israelis were busily at work on another ditch west of the village. This led to loud protests, but once a UN survey team had reported that the ditch would cause no harm to Arab land, and the Israelis had assured us that they did not intend to cultivate right up to the ditch, our inquiry found that the work was legitimate.

This ditch was to prove a bitter bone of contention. Once it became obvious that the Israelis had no intention of keeping their word to us and were set on appropriating and cultivating all the land west of the ditch, not surprisingly the Arab farmers were determined to hold onto their land and constantly crossed the ditch to plough their fields, where they ran into considerable intimidation from Israeli border police.

It became an everyday sight to see an Arab farmer working his ancient plough with a rifle slung across his shoulder; a lonely figure who probably drew strength from the knowledge that his activities were watched by the forward observation officers spotting for modern Syrian guns well back out of the forbidden zones on the plateau that overlooked the whole area. It is unlikely that these would ever have come into action had it not been for Israeli provocation. In December, we had to stop their digging another irrigation ditch. Constant interference with Arab farmers who were turned away from cultivating their own land created such bitterness that the Tawafiq area exploded on December 24 as the villagers opened up on the Israeli border police with rifles and automatics. It was four hours before our observers could arrange a cease fire; during this time an Israeli policeman was killed and an Arab slightly wounded.

The situation remained tense. Anxious to establish calm, Colonel Bertrand eventually persuaded the Arabs to suspend cultivation west of the ditch until further discussions could be held. The Arabs agreed to this reluctantly, making it clear their action must in no way be allowed to prejudice the eventual ownership of the land. This achieved a lessening of tension. But when the Colonel tried to get cooperation from the Israelis he looked in vain; his proposal to the Deputy Director of Armistice Affairs that the villagers of Lower Tawafiq and the settlers from the kibbutz should meet and talk things over was flatly turned down.

On January 8 (while the Arabs still kept their side of the agreement) he tried again. The reply from the Israel delegation to his own MAC took eight days, but when it did arrive, its tone was encouraging. The Senior Delegate thought that progress might be made through a personal talk, and suggested a meeting with the Colonel in Tiberias. This took place next day but proved a total failure when the Israeli asked for a three-day postponement because he was not yet ready for discussions.

It was not to be. That very afternoon an Israeli tractor had come lumbering up to the ditch to plough a strip of land close to its edge. Immediately the Colonel heard this news, he requested the work be stopped. His proposal was ignored; under the benign eye of the Israeli border police the ploughing continued for another two days. This was more than the inhabitants of the two Tawafiqs could bear to watch. On January 18 they crossed the ditch westward again to resume work on their fields before they were engulfed.

Next day the American Colonel Rickert, who was acting Chief of Staff in my absence, took Colonel Bertrand's place at a meeting of the MAC in Tiberias. The Israeli Deputy Director of Armistice Affairs was present and it soon became clear that what he called "the status quo" (in other words the agreement that Colonel Bertrand had obtained from the Arabs not to cultivate west of the ditch until discussions had been held) suited him very well. Until tension in the area had been reduced, he was not prepared to discuss proposals for a settlement.

This was typical Israeli "double talk." The tension would never have arisen in the first place had they not broken their word not to cultivate up to the ditch. In part this may have come about through the militant attitude of the kibbutzniks, but I personally suspected rivalry between the Foreign and Defense ministries. One had to remember, too, that Moshe Dayan (a great thruster and former Chief of Staff) was now Minister of Agriculture. Whatever the reason something had to be done quickly. As soon as I had had time to study Colonel Rickert's report, I communicated my findings to both sides. To try to arrive at an equitable solution, I decreed that subject to certain reservations, Arab cultivation on the west side of the ditch must not go farther than the immediate limit the Israeli ploughs had reached, and that for the sake of tranquillity they were not to use the land right up to the Israeli fields, but were to leave a ten-meter strip of "no man's land" between the two cultivated areas. I stressed that these findings would not impair a final settlement of the legal claims of either side.

I hoped that this decision would relieve the Arabs of any further apprehensions of being squeezed out of their land west of the ditch. I hoped, too, that both sides would now be able to carry on their activities in a more peaceful atmosphere. What actually transpired was quite the opposite; from that day onward we were showered with complaints from both sides.

Because the Israelis refused to allow our observers untrammeled access to the kibbutz or the disputed land west of the ditch, our picture during the next few days came mainly from an observer posted in Upper Tawafiq. On January 20, he reported that seven Israeli tractors accompanied by armed Israeli border police were ploughing beyond the limits I had laid down; the next day, he saw another Israeli tractor ploughing land the Arabs had cultivated only two days before.

On January 26 our observer saw an Israeli armored personnel carrier (forbidden under the Armistice Agreement) turn Arab farmers away from working their fields. As soon as it had withdrawn, they returned, only to be driven back once more when armed border police came on the scene and the carrier returned. On this occasion he reported three Syrian national guards carrying rifles and wearing battle dress and red keffias among the farmers. Up till now, despite Israeli complaints of Syrian troops in Tawafiq, we had seen only Arab farmers with rifles, ploughs, and cattle on the west side of the ditch.

We requested that the Syrians should remove these guards, and asked the Israelis to withdraw their border police and armored vehicles. Neither side complied, and on January 27 the crew of an Israeli armored car, mounting a light machine gun, was heard shouting at a party of Arab farmers. A few minutes later shots were fired from the vicinity of the armored car, which then moved away but remained in the area. The Arabs continued ploughing until more shots were aimed at them from one of the vantage points the Israeli border police had set up. As soon as this shooting started it brought an answering reply from the Tawafiq area, the farmers took cover in the ditch, and firing went on for nearly ten minutes.

During the next four days the situation deteriorated. The Arab farmers doggedly ploughed on, until intermittent shooting forced them to take cover, and our observers had a hard time arranging a cease fire. The shooting was mainly coming from vantage points around the kibbutz and the village of Upper Tawafiq, and before long tracer bullets and antitank shells thickened up the rifle fire. On January 31 Syrian mortar shells started landing west of the ditch. So heavy was the fire from both sides that one of our observers who had gone down into the disputed area was pinned down for some time before a cease fire could be arranged to evacuate a wounded Israeli. It did not last long and the day ended in a confusion of shooting that could not be accurately observed.

In Jerusalem, I informed both sides that I had instructed the Chairman of the MAC to arrange immediate visits for our observers to both the Syrian and Israeli positions to report whether armed buildups were taking place. I was certain both sides must have been moving troops and guns into the forbidden zone although it was probable the Syrians were the lesser offenders because their heavy guns on the high ground were well back out of the demilitarized zone and defensive area.

In a letter the previous day, I had appealed to both sides to solve their differences by peaceful means and I felt sure that the appearance of our observers would calm down the tension. I had, in fact, received assurances—in answer to an even earlier letter—of cooperation from both sides, and that very day the Israeli Director of Armistice Affairs indicated that Israel was prepared to meet Syria to discuss means of preventing new outbreaks of shooting. In typical fashion, however, this was qualified by a proviso that Israel would not discuss any issue with the Syrian authorities which might arise in the Demilitarized Zone west of the international boundary. Translated, this meant that they were not prepared to discuss the territory where the shooting *was going on* because according to their maps the whole area was conveniently, if theoretically, Israeli territory. I had had to write back asking whether I should interpret this as a refusal to comply with the Agreement we had wrung out of them in 1957 "that legitimate work in the disputed area should not be interfered with and that differences of opinion should be solved by peaceful means and that both parties should comply fully with the General Armistice Agreement."

I was not to receive their tortuous reply until the following day. But that night, a few hours after my letter requesting that our observers be admitted into the Israeli positions had been delivered (the delivery was "naturally" delayed by the "unavailability" of the Director of Armistice Affairs at the Israeli Foreign Office), our observers were reporting heavy artillery fire on Lower Tawafiq. Some came from the vantage points around the kibbutz (which no doubt had been reinforced from the illicit armory at Beit Katzir).

The really heavy shells that rained down on the village, however, came from Israeli gun positions near Porya southwest of the lake. A short time later the Israelis launched an attack in company strength and occupied the village. Heavy explosions were heard as they proceeded to blow up its houses. As violent flashes lit up the night, the Syrian forces on the high ground opened dense artillery and 120mm mortar fire on the Israeli troops, who then withdrew from the village.

Next morning four Israeli jet fighters flew over the Syrian positions farther back at Kuneitra; here they met strong antiaircraft fire. While our observers were trying to get close up to Lower

Tawafiq to arrange a cease fire, both sides counted their dead. The Syrians reported two Arabs killed and two wounded. The Israelis admitted to three dead and seven wounded and immediately arranged visits to the battlefield for journalists, service attachés, other diplomats, and even school children. Neither I nor any member of the United Nations were invited to these tours or even told about the elaborate display of weapons and material exhibited to demonstrate their "captures" in the village until we received a formal letter some days later.

Unofficially, we heard from the service attachés that the carefully mounted Israeli attack had not been entirely successful. By the time that this news filtered through we had been able to get our observers into Israeli territory where they confirmed that the assault must have been launched in company strength supported from several carefully prepared artillery positions. Meanwhile, although intermittent shooting was still going on around the Tawafiqs we had, on February 2 and 3, been able to get an observer into the lower village. Since the Israelis were insisting that it had been a heavily defended position, his instructions were to discover whether the village *had* been turned into a strong point and whether it had in fact been occupied by an Arab garrison on the night of the attack.

This observer was a particularly reliable Canadian officer and his report made interesting reading. He discovered that Lower Tawafiq consisted of two parts, the larger being circled by a shallow trench with a parapet of stones with firing slots for riflemen. At one side the trench continued on for one hundred and fifty meters until it entered the cover of a nearby wadi. The whole village was surrounded by barbed wire entanglements; no signs of bunkers or overhead cover were to be seen. Save for six or seven houses in the northern end of the village, the whole place was in ruins. The roofs had been scattered and the walls blown outward by heavy explosive charges. Although he searched the whole area there was no evidence that any fighting had taken place, no signs of blood, and only a few holes that could have been made by bullets. Not a bomb or shell crater could be found and the only evidence of occupation was a full light machine gun magazine and two quilts, which showed unmistakable signs of having been placed on top of some rubble *after* the demolitions had taken place. Two Arab witnesses told him that when on the Sunday night there had been rumors of an attack, everyone had withdrawn to Upper Tawafiq with the exception of those villagers who owned arms. These men had stayed until two Israeli tanks heading the attack had crashed through the wire under supporting fire from three more tanks outside.

One of an observer's most difficult and frustrating jobs is listening to and sifting evidence—invariably through an interpreter who may be distorting the story. But our officers, now experiencing these difficulties on both sides of the lines, could hardly have had a more frustrating time than mine in Jerusalem. During the next five days while sporadic shooting continued in the Tawafiq area, I had to fight a battle with Dr. Biran to persuade the Israelis to agree to attend a meeting of the Mixed Armistice Commission. Biran, who had now replaced Yosef Tekoah as Director of Armistice Affairs, was a neat, rather worried-looking little man who knew Palestinian affairs like the back of his hand. He had been in the country a long time and had worked as a civil servant in the days of the British Mandate. Like most of that breed, he had a fondness for sticking to the rules—especially if they happened to be his own, and he was determined now to meet the Syrians only on his own terms. "Peace" (which he professed himself eager to discuss) oddly enough did not seem to include the troubled Tawafiq area which, as far as he was concerned, was already Israeli territory. Under sustained pressure, however, he came up with an alternative suggestion for what he termed an "informal" meeting at which the Israelis would meet the Syrians on condition that the Chairman of the MAC ruled out of order any questions in which Israel considered Syria had no say. I turned this down but he then came back with another equally fatuous but calculated suggestion: the Israelis would be glad to meet the Syrians in the Mixed Armistice Commission "to discuss peace, complete peace, or, if not that, to discuss means to preserve quiet and tranquillity along the international boundary, as long as nothing pertaining to the Demilitarized Zone west of that boundary is raised."

While men were still dying around the Tawafiqs, Israel, through the medium of Dr. Biran, was playing its familiar game of trying to establish precedents that they could later use to advantage against UNTSO. The new State was quite content to play for time, comfortably aware that its unprincipled action had brought Arab farming to a halt amid the whip and crack of bullets west of the ditch. There was, however, no alternative but to submit Biran's proposals to the Syrians, who as far back as January 31 had been ready to attend a meeting. Not surprisingly, their reaction was unfavorable and they replied that they were ready to meet the Israelis at any time within the framework of the Mixed Armistice Commission to discuss the recent incidents and aggressive actions that had arisen through Israel breaking the General Armistice Agreement. But in order to ensure the tranquillity of the area problems affecting the Demilitarized Zone *must* be discussed.

I put this to Dr. Biran but met a blank wall of refusal. I was very angry. And with reason. The Israelis had broken the Armistice Agreement, broken their word, ignored my ruling of January 20, and were now blatantly disregarding the Security Council's ruling that they should attend meetings called by the Chairman of the Mixed Armistice Commission. It was stalemate; there was no alternative but to convene a meeting without them.

Two days before this took place a new fire fight broke out in another sector of the Demilitarized Zone well north of the Tawafiqs. Once again it was started by Israeli border police in an armored personnel carrier, interfering with Arab farmers. And once again the Israelis lodged a complaint and demanded an investigation.

Of course we complied, just as we did to a similar Syrian complaint. But before our observers' reports were received, the Mixed Armistice Commission had met at Banxat Yacoub on February 16 to consider the outbreak of fighting in the Tawafiq area. The day before it started, Israeli tactics were in evidence. Presumably wishing to insure themselves in case the verdict went against them in their absence, the Senior Israeli Delegate drew Colonel Bertrand's attention to the fact that the Syrians had not accepted their offer to attend provided no incident west of the international boundary was discussed. He even accused the Colonel of "taking up a position where there are basic differences of opinion," and claimed that he had *prevented* the Israelis from taking part in the meeting!

As the Armistice Agreement stated clearly that the Chairman of the Commission had the right to settle basic differences of opinion, Colonel Bertrand ignored this attempt to hold up the meeting. It took place without the Israeli Delegation.

Once the Syrian complaints had been considered and the observers' reports examined, the events that had led up to the incident were summed up in careful detail. It was recalled that the Israelis had broken the agreement reached in November 1957, had opposed the Chief of Staff of UNTSO's findings of January 20, 1960 by using force against the Arabs, and had used their regular armed forces to attack Lower Tawafiq, which had no fortifications other than a trench and some barbed wire entanglements. As a result of this premeditated attack, serious tension had been aroused in the area.

Although the Colonel made it clear to the Syrian delegates that they had been guilty of bringing troops and guns into the Demilitarized Zone, the onus of guilt fell fairly and squarely on Israel and the Commission condemned their attack on Lower Tawafiq. It further condemned them for a flagrant violation of the Armistice Agreement in allowing their four jet planes to fly over Kuneitra in Syrian territory a few days later.

These findings must have made disconcerting reading in the Israeli Foreign Office. As soon as they reached us in Jerusalem, the whole of my staff were set to work, compiling a detailed report for New York where the Secretary General would soon be placing the incident before the Security Council. Although the Old Fox was far from well, he stuck to his office until he had drafted a clear and cogent document, which set out the whole Tawafiq story in telling detail.

As we worked, a letter from Dr. Biran made us aware the Israelis were scenting trouble. He would, he announced, like to renew his proposal that I arrange a conference at a suitably high level between the Syrians and themselves to explore practical ways of restoring quiet and tranquillity. This was a distinct change from an earlier letter in which he had suggested that the Israelis bypass the United Nations and negotiate direct with the Syrians: a maneuver which would have suited them very well because had they ever got away with it, they would certainly have claimed it as a precedent for ignoring UNTSO. Guessing that the forthcoming meeting of the Security Council was weighing on his mind, I inquired whether such a meeting would still be inhibited from discussing incidents in the Demilitarized Zone.

Biran remained silent; but the Israeli information service was soon manufacturing a verbal smoke screen in case the verdict of the Security Council should go against them. As usual, while stooping to the most unscrupulous methods at home, the Israelis attached great importance to their public image abroad where it was vital to pose as a *parfait gentil* little state armed only with a slingful of pebbles against the massive club of an aggressive Arab Goliath.

It was, therefore, all the more vital that our report should reveal the impartial truth, and I was delighted with the lucid and detailed document that my staff produced. Once it had been published and distributed in New York there were two immediate reactions. First came a cable from Hammarskjöld, sending us his special thanks for "A thorough, well reasoned and well written report." Next, we began to receive visits from diplomats and journalists anxious to hear (in their own words) "the real and true facts from an impartial source."

Only a few months before, we had sometimes felt we were battling alone amid a fog of warped Israeli propaganda; now our point of view was being sought and listened to, and made known to the outside world.

Nothing could have stood us in better stead when a short time later the Security Council roundly condemned the Israeli attack on Lower Tawafiq. Although the Israeli newspapers and the whole machinery of its Information Service were turned full on to camouflage this blow to their international image, the facts spoke clearly for themselves and did them great damage. In UNTSO, we were relieved and delighted to discover that at last the truth had won out. From this time on, we noted a distinct difference in the attitude of diplomatic missions and permanent foreign newspaper correspondents.

These new relationships enabled me to develop a policy aimed at strengthening UNTSO's position. Over the past two years, I had been made vividly aware that noncooperation from the countries that had signed the Armistice Agreement was capable of virtually neutralizing the effective work of the mission. Unless UNTSO was to decline into an expensive but ineffective mission, it was vital that some local initiative be taken to manipulate strings which, when successfully pulled, would help the Secretary General to support us from New York. I was well aware how dependent the Israelis were on the good will of countries abroad, which either supported them politically or aided them with funds, supplies, and foreign loans. France and the United States were two of their most fruitful sources, and I now found it politic to establish friendly relations with their Consuls General in Jerusalem.

I soon extended this policy to cover the heads of the other foreign missions and although I had no intention of building UNTSO into a sort of unofficial pressure group, I found (and my subsequent experience on my return from the Congo proved) that we could obtain excellent results by dealing with them directly, if unofficially, and giving the Consul General clear and factual information about deliberate attempts to thwart our work; the gist of our conversations was reported back to their foreign offices, who were thus given a picture undistorted by propaganda; as a result pressure was often applied on Israel or the Arab States when we most needed it.

This policy undoubtedly helped Dag to help us, and certainly succeeded in infuriating and frustrating the Israelis. But it was often truly difficult to comprehend how they expected their actions to endear them, even to countries which were fundamentally well disposed.

The Gaza episode was an example. After the Security Council's condemnation, external political pressure exerted a restraining influence on their more militant leaders. The frontiers remained reasonably quiet, and in May, I was able to go down to Gaza where Prime Minister Nehru, who was visiting Cairo, was due to review the Indian troops who formed an important part of the United Nations Emergency Force.

Once again, the Israelis chose to demonstrate their contempt and dislike of the United Nations. The white UN plane carrying Prime Minister Nehru and General Gyani, the Indian Commander of the United Nations Emergency Force, was buzzed by an Israeli jet fighter just as it was coming in to land on the Gaza airstrip. The pilot of the jet fighter then proceeded to cement Israeli-Indian relations by an offensive and noisy low-level flight over the Indian guard of honor drawn up to receive Mr. Nehru. Sitting next to the Indian Prime Minister at luncheon later that day, I was interested to hear his comments!

A week later, I attended the Jordan Arab Army Day in Amman, and was impressed by the parade and the high standard of a battle exercise that took place with live ammunition. It was plain that the Jordanian army was benefiting from Brigadier Strickland's training mission, which had been sent out to Amman a year after General Glubb's dismissal. The British link had been firmly maintained, albeit on a new basis, their troops had been flown in to Jordan's aid at a time of crisis, and now that the unrest inspired by Cairo had quieted down, freedom from internal security duties had given the army the chance to get down to full-scale training.

I came back to Jerusalem to find more tension developing on the Syrian and Lebanese borders, owing to Israeli plans for diverting the headwaters of the Jordan away from the Arab lands to irrigate the Negev Desert. Toward July the situation became extremely tense, but somehow faded into the background once both Arabs and Israelis became aware that the outside world had suddenly lost interest in the Holy Land. For the moment international attention had become focused on the Congo.

Chapter Eleven

C'EST LE CONGO

FEW persons are at the top of their form in the small hours, and the news that hit me at 1.30 a.m. on July 13, 1960 had a gale-force quality about it. At this time I had been Chief of Staff of UNTSO for well over two years and was overdue for home leave.

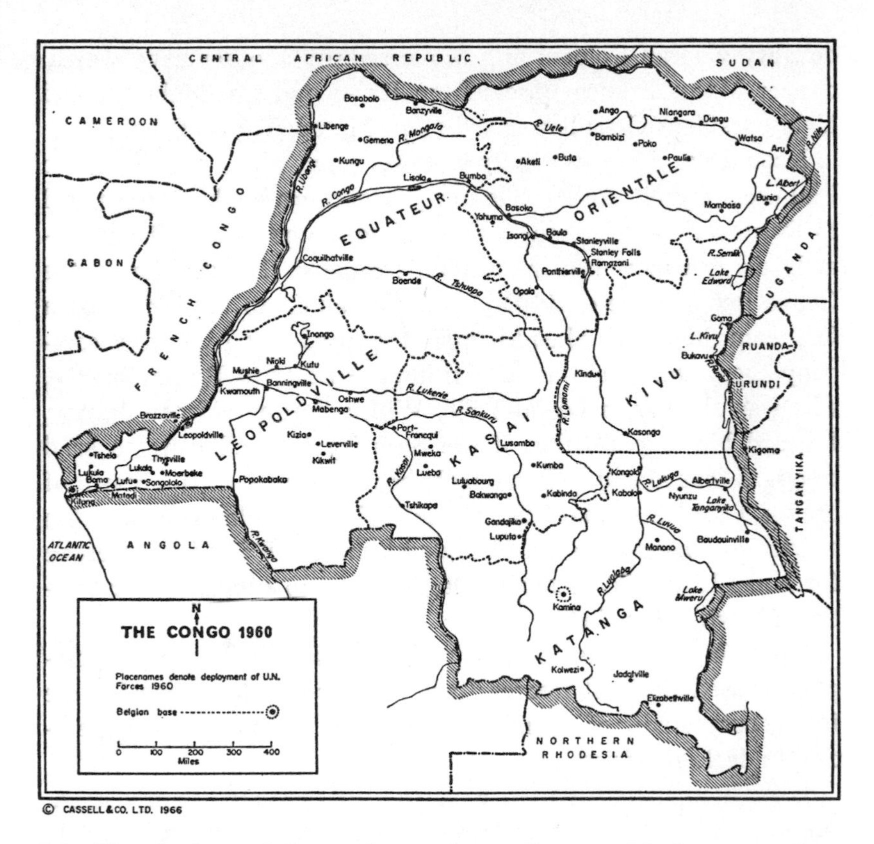

I had booked my ticket and was due to fly out of Beirut next day, eagerly looking forward to a real break with Scarlett and Johan at home.

Within a matter of minutes these plans were totally disrupted. True, there had been a hint on July 12 when a cable from Dag had ordered me to assemble a group of six observers for service in the Congo. After the chaotic buildup of UNOGIL I had drawn my own conclusions and, anticipating that any crash program in Africa was bound to follow the same pattern, took the precaution of doubling the number of observers and augmenting them with a team of communications personnel. In the short time available, I picked only officers with outstanding ability and resource. Among them was a first-rate Canadian Staff Officer, Colonel Johnny Berthiaume; Major Geoffrey Hunt, a resourceful, mustachioed civil engineer from the New Zealand Army Reserve; that doughty veteran Colonel Stig Mollersward; another cavalryman, dapper Major Franco Boschi from Italy; and a redoubtable and highly resilient Canadian guardsman, Major Wayne King.

I could hardly have chosen a better team had I been going to lead them myself. And at one thirty next morning, having listened to Dag over the telephone (who told me to get them off immediately air transport became available because the situation in the Congo had become critical), I was just about to tell him what a fine team they were when he broke the news that I was to accompany them and would act as Military Adviser to Ralph Bunche, who was already in Léopoldville. With a feeling akin to dismay, I heard him explain that if the Security Council were to send troops, I was slated to command them. Aware it was a waste of breath, I explained that I had a reservation on a plane home within a matter of hours; I even reminded him that I was long overdue for home leave. Courteously, Dag told me to cancel the reservation. He wished me luck.

I put the telephone down. His parting words: "Keep your fingers crossed till Hell freezes," sounded prophetic advice for the future commander of an unknown polyglot force in a crash operation in darkest Africa.

Eight hours later. I had handed over my command to my American Assistant Chief of Staff, Colonel Rickert, and we were ready for the plane. Meanwhile, my Administrative Officer, Jan Van Wijk, who had had to leave us for domestic reasons, had recently been replaced by a new man, about whom I was to hear a great deal at a later time.

It turned out there was no need for hurry. Although we sent an immediate signal to New York advising our space requirements, the whole of July 13 slipped by until eventually a message came in advising us to expect a plane the following day. This, July 14 and Bastille Day, sounded like an ideal operational code name for our arrival in the Congo, where the situation appeared to be growing worse hourly. Up till now, I had known little about the new Republic other than what I had read in the newspapers or heard on radio, but during the twenty-four hours before our plane was due to arrive, I managed to get a grip on the bare bones of the situation.

Thirteen days before (June 30) Independence Day had found the Congolese totally unprepared to shoulder the burden of self-government. This was hardly surprising for only a year earlier—on October 16, 1959—the Belgians had announced that 1960 was to see the establishment of a Central Congolese Government, and a four-year plan in the course of which the country was to advance gradually toward independence. On the face of it, this was a statesmanlike conception because although the Congo had the highest standard of literacy in Africa, it had never been Belgian policy to educate the Congolese much over the age of fourteen. With a few exceptions there was virtually no form of secondary education, and although the University of Louvanium had been opened in 1954, only thirteen Congolese had so far actually graduated from it. Politically there were plenty of parties, but not one of them commanded any broad national support. Nor was there any real sense of Congolese national identity; which was hardly surprising in a country whose population of just over thirteen and a half million came from more than two hundred different tribes.

Unfortunately the Congo was never to experience a gradual and peaceful transition during which a last-minute crash training program might have gone some way toward building up a new elite of Congolese civil administrators who could have grappled with the task of trying to run their own country. Such a breathing space would have been invaluable because the country, which was divided into six provinces, was still totally dependent for its civil administration, internal security, and economic welfare on Belgian experience, brains, and technical ability.

It had always been Belgian policy to keep power exclusively in their own hands and now the wheel was about to come full circle. With independence only four years away, every senior post and the vast majority of minor ones down to the most junior grades in the civil administration, armed forces, communications, medical and transport services were still held by Belgians while the economic resources of a country rich in natural mineral deposits were also either Belgian owned or controlled.

In a growing atmosphere of restlessness, however, and under the pressure of violent demands for immediate freedom, all hope of this invaluable four-year transitional period vanished overnight. Perhaps this was because the Belgians feared a second Indo-China or Algeria, perhaps they found themselves subjected to pressure from the Americans who wanted to obtain the good will of the Afro-Asian bloc in the United Nations; perhaps they simply panicked. Whatever the reason, a decision was suddenly taken to grant the Congo sovereignty within the staggeringly short space of five months.

A Central Government was rapidly established, and independence was duly proclaimed on June 30, 1960. But the new Republic of the Congo headed by Joseph Kasavubu as President and Patrice Lumumba as Prime Minister was soon in trouble. Within a couple of days, tribal disturbances broke out in the capital and other parts of the country, and two days later the very force that should have put them down, the 25,000-strong national security force (the Force Publique), had mutinied in many places, expelled its white officers, and was soon busy plundering and destroying European property and beating up and sometimes killing many of the unlucky one hundred thousand Belgians who had remained to run the country and look after their businesses. In part this may have been brought about by Communist agents, but the main reason seems to have been the sheer jealousy of the soldiers at the sight of Congolese politicians and administrators suddenly elevated to power, riding in large cars and drawing even larger salaries.

Under a treaty of friendship signed just before independence, the Belgians had been allowed to retain two large bases in the Congo. Now that their nationals were in grave danger and the country seemed on the verge of chaos, they vainly attempted to persuade Prime Minister Lumumba to allow them to bring back Belgian troops to restore order.

When Lumumba refused, they lost patience, flew in paratroops and other crack units, and restored order in several of the worst trouble spots while a mass exodus of badly frightened Belgian civilians flooded out of the country under their protection. Before long ten thousand Belgian troops were back in the country, the Force Publique had virtually ceased to exist, and President Moise Tshombé of the rich mineral province of Katanga had announced that he was proclaiming his province an independent state because

Lumumba was a Communist and he had no intention of allowing Katanga to become involved in the anarchic turmoil sweeping the Congo.

Since Katanga provided about half of the country's revenue, this secession was nothing less than a catastrophe. But there was little the Central Government could do to force Tshombé back into the fold. On July 11, however, Lumumba asked Ralph Bunche (the Secretary General's representative in Léopoldville) for United Nations assistance to restore order in the ANC (Armée Nationale Congolaise) as the Force Publique had been restyled on the transference of independence. Let it be noted that his request never even mentioned the Belgians, who were later to be blamed for everything. It merely stressed the unreliability of the ANC (whose new commander, Major General Lundula, had recently been promoted from warrant officer) which was totally unable to restore order in Léopoldville, let alone the rest of the country.

While we were waiting in Jerusalem on July 13 another cable from the Congo was on its way to New York. This time the entire tone of its appeal for help had changed. Signed by Lumumba and Kasavubu, it requested urgent UN military assistance in the face of Belgian aggression and support of the Katanga secession.

I had no idea that in between these messages the Congolese Cabinet had, in Lumumba's temporary absence, requested direct American assistance. Nor that on hearing about this on his return, Lumumba had been most displeased and had hastened to consult the Soviet Ambassador in Léopoldville. Even had I heard about the telegram to Khrushchev which Lumumba and Kasavubu were to send off two days later (which was to result in a flow of Soviet material), I should have been little the wiser, stranded as I was in Jerusalem.

Forty-eight hours went past without a word from New York. On the evening of July 14 there was still no sign or news of our plane. I sent an urgent signal, but the only result was an infuriating silence, made all the more frustrating as we listened to the news over radio and learned that, in New York, the Security Council had met and authorized the Secretary General to make arrangements for military assistance to the Congo.

Next day, July 15, the radio informed us that I had been designated Commander of the United Nations Forces in the Congo. We learned, too, that the response by Member States had been swift and impressive and that my force was destined to be one of the most polyglot in history, far surpassing the widely varying nationalities that had served with the United Nations armies in Korea. In the same fashion, we heard that Ghanaian and Tunisian troops were already being airlifted.

Before long the news leaked out that the commander of this remarkable force was stranded in Jerusalem. By this time we may have been becoming supersensitive, but it was difficult not to imagine a condescending note in the BBC announcer's voice as he broadcast this item four or five times a day. On July 16, as there was still no news of our plane, I sent a very rude signal to New York and then rang up the United States Air Attaché in Tel Aviv, who promised to provide air transport should it become necessary.

Around noon a chartered Norwegian DC4 plane turned up at Jerusalem airport in Jordan. We learned from the pilot that he had been diverted from his normal run flying caviar out of Iran because the Scandinavian Airlines plane, which New York had chartered for us, had been delayed in Oslo for an engine check and on finally getting as far as Athens, had been grounded because of engine failure. More startling was the Norwegian captain's strong advice to us not to attempt to fly to Léopoldville in his plane. It was, he explained, unpressurized, lacked the necessary maps and flight plan, and in any case was only capable of accommodating half our party.

After listening to the British announcer once more, I rang the United States Air Attaché in Tel Aviv, reminded him of his promise and was told that there was a plane ready in Libya which could come in to pick us up at Amman airport *provided* permission was granted from the "Golden Room" of the Joint Chiefs of Staff in Washington.

I immediately put through a priority call to Andrew Cordier in New York; no doubt my voice must have conveyed a good deal of the frustration I was feeling because the green light was not long in coming from Washington. Within a remarkably short time, a Hercules C.130 had taken off from the United States Wheelus air base in Libya—only to develop engine trouble over the Eastern Mediterranean and be forced to return to base.

After an assurance that a replacement would be available within a matter of hours, I put my convoy on the road to Amman without delay. At three o'clock on the morning of July 17, a giant Hercules appeared out of the night and we scrambled thankfully on board. After just over five days' holdup since Dag's message—we were finally on our way to the Congo.

After a stop at Wheelus, we flew on over the Sahara, nearly freezing to death in our light uniforms because the huge stern flapdoors of the Hercules refused to shut tightly over its heavy cargo. At Kano airport in Nigeria, it took us a little while to become de-iced in the big transit hall crowded with distraught Belgian refugees on their way out of the Congo and a horde of newspaper correspondents on their way in. While disgustedly watching some of these "hawks" pouncing on refugees and reducing many of them to tears in their determination to get a hair-raising story, I was approached by a very mixed party of United Nations career personnel who were anxious to thumb a lift in our Hercules. None of them knew anything about what was happening in Léopoldville and many of them turned out to be accountants rather than the experienced staff officers and technical staff I had hoped would be on their way to build up Force Headquarters.

Flying against the clock, it was two o'clock in the morning when we finally touched down at N'Djili airport outside Léopoldville. At this time it had one of the longest runways in the world, and as we taxied back toward the apron I noticed that we appeared to be being chased by an impressive line of moving lights. Stepping onto Congolese soil for the first time, I discovered these to be the headlights of a convoy of cars which turned out to contain Ralph Bunche, Dr. Sture Linner of Sweden (who was soon to become Chief of Civilian Operations), and a large mixed contingent of Congolese and United Nations personnel.

Ralph seemed delighted to see me, told me that I had a room at the Stanley Hotel, and that during my absence the Ghanaian and Tunisian troops had been commanded by the British General Alexander, who was now asleep worn out after his efforts. He also told me that a Moroccan battalion had arrived, that an Ethiopian

Brigade was on the way, and that its advance party had just landed "over there." Apart from telling me that there was an Ethiopian General with them, Ralph seemed strangely uncommunicative about the composition of my Force Headquarters or its signal facilities. Suspecting that this might be UNOGIL all over again, I told Colonel Berthiaume (whom I had appointed on the way out as my temporary Chief of Staff) to try to get some order out of the mass of men and material the Hercules was now disgorging, and asked Ralph to hold on while I went over to have a word with the Ethiopian General.

Minutes later, I began to wonder whether this had been a good idea. I had started off confidently, but now I found myself alone in the darkness on a vast expanse of concrete. The stars were unfamiliar in this latitude but there were plenty of lights flashing in the distance and a cheerful soul had told me just before I had set out that there were elements of the ANC, Belgian Metropolitan paratroops, and Ghanaian Brigade scattered somewhere around, and that all were "trigger happy." At this point I was relieved to notice lights coming from what dimly appeared to be a hanger. Squaring my shoulders and whistling "Colonel Bogey" (although it was unlikely to be familiar to the Ethiopians), I set off in that direction.

I was not challenged—let alone shot at! And in the hangar, I met the man who was soon to become my Chief of Staff and a very dear friend. Brigadier General Iyassu Mengesha made a remarkable impression even at that time of night. Later, in the light of day, I found his solidly built frame housed a martial spirit second to none. His complexion was light, his bearing upright and confident. He wore a narrow military moustache and hid fine eyes behind a pair of smoked glasses.

Iyassu would have done credit to any army in the world. Calm and collected, an officer and a gentleman in the finest sense of that much misused phrase, his training in the French Army and subsequent American staff training were to be a godsend to me in the troubled days ahead. At that moment he had not the faintest conception of where his incoming Brigade was likely to be sent nor even much idea of the role they were supposed to play other than to maintain some sort of internal security. Since I was unable to tell him anything except that his destination was Stanleyville, there was little to do other than exchange a few words before I left him to make my way back across the airfield to the convoy now formed up for the fifteen-mile drive back into Léopoldville.

Ralph did not talk much on this journey except to tell me that the situation in the capital was now more or less under control and that he had already dispatched a number of troops to towns in the interior. At some point along the route our driver lost his way and the whole convoy became bogged down in the satiny darkness. It took us some time to get back on the right road again, where we passed through several checkpoints manned by Belgian paratroopers.

At last we reached the city, and in the dawn light I was surprised at the width of its grass- and tree-lined boulevards, flanked on either side by tall, modern concrete buildings with acres of plate glass windows and flat-topped roofs. There was plenty of evidence of the recent disturbances; shops had been looted, windows smashed in, here and there the ground floor of a concrete building was blackened and stained, gutted by fire. Along the boulevards were scores of abandoned cars, some burned-out wrecks, others untouched just as their owners had abandoned them in a moment of panic. Finally, we drew up at the steps to the Stanley Hotel, which served as a temporary home for United Nations Headquarters.

The foyer of this tall, modern-looking building was virtually deserted and as Ralph looked rather forlornly about him, explaining that this *was* temporary HQ, I could hear Johnny Berthiaume in the background rousting out a sleepy hall porter to discover where we were supposed to lay our heads for the remainder of the night.

The Stanley turned out to be a complete shambles. Only one lift was working and inefficiently at that. Ralph's face looked creased and ancient with exhaustion in the indifferent light as he told me to come and see him first thing next morning.

"It's a difficult situation, Carl," he said, his voice hoarse from fatigue, "while you've been on your way here Lumumba has told us he is going to appeal for Soviet aid unless all Belgian troops are withdrawn within forty-eight hours."

On this note we parted. Ralph back to bed, I in search of mine. It was four a.m., we were deathly tired, and although the Stanley was nominally ONUC (Operation des Nations Unies au Congo) headquarters, we had the devil of a job finding somewhere to sleep. At last I was installed on one floor, my staff on another; God knows where my poor ADC landed up. Doubtless before independence the Stanley had been an excellent hotel. Eighteen days later this was no longer the case; as everywhere else in the new Republic, the vital services on which the amenities of modern life depend seemed to have come to a full stop. When I turned on the air conditioning to relieve the humid atmosphere, the only result was clouds of horrible dusty fumes. I turned in, dog tired, and snatched a few hours' sleep. When I awoke, it was to find the city outside bathed in fierce tropical sunshine.

I breakfasted in the main dining room, which served as a communal mess for the Mission and indeed everybody else in the hotel. Then off I went in search of my headquarters, only to discover that these were virtually nonexistent. My office turned out to be my bedroom and our operations room was the couple of bedrooms one floor down where my poor staff were crammed in like sardines.

As far as I could make out, this was the only space available to accommodate the large staff that should soon be building up to control a polyglot force which was going to speak a dozen different languages and whose operational orders would have to be drafted in both French and English. Looking at that cramped space, I turned nearly speechless.

I knew that were I to go and complain to Ralph it would be the beginning of a row. He had told me how difficult the situation was, and I had no wish to add to his troubles when he had probably been up all night. I felt I had to do something practical in order to cool off. So having discovered that General Alexander was living in the Memling Hotel, I decided to go and make myself known and discover what action he had been taking to restore order in the city.

I did not vastly enjoy this visit. While I had been waiting for that wretched plane in Jerusalem, General Alexander had been the only senior officer here. He had exercised untrammeled authority very dashingly to bring the ANC in Camp Léopold under control and was now visibly reluctant to give it up. Henry Alexander was not a United Nations choice. Dark-haired, of medium height, and stern-faced, he had been seconded from the British Army as President Nkrumah's Chief of Staff and had accompanied the Ghanaian Brigade (the first unit to reach the Congo) as his special representative.

At this time the Brigade was in the process of being "Africanized" and its senior officers were all Ghanaians who, although splendid soldiers, had virtually no command experience. As Alexander combined this essential with a naturally aggressive nature, it was hardly surprising that he had taken over the reins and was now reluctant to let them go. He was, too, at that time apparently much in Nkrumah's personal confidence, and it must have been hard for him to have to hand over command to a Swedish General who had suddenly appeared out of the blue from Jerusalem.

He received me in his bedroom while dressing, and told me that the key to restoring order in the Congo lay in swift action to disarm the ANC. He explained that during the last few days he personally had experienced little difficulty in bringing the ANC to heel.

I listened with interest. Although I had a feeling that I was not going to like the General, there was obviously a great deal of truth in what he said. My first impression was of a man who wanted my job (which I would gladly have given him). It was equally obvious to me that he was not fully aware of many of the pitfalls of UN service.

Although he hastened to tell me that what I *really* needed was a first-class field commander, I said that I hoped we would get on well together. As I left, I had the distinct impression that he intended to keep the Ghanaian Brigade under his own control.

Going back to the Stanley—which was just across the road—I discovered Ralph hard at work in his big converted bedroom, which up till now had done duty as the operations center for a remarkable feat of political and amateur military improvisation. Before I had a chance to inquire how I was expected to function without adequate headquarters, staff, or communication facilities, he drew me over to a rather pathetic collection of maps and explained what he had done so far.

One glance at the map on p. 141 will illustrate the intimidating nature of the task before us. Stretching over an area of 905,418 square miles, the Congo is larger than the whole of Western Europe. Scattered across its huge and complex terrain, which varies from crocodile-infested rivers and tropical jungle inhabited by cannibal pygmies to the beautiful open highlands and mining towns of Katanga, are the capitals of six provinces with satellite towns, river ports, diamond, copper, cobalt, and uranium mines, trading stations, and garrison posts. Eighteen days ago, the administration machine had functioned smoothly over all this territory. There had been a dozen goodish airfields and hundreds of lesser ones of varying quality. A network of roads (many badly surfaced), railways, and river transport (albeit hampered by many inadequate crossings) had linked the widely dispersed provincial towns and cities wtih the capital while an impressive system of telephone and telegraphic communications had connected the whole country. Now—in less than three weeks—this whole structure had collapsed, with the flight or expulsion of the Belgians.

Here and there, a few devoted specialists were still at their posts, "advising" their late Congolese employees, who were now the "new masters." But this was comparatively rare and throughout the whole length and breadth of the country, the experts whose technical knowledge and experience had been the lifeblood on which the system depended were gone and had, so to speak, taken their blueprints with them.

The newly proclaimed "independent" state of Kantanga was the sole exception; here the Belgians had been encouraged to stay. But in the other provinces—Léopoldville, Equateur, Oriental, Kasai, and Kivu—there was near chaos, complicated by outbreaks of tribal warfare, the uncertain loyalties of the ANC and the personal or secessionist ambitions of Congolese politicians. Overhanging all this was a growing hostility toward the Belgians. Inflamed by the reappearance of their parachute troops, this was threatening to erupt into something more terrible than the sporadic looting, beatings, and killings that had taken place so far.

Sitting hunched over his desk, Ralph told me that the UN

force building up in Léopoldville had been entrusted with four main tasks. First, United Nations troops were rapidly to replace the Belgian forces still maintaining law and order in the Congo. Second, we would have to take the place of the unreliable ANC troops, curb their undesirable activities, and eventually try to build them up into a reliable force. Third, we had to establish our own freedom of movement throughout the country. Lastly, since Lumumba's known Communist sympathies had already resulted in appeals for Soviet help, we must be ready to prevent any unilateral interference from outside.

Until recently the situation in Léopoldville had been critical and even the Stanley Hotel had been invaded and searched by armed parties of the ANC. As soon as an advance party of the Ghanaian brigade, seven hundred and seventy strong, had been flown in from Accra in British planes Ralph had called on General Alexander to take over the radio and power stations. More Ghanaians followed. And as Hercules aircraft of the US Air Force had flown in a battalion of six hundred Tunisians, it had been possible to restore an uneasy order in the European sector of the city and gradually bring the whole built-up area under some degree of control. The arrival of the leading battalion of a brigade of Moroccan troops had further eased the situation.

Although Ralph had had every cooperation from the Belgians, there were still Belgian troops in the city protecting their nationals and it was only now that the UN troops had got things under some control that they were being gradually withdrawn to N'Djili airport. Meantime the disgruntled ANC were still much in evidence and while the situation remained uneasy, Ralph was being deluged with appeals for help from Europeans in desperate straits all over the country. Although reinforcements were expected almost hourly, our forces were still desperately thin on the ground, and Ralph—under Alexander's guidance—had been sending out what men he could spare as and when they became available. The situation at this moment was as follows.

The Ghanaian brigade and elements of what Ralph called a Tunisian battalion were in the capital (they later turned out to include a first-class brigade commander and headquarters, who naturally resented being subordinated to a much junior colleague).

One company of Tunisians had been flown to Stanleyville to maintain order until the Ethiopian brigade, now in transit through Léopoldville, had arrived. A battalion of Moroccans were just about to entrain for Thysville and Matadi (Congo's only seaport) where the ANC had been running riot. As soon as the second battalion of this brigade arrived it was planned to keep it in the capital.

I listened to this account wtih a mixture of sympathy, admiration, and annoyance. Ralph had worked like a Trojan under exceptionally difficult circumstances, but inevitably in this crash operation troops were being flung out in penny packets without a moment's pause or the slightest chance to develop a central plan for the deployment of a highly mixed force on a basis designed to facilitate command problems and establish a proper system of logistical support.

I heard with apprehension that the Field Operation Service (a branch of the Administrative Services) was responsible for providing our stores and equipment and maintaining the whole force on an operational basis. What worried me most of all, however, as Ralph talked on, was my own job, its nature, scope, and definition. I found it difficult to visualize my exact role. In one breath, he told me that I had been awarded the euphemistic title of Supreme Commander of the United Nations Forces in the Congo. In the next, that over-all military command was vested in the Secretary General, and through him in his Special Representative or Officer in Charge—who turned out to be Ralph.

It soon became difficult to get any more information because, once the day's pressures began to bubble and simmer, Ralph's own peculiar working pattern rendered conversation virtually impossible. I had never seen this side of him before; during the next six weeks it was often to drive me to a pitch of frenzy. Not a telephone call, not a message, not an incoming signal, visitor, or interoffice memorandum escaped his conscientious and individual attention. His broad brow furrowed, his kindly eyes narrowed with concentration, he would sit there scribbling, usually in longhand, and doing his best to work himself to death.

I left him and went back to my own headquarters, where I found Johnny Berthiaume looking as smart and unruffled as though he was back at NATO HQ outside Paris. Somehow Johnny always reminded me of pictures of British officers in the first World War, neat, well turned out, indomitably cheerful in Sam Browne and well-pressed tunic, only the lines around his eyes betraying the strain he had been through. Now he had managed to establish some sort of order so that our cramped quarters at least would have done credit to a battalion commander's (if not a Supreme Commander's) office.

I was in a thoughtful mood. From the gist of my conversation with Ralph, I had realized that whatever rules were in the process of being drafted for ONUC in New York, I was going to have little over-all authority other than the tactical deployment of troops. Obviously the operation was creating new political and military precedents. At the moment it seemed that the best thing I could do, until the picture became clear, was to make contact with my troops. But when I asked about W/T communications, the head of the signal section I had brought out from Jerusalem told me with a rueful smile that although Bunche had a Dutch communications officer, this gentleman seemed to take no interest in military affairs. Our own little signal team had no sets capable of contacting units at long distances and we were certainly not likely to hear from them because they were all equipped with World War II sets incapable of transmitting over long ranges.

For the moment it looked as though we were doomed to remain out of touch with our troops, an ironic situation in a country which only three weeks ago had enjoyed a superb telephone service.

My signals officer, with all the weary scorn of a professional, showed me our only contact with the outside world—a wall telephone, more or less useless at the moment because of the hordes of reporters who were monopolizing the hotel switchboard below. He had, however, already spoken to the operator; for a suitable consideration, the line could be kept clear for the Supreme Commander!

Chapter Twelve

THE BLUE HATS

AFTER a disturbed night, during which a Russian air crew had blundered into my room in search of beds, I was summoned to attend a conference with the Belgian authorities. It was not an impressive setting. We sat cramped in Ralph's room around a table; Ralph, myself, the tall, pleasant, and polite Belgian Ambassador M. Jean van den Bosch, and General Gheysen, the resilient, clean-shaven commander of the Belgian troops in the Congo.

I was impressed by Gheysen. He appeared to be a capable, forceful, but also very well-mannered soldier who probably did not envy us our task. It must have been a most anxious and difficult situation for them. We were here to tell them to withdraw the troops they had flown in to protect their nationals. They knew, too, that they were about to be forced to give up their two permanent bases at Kitona on the Atlantic coast and Kamina in Katanga because Lumumba and the Congolese Parliament had refused to ratify the treaty of friendship, which had been signed before independence. Even more serious was the knowledge that Lumumba was threatening to call in Soviet aid were the United Nations tardy in ensuring that every Belgian soldier left the Congo.

Frankly, I had the gravest doubts about the wisdom of a pell-mell Belgian evacuation before our own forces arrived. As for the bases, it seemed madness to clear out their military and air force technical staff. Before long we would need to use these bases ourselves because their airfields alone would be invaluable for our own operations. And once we took over, we were likely to be in dire need of Belgian technicians. On our present showing, we had not the slightest hope of being able to staff and run them efficiently.

Despite some tension, the conference turned out an unqualified success. Both the Ambassador and General Gheysen agreed to complete evacuation in principle and assured us that they were ready to cooperate in withdrawing their troops once our incoming units were in a position to protect their nationals. As a start it was agreed that their troops should be out of Léopoldville by July 23. I could sense Ralph's very real relief; in yielding to our mixture of pressure and persuasion, the Belgians had strengthened his hand for negotiation with Lumumba and the Congolese Central Government.

Although Lumumba later never ceased to clamor for total and *immediate* Belgian withdrawal, the fact that we were able to announce that a complete evacuation was under way had marked results. These were immediately apparent in our relations with the ANC, to which turbulent force I had appointed Colonel Stig Mollersward as my personal liaison officer. Their Commander in Chief, Victor Lundula, was "not available" and was presumably still making his way toward Léopoldville after being captured but then released by the Belgians in Katanga.

Perhaps this was just as well. Lundula, a former warrant officer in the medical corps, was a woolly-headed squat African who had been Burgomaster of Jadotville when independence had been declared. He was a great admirer of Lumumba and totally unfitted by training or temperament for his exhalted post. In his absence, Mollersward had attached himself to a tall, well-built young man named M'Polo who, after eighteen days as Minister of Youth and Sports, had been suddenly pitchforked up to the rank of General and Army Commander. So far, he had cooperated with General Alexander in restoring order, and now with the aid of his Chief of Staff, Colonel Mobutu,* was struggling in a rather bewildered fashion to cope with his rapidly disintegrating command. Once Mollersward had made contact with him (no mean feat in the chaos at ANC headquarters), the two struck up a remarkable relationship in which the old veteran's feudal sense of decorum struck a reassuring chord with this young man who, totally devoid of military experience, was doing his best to bring some sort of order out of chaos.

* A remarkable man who, having retired as a sergeant major in the Pay Corps, took a course in journalism in Belgium—returning home to edit a paper. On independence he became Secretary of State for Defense.

Within forty-eight hours of our announcement, General M'Polo ordered the ANC to hand over their arms to our units. This was a godsend, and helped to simplify our task. Although the order was by no means universally obeyed, and whole sections of the ANC took off into the bush with their arms and ammunition (later to turn up at the bottom of most of the trouble) the units which still maintained some semblance of discipline handed in their arms. Doubtless they had been impressed, too, by our incoming units' obvious professional competence and discipline: an example which must have made its mark on men who, until a few weeks ago, had belonged to one of the best-trained forces in Africa.

At this stage, the UN troops had little trouble from them and were able to "borrow" much ANC transport and wireless equipment, which turned out to be of an exceptionally high standard. Taking advantage of what appeared to be a genuine spirit of co-operation, our commanders collected most of the ANC arms and ammunition and placed guards over their arsenals and ammunition depots.

Unfortunately an incident was soon to occur at the Regina Hotel in Lépoldville that put an end to this honeymoon with the ANC. This episode, which was to have a chain reaction, was sparked off by a Congolese cabinet minister, who entered the hotel at the head of an unruly mob of ANC soldiers to search the Europeans there. Fortunately, Brigadier Otu of the Ghanaian Brigade happened to be in the hotel and seeing a Congolese beating up a European, promptly disarmed him and sent him back to barracks.

Lumumba's rage when he heard this news (presumably through the cabinet minister) was great and he immediately sent for Otu and told him that from now on no more ANC troops were going to be disarmed by United Nations soldiers. Doubtless Otu immediately informed General Alexander, who decided the time had come for a somewhat unorthodox course of action.

There was no doubt about it; Alexander was an energetic and persuasive man. Whether he had already been to see the United States Ambassador, Clare Timberlake, before he came to see me, I do not know. At any rate, his proposals made extremely sound sense and would have been unhesitatingly adopted in any normal army. Unfortunately, we were not "any army"; we were a United Nations Force in which logic, military principles—even common sense—took second place to political factors. As I listened, I knew he was wasting his breath, even the seat on the plane to New York.

He had come here to get my agreement to let him fly there in order to convince Dag that only through the complete disarming, disciplining, and retraining of the ANC was there the slightest hope for the Congo. Unless this was done the authority of the United Nations would be undermined, our troops would face the possibility of not being able to carry out their task, and it was more than likely there would soon be full-scale civil war. This was something Ralph Bunche did not seem to comprehend. The solution lay in New York.

Alexander had other ideas, too; once he returned (and he appeared sanguine about the outcome of his mission) he told me that I was going to need an experienced field commander who could take operational activities off my shoulders and give me time for the complex politico-military duties of a Supreme Commander. It was clear who *he* had in mind, and I listened with growing amazement to that quick, rather clipped voice. Already the Ghanaian Ambassador in Léopoldville disliked the idea of a British officer leading black UN troops. And in New York, where the ambivalent Dag had to conciliate the permanent delegates of a dozen Afro-Asian states, the conception of this military scion of a colonial power being given *carte blanche* in the Congo was totally unthinkable. I could visualize the polite reception he would get, the courteous brush-off, the days wasted kicking his heels in impotent frustration.

As a soldier he was, of course, fundamentally right. I had no objection to his going to New York. But if I had had the slightest inkling of the press conference he was to hold enroute in London, I might have had second thoughts. In any event, we both set off to the pretentious glass and concrete building that housed the American Embssay to see Clare Timberlake. Timberlake, a forthright character who seemed brimful of energy and ideas, strongly supported the idea of Alexander going to New York and promised to arrange his passage.

I left the Embassy late that night with few illusions about the outcome of Alexander's visit. But I was preoccupied with the immediate situation. At the Stanley Hotel, it was rare to get advance notice of the national contingents which were beginning to come in thick and fast. The first we usually heard was a message from an overworked British Brigade Major of the Ghana Brigade, who had taken over control at the vital N'Djili airport, that "something" was likely to be landing within a matter of hours. This made our job difficult enough, but it grew worse and worse through sheer shortage of staff.

Time and again I had to detail officers I had brought with me from Jerusalem to accompany one of the incoming units up-country or on urgent missions. One of these was to Matadi to accompany a Norwegian shipping man who had volunteered to try to restrain the Congolese authorities there from letting their troops run riot. Gradually our meager strength was whittled down until I had only a couple of officers left, who had to make do until the trained staff officers (whom Ralph assured me were on the way) eventually appeared.

Working under nightmare conditions over the next few days, we succeeded in deploying the best part of six thousand troops. Crises came thick and fast. There were desperate appeals for help from the local Belgians, requests from our own units, and sudden outbreaks of trouble caused by tribal or political rivalries. In telling Ralph where I proposed to send each new unit, my decisions were governed by what information was immediately available.

It was the most difficult deployment I have ever had to tackle. At no time was there a hope of any advance planning because we had no notification of what units to expect, no idea of their strengths, organization, equipment, or armanents nor when they were due to arrive. When they *did* come, the planes carrying them either disgorged them at Léopoldville airport or, after refueling, flew on to their final destination. We could never partially unload and redistribute planeloads on a tactical basis because interior airlifts were banned; it was simply a question of "in" and "out" again.

I found it virtually impossible to advise incoming commanders what to expect up-country. Few of their units arrived with any transport except a few jeeps, while their food supplies were usually limited to four days' iron rations. All I could tell them was to forget everything they had learned about normal chains of command and supply in the field, and to use their own initiative, resource, and common sense. Each was naturally anxious to know who *were* the Congolese authorities with whom he would be dealing and what different there was between the central and provincial governments. Were they allowed to disarm mutinous elements of the ANC? Were the Congolese authorities to be permitted to arrest anyone they chose—and if not, what action should be taken to stop them?

Since Ralph himself had not yet made up his mind on all these issues, the only advice I could advance was the use of firm diplomacy; and once they had set off up-country, I could only hope that common sense and sound judgment would prevail.

During those early days the responsibilities these local commanders faced were formidable. With no W/T network over which situation reports could be sent back and orders requested, brigadiers and colonels found themselves out in the blue, entirely dependent on their own initiative and judgment. Yet within a remarkably short time these qualities were so admirably evident that they succeeded in restoring a degree of order in one dangerous, complex, and often baffling situation after another and often as a result became the uncrowned kings of huge stretches of territory.

We were particularly fortunate in the commanders we sent to two especially difficult places. Stanleyville, the provincial capital of Oriental province, was a Lumumbist stronghold, violently anti-Belgian, and a hotbed of trouble. There had been much violence, the ANC units were in a state of mutiny, and the provincial government was already showing signs of independent, if not secessionist, tendencies that were probably the work of agents from the Communist blocs known to have been infiltrated into the province during the last few months.

On his way there now, and soon to make his presence felt, was General Iyassu Mengesha with the Ethiopian Tekel Brigade, a mixed three-battalion brigade (two battalions were Imperial Guards while another, in contrast, was a line unit from the north) which was to have a stabilizing effect on the province although the activities of some of his troops were to expose them to fierce criticism from the Belgians.

The situation was also threatening to become critical in Thysville, a town in the Cataractes some eighty miles from Léopoldville where the leading elements of the 1st Moroccan Battalian were just beginning to arrive. Its commander, Lieutenant Colonel Ben Omad Driss, was an outstanding soldier who had seen plenty of action with the French Expeditionary Force in Indo-China before Morocco became independent. Not only was he under orders to restore order in the town, but he had the dual mission of pushing on to the port of Matadi where many Belgian civilians had been killed before their paratroops arrived to rescue them.

In both towns the situation looked extremely ugly; the Belgians were pulling out, the European inhabitants who had not fled were in terror of their lives, and mobs of Congolese, strengthened by dissident elements of the ANC, had begun to terrorize the area by way of celebration. As soon as his battalion had detrained in Thysville, Colonel Ben Omad Driss proceeded to make the presence of his Moroccans felt, setting up checkpoints, sealing off troublesome areas, and sending out patrols whose businesslike appearance had a remarkably sobering effect.

Once the city was under control, he left a garrison there and moved on to Matadi—with equal success. This was a remarkable feat and very valuable to us; quite aside from the need to restore law and order, Matadi (just over ninety miles from the mouth of the Congo and two hundred and fifty down river from Lépoldville) was vital as the only place in the whole Congo through which the United Nations Force could be supplied by sea.

The physical difficulties of sticking to the rules of peacekeeping became sharply apparent at Thysville. Our orders were specific; force was to be used *only* in self-defense, nor were we allowed any latitude however threatening the situation. As any soldier could have pointed out to Dag or Ralph (and Alexander had already done so—only to be brought up sharp and placed firmly under Ralph's control) orders like these present a commander with a distinct moral problem: whether to risk his men's lives by involving them in a situation where some of them are bound to get shot before having a chance to defend themselves—or whether to risk the failure of a mission (on whose success the lives of many civilians may depend) through a reluctance to expose his soldiers to what he considers an intolerable degree of risk.

This dilemma had never faced United Nations soldiers before; with no precedent to go by, Colonel Ben Omad Driss evolved a highly original solution. Faced with a threatening mob of Congolese who were on the point of rushing and overwhelming his section, one of his Moroccan corporals ordered his section to open fire. He had already warned the mob three times; where words had failed, bullets now cleared the street like magic, three shots were fired, one Congolese was killed, and order returned to that sector of Thysville.

The unfortunate corporal, however, very shortly found himself under arrest and facing a court-martial that promptly condemned him to death. While this grim news was being disseminated to Congolese and foreign correspondents in Léopoldville as an example that demonstrated beyond all doubt the strict injunctions on United Nations troops to observe the rules of peacekeeping, the corporal languished in jail sustained by the knowledge that a full report had been submitted by his commanding officer to King Mohamed of Morocco who, as Commander in Chief of the Moroccan Army, took a keen interest in the welfare of his troops serving with the United Nations. Nor were his hopes misplaced; in due course Colonel Ben Omad Driss was able to inform the corporal that a reply from the Palace had been received; its contents exceeded the corporal's wildest hopes—pardon, promotion to sergeant, and a medal which in due course was pinned to his chest.

Violence against our troops, however, was still rare at this stage; once the excited Congolese had grasped the fact that they were not Belgians or Belgian-officered units, there tended to be a temporary honeymoon marked by a degree of good will on both sides. But however much this spirit was in evidence during this period before feeling hardened against us, our commanders never found cooperation easy with the local authorities.

The reason was all too simple; the spirit might be willing but the flesh was weak. Lack of any training and experience almost invariably prevented them from exercising any real control in the chaotic areas for which they were responsible. In any case, however much they may have wanted to cooperate with us in restoring law and order, the means were simply not there; the civic administration had broken down, their soldiers were unpaid and could not be trusted, and whatever local police there had once been appeared to have vanished.

There was an atmosphere of fear in the air, too, which had been triggered off by the arrival of the Belgian paratroops and was now being fanned into hysteria by Lumumba and his supporters. Rumors spread with alarming speed—as into this electric atmosphere, where every new face was liable to be taken for a *"sale Flamand,"* * came a constant stream of American, Canadian, Russian, Ethiopian, Indian, and British planes bearing more and more United Nations soldiers. As we dispatched more troops by rail or river deep into the interior this danger became increasingly acute. Soon, it was not only the Swedes (a battalion of whom had been airlifted in from Gaza) who were likely to be mistaken for Belgian parachute troops; every soldier whatever his race or color ran the risk of being taken for a hated Belgian.

The unceasing task of receiving, briefing, deploying, and trying to supply this rapidly expanding force threw a tremendous burden on us at the Stanley Hotel. I had no clerical staff, no orderlies, not even a guard to stop strangers walking into our cramped bedroom offices until I borrowed one from the Ghanaian Brigade in Camp Léopold. Sheer unremitting pressure of work made it impossible even to think of long-term operations. (It was not until August that we were able to establish the force on a territorial basis.) We were forced to live in a constant aura of improvisation.

I had assigned the monumental task of supply and transportation to my mustachioed New Zealand Sapper, Major Geoffrey Hunt. One of his main headaches was how to supply our units up-country by rail or river (the planes flying UN stores and equipment into Léopoldville airport were not authorized to carry out regional distribution). We had already instructed our units to buy whatever supplies they could locally, but food was already

* This arose through the high preponderance of Flemish Belgians in the Congo. It is interesting to note that this hardy race provided nearly 80 per cent of Belgian soldiers and civilians before independence.

becoming short in certain areas and much of what was available turned out unsuitable or unacceptable because of national or religious customs.

There were virtually no Congolese supply or ordnance depots up-country on which they could draw and the possibilities of "borrowing" from the ANC was soon to be taken away from us by Ralph. So the main burden fell on Hunt at N'Djili, where he had the unenviable task of unloading, sorting out, and channeling up-country the food, stores, and equipment that normally arrived with no advance notice at the airport. His staff consisted of a young British captain, whom I had managed to "borrow" from the Ghanaian Brigade, and one male and one female missionary who had staunchly volunteered to help after visiting my office one day on personal business. No one could have been more welcome nor have done such sterling work as these two Good Samaritans, compiling endless lists, checking, sorting, and often physically manhandling crates and bales which had to be loaded into trucks destined for railway sidings and river barges.

Our whole supply system up-country was based on improvisation and a great deal of guesswork; at this stage of the crash operation it could never have been otherwise because, owing to the complete lack of W/T communications, the only information I received about the needs of my widely separated commanders was through letters brought in by African or European couriers who often had dangerous experiences getting through. We had no proper ration strength returns, no detailed lists of the stores and equipment which they had brought with them, and no comprehensive estimate of their requirements to keep operational.

I remember my fury one day in Ralph's office when Mr. Baumgarten, the Dutch civilian Chief Communications Officer from New York, proudly announced that he had succeeded in establishing ONUC's global communications. But my complaints proved a waste of breath; neither of them seemed capable of grasping the fact that while *they* might be in "global communication," out here in the Congo ONUC Force communications remained about as primitive as the Stone Age. On the face of it New York seemed totally oblivious of the serious implications of their failure to provide us in time with field signals.

Just how little conception they had over there was demonstrated by a message to me from the Administrative Services in New York (by "global" means) demanding a complete and detailed list of all our requirements *before* any action to meet them was taken in New York; obviously our field operations service had no idea of the true situation. While still totally out of radio contact with my units, I was even told to take a full inventory of all the vehicles they had brought to the Congo before submitting a list of unit transport requirements.

This total lack of realism, this passion for red tape was painfully reminiscent of stories of the Crimean war. Just how chaotic the situation *really* was out here was clearly demonstrated at N'Djili airport. I had gone there to ask for news of the Guinea battalion that was expected to fly in "some time" in the near future. All too often, the only notice we had of incoming troops was when their aircraft contacted the control tower ten minutes ahead of touching down; on this occasion, however, we knew there would be troops coming in over the next three or four days.

Arriving at the airport office, it struck me that the young British major from the Ghanaian Brigade, who was in charge of the airport, was showing unusual signs of strain. I was not mistaken; in reply to my inquiry, he reported that the situation was critical. This did not alarm me because N'Djili had at least a couple of crises every day. But when I asked what the trouble was, I was brought up sharp on hearing that the only civilian flight control official who had not abandoned his job in the control tower had announced that he was leaving next day and had there and then proceeded to get drunk. Even worse, the first flying boxcar was due to land in about an hour's time; from then on, troop planes would be arriving continuously over the next eighty-four hours.

I told the major to take me to the control tower immediately; once inside, I soon realized that neither force nor persuasion would do any good. The official, who had undoubtedly been through a grueling time during the past two weeks, was hopelessly and gloriously drunk; his only comment on the situation was: *"Je m'en fiche."* *

* Perhaps the politest direct translation is "I've had it." Hard-swearing soldiers (or anyone with a colloquial knowledge of French) would disagree strongly!

Emerging from the control room, I was about to descend the steps in search of help when I was lucky enough to spot a Canadian pilot whom I knew quite well. I shouted to him to go and fetch Squadron Leader Hlady, the commander of a flight of four Canadian planes that had recently brought in troops and were now due to return home. With a cheery wave and a twirl of his handlebar moustache, he set off across the concrete and soon returned with the squadron leader who, having listened to our appeals, unhesitatingly agreed to risk the wrath of the Royal Canadian Air Force by staying on and providing an officer to help us out until we found a replacement. To our unmitigated relief, the fellow was soon bundled out of his chair and within a remarkably short time the stage was set for the incoming planes; the stalwart Canadians stayed with us until the whole of the airlift had been completed.

The days when we were to be able to build up a permanent flight control unit with the help of the ICAO (International Civil Aviation Organization) were still far off. For the time being, we managed to keep operating with the aid of "borrowed" personnel who received magnificent cooperation and help from the Americans on the airfield. But our task was not made easier by the frequent appearance of groups of Congolese who resented the fact that under the July 19 agreement with General Gheysen, we had permitted a small Belgian unit to remain on the airfield to provide a refueling and staging post for the planes evacuating their troops back to Belgium. It proved quite impossible to explain that this purely technical unit was not only vital to, but was actually speeding up the evacuation. We were simply not believed and from now on were plagued by unruly squads of ANC who swarmed over the airfield—often led by one of their ministers or generals in person—on a "parachutist-chasing operation" which seriously endangered our efforts to fly in our own badly needed reinforcements.

"Les Paras Belges" had become a psychological obsession with the Congolese and our "distinguished" visitors, who had apparently no ministerial duties to distract them from heading mobs of soldiers onto the airfield (it became commonplace for ministers or generals to assure us that they had seen a parachute drop

"over there" thirty minutes earlier) became so frequent that I was forced to post Swedish soldiers around the airport. This led to a personal visit from Victor Lundula (who had now surfaced to resume his post as the Army Commander of the ANC) who protested bitterly that ONUC was collaborating with the Belgian imperialists by posting Belgian paratroopers around the airport. Although I pointed out the blue helmets, the armbands, even the identity cards of our Swedish soldiers, he remained totally unconvinced.

Before the operation was very much older, we became aware that certain African states (Ghana, Guinea, Mali, and later the United Arab Republic) were much concerned to insure the continued stability of the Lumumba government. And they had been bombarding Dag with cables, suggesting the political and military line that Ralph and I should be ordered to follow. (The gist of this was that ONUC should suppress the independent state of Katanga and forcibly expel the Belgians who were backing Tshombé.) These proposals had naturally been ignored: UN policy was governed by the resolutions taken in the Security Council and our own orders were explicit; United Nations forces were not to: "intervene in or be used to influence the outcome of any internal conflict, constitutional or otherwise."

This strong partisanship, however, alerted us to incipient dangers within a force contaning units whose member states had a direct interest in Congolese internal affairs. So when, on July 25, I welcomed the Guinea battalion and discovered that it had interpreted United Nations guidance "to bring light infantry weapons" by arriving equipped with heavy machine guns, mortars, antitank and light antiaircraft guns, I decided to send it on a mission where its heavy weapons would have the least possible chance of lethal employment.

It was an unusual battalion which I ordered to proceed to Banningville, conveniently surrounded by swamp and jungle some hundreds of miles away up a crocodile-infested river. Commanded by a lieutenant, its ranks included six political commissars with an appropriate number of acolytes, and I was glad to hand it over to that tough and indomitable Canadian Guardsman, Major Wayne King. Taking him aside, I told him to escort it to its destination in whatever boats he could lay hands on, copying, if necessary, the methods of Sir Garnet Wolseley in the Canadian Red River and Egyptian Nile campaigns * by recruiting local voyageurs; any improvisation so long as the battalion with its commissars and heavy weapons was removed rapidly from the vicinity of Léopoldville and ONUC headquarters.

They were hardly on their way before I received a desperate appeal from the Belgian ambassador, M. van den Bosch, to rescue eighty-five of his nationals who were reported besieged by mutinous ANC troops in an agricultural research station at Watsa in Oriental Province.

Unfortunately, Watsa was two thousand kilometers from Léopoldville. I was powerless to help. Our nearest troops were the Ethiopians in Stanleyville, separated from the research station by a huge stretch of difficult country. Even had I been able to spare them from their task, there was not a single plane available to airlift them into Paulis, the nearest town with an airstrip. M. van den Bosch, however, was desperately alarmed, and I knew that I could not abandon the wretched Belgians to the beatings, rapings, and killings that would inevitably occur once they had been overwhelmed. My only hope was rapid improvisation; Ethiopia was far closer to Watsa than Léopoldville and I lost no time in making use of Ralph's "global communications" and dispatching a signal to Dag asking him to cable Emperor Haile Selassie in Addis Ababa and request that he airlift in a company of Ethiopian troops.

The response was immediate; within thirty-six hours an Ethiopian company had been flown onto the airstrip at Paulis. Here a convoy of trucks awaited them, borrowed from Unilever nearby through the good offices of the local manager. Boarding the trucks, the Ethiopians drove at top speed to the threatened station—only to discover the Belgians in excellent spirits and adamantly refusing to be evacuated.

* In both these campaigns Sir Garnet Wolseley showed great initiative in recruiting local boatmen to ferry his troops on a riverine route. So successful was he in Canada with his locally raised "voyageurs" that a large number of them were shipped across to Egypt to assist him in his efforts to relieve Khartoum. Here they joined an amateur but devoted body of British "boatmen" raised from the battalions in the relieving force. History relates the British outswore their French Canadian colleagues.

They had, however, reckoned without the reaction of the Ethiopian company commander, who was patently reluctant to report to his Emperor that no one had been rescued. Having come all this way, he had no intention of returning empty-handed; a number of reluctant "refugees" were loaded willy-nilly into the trucks while the remainder were required to sign an affidavit absolving the United Nations from any responsibility for their future safety.

At the Stanley, we could not help feeling the operation had been rather a triumph of improvisation and cooperation, but the Belgians took a very different view; the ambassador's earlier desperate appeals were conveniently forgotten; before long both Ralph and Dag received strongly worded protests from Brussels.

Chapter Thirteen

RALPH BUNCHE

FROM the start, I had discovered that Ralph's views on how the Force should be administered and controlled were fundamentally different from mine. We had not clashed directly but I had a feeling the time would come. The reason was that Ralph was interfering in the day-to-day conduct of military matters. I discovered that his "wishes" were sometimes conveyed direct to the Ghana Brigade by Brian Urquhart without any reference to me. The result was most unfortunate. I was sometimes left totally in the dark about measures that Ralph had "dreamed up" and only learned about them in a roundabout way.

This passion for taking a hand in military affairs militated against my intention to create a strong, unified command, but I was, however, in a difficult position because the regulations that had been hastily drawn up to govern the whole ONUC operation made it absolutely clear that I was operationally responsible to the Secretary General through his special representative. In other words, I was responsible to Ralph who had full command authority and the right to instruct me where and how to deploy, organize, and control my troops.

This was a new precedent, totally different in concept to the command structure of UNEF in Gaza, whose commander had full command authority over his troops and was operationally responsible for the tasks assigned him by the United Nations. It is true that in the Congo ONUC was facing political problems that had never before arisen in the course of United Nations operations; the need for experienced civilian political guidance was only too clearly evident and I should have been the last to dispute it. Even under ideal conditions, however, the burden that falls on a civilian who has to assume authority for both military *and* civilian operations and somehow fuse the two activities into a successful working combination demands the most remarkable degree of understanding and knowledge in both fields. Unfortunately, Ralph knew little about military matters, and didn't appear to understand that *unless* there is real unity of command no force can operate with any degree of success.

I found myself in disagreement with some of his methods. But on the other hand, I had every sympathy with the difficult political situation he was compelled to face. I had already had a taste of what he was up against with the Congolese. One day in July (when Lumumba had departed abroad on one of his far-flung missions) I had accompanied him to a cabinet meeting, which had been chaired by the melancholy-looking Vice Premier Antoine Gizenga.* Time and again, I watched Ralph struggle to win their agreement and cooperation—only to be thwarted by the constant shrilling of the single telephone in the room. Invariably, Gizenga took it upon himself to answer each call, and though his sad face remained inscrutable, I was sitting near enough to discern a low-pitched female voice issuing from the receiver. I had little doubt that this must be that remarkable lady (known to us as the Black—and

* Antoine Gizenga was born in 1925 and educated in a Roman Catholic seminary. This serious, melancholy fellow, who was below medium height, had adopted Marxist principles after his return from visits to Eastern Europe in 1959. After Lumumba's downfall, he was to set up a "Central Government" in Stanleyville. Unfortunately his inability to control his soldiers led to total chaos and a mass exodus of the European population.

on occasion the Red—Spider) who was rumored to combine the dual role of the Vice Premier's mistress and political mentor.

Each time this happened, the other cabinet ministers would seize the chance to start violent arguments among themselves; it was soon apparent that secessionist ambitions in the provincial capitals was a very real issue. Poor Ralph would be cut off in mid-speech and the meeting remained in chaos until Gizenga had finished. Even then Ralph's careful reasoning met with a wall of naïve and hypersensitive reaction. But he would battle on, the telephone would shrill again, and then the ridiculous squabbles would recommence.

Hour after hour was wasted in this futile way and I returned to the Stanley Hotel with the feeling that there was not a grain of good will or common sense to be found amid the politicians of Léopoldville, these pathetically inexperienced creatures suddenly elevated to power, and whose personal ambitions, lack of judgment, and factional and provincial rivalries were bound to have the most tragic results for their own countrymen. Overlying this premonition was the more immediate suspicion that nothing any of us in ONUC could do or say was going to dissipate a mounting dislike and distrust of United Nations' activities.

The Congo was like some unexploded time bomb whose ticking was drowned out by loud voices wrangling through hours of interminable discussion. It only needed some sudden violent movement to bring the mechanism into play. All the ingredients for an explosion were at hand: hatred of the Belgians, hostility toward the United Nations troops, tribal unrest, secessionist aspirations—above all the unpaid, mutinous ANC.

I had had no dealings with Lumumba, the Prime Minister, but his outspoken hostility pointed to a time when we were going to find ourselves in the midst of a crisis with the Central Government. Once this happened, there was no balking the fact that all Alexander's warnings about the ANC would be justified, and I felt deeply relieved that the bulk of their weapons and ammunition were safely in our own hands.

Ralph, who had had considerable experience with Lumumba, disagreed because he believed the essence of the whole problem of the Congo was political and that once the political situation had been resolved, the military question would automatically be solved, too. I did not share his view; I did not believe that any degree of law and order could be restored other than through straightforward military control. Although we approached the problem from fundamentally different standpoints, I could not help but feel that there *ought* to be some meeting point between us.

Unfortunately, our relationship was never a happy one in the Congo. From the start, I had had the disturbing impression that his natural kindness and love of humanity, his deep-rooted belief in the *pacific* role of the United Nations, and his preoccupation with discovering a political solution to cure every evil combined to obscure the naked reality under his very nose. I had sat with him for hours one night, patiently explaining that the two- or three-page document which he had painstakingly drafted for distribution to every United Nations soldier in the Congo was unsuitable for troops operating under active service conditions. Ralph had looked at me in disbelief. Some of these soldiers, I told him, came from remote villages in the Moroccan hills or from the bush districts of African states where the schoolhouse had as yet made little impact. Faced with a hostile crowd, it was hardly likely they would remember Ralph's document—let alone thumb their way through pages of legalistic arguments. What was vital were clear, concise orders, which could be issued by word of mouth and memorized against the moment a crisis arose. Anything else would be unnecessarily jeopardizing ther lives.

For a moment, I thought that I had got through to him. He nodded as though he understood, but then his face crinkled as he picked up the document again. I listened as he began to talk about the legalistic aspect, knowing now that whatever I said was not going to prevent us from being burdened with that document and wondering, too, just how Ralph would react himself with a hostile crowd bearing down on him.

As I had suspected, the document was forced upon us, though I took comfort in imagining the uses to which it was probably put by some of my more experienced commanders hundreds of miles up-country and blissfully undeterred by Ralph's olympian ukase from ONUC headquarters. There was always a sharp and clear-cut contrast between the civilian element in ONUC and the soldiers, which was just as well in view of the realities the latter had to face and the crucial decisions that had to be taken without the luxury of recourse to legalistic argument.

I was lucky in my commanders. Fortunate to have men of such caliber as General Ben Hammou Kettani, who had been the senior North African officer in the French army and had commanded a division in Germany in the Army of Occupation. Now at the head of the Moroccan Brigade, his officers included men like Colonel Ben Omad Driss * at Thysville and Captain Bougrine, who had arrived at Coquilhatville with a young captain and fifty-six paratroopers to take over the trouble-torn Province of Equateur. Bougrine, a tough and first-rate soldier who had gained his battle experience with the French Expeditionary Corps in Indo-China, had rapidly dealt with riots and secessionist attempts in the capital. As soon as he was joined by reinforcements that brought his total strength to two hundred and fifty-two men, he moved out into the province to restore law and order over an area three quarters the size of France.

In Léopoldville, I had the excellent Ghanaian Brigade which, now that Alexander was in America, was commanded by Brigadier Joe Michel.** For a time the two-battalion Tunisian Brigade had been under their command, but this had led to friction because the Tunisians, under their much-decorated commander, Colonel Lasmar, senior in everything but rank, had resented Ghanaian control. Later we had dispatched them to Kasai Province, which was in turmoil now that its Prime Minister, Albert Kalonji, was about to declare the province an independent state.

Colonel Lasmar, who never wore one of his many decorations—not even a ribbon—but through whose open-necked shirt one could see a crisscross pattern of wound scars, took his troops into

* Colonel Ben Omad Driss proved an unusually capable and resourceful officer. Of medium height, slim and hard as nails, he was to survive a heart attack that invalided him out of the Congo. Later, during the short outbreak of fighting between Algeria and Morocco, Colonel Driss commanded the Moroccan forces with such success that he was promoted to General. At the time of writing he is Governor of Casablanca.

** Michel was a medium-sized, beaming Ghanaian whom General Alexander always considered "head and shoulders above any other African officer in the Ghanaian Army." Michel was certainly good, level-headed, dedicated, and fair-minded, and would have gone far had he not been killed in an air crash in September 1961.

the city of Luluabourg, disarmed the ANC, and through his firm but just methods soon earned himself the title of "Prince de Kasai." I was very proud of him and he became one of my most trusted officers.

This excellent pattern of local command in the field was not reflected in Headquarters at Léopoldville, where lack of clear-cut divisions of responsibilities between the civil and military elements often led to confusion and bad feeling. The result was a complete absence of any firm and definite policy.

In theory, ONUC was made up of three separate branches: political, civilian operations, and military. In practice, Ralph (who was responsible for the political side) controlled the whole Mission although both I and my fellow Swede, Dr. Sture Linner, had our own staffs. Linner was responsible for handling the huge influx of technicians from the United Nations specialized agencies who were about to be brought in to re-establish public administration, salvage the treasuries, restore the judicature, provide famine relief, organize agriculture, take over abandoned control towers and telephone exchanges, and restore communications. Experts from something like twenty-seven different countries were beginning to arrive or were en route to help the Congolese rebuild their country; a difficult and complex rescue operation under any circumstances, but which now, owing to the chaotic situation, was bound to be virtually dependent on the success the military were able to achieve in restoring law and order.

At headquarters we were well aware of this reality. We were quite sure too (despite Ralph's views to the contrary) that the political situation would become more stable once order had been brought out of chaos in the provinces where the Central Government appeared to have little or no control. True, we were operating on a military shoestring and still virtually out of touch with many of our units. Nonetheless, a great deal had been achieved in a remarkably short time, and as both the number of units and the strength of our staff built up, there seemed no reason why we should not eventually be able to establish the Force on a sound basis with provincial subcommands firmly linked to our central command in Léopoldville, *provided* we were given the necessary men and material and were not hamstrung by civil interference.

It did not take us long to realize that Ralph had no intention of letting us put our own house in order. I had already suffered from his tendency to issue orders direct to the Ghana Brigade through Urquhuart. Now I discovered that this habit was spreading to other units farther afield. The real trouble—whose implications I still did not suspect—had its roots in the fact that he virtually controlled all our communications with New York.

It was not a happy arrangement. No operational force has a chance to function under this sort of dual control. I had spoken to him very plainly about the inherent danger in what he was doing, but having so little conception about the basic principles of military command, he had no difficulty in shrugging off my warnings.

His passion for involving himself in the minutiae of administrative detail was a nightmare. Had he ever backed me up by insisting on the *immediate* dispatch of more trained staff officers, half our problems would have been automatically solved. Instead, Ralph would insist on my sitting up with him into the late hours in a listening capacity while he argued interminably over the phone to New York about discrepancies in the strength returns of incoming units which had been listed in New York as x hundred strong, but had turned up at N'Djili airport over or under strength. Half-dead with exhaustion after an exacting day, I used to watch Ralph's weary but still mobile features as he argued the toss over fifteen missing men; had he devoted ten minutes of his marathon telephone conversation to demanding (as I never ceased to advise) that there should have been *one* trained staff officer on duty in New York, capable of reliably transmitting the essential facts, we could both have conserved our energies for more essential tasks.

Any visitor who appeared suddenly out of the night would doubtless have been impressed by such obvious personal concern for the welfare of the troops; indeed, it highlighted the painstaking and conscientious side of a remarkable nature. But knowing Ralph so well, it left me cold. Besides, he understood as well as I where the root of the trouble lay. He had worked too long on the thirty-eighth floor not to be aware of the shortcomings of the Administrative Services. A stinging reproach delivered direct or a bitter and pungent complaint to Dag might have produced the necessary degree of consternation that would have galvanized them into effective action. But no amount of urging from me could persuade him to tackle the root of the problem.

During my entire six months in the Congo, the Force never enjoyed a satisfactory supply system because both its direction and application remained exclusively in civilian hands. Even when my own staff had been built up and the Field Operations Service in New York had come to rely to a large extent on the American Army for supplies, there remained a constant lack of coordination between soldier and civilian. But now—when we were still in the crash stage of the operation—there was chaos which Ralph managed to complicate further by decisions that bore little relation to the actual needs of the troops—whose numbers were beginning to approach nine thousand. At this moment, his Chief Administrative Officer announced that he had discovered a suitable building for ONUC Headquarters. This turned out to be the Royal, an ugly eight-story apartment block, most of whose inhabitants had not yet been turned out of their living quarters.

When I saw the bulding, I was horrified. There were no main staircases, only an emergency one so narrow that two people could not pass. Should fighting break out in the Capital it would be a death trap. I said so clearly and refused to have any part of it. But here I was smartly overruled, given a direct order, and told the matter was already settled. Gloomily, I contemplated an existence holed up in this totally unsuitable building. I was, after all, a soldier who presumably knew what he was talking about. But military logic carried little weight in the Congo.

The move was sanctioned, and at this moment when we were expecting Dag to visit us in Léopoldville, we received welcome reinforcements in the shape of two companies of Ghanaian police. No one could have been more welcome because the Swedish battalion that had taken over a sector of the city were in the happy position of never having seen a civil disturbance other than a difference of opinion at a soccer match. Under the command of their massive, barrel-chested Commissioner Madjitey, whose booming voice and majestic sense of humor made an immediate impression on the Congolese, the Ghanaians rapidly put on a demonstration of riot drill for the Swedes (and incidentally for the benefit of the local inhabitants too).

One platoon was soon on the scene equipped with riot sticks and wicker shields while their colleagues took over the role of rioters with the greatest enthusiasm. Soon a "hostile" crowd was bearing down upon the platoon in the most menacing fashion. The platoon commander halted his men, issued a stern warning that was noisily ignored, and then blew his whistle. Immediately, riot sticks were drawn and the platoon advanced upon the crowd; battle was joined and in the resulting free-for-all there were plenty of hard blows given and taken with every appearance of enthusiasm. I have often wondered who enjoyed that afternoon's entertainment most: the Swedish spectators, the duty platoon, the "rioters," or the Congolese; it was a remarkable performance.

We were expecting Dag at any moment now. But we were still sitting in the Stanley, our move to the Royal having been held up by its tenacious inhabitants. The security arrangements at the Stanley were totally unsuitable for guarding the Secretary General —even the ghastly Royal would be much better. If we *had* to go there it had better be at once and I insisted that our top echelon move right away. After an argument with Ralph, I got his agreement. The move was made right at the last minute and we settled into this gloomy place alongside a remnant of its volubly protesting inhabitants. At least we were able to seal off our own floors, bring in sentries, and set up a proper security drill.

It was only just in time. On July 28, Dag arrived from Brussels where he had been conferring with the Belgian Government over Katanga. It was not a propitious moment. Relations between the United Nations and the Central Government were already strained. Lumumba was in America (where he had flown with the Ghanaian Ambassador) to make an appeal for direct American help and aid. Although the United States Government was to treat him as an honored guest, there was no moving them from the view that *all* help must be channelled through the United Nations. As a result—at a time when American opinion was hardening against him as a result of the irrefutable proof the Belgians provided of the beatings, rapings, and killings of their nationals—Lumumba was to turn openly to the Soviet Union. By the time he came back to Léopoldville in July he had obviously made his mind up that the United Nations were not going to take the sort of action he considered necessary against the Belgians in Katanga. From that time on, he was to become an angry and suspicious man and relations were to take a significant turn for the worse.

At the moment, however, this mood was not yet reflected in Léopoldville. Early on the morning of July 28, a large party of high-ranking Congolese politicians and soldiers could be seen, milling in hopeless confusion around the Léopoldville landing stage awaiting the boats that would carry them across the Congo River to the former French Congo where Dag was due to touch down at the airport outside Brazzaville, its capital.

The complex business of embarking them on the ferries in correct precedence of brass and lesser brasslings turned into an involved and heated altercation, much complicated by continual onslaughts on the space on board reserved for VIP's by brightly clad women, clutching little black babies.

Once across the river, we drove to the airport where the diminutive, angel-faced President, Abbé Youlu, and a Guard of Honor of gorgeously attired Spahis were waiting to receive the Secretary General. Within a short time his plane touched down and Dag, looking desperately tired and drawn, was soon involved in the formalities of a full-scale reception.

I had never seen him look so exhausted, and once we had been able to get him safely away on board the river steamer, I was reluctant to break the news that there were still official formalities ahead on the opposite bank where a Guard of Honor of Ghanaian and Swedish troops were waiting to receive him. Poor Dag, who above all things detested military protocol, merely gave me a weary smile.

At the landing stage, we had great difficulty in getting him through the crowds of officials and Congolese spectators who pressed in on us. It was a relief when Major Otu (the brother of Brigadier Steve Otu) stepped up and reported the parade ready for inspection. We pushed through the crowds to the packed street where the Guard of Honor was drawn up. Before Dag commenced his inspection, I remembered to warn him to take care of his trousers as he went down the ranks of the Swedish unit. Unlike their Ghanaian comrades (whose rifles were pulled smartly into their sides) my countrymen, according to the Swedish Army drill manual, were holding their submachine guns with fixed bayonets at the trail. I had already had a word with their commanding officer earlier that morning and now, as Dag went down their lines, I was relieved to see the men tactfully dipping their rifle butts while continuing to stare the Secretary General firmly in the eye. Happily neither he nor any of his entourage fell victim to any scratches from extended bayonets.

ONUC Headquarters, where we drove once the inspection was over, could hardly have inspired Dag with the feeling that after his long and tiring journey he had reached the haven of a well-ordered organization. It would be difficult to imagine a building in the whole of Africa less suited to the immediate occasion than the Royal with its inadequate lifts and staircases.

Dag's quarters were on the top floor. And on reaching them he was plunged straight into a nonstop session of reports and discussions designed to bring him up to date on the situation before he left for the first of what was to turn out to be a marathon succession of interviews. Somehow, in the midst of all this, he still found time to spare a few minutes for me. He was looking pale and drawn, and when he asked me how things were going, I had no wish to add to his obvious fatigue by airing my own troubles. As we were alone, I told him that the operation had been a nightmare but that we were doing our best. He seemed grateful not to be bombarded with complaints and a faint smile brought back a semblance of the old Dag as he countered:

"But you remember my cable, don't you?"

I nodded: it had begun: "Remembering you for the sport you are . . ." I remembered, too, his final words over the telephone to me in Jerusalem: "Keep your fingers crossed until hell freezes." I was about to reply when he suddenly said:

"My God! This is the craziest operation in history. God only knows where it is going to end. All I can tell you is that I had no other choice but to lay it on."

Chapter Fourteen

KASAVUBU, LUMUMBA, TSHOMBÉ

JOSEPH KASAVUBU, President of the Republic of the Congo and "King Kasa" to his supporters, a portly, plump-cheeked figure, inordinately conscious of status and occasion, received us with considerable formality when we called on him at his residence at Stanley Falls.

Before independence, he and Lumumba had been bitter political rivals. So far, however, he had worked in surprising harmony with the Prime Minister, and now it was clear that they were entirely united over the Katanga issue. His attitude toward us became immediately apparent once the conventions of protocol had been satisfied. I had no part in the discussion which followed with Dag and Ralph, but I had the impression that the former was a little disturbed by the outspoken way in which Kasavubu expressed the Central Government's alarm and displeasure at the United Nations' failure to enter Katanga and expel the Belgians.

An experienced politician, who despite the smallness of his own party (ABAKO) was a well-known figure throughout the country for his opposition to the Belgians and his part in the Léopoldville riots in 1959, no one knew better than Kasavubu how urgent it had become for the Central Government to suppress the Tshombé regime before it had a chance to consolidate. Not without reason, he blamed the Belgians for the Katanga secession, which had deprived the new Republic of half its total revenue. Like Lumumba, he had looked to the United Nations for active intervention. And like Lumumba (who was soon to start on a tour of the African States to elicit the support which he claimed the United Nations had failed to provide) he had been bitterly disappointed.

I listened to Dag as he expressed his sympathy and concern, urging Kasavubu to be patient because the Katanga issue had to be handled with great caution. As always when under great pressure, Dag rose to the occasion with a virtuoso display of argument that appeared to cut no ice with Kasavubu. The latter, though invariably polite, evinced not the slightest sign of altering or changing his attitude. Toward the end of the discussion, however, it was eventually agreed that a Congolese cabinet committee should be set up to work with ONUC, that Dag should attend its first meeting the following day, and that we should all be guests at an official dinner that Kasavubu was giving in his honor that night. On this note, we parted; protocol became much in evidence once more and Kasavubu (whatever his private thoughts) bade us a stately farewell.

For the next few weeks, the Katanga issue was to be with us night and day. The dinner that evening was hardly an encouraging omen. It was an odd affair where, between courses of river fish and gazelle, the guest of honor found himself a target for harangues from members of the Congolese cabinet who would switch at a moment's notice from polite and almost formal conversation to impassioned arm-waving. As Dag wryly remarked as we left: "Not much progress so far."

The only bright moment throughout the whole dinner, so far as I was concerned, was an invitation from the West German Ambassador, Soehring, a former cavalry officer, to visit him at his home and make use of the horses in their excellent saddle club. It was an invitation I took up and vastly enjoyed until this gentleman chanced to go swimming in the Congo River where he vanished, an undoubted victim of the crocodiles.

Next day, Dag started his first session with the cabinet committee at which the gloomy Gizenga acted as Lumumba's deputy while around the table sat the stout and (outwardly) affable Justin Bomboko, the Foreign Minister, General M'Polo, Gbenye, Kanza, and Mwamba. I imagine that Dag's tactics must have been very similar to those he used with Kasavubu—and equally unsuccessful: caution and restraint were the last things the Congolese wished to hear about; pressure on him to enter Katanga remained fierce and sustained.

I had little means of knowing what was said at this or any subsequent meetings. But their results were reflected in my conversations with Dag over the military implications of UN troops entering Katanga. Unfortunately, we had no knowledge of the sort of reception they would be likely to encounter. Dag's mandate from the Security Council, too, made it impossible to make a realistic military appraisal because it still ruled out any intervention in Congolese internal affairs. If an entry *was* to be effected, it would have to be through political pressure. He had, however, obtained assurances from Brussels that Belgian troops would not oppose our entry.

Although he was hoping for cooperation from Tshombé, there was no news from Elizabethville, where, to put it mildly, the reaction was hardly likely to be favorable. Meanwhile, Dag was under unrelenting pressure from the Central Government, and was well aware of the campaign being mounted against him in New York by a combination of Lumumba, Ghana, and the Soviet bloc. And on top of it all now was the increasing threat of Russian intervention, which would be warmly welcomed by Lumumba, but would plunge the United Nations operations into chaos.

I told him that even were he to secure a mandate from New York to use force to enter Katanga, it was simply not a practical proposition. The operation would necessitate the use of a force of between four and six self-contained and properly equipped brigade groups. In the unlikely chance of such units becoming available, I had the gravest doubts whether New York would be capable of supplying them on an operational basis. Dag nodded, and asked how I would suggest using our existing forces were Tshombé not to oppose us. I said that at a rough estimate it would mean diverting over a third of our troops from their present duties. Although we had just been reinforced by another Moroccan and an Irish battalion, we were still desperately thin on the ground.

Despite this warning, I was told to work out plans on the assumption that Tshombé would decide to let us enter Katanga. For the first time, I now had a few trained staff officers who had at long last made their appearance. Our headquarters was also beginning to take shape and form; General Kettani had been appointed my Deputy Commander while as Chief of Staff I had Brigadier Iyassu Mengesha, who had come down from Stanleyville. I could hardly have been luckier in these two remarkable men, each a tower of strength. And now to my delight, a plane touching down at N'Djili airport brought in Colonel Justin MacCarthy of the Irish Army, whom I had known in UNOGIL and had brought across to UNTSO where, for a time, he had served as my Chief of Operations. I made him deputy to Brigadier Iyassu Mengesha, and like the rest of us, he was soon involved in our complicated but necessarily makeshift planning for moving selected units by plane, train, or barge toward the Katanga border.

During those few hectic days I saw little of Dag. He seemed to move from one crucial meeting to another in an atmosphere that was steadily becoming more tense as our relations with the Central Government deteriorated. At an official reception on July 30, he had been disconcerted by an outburst from his host, Vice Premier Gizenga, who had accused him of disarming Congolese soldiers who were only defending their homeland against Belgian "aggressors" whom the United Nations did nothing about. Poor Dag must have had a difficult time; the only agreeable occasion I can remember was when he was wielding the conductor's baton at a party he gave for the Congolese, relaxed and happy under the beaming gaze of our Ghanaian bandsmen who took it in equally good part when Ralph and I took over to conduct in turn.

On August 1, I was able to write in my diary: "Tonight I managed to get to bed at midnight for the first time in twenty-two days." Next morning, it appeared that there was little chance of this happening again. Under unrelenting pressure Dag had taken the decision to go into Katanga and announced that Ralph and an advance guard of United Nations troops were to arrive in Elizabethville by air on August 5. Even more disturbing was the news that our troops were to enter Katanga in force the following day. Fortunately, however, he had refused Gizenga's demand that Ralph should be accompanied by a number of ministers of the Central Government.

This infuriated Gizenga, who claimed that the United Nations were treating the Congolese Government like children. But his rage and the hardening tension in Léopoldville were like the trembling of a leaf compared to the storm that this news aroused in Elizabethville, where the Tshombé government was convinced that the entry of UN troops would mean the end of their independent state.

Cables of protest were dispatched all over Western Europe: the Katanga delegation in Brussels was ordered to proceed immediately to Paris and then on to New York; another delegation was hastily assembled in Elizabethville and put on board a plane for London. On August 3 Godefroid Munongo, the Minister of the Interior, called for general mobilization and announced that Katanga would resist United Nations troops with every means in its power. Finally a telegram arrived for Dag, repeating this declaration, and warning that the entry of our troops would set off a general uprising.

The telegram, however, contained a less belligerent postscript; the Katanga government was prepared to meet the Secretary General's special representative and discuss "any formula of cooperation with other sovereign States of the former Belgian Congo." This led us to suspect the talk of force had been a bluff. We knew that the Belgian troops there had no intention of hindering our entry; what we could not judge were the reactions of Tshombé's gendarmerie and paramilitary forces, which were officered by Belgian soldiers and volunteer civilians.

Again Dag asked my advice, and I had no alternative but to tell him that if we went in and then become involved in fighting, there was no chance of our making headway; nor were we in any position to supply our forces. Even as I was talking, however, I sensed this warning was superfluous; Dag had no intention of becoming involved in a shooting war without a new and explicit mandate from the Security Council. I could see that he was disturbed at the turn events had taken, and I suggested that when Ralph did go up to Elizabethville, he should make every effort to weigh the possibilities of armed resistance.

This task was to fall on Ralph's shoulders within twenty-four hours after Dag had sent a stiff reply to Elizabethville informing them that his special representative would arrive there on August 4. Although Ralph was instructed to make contact with General Gheysen to insure that all Belgian troops were withdrawn to the Kamina base, his primary role was to gauge the temper of the Katanganese. I wished that I or one of my more experienced officers had been allowed to go too, but our arrival in Elizabethville would have led to another storm. The reconnaissance had to be left to Ralph who did not have the requisite training and background for making military judgments.

I do not know what transpired in Elizabethville, but on August 5 Ralph returned a shaken man. The "hostile" reception that had greeted him at the airport had turned out to be only a prelude to verbal assaults and hair-raising warnings from every African and European whom he had met. Munongo had regaled him with vivid descriptions of the measures in hand to prevent our planes from landing, and had painted an alarming picture of paramilitary units fighting to the last man, backed by hordes of tribesmen. From what he had seen, Ralph had no doubt at all that our troops were likely to receive a hot reception.

Our discussions lasted long into the night with Ralph remaining adamant that after what he had seen, the Katanga operation must be called off. Whether his judgment was right or wrong, I was extremely relieved because I knew we simply did not possess the resources to face any sort of opposition. After listening to us all, Dag summed up the situation; in view of Ralph's report he did not feel that his mandate covered the use of force. There was no alternative but to cancel the operation; he would return to New York and report to the Security Council.

He left next day. Once the news broke the Central Government accused us of capitulation to Tshombé, and Léopoldville became full of disturbing rumors. We had no doubt now that appeals to Russia for help would be intensified, and therefore kept a close watch on the Soviet and Czech embassies whose staffs had soared to unprecedented numbers during the past weeks. After consulting Ralph, I took the precaution of strengthening our guards around both these building so that we could keep a careful watch on their comings and goings.

Within a few hours we received a telephone call from the new Russian Ambassador, who wanted to know what was going on. He was told that more sentries had been posted for his protection because conditions in the city were becoming disturbed. Before he rang off, he was polite enough to express his thanks.

Despite rising tension, I felt that my new staff was working smoothly enough to allow me to snatch a few hours to visit some of my troops. Hitherto, circumstances had made it impossible to leave headquarters. Not only had I been permanently at Ralph's beck and call, but I always had an uncomfortable feeling that were I to be away something was bound to go dreadfully wrong.

Every problem seemed to come home to roost firmly on my shoulders. I doubt whether many soldiers can have been saddled with such a complex, frustrating burden. Certainly few could have been handed such a polyglot force nor so ill-defined a mandate to keep them operational over vast distances without the beginnings of an adequate supply system. And doubtless because it was virtually impossible for anyone on the outside to realize the magnitude of what I was up against, I had come under heavy criticism for not behaving like an ordinary commander with the advantage of a tried and tested army structure behind him.

As I flew down to Matadi in our staff plane—a Swedish Metropolitan—to visit Colonel Ben Omad Driss' Moroccans, it was difficult to forget how strongly I had felt about the military correspondent of the London *Daily Telegraph*. Normally, I do not like journalists; I have suffered too much from their tendency to distort or elaborate on interviews given in the best of faith. But among the horde of journalists who inhabited the Memling Hotel in Léopoldville (at Headquarters we used to call them the Memling Brigade) there had been a man whom I believed an exception to this rule—if only because he had been a regular soldier. Brigadier W. F. K. Thompson, who represented *The Daily Telegraph,* was someone whom I instinctively liked and trusted, and I had had none of the usual inhibitions in explaining just how chaotic the situation was nor what appalling difficulties I was experiencing in trying to maintain and supply our units.

By the time I had finished, he knew just how many amateur staff officers I had, was aware of our almost total lack of communications and knew, too, just how closely my hands were tied by Ralph. He expressed concern and sympathy; the next I knew was a scathing article in *The Daily Telegraph* datelined Stanleyville (where I presume he must have thumbed a lift in a UN plane) describing the concern prevalent amongst the Ethiopian troops there owing to the fact that their Commander had not troubled to pay them a visit. There was more in this vein, and the implication was that I should have been out in the field leading my troops in an aggressive fashion that would have clamped an iron control over the whole province. Thompson saw the problem in terms of a straightforward military operation and appeared to be unaware of the shackles a UN Commander puts on with his blue beret. I threw his article into the wastepaper basket.

This episode was to have an amusing sequel when the Chief of Staff of the Nigerian Army, Major General Foster, came down some months later to visit the excellent Nigerian Brigade that was serving with us. One night, when we were discussing the iniquities of journalists, I told him how bitterly I had resented this incident. General Foster listened with sympathy; his only comment was "Brigadier Thompson happens to be my brother-in-law."

I was heartened by my visit to Matadi; everything seemed under control. A trickle of supplies was beginning to come through from the port that was scheduled to become one of our major supply points once the American General Wheeler arrived to get the installations on a working basis again. It was the same at Thysville where I went on to thank another Moroccan detachment for their sterling work during the difficult early days. Even the local ANC commanded by Colonel Bobozo (a regular who had reached the rank of warrant officer under the Belgians) appeared to be modeling themselves on Colonel Driss' troops.

Back at Léopoldville, I discovered the Central Government had now started a full-scale campaign to oust Ralph. Dag meantime was in New York, struggling to obtain a new mandate from a divided United Nations while Lumumba was in the throes of an African tour. Its repercussions were already beginning to make themselves felt at ONUC headquarters.

Sekou Touré, the President of the Republic of Guinea, announced that he was ready to put his entire armed forces at the disposal of the Central Government should the United Nations hesitate over entering Katanga. President Nkrumah hastened to back him up, and within a few days President Nasser (whose UAR parachute battalion had just arrived in Léopoldville) was to follow suit.

Although our relations with the Central Government were going from bad to worse, the news from New York was heartening. On August 9, after a difficult session in the Security Council, Dag had finally succeeded in obtaining a new mandate which, although it contained no mention of the use of force, gave him clear authority to enter Katanga. On the same day, Tshombé announced from Elizabethville that he was prepared to admit UN troops, but listed some ten conditions, the principal one being that no UN planes or vehicles were to be used to transport officials of the Central Government into Katanga. Dag replied from New York that he could not accept any conditions but was willing to come to Elizabethville for discussions; his suggestion was accepted; on August 11 he flew back to join us in Léopoldville.

Although I did not accompany him on August 12 when he set off for Elizabethville with his military adviser, the Indian General Rikhye, General Kettani, and two companies of Swedish troops drawn from the Léopoldville garrison, I had been instructed that our troops were to be ready to enter Katanga on August 15. Our plans for this move had already been drawn up, my improved staff functioned well, and now units from all over the Congo began converging on the Katanga border by road and rail. Although we kept aircraft standing by to fly in as many units as possible, the bulk had to move overland.

Our plans for establishing a skeleton task force in Elizabethville, Kamina, Jadotville, Manono, Kolwezi, Albertville, and Kabolo were necessarily ambitious, and in order to assemble sufficient troops we had to denude the other provinces of four thousand troops out of a total garrison just under twelve thousand strong. We set the Irish in motion from Kivu Province, the Malis from Léopoldville, elements of the Ethiopian Brigade had to come right across from Oriental Province, Swedish troops from Léopoldville and Moroccans from the Lower Congo. With our inadequate system of communications, it seemed almost a miracle that everyone was alerted or already on the move. I was still wondering whether the Congolese-controlled railways might not land some unlucky unit up against the Sudanese border when I was ordered to fly to Elizabethville to "lead" my troops in person on August 15.

I flew up in the early hours of the 14th, taking a couple of officers to form the nucleus of an operational staff that would have to be built up from the units as they came in. I brought with me, too, a list of the minimum number of troops and ancillary and supply units that I considered essential for operational efficiency in the Congo now that we had added some 190,000 square miles of potentially hostile territory to our already overextended command.

I was glad to see Dag who, now the immediate strain was over, looked more like his normal self. I was more than interested, too, to meet President Tshombé, who struck me as a clever, able, and adroit man with visible signs of more "background" than I had so far encountered among Congolese politicians, and Godefroid Munongo, his Minister of the Interior, who was reckoned to be the strong man behind him. Munongo impressed me as nothing more or less than a man drenched and impregnated in evil.

Once we had dodged our way through swarms of reporters and driven to Dag's billet in a guest house of the Union Minière,* I finally found myself alone with him. Possibly I was not in a good mood. On the way in I had been waylaid by two press correspondents who, after my refusal to comment on the situation, blatantly announced: "Why on earth don't you give us a statement? It's far better you should because we shall quote you whether you talk to us or not."

Maybe I was on edge. I was sorry to have to worry Dag but there was no alternative but to bombard him with military home truths. I knew his troubles had hardly started. We might be on our way into Katanga but within a matter of days Lumumba would be back in Léopoldville, furious because Dag had refused to allow any members of the Central Government to accompany him to Elizabethville.

There were plenty of shadows on the horizon. We had just heard that Lumumba had arranged a meeting of the heads of all African States in Léopoldville for August 30. Nonetheless, Dag looked remarkably relaxed, almost carefree, until I broke the calm by an-

* The Union Minière was, and still is, one of the most powerful of the Belgian-based companies that control the mineral resources of the Congo. Recently (before ceasing to be Prime Minister) Tshombé threatened to nationalize its vast holding. At present, however, this immensely powerful company, whose subsidiaries and ramifications stretch into every exploitable interest in the Congo, remains on good terms with the Government. This is understandable. Its activities provide nearly 50 per cent of Congolese revenue.

nouncing that even were the operations scheduled for tomorrow to go off smoothly, the maintenance of our units there was bound to create a terrible headache.

I told him categorically that despite what some of his people might tell him to the contrary in New York, it was going to be a fantastically difficult task to supply the troops—widely spread as they were bound to be—over a huge area. I told him it was useless to rely on assurances in New York; the people there were totally out of touch with the actual situation. What we had to put up with had been horrifying enough while we had been operating under comparatively peaceful conditions. But were we ever to find ourselves at war with the Katanganese, we had neither the arms, ammunition, equipment, food reserves, or communications to maintain ourselves, or the faintest confidence that we could command adequate logistic support from New York. On top of the chaos which we knew existed there, there were still no clear orders about when and how we were permitted to defend ourselves. Unless these were rapidly forthcoming, I foresaw a sharp drop in morale.

I remember saying: "I'm afraid this is a pretty tall order," as I handed Dag the list I had drawn up to cover a sound operational role in the Congo. Large it may have been, but at least it was realistic. I had asked for five to six brigades, at least one squadron of tanks, two reconnaissance units, several field and antiaircraft regiments, and an air element composed of reconnaissance and fighter planes and sufficient transport squadrons to maintain a thoroughly adequate airlift.

Dag read through the whole list carefully, threw it down on the table and burst out laughing.

"Are you mad? Do you think I want to start an armaments race?"

"No," I said, "I'm sure you don't. But if you want to control the Congo that's about what it comes to."

"Let's hope things never get as bad as that," he said.

Just as I had begun to ask him whether this hope wasn't wishful thinking, he cut me off in midsentence and began to talk about the evacuation of the Belgians. I was aware that he had already had talks with General Gheysen; I knew, too, that he was under tremendous pressure to get all Belgian soldiers and officials out of

Katanga. But on this I had my own views; having seen the chaos in the other five provinces that had followed the flight of the Belgians, it struck me as little short of madness to contemplate disrupting a well-organized state like Katanga. I had always spoken frankly to Dag, and now I asked him whether he really believed it right to kick out every Belgian soldier and civil servant when we were incapable of bringing in replacements soon enough to prevent a total collapse of the civilian administration.

Since I knew very well that the real pressure for this stupidity came from the newly emergent states in the United Nations, I also asked him whether in his own heart he did not think it a farce that these states should have the same voting power as more mature nations. Should there not, I suggested, be some sort of test of political maturity? . . .

I was unable to press this point because Dag became extremely angry. In an icy but controlled voice, he informed me that there was no alternative to expelling the Belgians. And the edge in his voice became even more glacial as he reminded me that the principle of one state one vote was the essence of the whole idea behind the United Nations.

That night I saw him off for Léopoldville. And the following morning our troops entered Katanga by air and rail. The unwanted "peacekeepers" were hardly accorded a warm welcome but there was no active opposition and very few hostile demonstrations. The only exception was Goma, where a large crowd, waving an assortment of lethal-looking weapons, had assembled on the airfield to give our troops a hot reception.

Yells of rage and defiance greeted the big American planes as they touched down and taxied up the runway, turning to gasps of wonderment as the huge doors of the first plane swung open, the ramps came down, and out marched the pipe band of the Irish 32d Battalion with saffron kilts swinging and pibrochs wailing.

For a moment savage black faces stared at the bulging cheeks of the pipers, the brave expanse of pink knees, the impressive flourish of drumsticks; the skirling of the pipes assailed their ears. And then—as though by magic—the hostile reception changed into frenzied welcome, pangas were stuffed back into waistcloths, the crowd surged forward for a closer look at this remarkable "enemy" who had dropped out of the skies. Without drawing breath the pipe band marched out onto the road for Goma while the rifle companies discreetly descended from their planes to follow in its wake. At times the pipers were almost obscured by the dancing, singing crowds that accompanied them the whole way into the town.

There was no trouble with the Belgians in Katanga. General Gheysen proved thoroughly cooperative, and it was arranged that all Belgian troops were to be withdrawn to the Kamina base by August 19, prior to being flown out to Belgium. Gheysen was a remarkable man in his own way, and his views on the best means of maintaining order struck me as effective though possibly a trifle questionable. I remember his friendly advice just after I had reviewed a very smart outgoing reconnaissance regiment. Dispersing an unruly and hostile African crowd was, he explained, a simple business; all that was necessary was plenty of tear gas and riot sticks, but it was wise to sprinkle a few fragmentation grenades in with the lachrymose ones. *"Parce que,"* and he did not blink an eyelid, *"il faut frapper, il faut frapper."* *

During the next few days, I visited the Ethiopians who had begun to arrive at the huge Belgian base at Kamina (which at that time had one of the longest runways in the world). From Kamina I went on to Kolwezi and then to Jadotville; at the latter, the situation seemed peaceful enough (though a year later the Irish here were forced to surrender to Tshombé's forces). Indeed, every place I visited was destined to become the scene of violent trouble. Even then I was acutely conscious that my warnings to Dag had not been overdone; if anything, I had understressed the dangers. But I had hardly had time to see my troops settled in before I was urgently recalled to Léopoldville.

* "You've got to hit them, and hit them hard."

Chapter Fifteen

MAINTAINING ORDER

At N'Djili airport the guards had been strengthened and there was an uneasy atmosphere that one could sense immediately on leaving the plane. I soon discovered the reason. The previous day a tremendous swarm of Congolese "para hunters" had invaded the field and surrounded a United Nations C.119 that had just landed. Beneath the passive gaze of a Ghanaian guard, this rabble had proceeded to interrogate the crew and had then dragged out four bewildered Canadian signalers on the pretense they were Belgians. In no time these luckless men (who were badly needed at Force HQ) were being savagely beaten up in true Congo style. Not until they were virtually unconscious had the Ghanaian guard belatedly come to the rescue.

This tardy arrival did not pass unnoticed; Ralph reported the lapse (which might have cost the Canadians their lives) to New York. Reaction was swift; a strongly worded protest from Dag to the Central Government arrived simultaneously with a sharp rebuke for the Ghanaians. From what I could learn, it was well merited; the Ghanaians were a highly trained and disciplined unit and there was no excuse for their not intervening earlier. General Alexander, however, took a different view. His report—forwarded to Dag through President Nkrumah—acknowledged the incident but strongly repudiated any criticism of Ghanaian officers and men.

This proved to be just a prelude to a bitter tirade; Alexander once more stressed the crucial need to retrain and discipline the ANC and warned that there could be no hope for the Congo unless this was done.

"The situation," his report concluded, "is not irretrievable, but it will certainly be hopeless unless something drastic is done to deal with the ANC problem."

Logically this made sound military sense, but there was nothing logical about our military status in the Congo. Alexander, however, seemed undisturbed by New York's rejection of his ideas, and now criticized me for putting his Ghanaian troops in an impossible position; he also claimed that I had never given specific orders to any of my contingents and had throughout shown unwillingness to exercise any authority.

I found this hard; what he was getting at was the same problem of when and how to use force that I had argued with Ralph into the depths of the night. I felt like sending him a copy of the ONUC regulations; my subordinate position to the civil element, the fact that *all* command authority had been vested in the Special Representative ever since I had arrived was set down clearly as refutation. But while the action he advocated might have made sense in a normal military operation it had no validity here in the steamy Congo where the United Nations had established its own conception of Alice in Wonderland. Wisely Ralph rejected Alexander's criticisms as unjustified and not in keeping with the goals of the United Nations Force, which was supposed to be a peace force and not a fighting organization.

Tension, however, was not confined to soldiers. On Dag's return to the capital from Katanga, he discovered Lumumba furiously claiming that we had dealt with Tshombé as though the Central Government did not exist. Five angry letters passed between them in a single day. Lumumba insisted that the people of the Congo had lost all confidence in the Secretary General and made it quite clear that help would have to be sought elsewhere. From this moment onward Dag was to make no effort to hide the gulf between them; I gathered from Ralph that he considered the Prime Minister a potential dictator bent on wrecking our operations.

Whatever his shortcomings, there was no doubt that Lumumba was a remarkable man, but his driving, volatile nature had its own drawbacks. From the intelligence we were able to gather, it appeared that during his absence on his African tour a number of Congolese politicians had seized the chance to consolidate an anti-Lumumba movement that had its roots in a combination of long-standing political rivalry and a genuine fear that the Prime Minister's monomania would burgeon into a communist-dominated Congolese dictatorship. Lumumba had scented out this antagonism within days of his return; several newspapers were closed down and the jails received their first quota of "free Congolese" prisoners.

Now I was back, I was determined to get to the bottom of a problem that had long been nagging me. Ever since Ralph's "global communications" had come into operation, I had had an increasing suspicion that parts of my cables to New York had been "doctored," and now I decided to create a test case to discover what was going on. Although I had long felt certain something was wrong because of the total lack of response to certain points I had stressed and the curious delay in any sort of satisfactory replies, I had hesitated to accept my staff's suspicion that the man I was working with so closely might be quietly censoring my cables behind my back. As I knew to my cost, Ralph had his infuriating side, but I was personally very fond of him, and a pattern of behavior like this seemed quite out of character.

I was determined to find out. On August 12 I drafted the following cable to David Vaughan via Andrew Cordier. I quote it in full because it was later to be suppressed by Ralph.

Withdrawn at Dr. Bunche's request.

OUTGOING MESSAGE

TO: Cordier
FROM: von Horn
DATE: 12 August 1960

For Vaughan. I thank you for your personal note assuring me of full support. In view of the enormous task and complicated problems that we have to face and tackle here I feal I cannot conceal from you the fact that the administrative contribution here in spite of all personal ambitions and efforts is NOT repeat NOT up to standard and therefore on the 29th day of the operations jeopardizing its success. Even if you feel it hard to face it is my duty NOT to conceal from you the hard verdict that "never have so many people managed to produce so few results in so long a time."

For political reasons, the whole operation had to be laid on in an "inverted order" creating operational and technical problems which call for administrative imagination and above all drive. This has been and still is lacking. Unless at all levels initiative, common sense and drive are used to achieve our common aim the success of the whole operation will be imperiled. As Supreme Commander I would like to know which limitations are likely to be imposed upon me in the execution of my duties. I wish to emphasize strongly that the United Nations do have responsibilities towards the governments who willingly and at great expense have so generously contributed to the operations in the Congo. We are not giving them what they are normally entitled to get even on a wartime basis.

I realize fully that in the initial period the provision of these minimum facilities is likely to be costly and that because of the fluid situation non-recoverable expenses are likely to be made. I would like to point out to you that the standards and criteria used in UNEF and UNOGIL are NOT repeat NOT automatically applicable here. What is required here is immediate and positive action. Ways and means must be found to achieve this goal. Whatever the concerted military and technical administrative and organizational build up will be, I request as personal administrative assistant JAN VAN WIJK the only one who in the field so far equals my repeat my administrative requirements in an emergency. Please let me know where I stand.

My military assistant delivered this signal personally, I told him to keep a check on it for coding and dispatch. When, twelve hours later, it was located languishing in the communications office, I sent for Mr. Baumgarten, the Chief Communication Officer, and told him to send it off immediately. Poor Baumgarten now found himself in an embarrassing position; he hemmed and hawed and squirmed but was unable to conceal the fact that this simply could not be done. Under steely cross-questioning, he reluctantly revealed the reason; *all* incoming and outgoing code messages had to be personally signed by Dr. Bunche!

I left him and told my staff to root out the Chief Administrative Officer. Before long this gentleman appeared between two of my officers. He appeared highly alarmed, confirmed what Baumgarten had told me and, in response to my furious query how such a monstrous rule could have been put into operation without my knowledge, seemed totally at a loss.

I sent my two duty officers off again to roust out Brian Urquhart, one of Ralph's most trusted political officers. I felt sure he would know a lot about this business, and I was not mistaken. Urquhart knew all about it and was very angry at being awakened. Spluttering with rage and resentment, he made no bones about Ralph having initiated the order. From his bearing and behavior, I gathered that he personally thought it was a very good thing.

I looked at him coldly; at this stage I felt almost past speech. It was as though I had been plunged back into the nightmare atmosphere of my early battles with the Administration in Jerusalem, only this time it was far, far more serious. I looked at my watch—it was now 4 a.m. I had not the heart to wake Ralph out of his exhausted sleep, but I told Urquhart to see that the message was presented to him for clearance on the dot of 7 a.m.

At half past seven I was summoned to Ralph's office. I could see at once from the tight lines around his normally good-natured mouth that my outspoken signal had shaken him. We were both tense, facing each other across his desk. But although I had known Ralph to use forcible language on occasion, this was evidently not one of them. His voice was more sorrowfully earnest than angry as he said:

"I have just been reading your signal, Carl. I am very sorry to find it so bitterly critical of me. I can't stand for this sort of behavior. If you insist on sending it, I shall have no choice but to resign."

"Look, Ralph," I said, "I came here to resign myself because a few hours ago I discovered that I'm not allowed to communicate with New York direct. I've suspected this for some time, I sent that signal as a test, knowing that if you saw it you were bound to suppress it. Now I know where I stand. What you don't seem to realize is that no responsible Force Commander can tolerate this sort of censorship. If *you* persist in it, then I think there are other places for me than Léopoldville."

There was a long silence during which we looked at each other; for my part, I was very conscious that Ralph was brimming with those qualities of loyalty and devotion that the United Nations badly needed; of course, he had shortcomings, but his burden during the last weeks had been heavier than mine. Finally, I said:

"It looks as though Dag is going to have a couple of resignations on his hand. I think we'd both help him best by deferring them and trying to work together . . . at least for the time being."

"I agree," Ralph said. And then fingering the signal: "I take it that . . . ?"

I nodded.

Unfortunately this episode was a prelude to the major clash that was now only days away. But during the weeks he was still with us, I heard nothing more about censorship. Good old Ralph —I have never met a more sensitive or kindly man; the following morning, I overslept through sheer exhaustion and so missed "morning prayers"—the daily staff meeting in his office. Within a matter of minutes of arriving belatedly at my desk, a personal letter arrived by hand, expressing the hope that my absence had not been motivated by any personal feeling.

Ralph's days at ONUC were now numbered; under tremendous pressure from the African States, who claimed he had far too many "Western" advisers in the Mission, Dag decided to replace him with the Indian Rajeshwar Dayal—to whom they could hardly object.* But there was still a little time to go, and Ralph remained under constant pressure from Lumumba, who had secret plans for independent action and was consequently insisting that the arms and equipment the ANC had handed over to us must be returned. I do not know what discussions took place; the first I heard was one dismaying night when Ralph came into my office.

I had no premonition of what he was about to say, but I listened with growing incredulity as he told me that a political decision had been taken to hand back all the ANC arms and equipment under our control. I remember staring at him as though he must have taken leave of his senses when I heard him say:

"I want you to give the necessary orders, Carl. This has to be done right away."

"Have you gone mad, Ralph?" I asked. "Don't you realize that this will mean civil war? Haven't I explained to you that the

* He was, after all, an Asian, a distinguished and able administrator who, though he had been educated under the British (doubtless a vast advantage to him personally) had held high office, his last post before he was seconded to the UN having been Indian High Commissioner to Pakistan.

ANC is just a rabble, not a disciplined body? As long as we keep their arms locked up they can't do much harm, but once they lay hands on them then God help the civilian population—let alone our own troops."

"I want you to give the necessary orders."

"Look, Ralph," I said. And then, I made him sit down and listen while I talked.

But even as I explained just what an incredibly dangerous act this could be, I sensed that his mind was already made up, that my arguments would have no more force than raindrops bouncing off armor plate. But I was his Force Commander, responsible for the lives of more than twelve thousand men and entrusted with the task of maintaining order, if not law, in a huge and uncivilized country where the lives of thirteen million Congolese would be irreparably plunged many steps backward once the delicate balance had been disturbed. Life was all too cheap in the Congo already, and I warned Raph that he would undo everything we had achieved, that every rifle handed out was certain to be used and that once tribal and civil war had started, we would have blood on our hands.

Ralph remained silent. Looking at those kind and familiar features, I knew exactly what he was going to say and I knew, too, what my answer was going to be. When he told me once again that this was a political decision which he, as the Special Representative of the United Nations, had every right to take, and told me categorically that I was to hand the arms back, I looked him in the eyes before I said:

"I have warned you, Ralph—and warned you very clearly. I am your Force Commander, and since you refuse to listen to my advice, I must tell you that I utterly refuse to give such an order to my troops."

Ralph has big, warm, affectionate eyes—but there was nothing warm or affectionate about them at this moment. We parted very coldly. I had had plenty of trouble during my thirty-nine years soldiering but never anything quite like this. I had deliberately refused an order and in my opinion I had been absolutely right; what worried me was a suspicion that this was not the end of it. I had a quick word with my staff, and went to bed extremely disturbed. But it was nothing to my perturbation next morning when Justin MacCarthy and Johnny Berthiaume came in to see me and told me that Ralph had already summoned them to his office and had instructed them to pass on the order to the troops. When I asked whether they had done so, both these stalwart characters shook their heads; their answer, I gathered, had been exactly the same as mine.

When I heard of the signals that had been sent direct to my unit commanders in the name of the Secretary General's Special Representative, I had little doubt that the order would be obeyed; Ralph was, after all, within his rights and was technically justified in going over my head now that I had refused to obey his orders. I must admit I cherished a small hope that some stout-hearted commander would foresee the consequences of what he was being ordered to do and take the same lonely course we had adopted in Léopoldville. But I knew it was vain to hope; political and racial factors were involved and commanders might well find themselves in danger of flouting the policy of their own governments as well as that of the United Nations.

As the day wore on it grew clear that the dragon's teeth had been sown. Nowhere were the results to be more tragically in evidence than at Luluabourg, where Colonel Lasmar, "Le Prince de Kasai," and his Tunisians were forced to hand over the carefully guarded armory to the local ANC.

It was from this city that Lumumba was about to launch a private offensive against Katanga that was doomed to peter out into the nearest thing to genocide the Congo was ever to experience. Without the rifles, automatic rifles, and machine guns the Tunisians were now handing over to an eager crowd of ANC this tragedy need never have taken place.

I have often wondered whether Ralph realized the full implications of what he was doing; I thought I had explained these clearly enough, but I am convinced that he must have seen the whole decision as a political issue. Although he demonstrated an extraordinary mixture of shrewdness and realism on occasion, he nonetheless was essentially a politician with much of that species' dogged adherence to the belief that no problem exists that cannot be solved by political ends. Undoubtedly, he was hampered by the UN directive *not* to interfere in Congolese internal quarrels, and it may have seemed to him that Lumumba's demand to control an armed ANC had some validity.

I do not doubt that Ralph honestly believed his action would result in a more stabilized situation although how he reached this conclusion in the teeth of my warnings is hard to understand. In any event, the results were just as I had foreseen. He left us too early to reap the whirlwind, but the blood and suffering that followed could not possibly have occurred without those arms in the trigger-happy possession of the ANC.

On reflection, I think I should have resigned on this issue, but at that moment there seemed little need because in Elizabethville I had already told Dag that I would like to be relieved of my command. It might have been different had I been aware that Lumumba had already ordered the excitable and devoted General Lundula and Colonel Mobutu (who kept his own counsel) to work out plans for an attack on Kasai Province, where President Kalonji had just proclaimed an independent state. Nor had we any suspicions that the hundred trucks we were expecting as part of the Soviet Union's contribution had been diverted up-river to Port Francqui in Kasai, while some fourteen Ilyushin planes were standing by to airlift Central Government troops into Luluabourg.

Ralph's departure was scheduled for August 28, and I felt that in view of our strained relationship, I would be well out of Léopoldville. I knew that Andrew Cordier was due to fly in as a temporary stopgap before Rajeshwar Dayal arrived. In Léopoldville, the African States had started their meeting earlier than we had expected, and the situation was temporarily quiet; I took the chance to fly up to visit a detachment of Moroccans in Equateur Province.

This was the unit, commanded by Captain Bougrine, who had long been holding down a huge area of difficult country with a handful of paratroopers. I was most impressed by the turnout of his men. Except for the youngest, they had all had long service in the former French Colonial Army, and as Bourgrine told me about the variegated tasks he had had to tackle, I had the distinct feeling that this sector of the Congo was in extremely capable hands.

I went on to visit another parachute battalion, in Equateur Province. But here one sensed immediately the divided loyalties that arose from Member States' direct interest in Congolese internal affairs. Colonel Shazli and his UAR (United Arab Republic) "Sheitan" parachute battalion made a good enough impression, but I was to have plenty of trouble with them in the days ahead. Even before their arrival, President Nasser had suggested to Dag that they should be stationed at the big Belgian base of Kamina. From a technical point of view, this would have suited us well enough because Kamina had been the training base for Belgian paratroops. But at that time we considered that the Congolese mania for "para hunting" * would be exacerbated by the arrival of a fully armed and equipped parachute battalion whose far from African appearance was bound to arouse suspicion and alarm.

Accordingly the "Sheitan" battalion had been posted to Gemena and Lisala in Northern Equateur Province with one reserve company stationed in Léopoldville to help guard the airfield. The battalion had not greeted this decision with great enthusiasm, but as I inspected them, they seemed well disciplined and were obviously capable of playing an adequate role in the area.

I flew on to visit my Irish units in Kivu and Katanga. I had allowed myself three days, but had hardly started before I was summoned back to Léopoldville. On landing, I discovered that there was another crisis. Three days earlier Russian planes had begun airlifting Central Government troops from Léopoldville to Luluabourg while other troops were being ferried up by barge. While these preparations for an attack on the secessionists in Kasai Province were going on, Lumumba had flown to Stanleyville. More Russian planes were expected here and just before his arrival an American Globemaster had touched down on the runway with reinforcements and equipment for the Canadian signal squadron that was now virtually running the whole of ONUC's communications.

* This had become a murderous national pastime, egged on by politicians who felt their own positions in danger. *Anyone* who looked remotely like a Belgian soldier became suspect as a paratrooper—the "Paras" who spelled the return of Belgian colonialism. Even a mention of their presence was enough to produce a Congolese mob.

A rumor—the city was enthusiastically awaiting Lumumba's arrival and the "para hunting" mania was at its height—spread that the Belgians had come to arrest the Prime Minister. A huge crowd of Congolese police, soldiers, and civilians rushed onto the field and dragged out the Canadians and the American crew. Unfortunately, the luckless Canadians were wearing the parachute wings of their own airborne training and were savagely beaten up and dragged away to jail before the Ethiopian guard could arrive.

Their fate might have been worse had not an Ethiopian nurse resolutely followed the jeeps carrying the battered victims off to prison. She was stopped outside the jail by Congolese police, who showed every sign of dragging her in too. But before they could lay hands on her, she turned her own jeep around and drove back at breakneck speed to the Ethiopian Brigade Headquarters. A detachment was sent off immediately to rescue the Canadians, and brought them back to the hospital. Next day the badly injured men were put on a plane for Léopoldville.

This incident had a profound effect on everyone in ONUC. I know it affected me personally and from that time very few of our people troubled to disguise their hostility toward the Congolese. Probably it had been latent for a long period but now it had certainly come to the surface. I strapped on my own pistol before going out to the airport to see the Canadians flown in.

There was to be little need for it; the only aggressive action I took that day was to prod a member of the "Memling (Press) Brigade" smartly in the rump when I found him blocking the passage of the stretchers. Once inside the hospital, I found the Americans and Canadians in surprisingly good heart; all they could talk about was the Ethiopian nurse whose determined action had saved their lives.

I have seldom felt such a surge of relief as I experienced when Andrew Cordier stepped out of his plane August 28. The sight of Cordier's bulky, determined figure put new heart into me; I knew that at last there was a genuine realist among us, and his huge hand clasping mine felt like the reassuring grip of a guide who had come to lead us out of the nightmare we had been living in too long. I returned to ONUC headquarters feeling events had taken a distinct turn for the better.

Cordier was plunged straight into a series of meetings, instigated by the African States in an endeavor to cool down the tension between ourselves and the Central Government, and I took the chance to move into a private house my staff had discovered in the Parc *Salemba.* I had always hated the Royal. And now that Ralph, looking very old and shaken, was packing his bags for the trip back to New York, there was nothing to stop my moving into this new residence, which we christened "Flagstaff House." It was a pleasant place that had originally belonged to the Belgian holding company C.C.C.I., which had left it deserted in the first wave of panic flight.*

Here I settled down with my ADC, a Canadian cook steward, a Canadian batman, and three Congolese servants. I kept on my operational HQ at the Royal. But it was a great relief to come back to the Parc *Salemba* at nights. It proved a refuge amid a mounting sea of trouble.

The African States, which were just completing their meeting in Léopoldville, had on the surface succeeded in exerting a restraining influence on Lumumba. But it was already too late; Russian planes were flying reinforcements into Luluabourg from Stanleyville (where Lumumba's visit had been the occasion for fevered planning to start an uprising among the tribes unfavorable to Tshombé in Katanga). Nor had Victor Lundula and Colonel Mobutu been wasting their time in Léopoldville; a concerted drive into Katanga had been planned through North Katanga and Kasai Province.

In Kasai, there was bitter hostility between the Lulua and the Ba-Luba tribes. The Ba-Luba, who supported Kalonji (and through him President Tshombé), had already been active against the Lulua. Now, with the arrival of the Central Government troops, the pendulum swung the other way; the Ba-Lubas' ancient shotguns proved no match for the ANC's modern weapons and a blood bath ensued.

The Central Government troops had no supplies or commissariat, and pillaged the land through which they passed; village after village went up in flames, the terrified inhabitants fled to the

* It was a property belonging to the C.C.C.I. (Compagnie Congalaise de Commerce et d'Industrie).

jungle, Kalonji and the remnants of his government took refuge in Katanga, and the whole province was plunged into the horrors of a civil war.

Cordier could hardly have arrived at a more crucial moment. As we saw Ralph off on August 30, we were aware that the Russian planes and trucks supporting Lumumba's troops had made outside intervention an inescapable reality. We anticipated, too, that this was only a step toward more active support.

It could be argued that Tshombé had already set a precedent for foreign aid. But Tshombé, on the surface at any rate, was collaborating with the United Nations. Lumumba, on the other hand, was bitterly hostile. Although the African Congress had persuaded him into making conciliatory gestures toward the United Nations, his discussions with Cordier soon made it clear that we were up against the implacable hostility of the Prime Minister, his government, and a very considerable weight of opinion in the country. On our side, there was no use disguising the fact that from Dag downward there was a marked distrust and dislike of Lumumba.

It seemed only a question of time before relations with the Central Government broke down and the situation entered a new and dangerous phase. We had, however, reckoned without the bitter domestic political rivalries about to erupt in Léopoldville.

Chapter Sixteen

CIVIL WAR POLITICS

THERE was little warning. On September 5, a telephone call summoned Cordier to the Presidential Palace. Although there had been rumors that Kasavubu was growing disturbed at Lumumba's determination to go his own and increasingly violent way, Cordier was taken by surprise when the plump president confidently informed him that he was launching a *coup d'état* that night; handing him a typewritten list of names, Kasavubu told him that these were the men whom he wanted ONUC units to arrest to insure everything went smoothly.

The list made interesting reading; starting with Lumumba, it continued like a roll call through the ranks of his most influential supporters. After a moment Andy Cordier handed it back; he was not allowed, he informed the disappointed president, to intervene in Congolese internal affairs and had no mandate that permitted him to arrest people in this way.

Kasavubu appeared a little shaken, but after some hesitation, told Andy that he intended to go ahead just the same. Since the United Nations refused to support him, it might be necessary to alter the timing of the *coup d'état;* in any case, he reserved the right to call on us for his personal protection should events make it necessary. Cordier agreed that this would certainly be forthcoming. Having bade the president (who obviously had other things on his mind) farewell, he drove back to the Royal at top speed.

I was called in to see him immediately; what worried us most was the exact turn events were likely to take were civil war to break out in Léopoldville. It was impossible to guess what sort of popular support Kasavubu was likely to command or whether he had enlisted the collaboration of the ANC. Although General Lundula was a Lumumba man, we were not so sure about Colonel Mobutu. But whether the troops supported the *coup* or not, Lumumba was certain to react violently. In the event of fighting breaking out he was almost certain to use Russian planes to airlift reinforcements down from Stanleyville.

There was little we could do, immediately, other than strengthen our guard units at the airfield and alert all troops in the capital; we just had to sit tight and await events. We informed New York of developments and, as the hours dragged on, began to wonder what Kasavubu was up to in his Presidential Palace, surrounded by his closest supporters and doubtless in touch with the Abbé Foulbert Youlu across the river in Brazzaville (an astute and pro-Western politician who was to be of great service to him in the days ahead).

It has been claimed (in view of what happened later that night) that Kasavubu had the connivance and help of the United Nations in his *coup,* but the hours we spent waiting in the Royal in complete uncertainty are sufficient refutation of the charge. Whether he had consulted and obtained the tacit blessing of Clare Timberlake, the American Ambassador, seems possible but unlikely. At ONUC we had no means of gauging his movements or intentions; we were preoccupied with our own problems.

Unknown to us, Kasavubu had not been wasting his time; under the constitution he had as President the power to appoint or dismiss prime ministers, and he had already drafted a proclamation dismissing Lumumba and six of his most trusted ministers from office and appointing Joseph Ileo (a member of his own ABAKO Party), as the new Prime Minister.

At exactly 8.15 p.m., we heard Kasavubu announce this action in a broadcast that set out his reasons. These were short but concise; Lumumba, he claimed, was arrogating too much power to himself and was on the verge of plunging the country into civil war.

The broadcast ended abruptly; looking around the room where we were gathered about Uncle Andy, it was impossible not to detect an atmosphere of relief, almost of satisfaction. I caught myself wondering whether someone might not have guessed this had been in the air. And yet it was impossible to detect. I saw the inscrutable oriental face of a Formosan Chinese, the dark features of a Haitian, the hard controlled features of the western types. Had they known? Had they guessed? Even to this day I do not know.

By the time Lumumba got wind of the broadcast and was hurrying to the radio station, Kasavubu had gone quietly back to his home whence he put in a telephone call requesting UN protection. We sent a detachment of Moroccans, which was already on its way to his residence, as Lumumba arrived at the radio station to launch the first of three counterbroadcasts denouncing Kasavubu's action.

Claiming that the President had no right to dismiss a prime minister and was, in any case, nothing better than an imperialist stooge, he assured his listeners that *he* was dismissing Kasavubu and warned the United Nations and the Western Powers to stand right outside the issue—in which they had no right to interfere.

This was repeated three times on an increasingly hysterical and hostile note between nine o'clock and ten thirty. It left us with an uneasy feeling that the next step was likely to be the arrival of Russian planes from Stanleyville at N'Djili airport, landing disorganized mobs of ANC, who would pour into the capital. Overhanging this disquieting prospect of civil war was the suspicion that the Russians might soon launch out into a major airlift to support Lumumba. Now the die was cast, he was certain to turn to them for help. Once that happened, ONUC would be in real danger of losing control.

My own reaction was quite straightforward; when Cordier asked for my opinion, I told him that it was essential to prevent interference with our air communications. I could see no other way out but the immediate closing of all main airports, and I felt certain that, in our own interests, we had no alternative but to act swiftly. Cordier listened and nodded; at this crucial moment he was as solid and immovable as a rock. Calm and objective, he took his time in weighing up the problem. Nothing could hurry him, but when at last he had made up his mind, his voice was firm and incisive, his orders clear and to the point. There was no shilly-shallying, no last-minute agonized reappraisal. He simply told us to close all the airfields except to UN traffic. He had no time to consult with Dag; it was his own decision, and the orders went out immediately.

At ONUC, we were 100 per cent behind this action. We were proved right the following morning when at a much reduced cabinet meeting Lumumba took his own emergency measures, imposed a curfew in Léopoldville, and, too late, announced that he was taking over control of all internal and external communications. Throughout that morning a stream of violent denunciations poured out from the broadcasting station, becoming so inflammatory that Cordier decided they were a direct incitement to civil war and, at lunchtime, ordered me to send troops to take over the station and suspend all broadcasting.

This was an extremely tricky operation. Because we did not want to precipitate fighting around the studio, we sent in a UN expert accompanied by a guard, who removed a "vital element" from the transmitting station. It was swiftly done, and avoided a clash that might have placed us at a serious disadvantage. The air, however remained very much alive. Soon the wavelengths were filled with rival broadcasts by Kasavubu and his supporters from Radio Congo over the river at Brazzaville. Perhaps this was one of the reasons why Cordier's action has been attacked for hampering Lumumba to Kasavubu's considerable advantage. As it turned out, this may have been the way the cards fell, but never for a moment had there been any political bias in his decision; it had been motivated solely by the urgent need to prevent civil war and safeguard our own operations.

The success he achieved was evident in the lack of disturbances in the streets and boulevards during the next few days (despite feverish activity behind the scenes by Joseph Ileo to form a new cabinet). An uneasy peace brooded over the capital, a half silence in which the oversensitive UN ear might have detected the distant sound of knives being sharpened for Cordier in New York where Dag, who had backed him staunchly, was facing a mounting offensive from an infuriated Soviet bloc, and was under heavy pressure from the African States.

On September 8, Dag's new special representative Rajeshwar Dayal arrived, a hawk-nosed Indian of great personal charm, whose calm and aloof bearing was often mistaken for arrogance. I remembered him well from UNOCIL days where his maxim had always been: "Never get excited. Once people lose their heads, it's impossible to make sense." I had the feeling that he was going to be hard put to it in the Congo where everyone invariably got excited.

Although I was glad to see him I was very sad to see Cordier go. We had been through a tough time together, and I would never forget him as a fearless, altogether splendid chief. But as I said good-bye it was difficult to escape the suspicion that his resolute action had not set the seal on a distinguished United Nations career; he had done the right thing, but we knew, too, that it would be held against him; there was no doubt in any of our minds about that.

Dayal set out immediately to call on Lumumba and Kasavubu,

but the result could only be described as "a mixed bag"; Lumumba accused the United Nations of gross interference in Congolese internal affairs; Kasavubu merely informed Dayal that it was a waste of time to bother with Lumumba since his Government had ceased to exist. Dayal, however, is not a man who is easily discouraged and set himself to discover a formula that would allow us to reopen the airports and the radio station without precipitating some fresh outbreak of trouble between the two rivals. Not that the prospects looked promising; on September 9, we learned that the ANC had refused an order from Lumumba to retake the airport. Two days later a Ghanaian guard under a redoubtable British subaltern had to restrain Lumumba and his bodyguards from forcing their way into the radio station.

On September 12, however, the radio station *was* reopened, and over the next two days all airports were opened up to normal traffic again. By this time Lumumba was no longer in any position to exercise much authority. On the 12th he had been arrested by units of the ANC which supported Kasavubu and taken to Camp Léopold, but had shortly afterward been set free by a group of the ANC.

After this episode, he became preoccupied with an attempt to persuade Parliament to ignore the new Ileo Government and grant him full power to resume his old authority and position. Partly because of his eloquence and the very real following he commanded, and partly because he had taken care to pack the Assembly Chamber with large numbers of voteless but none the less persuasive ANC supporters, he got his way although there were certain strings attached. But his triumph was short-lived; the following day, Kasavubu riposted by dissolving Parliament.

Into this stalemate stepped a figure I had come to know quite well. Colonel Joseph Mobutu, who hailed from Equateur Province, was a serious-looking man, a devout Catholic, and virtually the only Congolese officer who was capable of exerting any real guiding influence over the ANC. Mobutu, an emotional type, was on excellent terms with the only two really efficient officers in the ANC—Colonel Kokolo, who commanded the garrison in Léopoldville, and Colonel Bobozo, in Thysville. Both these officers were command material even though their experience had hitherto been on the NCO level. As Victor Lundula, the Commander in Chief, was still stranded up in Stanleyville, Mobutu found himself in a position of strength.

Toward evening on September 14, his voice came clearly over the air from the reopened radio station. His message was short but dramatic; he was staging a "peaceful revolution," had decided to "neutralize" Kasavubu, Lumumba, Ileo, and the Houses of Parliament for a period of three months, and would call in technicians to run the country and get it out of its present difficulties.

This news was surprising but not unwelcome. From General Kettani, my Deputy Commander, who had recently been appointed to reorganize the ANC, I gathered the *coup* was a result of a meeting of officers in Camp Léopold that had been going on all that morning and afternoon. Passions had run high among the ANC, which now contained not a single private—everyone had promoted himself one rank up. Still unpaid, they cherished the utmost contempt for politicians, and were all for violent action. A moderate man, Mobutu had been alarmed at some of their suggestions; since it was plain a revolution of some sort was inevitable, he had decided to take the plunge while there was still a chance of keeping it under reasonable control.

Kasavubu and Lumumba were both taken completely by surprise, but the most striking evidence of the new regime was a message that night to the Soviet bloc embassies that they had exactly forty-eight hours in which to pack up and get out of the country.

At ONUC, we had a flood of calls from alarmed satellite diplomats requesting official protection. Before midnight extra Ghanaian guards had been posted at the Soviet and Czech embassies; Kasavubu remained discreetly in his guarded residence, but Lumumba rushed up to Camp Léopold to search for Mobutu. Unable to find him, he unwisely stayed the night and next morning. Ghanaian troops had to rescue him from a crowd of infuriated ANC who blamed him for the deaths of their fellow tribesmen in Kasai. During the *mêlee* his briefcase vanished; its contents—including appeals to Russia and China and the famous letters from Nkrumah advising him how to set up a Congolese dictatorship—found their way to Mobutu; published soon afterward, these documents—which included recommendations for torture—caused a wave of hostility at home and abroad.

There was an excessively turbulent atmosphere about the next few days. Then tension could almost be felt in the air. On the afternoon of September 15, Dayal refused Kasavubu's and Ileo's request that he should arrest Lumumba. Next day Mobutu and his ANC arrived at the parliament buildings and forcibly ejected a stream of volubly protesting deputies and senators. By this time our units in Léopoldville were tightly stretched, patroling the streets, guarding the radio station, and "protecting" a dozen or so cabinet ministers, and the Russian, Czech, Ghanaian, and Guinea Embassies—where a flurry of hasty packing was going on.

Fortunately there was now an excellent Sudanese battalion out at N'Djili airport, magnificently proportioned and disciplined soldiers whom I discovered had come straight from a remote garrison in the Sudan's deep South without having had a chance to set eyes on their wives and families for the past eighteen months. But our job of forming a tight protective screen around the airfield was complicated by the arrival in my office of Colonel S. Shazli of the UAR battalion with the highly unpalatable information that should his company of Egyptian paratroopers, which was stationed there, be called on to use force, his "orders" were that they were not to open fire.

I was amazed to see him; he should have been seven hundred miles up-country with his battalion at Gemena. But once I had told him what I thought about his interpretation of his duties, I agreed to withdraw the company into a temporary camp from which they would be sent up-river again. Shazli's "orders" had clearly come direct from President Nasser. It was a waste of breath to argue with him and I told him to return at once to his battalion up-country.

Several days later, I was outraged to discover him still in Léopoldville, ardently requesting that his company should remain in the capital. This time, I did not mince words. He left abruptly, and a day or so later my staff informed me that the company had returned up-river. A week went by before it was found that they were *still* in the capital. On inquiry, we discovered that this was not the original company but another that had sneaked downriver, on Cairo's orders, to replace it. I immediately asked for Shazli to be sent home to Egypt.

Lumumba's downfall had a sharp reaction on the behavior of other UN units. My next visitor was a melancholy five-star general whose suggestion that I sign him on as a sort of personal military adviser had been discreetly rejected a month earlier. General L. Diane of Guinea, who had been a veterinary surgeon's assistant before embracing the *servitudes et grandeurs* of the military life,* was President Sekou Touré's personal military "private eye" in Léopoldville. Now he told me that the Guinea battalion was itching to abandon its swamps and jungles around Banningville and Mushie to return to a more active role in the capital.

With visions of their antitank and light aircraft guns, their heavy mortars, machine guns, and plethora of commissars, I was determined that this was the one thing they were *not* going to do; I had no intention of exacerbating the situation in the capital by providing the ex-Prime Minister with a private bodyguard. I expressed my regrets, but told Diane that I was distressed to see him looking so pale and unwell, a stratagem that elicited a rapid switch to a more personal vein.

He was, I gathered, a devoted family man with eleven children who found the burden of separation hard to bear. There were, too, a number of other factors, which I have forgotten now, contributing to his general antipathy for the unsympathetic climate of Léopoldville. I assured him that I would do everything in my power to arrange a respite for him in his own country, so that he could make his brood a round dozen strong! Diane departed with a much more springy step; the Guinea battalion remained among its swamps and jungles.

General Mobutu's *coup* brought a marked, if temporary, degree of stabilization. On September 17, N'Djili airport saw the mass departure of the inflated staffs of the Soviet bloc embassies. The following day we held a conference with Mobutu and were successful in persuading him to withdraw the ANC from Kasai and call off the attack on Katanga.

I was impressed with his attitude. He was realistic; his dark,

* See Alfred de Vigny's classic, though I doubt whether even he could have visualized the *demands* the Congo made on a soldier's sense of duty! *Author.*

rather melancholy face would light up occasionally with a flash of humor, but it was obvious that he was a dedicated man who had his country's interest at heart and was not afraid to face up to unpleasant facts. I had the distinct impression that he was deeply chagrined at the failure of the plans he had carefully worked out for the attack through Kasai—only to see them disintegrate through the total incapacity of his troops.

For the moment it seemed the capital was likely to remain quiet. Mobutu was soon busy creating a "College of Commissioners," an elite corps of young educated Congolese who were to take over the administration, and I took the chance to fly up to Kasai where Colonel Lasmar and his Tunisians had been having a difficult time.

I sent a signal advising him of my arrival in Luluabourg, but the state of our communications was still so unsatisfactory that it was not to arrive until an hour before I was leaving at the end of my visit. Although he was not expecting me, I found Lasmar very much on his toes. Until the Central Government offensive had started, he had had little difficulty in preventing outbreaks of tribal trouble. But once the arsenals had been opened up and the rifles, mortars, heavy machine guns, and armored cars handed over to the ANC, there had been little the Tunisians could do except protect the hordes of refugees. As more ANC troops had been airlifted in from Stanleyville, Kalonji had fled into Katanga and the BaLuba who supported him had been shot in droves or speared and hunted through the jungle by the ANC and bands of triumphant Luluas. A trail of burned villages and looted European houses had been blazed across the diamond province right up to the Katanga border.

Now that the ANC were about to pull out there were new troubles. Large bands of well-armed tribesmen, led by European officers, were pushing in from Katanga and it seemed likely the Luluas were about to be slaughtered in their turn. It was a bloody and unpleasant war and had virtually severed our rail connections from Port Francqui to Katanga and Kivu provinces. Lasmar had done his best to control the situation where the river barges coming up from Léopoldville unloaded supplies at the vital railhead of Port Francqui—but it was one thing to keep order in the town;

once out in the country all the rail routes had been cut or disrupted.

I visited the hospital where numbers of wounded Tunisians and Congolese were evidence that Lasmar had been exercising his own discretion as to when and how UN troops could defend themselves. The patients appeared blissfully unaware of any international complications and looked remarkably cheerful. Although most of the Tunisians were illiterate, I knew they must be missing news from home penned by the local letter writer or read aloud to them from the local newspapers by their more educated comrades. Unfortunately there was no mail and no papers—a blight that extended all the way through our units in the Congo.

Wherever I went, I was surprised at the high morale despite an almost total lack of the basic amenities that keep a soldier happy and contented. Letters—when they did eventually arrive—were often months late, there were few local newspapers (or even national ones) flown out from home, while their allowance for the dangerous and exacting work they had to do was a meager sixty-five Belgian francs a day—it had been only forty-five until I had had a stand-up battle with New York—compared with the three hundred drawn by civilian ONUC personnel, who for the most part sat in offices in comparative peace and comfort.

Even when they had been paid, there was little the troops could buy. For weeks I had been battling with New York to set up PX shops throughout the provinces, but so far only one had been opened in Léopoldville. I had issued strict instructions that no military or civilian personnel at Headquarters were to use it until arrangements had been made to distribute supplies up-country; with our dear civilians at the helm, this had been totally ignored.

All that my soldiers could spend their money on were a few necessities, toothpaste, cigarettes, and a little extra food while stocks remained in the few European shops. At the moment there was not the faintest prospect of leave in Léopoldville for shopping and recuperation. And yet they managed to remain cheerful and uncomplaining in a climate that was rapidly approaching the damp and humid season.

I found a similar stout-hearted spirit at Stanleyville when I flew on for a brief visit to Ethiopian Brigade Headquarters, which gave me the chance of thanking the brave Ethiopian nurse who had saved the lives of our Canadian signalers and American air crew such a short time before. She was a remarkable smiling girl who seemed to see nothing unusual about the risk she had taken.

I was deeply impressed by the Ethiopian Commander, Colonel Woldeyohans Shitta, who knew he was sitting on a powder barrel, but seemed as calm, collected, and well informed as though on peacetime maneuvers as he told me about the Lumumbists who were starting to arrive from Léopoldville. Colonel Shitta was skeptical about Mobutu's chances of being able to bring the provinces under control; he thought that everything from now on would hinge on tribal allegiances and pointed out that with two hundred tribes in the Congo, its evolution was destined to revert to a distressingly primitive stage.

I liked the Ethiopians very much. After a quick trip to another battalion at Bunia, I flew on to Kivu Province over country that suddenly ceased to be jungle and became a great vista of savannas and pastoral valleys dominated by the towering volcanic Ruwenzori Mountains in the distance.

It was not a pleasant trip; we had cracked a window on take-off, and as we began to climb through heavy cloud toward a pass in the mountains, it was unnervingly borne in on us that we were no longer pressurized. I don't know whether the sight of some unconscious bodies slumped in their seats or the knowledge that our pilot was flying blind frightened me most. Eventually, he negotiated the pass, brought us down into bright sunlight and there, on the Goma airstrip, were the saffron kilts and emerald-green doublets of the pipe band of the 32d Irish battalion.

Colonel Murt Buckley of Cloghan Offaly may have been surprised at the fervent warmth of my handshake; I was pleased to see him, but even more delighted to be on the ground again. I spent a day with his battalion, which organized a magnificent singsong; listening, I was again impressed by their high morale—though God knows they had plenty to complain about. Their private views on the Congo and United Nations service were something they stoically kept to themselves or doubtless reserved for Buckley and the Rev. C. P. Cream, their chaplain who, as father figures, played an admirable role.

The men had arrived dressed in thick serge uniforms that conjured up visions of the days when Irish soldiers in the British regiments had fought and sweated and dropped from heat prostration under burning Indian skies. Since ONUC was unable to provide them with tropical kit, Buckley had made use of his authority to purchase local supplies, and every European and Congolese with any knowledge of tailoring in the district had been pressed into service. The result might have been frowned on in colonial days, but with a few tucks here and there, the battalion looked smart and serviceable and could operate in comparative comfort. But here again, off duty, there was no mail, no local papers, and only a few copies of the ONUC news sheet, *Tam Tam,* hastily compiled by journalists with little experience of the sort of news soldiers really like to read.

At Kabalo, I visited a unit I was very sorry to be losing, but the breakup of the Federation of Mali meant that the Sudanese and Senegalese who composed the Mali battalion would soon be going home. Although I could give them no news in reply to their eager questions, there was no shortage of beaming grins on the otherwise ferocious faces of these gigantic warriors. The huge Sudanese looked quite short alongside the towering Senegalese, whose filed teeth glinted in the sun. This was a first-rate battalion, and I hated to see them go. Under the able guidance of Colonel Mademba Sy their very appearance had been enough to instill order into the most troublesome district.

At Albertville, a pleasant town on the edge of the great lake, I found Lieut. Colonel Dick Bumworth of Clontarf, near Dublin, with the 33d Irish battalion. Albertville is a town of some importance and forms the Katanga end of the ship link to Kigoma in Tanzania on the other side of this huge inland sea. From Kigoma, seven hundred and eight miles of railway wind down to the deep ocean port of Da-res-Salaam. This was the real way in for the Malayan and Indonesian battalions, which I knew were on their way by sea to reinforce us.

We needed them badly and I had suggested that they should be brought in over this quick and effective route. New York and Washington, however, had other ideas; just before leaving Léopoldville, I heard that the battalions had been routed round the

Cape to Matadi, which meant wasted months before we saw them in Katanga. From Matadi the railway runs only to Léopoldville; unless there was air transport available, the remainder of the journey would have to be made by slow-moving river barge.

Time and again I was delighted with the humor that seemed to keep the Irish going under handicaps that would have driven the average European to despair. Colonel Henry Byrne, from Rathgar near Dublin, was a typical example. I stayed with him a night on my way through Elizabethville. Henry commanded all our forces in Katanga. His headquarters were in a *Union Minière* building, where he was operating under great difficulties and having to make do with what he could purchase locally. Transport was an especial nightmare; the average battalion needs about a hundred vehicles to keep operational, and our units had arrived with only a few jeeps. It had been possible to purchase a number of trucks locally, but the shortage of spare parts was proving a nightmare. Byrne told me it was impossible to mount the number of patrols that ought to have been going out—an unsatisfactory state of affairs that was to lead to unnecessary losses later on.

The troops were often suffering a considerable degree of physical discomfort; the food and clothing bought locally was usually of poor quality and there was an acute shortage of bedding. Although many Belgian houses were still standing empty, the majority of the men had been billeted in schools, church halls, or empty administrative buildings where most of the Irish were sleeping on stretchers.

As I listened to Colonel Byrne, it was difficult to disguise my own resentment at this evidence of the inefficiency of the Field Operations Service. I told him of one of my own experiences in Léopoldville during the early days when my supply staff had consisted of two officers and my two missionary helpers. It had begun with the arrival of a large consignment of tinned food, which had a remarkable history. The story had started when New York accepted a tender from a Hamburg firm for large quantities of tinned fruit, vegetables, and fruit juice. As soon, however, as it was discovered these had been tinned in Israel, the order had to be canceled. Even New York realized what the reaction of the large numbers of Muslim troops were likely to be on being issued tins bearing Israeli labels.

However, hardly had the cancelation been made before the outraged cries of Jewish businessmen were heard, to such an extent that the Israeli Permanent Delegate in New York was soon accusing the United Nations of racial discrimination. This indictment fell like a thunderclap on oversensitive UN ears, the cancelation was hastily rescinded, and in due course the tins, with their vivid Israeli labels, appeared at N'Djili airport with orders that the Supreme Commander should have them relabeled and issued to the unsuspecting Muslims. Specially printed labels were flown out, and Geoffrey Hunt and his staff of four (assisted by an apathetic squad of indolent Congolese) were faced with having personally to relabel thousands of tins at a time when their entire energies were needed to instill order into the chaotic jumble of stores and equipment being unloaded every day for transit up-country by rail or barge. Both Byrne and I smiled wryly; there was little one could do in the Congo but grin and bear it.

Chapter Seventeen

FINANCING FIELD OPERATIONS

As our plane came into sight of the familiar high concrete buildings of Léopoldville and its suburbs stretching for eight miles along the mud-colored banks of the Congo River, I wondered what new crisis might be waiting. But there was an atmosphere of tranquility at the Royal, Dayal was his normal, imperturbable self, and I learned that Dag had won a major victory in the General Assembly, obtaining a vote of confidence despite a full-scale attack launched by Mr. Khrushchev and the Soviet bloc over Cordier's handling of the September crisis.

Although Dag had been backed by the African States, relations with our own African opposite numbers in Léopoldville were not encouraging. Mobutu's close alliance with Kasavubu, reflected in the ring of ANC troops which acted as a sort of outer perimeter to our own Ghanaian guards around Lumumba's residence, had caused a deep split that was particularly evident in the provinces. Only Equateur seemed anxious to collaborate with the new regime; Oriental was already a Lumumbist stronghold, despite an attempted *coup* by pro-Mobutu troops in Stanleyville. One reason was immediately apparent. Mobutu's "young men," who had been drawn from the ranks of a paucity of Congolese graduates, were willing enough to try to govern, but their complete lack of practical experience had resulted in an influx of Belgian advisers; indeed, one's first impression in Léopoldville was that the Belgians had returned in strength. Nor were they at all well disposed toward us; whereas a couple of months ago they had greeted us as saviors, offered us their homes, cars, and worldly possessions—anything so long as it could be got under UN protection—there was now a very different attitude, a resentment fast turning to hostility and already hampering our civilian operations, which Dayal had now taken under his personal wing.

Their return had sparked off violent repercussions among Lumumba's extremely strong and numerous supporters. Scenting trouble, I was anxious—after what I had just seen up-country—to insure that our troops were properly equipped and at a high pitch of readiness. But although I discovered Dayal a satisfactory man to work with, and was no longer tied by an umbilical cord to Headquarters, the factors mitigating against our supporting and maintaining them on a satisfactory operational basis remained implacable as ever.

Language in itself was a problem. ONUC was now composed of individuals and units drawn from twenty-nine nations. Although our basic working speech was English, I had instituted a bilingual procedure whereby all orders and instructions from headquarters were issued in English and French. Unfortunately, we were so short of bilingual officers that translation was often delayed over forty-eight hours, and the task threw a tremendous burden on the few officers proficient in both languages. We suffered a similar shortage of bilingual staff officers in the provinces, where French was a necessity for dealing with the local Congolese administrators and ANC commanders. By now we had set up territorial commands with their own headquarters situated in each provincial capital. But although these were now in more or less satisfactory W/T communication with Léopoldville, they were frequently out of contact with the short range, organic sets of their units out in the bush or jungle.

Our territorial commands were hampered, too, by lack of close consultation and collaboration from the Civilian Operations teams although they often shared the same buildings. Controlled from Léopoldville, where Linner and Dayal were already at loggerheads, these teams consisted of a political officer, a civilian operations official, and an administrative officer. In theory, they should have worked hand in glove with our local commanders—and in one or two places this did happen, to mutual advantage. On the whole, however, the two organizations tended to work in separate compartments. The result was that much information gathered by the civilians, which would have been invaluable in helping our commanders to anticipate events and plan a suitable course of action, was simply channeled back to Léopoldville, and too often became lost in the cavernous depths of filing cabinets.

Early on, we had gleaned invaluable information from monitoring the ANC sets. But Intelligence was a dirty word in the Congo, and monitoring was taken over by the civilians. From then on nothing they learned was ever passed back to us. I was disappointed to get very little help from Brigadier Rikhye in trying to solve these difficult problems. When, after coming out with Dag to Elizabethville as his military adviser, he had stayed on in Léopoldville with a sort of watching brief, I had felt confident that I would have someone to turn to for support who, as an experienced soldier, would appreciate the serious drawbacks that were hampering our operations.

I had know Rikhye as General Burns's very capable Chief of Staff in Gaza. I had liked him and always thought him a practical soldier. But it did not take me long to realize that, in the course of his climb into the rarefied atmosphere of the Secretariat, Rikhye's ideas and attitudes had undergone a subtle change; like other soldiers before him, he had developed political ambitions. I discovered, too, to my dismay that he had adopted Ralph's method of issuing orders direct to my staff.

How different it might have been had he tried to help me with our urgent problems instead of sitting at Dayal's right hand at the political high table. His assistance would have been invaluable in trying to make New York understand what we were up against.

The rainy season was almost on us; soon the sandy tracks linking the few main roads in the interior would become a sea of mud, despite the efforts of our men to bind them by cutting down the high grass that towered on either side. Supply was bound to become a nightmare; we had only two of the eight movement control teams we had asked for, since most of the other personnel that had arrived had proved so unsuitable that we had had to transfer them to other jobs.

Matadi, where the port had been opened and more than twenty steamers had come in to dock, was now our main source of supply. Once the stores had been unloaded here, the railway functioned reasonably well up to Léopoldville, but from then on everything had to be sent up-country in big river barges towed by diesel tugs. It often seemed a miracle that so much got through; all but a handful of the Belgian skippers had left, and we were functioning haphazardly because we did not have a single experienced water transport officer who could take over and coordinate the barge traffic. So far supplies were reaching our units in Léopoldville, Equateur, and Oriental provinces, but beyond River Head at Port Francqui our supply system into Kasai, Kivu, and Katanga had been seriously disrupted.

As a result, our units in these provinces were heavily dependent on air transport. From the beginning we had had to rely far too much for my liking on aircraft chartered from the local airline—a subsidiary of the Belgian Sabena Air Company—still operating in the Congo. Although we were using a number of our own C.119s (now nearly obsolete). a serious shortage of spare parts made it a constant nightmare to keep them operational.

Ever since I arrived, I had pointed out that the only basis on which our air component could function satisfactorily was through member states providing their own ethnic squadrons complete with flying personnel and ground crews. But up to this time we had been given only one Indian and one Italian C.119 squadron. And we had been told to create transport and recce-liaison squadrons out of a heterogeneous conglomeration of jet fighter and transport pilots, whose varied languages created a Tower of Babel atmosphere. We were also badly in need of new reconnaissance and fighter squadrons to replace our short-range Otters, Super Pipers, and Beavers. And coming back to our vital airlift problem, the real need was to replace our C.119s with C.124s (the ideally suitable new Globemasters) that would virtually double our carrying capacity, halve our present transport problems, and make shortages of outdated spare parts a thing of the past.

Objections, based on financial grounds, came in thick and fast from New York. These were doubtless valid enough in view of the vast amounts the Congo operations were costing, and I could accept them reluctantly although I knew that sooner or later sheer force of circumstances would impel a change of attitude whatever the financial burdens. By contrast, I found it impossible to accept the sort of stinting that was bound to have an adverse effect on the morale of the troops.

Here I had to fight a lonely and unceasing battle. I knew only too well that the troops had begun to look on themselves as second-class UN citizens. Living expenses in the Congo were high and their special allowances (which I had had to battle like a tiger to get increased) was only sixty-five Belgian francs a day, the equivalent of $1.25. This was little enough to supplement our own tottering supply system and a diet of local produce thickened up with refrigerated meat, corned beef, sardines, dried peas and beans, and a meager issue of tea and cocoa.

Food aside, I had wrung agreement from New York to bear the expense of having magazines and newspapers flown out from home, but my request for an adequate supply of 16mm movie projectors had fallen on deaf ears. A weekly film show would have given our soldiers enormous pleasure and an event to which they could look forward. Instead there was virtually nothing to occupy their leisure hours; not surprisingly, reports of drunkenness and traffic accidents while under the influence of imported or local firewater were beginning to multiply.

Despite all these difficulties, our soldiers' health remainded surprisingly good. (I had long ago co-opted the senior Medical Officer of the Ghana Brigade to organize hospitals on a territorial basis to supplement the efforts of the hard-worked unit medical officers.) He had done sterling work. And when he had gone, Colonel B. L. Kapoor, a very capable Indian medical officer, had taken his place. His task had been eased by the arrival of the 152d Indian Army General Hospital, whose commander, Lieut. Colonel H. J. Bannerjee, established a main hospital in Léopoldville with smaller hospitals at Luluabourg and Coquilhatville. We were fortunate in having a Swiss hospital in the capital, too, although, since Switzerland is not a member of the UN, this was not under our command.

Later on, we were to be well served by an Italian hospital in Katanga and an Austrian one at Bukavu in Kivu Province. But just now we were very hard pressed and with the rainy season on us, plus the increase in humidity and the unwelcome appearance of a plethora of mosquitoes, poisonous spiders, hornets, and snakes, I was hardly anticipating a sharp rise in morale. I had issued all units with an adequate supply of vitamin pills to make up the deficiencies in their diet, but the hard living conditions, lack of amenities, and the necessity to remain constantly on the alert, were bound to take their toll in a sharply rising sick list over the next few months.

Although long-term measures were hopelessly hampered by the lack of reality in New York, I concentrated on two immediate short-term priorities. First, I wanted to establish the troops in suitable camps or barracks, where mutual proximity would decrease the feeling of being left out alone in the wilds, and make it easier to maintain *esprit de corps*.

In Léopoldville, most of our men were living in private houses, good enough accommodation, but often widely scattered. To bring them closer together, I had already selected an excellent site for a concentrated camp at Limete. Unfortunately, the Administration was so slow that it was snatched from under our noses by the ANC, whose own quarters at Camp Léopold and Luluabourg were remarkably luxurious. Not even in the prewar barracks of the German Wehrmacht had I seen anything to equal them; each private had his own washbasin, and the rooms were the height of comfort and privacy. In contrast, our own troops remained doomed to less affluent conditions; apart from five seven-story buildings opposite the Royal commandeered for headquarter units, they were destined to occupy makeshift quarters until the whole unhappy Congo operation petered out to its predestined end.

My second priority was based on something dear to most soldiers' hearts. Jokes abound about "fruit salad" on the military chest, but I have never yet come across a soldier who did not like to feel that hardship and risk deserve recognition. I knew what a powerful stimulant to morale the news would exert that a special bar was being struck for service in the Congo. It would add luster to the general blue and white UN Medal, something quite special that "old Congo hands" could show their children, denoting service in the Congo. But I had reckoned without Ralph Bunche's firm belief that the cause of peace needed no "campaign" flavor to distinguish service that *should be* an honor in itself. He raised a string of objections that delayed the whole project until the Swedes in Elizabethville lost patience and commissioned a medal complete with bar of their own. It was struck in Stockholm and flown out with the familiar ribbons in the space of four weeks at a cost of $0.53 each. Seldom have troops stumped up with such alacrity. But even faced with a *fait accompli,* Ralph refused to capitulate until long after I had left the Congo.

Had there been time to brood, I don't doubt I should have become a chronic martyr to frustrated indigestion during these critical months. But the fact that my advice was consistently disregarded by New York—which seemed blissfully out of touch with reality—merely stimulated me into a permanent state of rebellion.

I realized nothing was going to divert New York from trying to run ONUC as though it were a sort of glorified UNEF or UNOGIL: duplicating their mistakes but never emulating their merits, or showing signs of the fresh and original thinking that was so desperately needed. Even though it meant battering one's head against a brick wall, I was determined never to cease trying; demands of conscience—above all my obligations to my long-suffering troops—made the eternal struggle infinitely worthwhile.

There were lighter moments. While Dayal remained closeted in the Royal, composing a monumental report for New York, and

Mobutu temporarily turned his attentions from politics to trying to reorganize the ANC, I had the pleasure of welcoming an advance party from the Indonesian 2d Garuda Regiment, whose inquiries about recreational facilities (in other words, dancing girls and other shapely home comforts) I found politic to refer to my staff. Somehow, I felt they were unlikely to discover much talent in the outstations I had assigned them around Coquilhatville. But I awaited news of their prowess up-country with a certain trepidation because their predecessors in UN service—the 1st Garudas at Gaza—had left us with the impression that every Indonesian battalion required the ancillary service of a full-strength company of military police.

My fears turned out to be ill-founded. After the 2d Garudas arrived at Matadi and were posted up-country, we discovered ONUC had acquired a very valuable asset. When my plane touched down at Coquilhatville on a visit to them a month later, an impressive Guard of Honor was waiting. So impressive was the array that when Captain Tendy advanced toward me, short, barrel-chested, muscular. stern visaged, and bearing a heavy, broad-bladed sword, I had a momentary pang lest I were due for decapitation! He had, however, merely come to invite me to inspect the Guard, and as I followed him down those ranks of short, tough, and immaculately turned-out men, I had the distinct feeling that these were soldiers who had learned their trade the hard way. Nor was I mistaken; the training displays exhibited later beneath the respectful gaze of a large crowd of local ANC were admirable.

Their quarters, too, were spotless. When I complimented their commander, Lieut. Colonel Solichin, on the high standard of turn-out and the obvious ability of his men to take care of themselves in a tight corner, I was hard put not to try to discover something about the experiences that had gone into the making of such a first-class unit. With a suspicion of a smile, he gave me the answer in a nutshell.

"Well, sir. It was like this. First we were trained by the Dutch, then the Japanese, and finally the British—and we fought them all!"

The Indonesians soon compelled the respectful cooperation of the local ANC through beating them at soccer and the sheer meaningful purpose of their disciplined bearing. But in Léopoldville our relations with this turbulent force were still unsatisfactory. For some weeks now General Kettani and a number of officers, seconded from the Royal Moroccan Army, had been established in Camp Léopold. But their efforts to reorganize and train the human material there had been gravely hampered by the ANC's disorderly habits.

It was their normal custom to turn up only when they felt like it—so that most units undergoing retraining were short of about 50 per cent of their effective strength. There was, however, one exception; ever since the withdrawal of the Belgians, the burning ambition of the Congolese had been to have their own parachute units. Here, at least, Kettani's instructors were not hampered by a shortage of recruits; one para commando unit was almost ready to do its practice drops; others were approaching a reliable state of discipline and training.

Unfortunately, Kettani had found it impossible even so much as to lay the foundations for a reliable gendarmerie. The need was vital but the task hopeless; new recruits would be signed on, drill for a couple of days, then melt away to their homes, taking whatever equipment they had been able to acquire with them. Having joined dissident elements of the ANC, they would be out in the city within days on private looting forays.

The situation became so acute that Kamitatu, the premier of Léopoldville Province (who was still, on paper at any rate, one of Lumumba's ministers) accused Mobutu of being incapable of keeping order and called on us to police the whole city. As he qualified this with the ominous warning that unless the situation improved, provincial governments would be justified in mobilizing their own citizens to protect property, it was hardly surprising that Mobutu clapped him under arrest. Prudently, however, he succeeded in patching up the quarrel and was soon in circulation again—unlike General Victor Lundula who had slipped away to the Lumumbist stronghold of Stanleyville to raise the province against Mobutu.

We soon heard that Nasser had provided Lundula with sufficient funds to pay the ANC in the city, who celebrated this unusual occasion by suppressing the last signs of a pro-Mobutu *coup*.

Within days Oriental Province was in ferment, and contact between Stanleyville and the capital ceased. Soon our units were reporting that the Lumumbist regime was in control of the entire province.

At headquarters it was difficult to escape the feeling that the whole country was coming apart at the seams. Dayal consistently refused Mobutu's demands that he should arrest Lumumba and almost appeared to ignore him. It was not that Mobutu's new young men of the College of Commissioners lacked the spirit to take over the country. Often they had outstanding qualities and their lack of experience was compensated by shrewd Belgian advice; the tragedy lay in the fact that the means simply did not exist. At places where Mobutu had scraped up sufficient money to pay the ANC there was a degree of what passed for authority; at others the troops remained apathetic or simply faded into the bush to rejoin their tribal relations at the first sign of a call to duty.

Although fighting between anti-Tshombé tribesmen and the gendarmerie dragged on along the Katanga border, and General Rikhye had to fly up there to establish a neutral zone on the northern frontier, the real struggle for power was in Léopoldville where it was becoming increasingly apparent that Dayal had made up his mind not to cooperate with Mobutu's College of Commissioners.

When he finally sent his report to the United Nations outlining his views, there can be no doubt that its tone and contents came as a very real encouragement to Lumumba and his supporters. Dayal was a man who certainly knew his own mind, and his report burst like a bombshell in the troubled capital. It plainly had no time for and virtually denigrated Mobutu, bitterly attacked the Belgians both in Léopoldville and Katanga as the prime cause of the bad relationship between the Congolese and ONUC, and stated flatly that the reappearance of Belgian advisers had exacerbated unrest in the ANC.

Dayal was quite specific in his recommendations. His view was that the only two institutions through which a peaceful settlement between rival politicial interests could be reached were the Head of State and the Houses of Parliament. In other words, he completely rejected the authority of Mobutu and his College of Commissioners and added fuel to the flames by violently criticizing the discipline of the ANC which Mobutu, nominally at any rate, controlled.

The uproar was terrific. The Belgians were bitterly offended, and the Americans—who had placed great hopes on the Mobutu-Kasavubu Alliance—took umbrage. Mobutu's own reaction was predictable. The celebrations of October 24, when elements of all the UN national contingents marched smartly past the saluting base beneath the fluttering UN flag, were firmly boycotted.

I do not know whether Dag approved Dayal's report. I have a feeling he may have felt it unfortunate and mistimed. Certainly, we felt that Dayal had not displayed much talent for "making friends and influencing people." Even before its appearance our relations with the Tshombé regime had been badly strained, while the Lumumbists in Oriental Province frankly looked on us as enemies. Now on top of all this we would be facing outright hostility in Léopoldville.

Dayal's report—whether right or wrong—was, of course, a signpost along what would eventually become the blood-stained route into Katanga. But at this moment his refusal to recognize Mobutu and his College of Commissioners had the immediate effect of embittering feeling against us. Dayal might take the view that Mobutu, his Commissioners, and ANC had no legal status but for all practical purposes they were still in power in the capital.

It was difficult to assess what repercussions the report was likely to have in the provinces where secessionist tendencies, sparked off by the actions of the Lumumbists in Oriental, were adding to the general chaos. Although actual fighting was going on only in North Katanga and along the Kasai-Katanga border, it looked as though tribal loyalties and political rivalries were fast setting the scene for chaos and civil war throughout the whole country. Once this happened, our supply lines were bound to become seriously disrupted and we would become virtually dependent on air transport; If our units were drawn into the struggle, the means simply did not exist to keep them operational.

It looked as if all the chickens I had gloomily prophesied were coming home to roost at ONUC Headquarters. Our first shock came within a week of Dayal's report when we learned that a patrol of the 33d Irish battalion had been wiped out by tribesmen near the Katanga border. No doubt this sort of misfortune would not have happened to the battle-experienced Tunisians or Moroccans. But, although the Irish had no combat experience, one of the contributing causes was the shortage of vehicles that had precluded any chance of their being properly trained in patrol work.

For all I know, Lieutenant Kevin Gleeson and his ten men may have been on their first patrol when they drove up to inspect a damaged bridge fourteen miles south of Niemba. Although he knew there were tribesmen about, Lieutenant Gleeson and his men dismounted from their jeeps and walked toward the bridge. Not a single scout preceded them, and when Gleeson noticed a tribesman standing on the bridge, he greeted him with a cheery wave. The next thing he must have known was an arrow in the armpit while a hail of barbed shafts descended on his unsuspecting men from two hundred tribesmen waiting in ambush on either side of the road.

The Irish put up a brave fight, firing back from whatever cover they could find and killing eleven tribesmen before perishing in a last-ditch stand. Only one survivor crawled out of the bush when a relief patrol belatedly arrived; another was discovered two days later with severe head wounds and two arrows still embedded in his chest.

We had great difficulty recovering the bodies of those other gallant men. Eventually we were able to send them back to Dublin for an official funeral. One of them, Trooper Anthony Browne from Dublin, who had been only nineteen years old, was sadly mourned by ten little African orphans he had taken under his wing back at the base.

I admired the dignified way the Irish people took this news, but I found it impossible to escape a deep sense of involvement and I felt personal tragedy. This was heightened, no doubt, by the death of another splendid Irishman ten days earlier. Colonel Justin MacCarthy had been a personal friend as well as a trusted Deputy Chief of Staff; his death in a road accident had deeply saddened us at headquarters.

I felt it imperative to get away for a time and be with the troops, to escape from the stultifying atmosphere of the human antheap in the Royal. A couple of weeks before, I had revisited Colonel Lasmar in Luluabourg where his Tunisians were due to be relieved by Ghanaians. Taking my new ADC, Captain Bob Dontoh,* whom I had obtained after a bit of a struggle with General Alexander (who wanted me to house a British officer from the Ghana Brigade), I had driven with an armed escort through sixty miles of dense jungle to meet "Le Prince de Kasai." All along our route tribal fighting had left burned-out villages, and burned and looted cars had littered the road as we came out into fine rolling tableland.

Only on reaching Lake Makamba, some sixty miles from the city, had we discovered signs of peace and order again. Two bands (bugle and drums and brass) had greeted me with the Swedish National Anthem. And over a good lunch of mussels, lobster salad, chicken, cheese, fruit compote, coffee and cognac, it seemed as if war had temporarily receded in this haven of ordered existence.

It was only a fleeting moment; Lasmar's quiet résumé painted a picture of armed bands running wild along the northern border, tribal fighting, streams of refugees. It was clear the Ghanaians would have their hands full. For once, however, the ANC in Luluabourg were giving no trouble; Mobutu had found money to pay them and for the first time since Independence, they had something to spend.

Moments like these among my troops were precious. As I set off again this time, I found myself reflecting that, although there were nearly seventeen thousand of them here now, this was still ten thousand less than the Belgians had considered essential to control the Congo in peacetime. But quality can make up for quantity and the Moroccans whom I visited in Thysville with General Kettani were an excellent example as they swung past the saluting base at a lively French marching step. I could see that the martial strains of the band and the discipline and bearing of the troops were having a marked effect on the Congolese who had turned out to watch in great numbers. Of course, Kettani and his officers were well known to the ANC through their training cadres in the capital.

But at Thysville there seemed to be a special relationship, which

* A tall, likable Ghanaian captain.

I doubt existed anywhere else. This may have been helped by the influence of Colonel Bobozo, the local ANC commander (a regular who was soon to rise to the rank of Major General), but I had the impression that it went much deeper and sprang from a genuine admiration of the Moroccans' military qualities which the Congolese genuinely tried hard to emulate. How long it would last was another matter.

Next day I flew to Kindu in Kivu Province to say good-bye to the Malis, who at long last were to be relieved by the Malayan Battalion. Five hundred and twenty-seven strong, they were drawn up for inspection on a football field outside the town and I made them a farewell speech in French, which Johnny Berthiaume, my Military Assistant, had prepared. Because they had no band, they had chosen to march past singing. And now, company by company, they swung by, Sudanese and Senegalese in turn, singing in deep bass voices with a verve and purpose that moved one's heart.

I could not let them go without some token appreciation. And because my battle with Ralph was still raging over the medals, I had brought six ordinary UN medals that I had scrounged from UNTSO. I pinned them to the chests of two officers, two non-commissioned officers, and two privates—and how I wished I had had five hundred and twenty one more! Needless to say, they had managed to acquire a supply of champagne for luncheon where we were royally entertained with a ritual fire-eater's dance. I was glad that our three Congolese guests did not stay long.

Later, as respective District Commissioner and commanders of the local gendarmerie and ANC, they were to be responsible for dragging nine Italian airmen out of the Malayan battalion's mess at Kindu and hacking them to pieces. No suspicion of tragedy, however, marred the Malis' wonderful farewell singsong. I left them with real regret, having been made to promise never to visit Dakar without contacting the Old Comrades Association they were already busy forming: *L'Association des Anciens Berets Bleus*—an invitation I intend to keep.

Back in Léopoldville there was, for once, a pleasant surprise. Although General Alexander had now returned to Ghana, he often came down to visit the Brigade. By chance, he was in the capital now and apparently anxious to talk to me on a personal matter.

I was not sure what this presaged, but was quite ready to see him. Just before Johnny Berthiaume ushered him into my office, however, a sudden thought struck me.

"Hang on a minute," I said, and turned a heavy African panga, that was lying on my desk, so that it pointed to the door in the time-honored fashion of court-martial procedure when a verdict of "guilty" has been reached.

General Alexander never misses a trick. Those alert eyes took in the panga blade immediately. For an instant they lingered, then he looked at me.

"Good morning, General. I have come to apologize and make peace."

"Just a moment," I said, leaning forward to reverse the panga blade, "that makes all the difference." And then, looking at that familiar face: "I have been very disappointed at your behavior. But if you really mean what you say, I'm prepared to forget all about it, *provided* there is no, repeat no, recurrence."

Alexander lost no time in assuring me that he meant what he said. He made it plain, too, that from now on I could count on all the support he was able to give me. I do not know what had brought about this change of heart, but I welcomed it. For the first time since we had met, we were able to have a really candid discussion which we continued when he came to lunch with me at Flagstaff House.

Next day, at a return lunch given by my Ghanaian friend, Brigadier Steve Otu, it was obvious the Alexander-Horn peace treaty had become a working reality. It was a pleasant moment, but I have a feeling that the most relieved and delighted unit in the command was undoubtedly the Ghana Brigade.

Chapter Eighteen

SAYING GOOD-BYE

It seemed that nothing we could ever do in the Congo would make us either loved or wanted. In early September Andy Cordier's resolute action had made us a target of hatred for the Lumumbists and had created a lasting scar that would remain inflamed and ugly until the end. Now, two months later, Dayal's report had antagonized another powerful and resourceful element.

In a different way, Dayal had written *finis* to his consulship in the Congo as irrevocably as Cordier had ever done. Since the publication of his report, the Léopoldville radio station had poured out a stream of venom against Dayal in a steadily mounting offensive. Each broadcast was an incitement to violence in itself so that rumors of *coups* and "pushes" against ONUC headquarters were constantly circulating in the city. Our relations with Mobutu and his College of Commissioners had virtually ceased to exist. In fact at times Johnny Berthiaume was the only man through whom Dayal could contact them at all.

The Congolese flatly refused to deal directly with the special representative or his political assistants. In that damp and humid atmosphere, it was not difficult to imagine a new outbreak of violence that might isolate us like so many small besieged garrisons throughout the city. This could be only temporary. Our discipline and training would soon enable us to get the upper hand, *provided* our ammunition did not run out and we could hold the route open to N'Djili Airport fifteen miles away. But our rail communications with Matadi were certain to be cut and, although second-sight did not enable me to foresee the fate of the Irish at Jadotville the following year,* it required no psychic powers to realize that we were likely to find ourselves in a very tight corner.

One thing and one thing only counted in Léopoldville, where flowery diplomacy and the political acrobatics so beloved in New York were a pathetic waste of energy and breath. We might be here as peacekeepers, but we would have been very odd soldiers not to know that force was the sole element that impelled respect in this primitive country.

At the height of the tension—when rumors and counterrumors were running riot—I was relieved to welcome the Malayan battalion as it marched through the streets on its way from the railway station. From the outset, one could see this was a unit that meant business. Eighteen Ferret scout cars, with workmanlike-looking guns swiveling from their turrets, led the well-trained, disciplined companies of Malayans through the main streets and boulevards toward their quarters at the Chanic Building. The impression created was extremely marked and, although the inhabitants of Léopoldville consistently disliked them and nicknamed them *"Les sales Chinois,"* their arrival brought a lowering of tension in the capital.

Night after night, the new arrivals sallied out to inspect the delights of the city in threes, unarmed save for a broad-bladed, wicked-looking kris. But not a single Congolese hothead ever appeared anxious to pick a quarrel; much, I gather, to the disappointment of the Malayans, who regarded the Congolese as an inferior race sadly in need of being taught a salutary lesson.

This relaxation of tension gave me a chance to pay a brief visit to the UAR "Sheitan" battalion, seven hundred miles up the Congo River at Gebena. Colonel Shazli was still about and on arriving at Lisala, I was interested to observe the remains of a pancaked UAR plane that had certainly never been featured on our ONUC list of aircraft. I could not help wondering whether Shazli was still up to his old tricks.

* On a direct order from New York the ONUC command sent a company to Jadotville in September 1961 to protect white people. The allegations of these being threatened were later established as unfounded. The company was cut off, attacked, and after a week forced to surrender. Fortunately there was no loss of life—unlike the horrible incident at Port Francqui the same year when 120 Ghanaians and their British officers were killed.

The battalion was responsible for the two northwestern districts of Ubangi and Mongala, with detached companies to protect the airfields at Lisala and Libenge. As I took the salute at their headquarters in Gebena and watched the troops march past in commandeered transport or on foot at a not unimpressive "parachute trot," I would have been interested to know whether they were still receiving those "unofficial" orders that had already clashed radically with mine.

Later, as particular trouble was taken to divert me past a solid-looking building that turned out to be the jail, I had even more misgivings. It occurred to me that the inmates were unlikely to include anyone of pro-Lumumba sentiments. Nor, I imagined, could Linner's local political officer be having a very easy time. Politically we were, to all intents and purposes, inside an Egyptian sphere of influence.

The behavior of the "Sheitan" battalion is an object lesson to students of the troubles likely to beset any future United Nations force that includes units sent by Member States with a direct interest in their host country's internal affairs. I had learned the hard way what an adverse effect this could have on the conduct of operations. But despite my very frank report the Egyptian battalion was still firmly with us, and I doubted whether political factors would not always inhibit New York from drawing the obvious conclusion and taking steps to lay down some rule governing the national composition of the next mission that might have to be hastily scraped up and sent out whenever a new outbreak of trouble flared up in some distant but politically explosive corner of the world.

On the other hand, there was no doubt that the Congo would impose *some* lessons. The more one saw of the operation the more one came to feel that this was something unique, something so unusual and bizarre that it created a watershed in UN military history. From its inception it had been a hodgepodge, an intensely amateur throwing together of totally differentiated units. Accordingly, although on paper some norm might appear to exist, there was in practice such a variation of national, racial, and educational standards between units that every individual battalion must have stamped its own characteristics in coin of human behavior on the local population, which naturally accepted this as "United Nations behavior." Whatever reports and documents eventually emanated from New York to form the basis of the history of our operations in the Congo, the true feeling of these primitive people would never find its way into print; no intimate looking-glass mirror showing warts and all was likely to be held up from the Congo.

Even so, an intelligible if murky picture would get through. But who was going to face the truth, and build a new Jerusalem from unpalatable facts? Who, in the hothouse atmosphere of New York, was going to be brave enough to admit the truth—that our success in saving thousands of lives had rested exclusively on Western military discipline, training, technique, and know-how or on those same qualities the new National units had inherited from the old colonial armies?

We had come in many guises—not all of them agreeable. On the one hand, there had been the dead Trooper Anthony Browne—and so many others like him—with his concern and affection for ten little adopted orphans. On a different level, there had been the stern paternal discipline that brought peace and stability to chaotic areas. On the other hand, we had had our failures. I still did not like to think of the reports on my desk, outlining what had happened to the prisoners taken by a company of the Liberian battalion in Kasai Province. How these prisoners had come to be arrested had never been fully cleared up; why they had been herded into railway boxcars under a tropical sun, in conditions rivaling the Black Hole of Calcutta, was still a mystery that the American-trained Liberians appeared to have every intention of keeping to themselves.

I could not help wondering whether, had we been in a position to take drastic action against the individuals involved, there might not have been outraged voices alleging racial discrimination; yet it had been fellow Africans who had died in those red-hot boxcars.

It was a strange mixture of human material, an odd combination of totally different types of men that made up my command. Perhaps one of the most heartening aspects of the whole operation had been the unhesitating way in which their commanders had accepted—and so seldom abused—the virtual autonomy thrust on them in great stretches of isolated territory that had reverted to primitive conditions.

Each individual command, whether at company or battalion level, had had its own unorthodox problems amid a welter of bitter political strife and conflicting tribal allegiances. Restoring order and saving lives had been a thankless task—even at the beginning when there had still been a veneer of good will toward us. Now—with a hopeless mandate that made us everybody's enemy—our relationship with the people we had come to help was becoming corroded with a new bitterness. We seemed doomed to exist in a perpetual aura of hatred. And our role under conditions like these imposed a continual strain. Sooner or later, our units were bound to come to hate the task they had to carry out. Had our men been conscripts, I doubt whether they could have weathered the burden. Our strength in this increasingly hostile country sprang from the fact that our men were mostly long-service regulars with a tradition that had its own inner strength and was powerful enough to survive the anomalies this strange peacekeeping role was heaping on our heads.

Back in Léopoldville, I could see the time approaching when this discipline would be put to fresh tests. I had come from Elizabethville, where I had been saying good-bye to the Swedes who were about to be replaced by another Swedish battalion specially raised for service in the Congo. I had noticed their specially manufactured Congo medals. But here—in the capital—there were no medals, no word of thanks; only the endless round of guards and patrols drawn from Colonel Lasmar's Tunisians, who had taken over from the Ghanaians.

A fresh batch of cables from New York expressed concern over Mobutu's intention to hold a ceremonial parade of the ANC in Léopoldvile, followed by a drop by a company of his newly formed parachute unit somewhere out near the airfield.

I, personally, had a great deal of admiration for Mobutu. Unlike Lumumba, he struck me as a genuine Congolese patriot with no time for playing politics with Communist theories or alliances that held no true future in the Congo. His new regime at least gave hopes of some centralized authority. He was dedicated, aloof from self-interest, essentially the soldier who had stepped in to prevent his country from disintegrating into chaos.

Admittedly, there were drawbacks: there always are when a

soldier whose only previous experience has been in the ranks steps in to take control. He had no legal recognition, was accused of dictatorial ambitions, was at loggerheads with us and Lumumba, and could hardly control his own ANC. Nevertheless, he represented the only stable element, and it was difficult not to sympathize with him at this particular moment. His ally, Kasavubu, was out of the country engaged in a crucial struggle to insure recognition for his own delegation—rather than Lumumba's—at the General Assembly. For Mobutu at this moment—despite Dayal's disapproval—it must have seemed vital his ANC should lay the ghost of the Belgian "paras," show the country they were a force to be reckoned with, and demonstrate their ability to enforce the regime of the College of Commissioners.

The curious battle going on in the General Assembly over the credentials of the rival Congolese delegations must have thrown New York into a furore. At first, our orders were implicit and it was difficult not to suspect that they emanated from a direct desire to deflate Mobutu. We were instructed to prevent the parade and the parachute drop from taking place—orders we had no chance of implementing. I think Dayal would have liked to see this done, but the truth was that we were in no position to tell the ANC what they could or could not do. It was too late; we had never been given any command authority over them, and who were we, when Alexander's recommendations had long ago been cast aside and Ralph had given them back their arms, to object to their undisciplined soldiers running riot in the city and, at the same time, compel them to desist from the retraining and reorganization we had urged so long.

The situation was immensely complicated because behind New York's concern lay the undoubted personal antipathy between Dayal and Mobutu. Personally, I had little doubt that official anxiety reflected little more than Dayal's determination to deflate the colonel. Dayal was a very proud and sensitive man, and I sometimes wonder whether his personal emotions did not tend to override his political judgment. It was not easy to judge what was really going on in his mind at this moment, because he was no longer with us, having been summoned to New York to discuss the implications of his report.

He was destined to be away throughout the crucial time that followed and behind him, as acting special representative, he left the ubiquitous Rikhye,* who at first was inclined to look down his nose when I suggested that Mobutu should be allowed to hold his parade and that we lend him an old C.119 to help with the parachute drop. As a newly fledged political soldier, he was anxious not to make a wrong move. I did not blame him, but I made no bones about my own opinion. If we forbade the parade, it would take place just the same, and we would be made to look ridiculous and incur even more loathing than we enjoyed now.

Rikhye listened, dubiously at first, but gradually I wore him down in one bitterly argued discussion after another. At last, his military logic got the better of his doubts and fears, and he began to support me. And so the cables flew back and forth to New York, and in the end sheer common sense prevailed.

I had few fears about the result. For months past, I had had Kettani's reports, and was well informed on the ANC's morale and efficiency. Some time before, a Swiss officer who had been loaned to us under the technical aid assistance program had spent a short time endeavoring to retrain them before throwing up his hands in horror and departing. I did not blame him, and could only admire the long-suffering officers, seconded from the Royal Moroccan Army, who had this thankless task.

The parade, which took place on November 17, created no trouble. As infantry and armored cars, 25-pounders, AA guns, and paracommando units marched past in an odd mixture of half slouching, half defiant bravado, it was plain enough that this disorderly procession concealed a wealth of splendid human material.

Their marching, thanks to years of Belgian training, was magnificent. But the parade itself was little less than a ghastly shambles. It was not unexpected, but it looked bad. Sheer lack of experience turned the march into a veritable traffic jam with infantry, guns, and motorized elements all treading on each others' toes, until what ought to have been an impressive spectacle bogged

* Brigadier, later Major General Indar Jit Rikhye. An Indian officer commissioned 6th D.C.O. Lancers, served in Italy in World War II, COS, UNEF in 1958; while taking over a brigade on India's frontier August 1960 appointed Military Adviser on the Congo operation to Hammarskjöld, confirmed in position by U Thant with extended responsibility.

down into a shuffling military farce wherein the only saving grace was the sheer physical caliber of the troops themselves. This was not enough, however, and of one thing I was absolutely certain; only the return of experienced Belgian or European officers was ever likely to restore the ANC to a vestige of the outstanding force it had once been. And since this would have been heretical talk, coming from the Force Commander of the United Nations troops, I kept it to myself, knowing that sooner or later circumstances would prove me right.

It was the same story with the parachute drop that took place the following day over a deserted moor thirty miles outside Léopoldville. This was not so much a demonstration as a vindication of a few devoted troops and the even more devoted efforts of General Kettani's officers from the Royal Moroccan Army. Essentially the maneuver was designed as a psychological boost to Mobutu's army's self-respect. As I watched a couple of brave black soldiers launch themselves from one of our decrepit planes, my heart went out to them beneath their burgeoning silk canopies. Once on the ground, they proved to be not particularly impressive. But at least they were there through sheer guts, determination, and devotion to their new republic.

It was a foretaste of the shape of things to come. Not long after my departure, the Israeli army took over their training. From then on the "Paras" trained in the Holy Land, and returned to instruct a steadily growing corps, until, in 1964, a very different demonstration took place outside Léopoldville that brought impressive applause for a Congolese unit that was to be reckoned with.

On November 21, I was taking my usual siesta after lunch and, while half dozing, was surprised to see a Canadian captain of our headquarters medical staff walk in unannounced and settle himsef at my bedside as though he had arrived for a prearranged consultation.

I did not suspect it at the time, but this was exactly what it was; my long-suffering staff had summoned him on their own responsibility. He had hardly begun to take my blood pressure before the door opened and he was joined by Colonel Kapoor, my senior Indian medical officer, who also appeared to take it as a matter of course that he should have dropped in at this convenient moment.

I had recently become aware of a dragging, debilitating exhaustion, hardly helped by the humidity of the atmosphere. And I felt too lethargic to argue. Nor, oddly enough, can I remember feeling particuarly disturbed when they informed me that my blood pressure had become dangerously high. It merely seemed odd that it had not exploded long ago in the course of my protracted battles with Ralph. When they told me it had been brought about by cumulative stress, I was almost inclined to chuckle.

I was not so pleased, however, when I was sternly told to stay in bed and advised that the sooner I went on leave the better. Nevertheless, the import of what they were saying sank in, and I must admit to a sense of something very close to a feeling of relief and peace as though—I mused sleepily, like an old crusader—I had already been placed to rest with my sword on my chest and a faithful dog at my feet. Unfortunately, a moment or two later, this delightful decadence was shattered when the "old crusader" looked up and, through the open door to his bathroom, spotted a six-inch cockroach mocking him from the edge of his bath tub. Immediately the offensive spirit came to the fore in Swedish martial style. Bedclothes went left, right and center as I sallied out to assault the enemy, unhampered by UN strictures on military initiative.

I had hardly completed my punitive expedition before a telephone call from Colonel Lasmar brought me sharply back to reality. "Le Prince de Kasai" wanted to know whether he wasn't wasting his time mounting guard over the residence of the Ghanaian Ambassador, Mr. Andrew Djinn (who, he claimed, was a positive menace to what little remained of our relations with Mobutu's regime).

We all knew about Djinn's role as Lumumba's *eminence grise* and it had hardly come as a surprise to hear Mobutu had recently declared both Djinn and Nkrumah's special representative, Mr. Nathaniel Welbeck, *persona non grata.* I had, however, received no instructions to relax the guards on duty outside the Ghanaian Embassy. Possibly because I was feeling unusually drowsy—the doctors had insisted on giving me a strong dose of sedatives before they had departed—it occurred to me that there might have been some last-minute change in instructions from the Royal. I told Lasmar that I would telephone to find out and ring him back.

But everything was just the same; I was informed that diplomatic relations with the Ghanaian Embassy were very much in force and we were under every obligation to oblige them with an armed guard around their embassy. I rang Lasmar back and told him this, stressing that whatever his personal opinions about the activities of the ambassador and his staff might be, our main duty was to insure that no fault in our own arrangement led to a break in official relations between Accra and Léopoldville.

I heard Lasmar's grunt of disapproval, but I knew I could rely on his Tunisians to carry out their orders to the letter. I had no premonition that they were about to do so to the death. Nor had I heard that that very morning an unusual omen had been reported; crocodiles had been sighted—at a spot where no crocodiles ever normally appeared—in the stretch of the Congo River not far from the Ghanaian Embassy.

Later that evening, heavy firing awakened me from my drugged sleep at Flagstaff House. It appeared to be coming from the direction of the Ghanaian Embassy and was loud enough to convince me that this was no sporadic *feu de joie*. Soon, I could hear the unmistakable chatter of automatic rifles and light machine guns. I told Bent Fredriksen and Bob Dontah, my two aides, to phone Johnny Berthiaume to find out what was happening, but I was not destined to receive a report that night. The drugs those medicos had given me proved too strong; I fell back into a deep and untroubled sleep through which the sounds of battle could not penetrate.

But morning found me smartly out of bed with a difficult, even embarrassing day before me. Colonel Kokolo was dead; and Colonel Kokolo, besides being the commandant of the ANC in Léopoldville, happened to have had a very considerable reputation as an amateur witch doctor. I realized that something must be done, and quickly—otherwise we were likely to find ourselves facing some unorthodox accusations.

According to the reports now available, it had been a turbulent evening. Toward sunset, the Tunisians around the Ghanaian Embassy (who had plainly felt there was something unusual in the wind) had opened fire on a large snake in the Embassy gardens. It had apparently taken a considerabe weight of fire power to down the serpent, and the fusillade was hardly at an end before two officials sent by Mobutu appeared demanding to talk to Mr. Djinn, whom they had come to instruct to leave the country with the minimum of delay.

The Tunisian guards refused to let them in. The officials then threatened to use force, and they had all been talking and arguing when a party of ANC had opened fire from their hiding-place in some neighboring bushes. A short, sharp rush toward the embassy followed, which the Tunisians were easily able to repulse. From then on shooting continued despite repeated efforts by UN officers to bring about a cease fire. Fresh outbursts of fire foiled them every time, and before long the ANC were endeavoring to install themselves in our main ONUC hospital, which occupied a commanding position overlooking the embassy.

Unsuccessful here, they had returned to do battle in the gardens, shooting had continued throughout the rest of the night, and it was only toward morning that the attackers panicked, fled down to the river, but soon returned in a wet and dejected state in hot retreat from the attention of the crocodiles.

When dawn had risen Mr. Djinn and Mr. Nathaniel Welbeck were still inviolate within the safety of the embassy. Lasmar's casualties, however, totaled one dead and seven wounded. Although everyone felt certain the ANC must have suffered much heavier losses, the only corpse that could be immediately discovered proved to be that of the redoubtable Colonel Kokolo.

Tension ran high throughout the city. All day, incidents multiplied and it was soon apparent that it was unwise for UN personnel to venture out alone. Although we took immediate steps to send out patrols to cope with the situation, we were equally concerned with keeping the colonel's body in a good state of preservation. Already questions were being asked about his whereabouts at the Royal where Rikhye's and Dayal's staffs considered it wise to profess a diplomatic lack of knowledge—an approach that entirely failed to satisfy the questioners who, in a transport of rage and frustration, accused them of having murdered *and then eaten* their missing commandant.

Fortunately, unknown to them, poor Kokolo had been safely laid out in the temporary morgue attached to our hospital. Even in death, he had become a victim of administrative chaos. Inquiries at the official morgue had elicited the fact that their freezing apparatus had not been functioning for a long time, and now it was discovered that a breakdown in the electricity supply had led to a temporary absence of this highly necessary facility in our own ONUC hospital. Nevertheless everything that could be done was performed with suitable decorum.

Kokolo had been one of the few outstanding soldiers the ANC possessed and the reaction to his death was much as I had foreseen. An influx of his tribal supporters invaded the city and the accusations of UN cannibalism were heard far and wide. Even Rikhye, who was now in a genuine political hot seat, must have heaved a vast but doubtless disguised sigh of Indian relief when he found himself able to tell them that they would be able to see for themselves that this was not the custom of United Nations troops. The colonel's body was ceremoniously handed back in an uncommonly good state of preservation. Understandably, we did not attend the state funeral a few days later, but I gather that it was an impressive function—though hardly guaranteed to enhance our popularity in Léopoldville.

I was not, I discovered, now in very good shape to attend any more functions. It was as though the arrival of the doctors the day before had suddenly released a mainspring that had been wound too long under too great pressure. I could hardly summon up the strength to drag myself about. I felt drained, sapped of all energy, totally burned out. It came as no surprise to be told that I was being sent on leave; it seemed a century, rather than a few months ago since that evening in July when Dag's telephone call had put an end to all thoughts of the seat booked for me on the plane from Beirut to Sweden.

We did not know yet who was to take over from me, but I was aware the changeover would put a heavy burden on my Deputy Commander and Chief of Staff. While I still had the authority, I made sure that General Kettani and Brigadier General Mengesha took home leave immediately so there should be no break in the continuity of command and staff work. Whoever came after me would be fortunate in inheriting two fine associates of quite outstanding quality to guide him in the early days. Each was a paragon of all the military virtues and each has now, as he had then, a very warm corner in my heart besides a distinguished place in the history of International soldiering.

Although my own task here was almost at an end there was to be little or no rest for ONUC. Conditions in Léopoldville were hardly back to normal before we learned that Lumumba had escaped through the ring of ANC outside his residence, and was believed to be making his way toward Stanleyville.

We had known for some time that he and his supporters had been making plans to set up a new regime there in Oriental Province. But doubtless lingering hopes of a *coup d'état* or a compromise with Kasavubu had kept him in Léopoldville. Suddenly, events turned against Lumumba. Although he still commanded plenty of support in the capital, I have no doubt that the events that finally induced him to take the plunge were the expulsion of Andrew Djinn and Nathaniel Welbeck, which had followed the shooting affray at the Ghanaian Embassy, and the decision in New York to seat Kasavubu's delegation in the General Assembly.

On that very same night, November 27, Kasavubu had returned in triumph from New York. And while a grand reception was being held to celebrate his victory and cement the Kasavubu-Mobutu alliance, Lumumba had quietly chosen to vanish. The UN guards around his residence had orders to protect him but no instructions to stop the closed car that seems to have failed to attract the notice of the outer ring of ANC.

By morning, it was clear that he had gone although the escape was not officially confirmed until that afternoon when Mobutu's men had been permitted to enter his residence. It was further discovered that a number of his close supporters (including General M'Polo who had collaborated with us so effectively during the early days) had vanished with him. Within hours, poor Rikhye, who was really going through it, was being bombarded with demands from Kasavubu and Mobutu who wanted him arrested; it was an urgent matter for them because they knew Lumumba would be making his way toward Stanleyville.

Doubtless acting on Dayal's instructions, Rikhye remained firm; the orders we received from him, and which we passed on to our units, were explicitly in line wtih Dayal's policy not to interfere in internal affairs. Units were ordered not to interfere either with Lumumba's movements or with those of his official pursuers. It was a decision that must have put a strain on the Ghanaian units in Kasai where, on November 30, a Congolese plane reported a column of cars moving toward Mweka. All Mobuto's ANC troops in the area were alerted. On December 1 news was received that Lumumba and his companions had been arrested by the ANC.

There were mixed feelings at ONUC headquarters. A small minority were plainly alarmed and dismayed. But most of us felt quite rightly that there was now a genuine chance of the Congo returning to some degree of tranquillity. To put it frankly, had Lumumba got to Stanleyville, the whole Congo might have gone up in flames.

We counted ourselves fortunate, but had no illusions about the repercussions this news would have inside our own ranks. The Ghanaian reaction was immediate and took the shape of a request from their local commander in Kasai for permission to rescue Lumumba. At headquarters, we passed this immediately to Dayal. I do not know what arguments and counterarguments may have raged over the telephone to New York, but the end result was clear enough. We were instructed to refuse the request and issue orders to the Ghanaians not to intervene.

Lumumba was flown back to Léopoldville the next day and our troops at the airport noticed that he seemed to have been beaten up by his captors. Within twenty-four hours, he had been transferred to Camp Hardy in Thysville. Some of his supporters, however, had succeeded in getting through to Stanleyville. Although there was great rejoicing among Mobutu's and Kasavubu's followers in Leopoldville, the reaction in Oriental Province was swift and disturbing.

By December 9, when I went out to say good-bye to the Malayan battalion at the disused Ndolo airport, not far from Léopoldville, the self-appointed authorities in Stanleyville had already threatened to arrest all Belgians unless Lumumba was released within forty-eight hours. It was hinted, too, that executions might follow. It was obvious our Ethiopians up there were in for an extremely difficult time.

For the moment, however, despite my shaky legs and the waves of exhaustion that attacked me, I was determined to enjoy what I knew would be my last contact with the troops whose endurance and loyalty had been the one thing that had made this long Congo nightmare worthwhile. For a finale, I could not have picked a more outstanding unit. Colonel Mobutu was among the spectators, and the Malayans had put on a parade that still lingers happily in my mind as an example of the panache and bearing that distinguished our forces who wore the blue beret.

Under the eagle eye of Colonel Ungku Nazaruin the Malayans had marked out a parade ground on the disused airfield that exactly matched the dimensions of Horse Guards Parade in London. A dais had been erected, and once I had mounted it and stood flanked by stick orderlies in front of the flags of Malaya, the United Nations, and the Congo Republic, facing rank after rank of stocky, tough-looking soldiers in jungle green, I saw Colonel Nazaruin approaching across the parade ground accompanied by a subaltern who was carefully bearing a silk cushion. On it lay a blue beret with the dark blue hackle and cap badge of the Malayan Infantry and Reconnaissance Corps. I was proud to take my own off and don this in exchange, and throughout the inspection which followed, I became increasingly proud.

It is not often that an old soldier's eye fails to alight on some minor blemish or fault, but going down those immaculate lines of Malays, Sikhs, Chinese, and Eurasians, I simply could not find a single fault. Finally—just to save my own face (an inspecting General *has* to find *something* wrong)—I managed to spot a missing muzzle cover on one of the Reconnaissance Squadron's smoke grenade projectors. But when, after a march past that would have done credit to the Brigade of Guards, and three loud and patently heartfelt cheers that sent a tingle down my spine, I saw Colonel Nazaruin advancing across the parade ground again with another subaltern carrying another silk cushion, I began to feel that if anyone deserved fresh honors, it was the battalion rather than the Force Commander.

On this cushion lay a beautifully worked old gold and jewel-studded Kris that had been specially flown out from Malaya. I doubt whether the words I found to express my thanks came anywhere near revealing my true emotions. When it came time to say good-bye I knew this would be the last chance I would have of talking to my own troops in the Congo, and I was glad I had rehearsed a little Malay in which to begin and end my speech. The rest of what I had to say came to them through interpreters, but every word originated from the heart as I told them:

"I am glad you came. I feel proud of having you under my command. I feel honored and moved by your gifts. Don't forget that soldiering for peace is in some respects even more difficult than for war. In addition to the standard soldier qualities, it calls for not only unyielding firmness but also infinite patience, restraint, tact, tolerance and understanding.

"The UN Force came to the Congo in order to assist the government in the restoration and maintenance of law and order and particularly to take all possible measures for the protection of life. In view of the strength of the Force and the size of the country it is a big order and our task is a thankless one.

"Do not expect either reward or gratitude. Soldiers from all contingents of this twenty-nine-nation force can tell you that those who one day beg you to protect them and their property do not hesitate the next day to accuse you falsely of inactivity, partiality, interference, maltreatment, theft, and even capital crime.

"This is hard for good soldiers to take. But it goes with the job. There is not a single contingent in this Force which has not been subject to unjustified and false accusations during the past four months."

I was very, very tired by the time that the farewell ceremonies were over, and yet curiously exalted. In these last minutes I had realized that the endless battles I had had to fight with New York, the struggles with Ralph Bunche, the nightmare frustrations whose cumulative effects were reflected in my physical condition—all had been infinitely worthwhile if, in some small measure, they had helped to lighten and alleviate the hard burdens that had been so cheerfully accepted by the thousands of fine soldiers who had come from so many lands to wear the blue beret.

I had been proud and honored to command them, to come to know them, and try to make their lot a little easier in this hard and unrelenting country. And when, the following day, I held a reception for senior officers from every nationality represented in my headquarters, I was very conscious of the loyalty and soldierly qualities that had made our joint effort possible. I had, by this time, acquired a few advance boxes of the standard United Nations medal with the Congo bar (its creation had been a campaign in itself). In the garden of Flagstaff House, I was able to present these first tokens of recognition which I hoped would very soon be reaching the troops.

Even this pleasant ceremony exhausted me completely, but it was only a matter of hours before I would be on my way home. In the little time that remained I was delighted to meet General Sean McEoin, Chief of Staff to the Irish Free State Army, who had come to visit his battalions in Katanga. Neither of us knew then that he was to replace me as Force Commander.

On the evening of December 12, I drove out to N'Djili airport. There were farewells, a Guard of Honor and then, at last, our plane was circling the green hills around Léopoldville and there, down below, was the troubled capital stretched along the mud-colored Congo River. I thought for a moment of that classic story that old hands claim depicts the spirit of the Congo. It concerns a tarantula who approached a hippo to carry him across the Congo River on his back. "Certainly not," cried the hippo indignantly, "you'll sting me as I'm swimming and I shall drown." But the tarantula insisted he had no such evil intention. "I *promise* not to," he cried, "and besides, why should I? I can neither fly nor swim. If I sting you, we should both drown."

Although this seemed logical, the hippo still took a lot of persuading. But at last he entered the river with the tarantula comfortably seated on his back. Half way across, he was horrified to feel a deadly, poisonous sting. As he sank with the tarantula on his back, his last indignant words were: "But you promised! And you can't swim!"

"That's true, my friend," gulped the tarnatula as he, too, sank to a watery grave, "But *you* forgot. *C'est le Congo*."

"C'est le Congo!" The mud-colored river stretching through junge lay beneath us. But it was over now. And all I longed to do was sleep.

Chapter Nineteen

THE GLASS BUILDING

It was good to be home, to sleep untrammeled for twelve solid hours at a stretch and to sit dozing in my armchair, knowing I had only to glance through the windows to see that winter had already touched the familiar Swedish countryside. In the distance, I could see the rooftops of the good old city of Malmö. Its skyline of mellowed old houses, spires, and warehouses had changed since I had been away, was constantly changing as rebuilding turned the old seaport into a blooming city.

But it was rather different in my own home. Even when I had first arrived I had sensed through my exhaustion that Scarlett was far from well. I could see it in the lines now etched into that lovely face, the new weariness with which she moved and talked. It was as though a light was going out inside her. As each new day brought an improvement in my own physical condition, it was plain that there was something seriously wrong. Even now, it saddens me to write about it. But every family experiences its tragedies alongside its moments of happiness, and ours was to be no exception. Until now I have always believed that such moments are an intensely private and personal prerogative, which have their place in the heart rather than the cold light of print. But the troubled events that were to mark the next two years became so closely bound with private tragedy that the latter becomes an integral part of this story.

I knew that before long I was bound to receive a summons back into harness. Not, thank God, to the Congo, but to UNTSO. Dag's calls to duty were very hard to refuse; their quiet urgency concealed an imperative need. Ever since I had gone to the Congo, I had been receiving disturbing letters from Jerusalem. I knew, too, that Henri Vigier had written a personal letter to Dag, making no bones about the deteriorating situation there, and urging my return at the earliest possible moment. Now that it was only a question of time before I was fit and well again, I had no doubt that the moment of recall was very close at hand.

It came more swiftly than I had anticipated and I did not find it an easy situation to have to face. In the ordinary way soldiers' wives are accustomed to brief leaves and sudden departures, but this was no ordinary occasion. Although the doctors could discover nothing seriously wrong with poor Scarlett beyond a general weakness complicated by consistent attacks of arthritis, and were insistent that the malaise had been brought on by strain occasioned by worry about me in the Congo, I could sense that there was some deeper, more intangible factor at work and became deeply concerned over leaving her, insistent that she should come with me so that at least I could take care of her in Jerusalem.

But at first nothing I could say would move her; she was determined to stay in Malmö until Johan had finished at the State Grammar School, where he was growing up into a tall, good-looking boy with all a boy's deep interest in railways, photography, and soldiering. Scarlett had never wanted to leave him on his own, although he was remarkably well balanced for his age, had a grand sense of humor, and was an excellent mixer. But gradually for her own sake I succeeded in persuading her to change her mind and come out and join me once I had settled back into my quarters in Government House.

It was a place she loved and knew well from previous visits; indeed, the gardens around Government House were eloquent testimony to her love of flowers. It had been her idea to introduce a profusion of Dutch tulips and encourage Ahmed, the old head gardener, to plant great swaths of her favorite marigolds. There was nothing that gave her more pleasure than a riot of color against the background of those smooth green lawns.

Although I still felt uneasy, I was now happier, believing that the change to the hot Palestinian sunlight might work a profound improvement in her health. In a way, I think that I convinced myself that this would be what would happen; partly because I could never really crystallize my fears, partly because I knew myself already committed.

At the end of January 1961, half fearful still, but conscious my own health had undergone a change for the better, I flew back to the Holy Land. I landed at Beirut and flew on to Kalandia, Jerusalem, where nothing, not even the flowery speeches of welcome, had changed; and I was soon driving up the winding road from the Jordan Valley until the familiar square tower and outlines of Government House beneath its UN flag came into sight again.

After the Congo this was almost like coming home. But although the faces in Government House were familiar, I found a very different atmosphere. I was greeted with such voluble relief by Henri Vigier, my political adviser, and the members of the Fifth Republic that I might have been Joan of Arc before the gates of Orleans. Colonel Rickert, too (who had acted as Deputy Chief of Staff in my absence), was patently glad to see me; his handshake was warm and fervent.

Hansen hurried forward to greet me, a physical shadow of his old self but still a sterling, if frustrated, Chief Security Officer. Colonel Pirlot, my Operations Officer, was there too. All seemed delighted to have me back among them. The Chief Administration Officer, who had replaced Jan Van Wijk shortly before I had left for the Congo, stared at me as if I were a ghost.

I was soon to learn why. During the next few days, everyone was bursting to relate his own version of what had been happening in my absence. It soon became clear that I had come "home" with a vengeance. No situation could have illustrated more clearly the impossible anomalies of UN service. But by this time I had become so accustomed to the ridiculous that it no longer seemed strange that internal trouble should take precedence over the Mission's primary task. For the time being, I had no option but to divide my energies between two conflicting demands: on the operations front, I was briefed on the latest news of incidents at sensitive spots along the frontiers; on the "home" front, I had to listen to the story of an internal struggle within the framework of UNTSO itself.

From the reports I received it became apparent that the new Chief Administrative Officer had turned out to be a seriously disruptive influence. Before I had left for the Congo, I had managed to get the Mission into relatively efficient operational condition. Yet now—seven months later—Vigier, Albert Grand, and Hansen were in a state of despair, the security system that I had so carefully built up had deteriorated sharply, and morale had sunk to something close to zero.

I learned that Van Wijk's replacement had been trying to run the Mission over Rickert's head, had been bypassing the channels of authority I had established, and had been steadily arrogating more power into his own hands. He had managed to place Hansen's security work directly under his own supervision and was highly successful in securing control of all Mission communication, with the result that Hansen was blocked off from all official sources of information.

Unfortunately, I did not have a great deal of time in which to discuss the situation with this remarkable man. Our first meeting was brief and hardly marked by an abundance of good will on either side, and he had not a great deal to say. On subsequent occasions when I summoned him to my office, he was even less communicative. I soon discovered the reason; high-powered, but also high-strung, he felt himself overwhelmed by misfortune and had had a nervous collapse.

There was no question but that he would have to go. I discussed the whole matter with Vigier and Rickert and then, heavily briefed, drew up a report. It was hardly on the way to Cordier in New York before the fellow requested permission to take leave "outside the Mission area." I was, of course, happy to let him go. Later on, I learned that he was appointed Chief Administrative Officer to other UN missions, and today, as far as I know, he is still serving in the organization.

His replacement, Victor Mills, a hard-working, pleasant American, came into our midst like a breath of fresh air. This outstandingly able executive cooperated wholeheartedly with me and the rest of my staff with the result that there was soon a marked rise of morale within the Mission. Restoring things to normal, however, took a little time.

Fortunately I had come back to Jerusalem during a period of comparative peace and quiet; so much so that during those early days, the Holy Land seemed almost like a bed of roses after the Congo.

For the time being Israel had come to the reluctant conclusion that a seemingly unending succession of border incidents no longer aroused much sympathy in Europe or America. However carefully the Israeli Information Services might exploit them, the Powers had grown weary of listening and had begun to question much of their authenticity besides reacting critically to some of Ben Gurion's and his ministers' more militant speeches. The Holy Land had been almost forced off the world stage by the upheavals in the Congo. And now that the impending trial of Adolf Eichmann was likely to center political interest on Israel again, the Govenment decided that it would be unwise to allow a sudden recrudescence of incidents lest they divert attention from preparations for a dramatically staged reconstruction of Nazi persecution.

Ben Gurion had personally planned this vast, histrionic set piece, which was designed to attract the sympathy and horror of the whole civilized world, and the trial (at which many hundreds of foreign journalists, commentators, and spectators would be present) was due to open in Jerusalem on April 8. Already, however, the Israelis had been dismayed and not a little startled at the weight of criticism over their violation of Argentinian sovereignty. Were the trial to be interrupted by news of blood forays within a few miles of the courtroom, the truth (always difficult to disguise at such short range), might somehow filter through to the mass of visitors and even inculcate a suspicion that Israel herself was not immune from perpetrating her own atrocities for national ends.

It was a difficult year for the Israelis; the sordid echoes of the Lavon affair were still to be heard in the Knesset. Some time ago —in 1955-1956—an Israeli espionage ring had been discovered in Cairo, a full-scale trial had ensued, and several of the offenders had been hanged while others had been sentenced to long terms of imprisonment. The trial had shown, however, that this had been no routine case of espionage; the activities of the group had been devoted to fomenting anti-American sentiment among the Egyptians (and not without success because the United States Information Service Offices and Library in Cairo had been set on fire).

It had been an interesting revelation, and when the blame had been put fairly and squarely on the Israeli Intelligence Service, its directors hastily took refuge behind the Minister of Defense who, they claimed, had signed the authorization for the whole operation. True enough, his signature *was* on the document, but subsequent investigation revealed that it had been forged. Despite Israeli dependence on American good will, the real truth has never been revealed. But the affair was to provide capital for political infighting in the Knesset for years to come and left an unpleasant dent in Israel's public image which, with the Eichmann trial en train, they were very anxious the outside world should forget.

Although UNTSO derived some indirect benefit from this more subdued attitude, there was little relaxation in the day-to-day personal animosities, distortions, and underhand deceptions that characterized the Israeli attitude in their relationships with the Mission. Indeed as time went on, it seemed as though much of the rage and frustration they would have liked to vent on the Arab States had now been transferred to us.

In the early days following my return, the Scopus enclave figured largely in our negotiations. But although I was greeted by Mrs. Meir on this occasion with the loaded comment: "Well, General. It's clear *you* are back again," their real invective was reserved for the formidable arguments that raged later in the Jordanian-Israeli Mixed Armistice Commission over the Israeli intention to hold another Independence Day Parade in Jerusalem.

We could all remember the last one only too clearly, and were hardly surprised when the Jordanians formally protested well in advance. Since the Parade was a violation of the Armistice Agreement, it was obvious that the MAC must automatically condemn it, but this did not stop the Israelis from resorting to a mass of legalistic argument to ward off a condemnation *before* the parade actually took place.

But the MAC went resolutely ahead—a decision that brought down venomous attacks on the heads of Vigier, myself, and Colonel Owen Burn (the New Zealand Chairman of the Jordan-Israeli MAC) in the Israeli press. Just because I had carried out UN policy in accordance with an Armistice Agreement that the Israelis had signed, I found myself described as: "General von Horn who, after a number of failures here and in the Congo (from which he was recalled) seems anxious to make himself seem important and exert influence. He conjures up imaginary terrors and creates tension and antagonism where before complete tranquillity and mutual understanding reigned."

This was, perhaps, one of the more kindly worded comments in a mass of hostile print. Poor Vigier, the "Old Fox" and senior member of the Fifth Republic, caught it too: "Henri Vigier, who once played an important role in the United Nations service, has recently come to feel himself more and more out of the way here. Once, however, the international spotlight began to focus on this out-of-the-way corner, he was unable to withstand the temptation to thrust himself forward. Ambitious to secure power, an intriguer, he cannot resist "advising" UNTSO to take totally uncalled-for and unnecessary measures."

In retrospect all this may seem trivial enough, but it highlights the sort of difficulties that descend like a swarm of hornets on the peacekeeper. I doubt, however, whether many other countries could have been *quite* so infuriating as Israel for the international soldier. Nor for the international civil servant. Although the outcome was bound to result in a condemnation by the MAC unless she agreed to call off the parade, the Israelis nonetheless managed to string out a meeting from 9 a.m. on April 17 until 2:30 the following morning.

The only reason it eventually broke up was because the Israeli delegates, having exhausted every technique of procrastination, finally walked out, leaving six UNTSO secretaries in a state of exhaustion after transcribing a torrent of rhetoric into shorthand. Left alone, Colonel Burn and the Jordanian representatives automatically condemned the Israeli action. From that moment onward UNTSO was blamed by the Israelis as the prime cause for the criticism that descended on the new state from the outside world.

We were still fortunate, however, in that world opinion had ceased to worry about comparatively small affairs such as the Jerusalem parade, and the Israeli Information Service began to have an increasingly hard time in disseminating its anti-UN propaganda to the press overseas. Even the network of Jewish publications that specialized in presenting a picture of their own version of the situation in the Holy Land were much more interested in telling their readers about the dramatic trial which was taking place in Jerusalem.

For once we were almost in the happy position of being forgotten. And I welcomed this unfamiliar state of affairs because I was now deeply immersed, drawing up an extensive report based on my experiences in the Congo. When it had been completed, I sent it, together with several copies, to Dag, in the hope that its conclusions might make some useful contribution toward the future planning of UN operations.

I was well aware that it would cause some fluttering in administrative circles on the twenty-first floor, but this seemed unimportant in the true interests of the organization. It was essentially a constructive report which no organization, faced with the prospect of mounting new operations in some other unexpected corner of the world, could safely afford to ignore. I had been, so to speak, one of the pioneers who had been thrust into a command role in an unforeseen crash operation, and I had had to fight my way through a maze of difficulties and hard experiences which I hoped would never be the lot of any other international soldier. I had drawn on my own experiences to make many suggestions, draw a number of conclusions, and make constructive and helpful criticisms. I believed the report *ought* to be of real value; certainly it deserved a place in the UN archives once it had provided a basis for a study for future United Nations military planning.

I was to be disappointed. As time went on and the whole Congo operation came to an end and took its own odd place in international history, I began to receive more and more visits from members of officially appointed study groups engaged in compiling histories or critical studies of the UN operations in the Congo.

Almost all had been to the United Nations as their first port of call, and although I realized that a number of documents would not be available for release until a certain period had passed, I was nonetheless puzzled to discover that not one of them had ever seen or even heard a mention of the report which I had labored over so long and hard.

At first, I imagined it must have been classified as secret material, but when, shortly after Dag's death, I learned unofficially that it had been bundled up with all his private papers, classified as "storage," and sent back to Sweden, I soon realized what had happened. On my next visit to New York, I decided to make quite certain, and sent my Military Assistant to get hold of a copy "for consultation." As I had anticipated, he returned after a lengthy search with the information that no such report was in existence. Frankly, I knew it hopeless to persist; by this time there were too few men left in the glass building who would give a damn about my report.

I merely recall the episode because of the light it sheds on an apparent official unwillingness to assess the Congo operation in its true light, and (far worse) the seeming indifference of the UN's present military advisers to any opinion other than their own when assessing the mistakes of the past, which must be avoided in any successful planning for the future.

In May, I had another saddening insight into the inner pressures mitigating against continuity in the Secretariat. I had not seen Andrew Cordier since that momentous week the previous September when his resolute action had marked him out for mounting attacks by the countries in the Soviet bloc. Officially, Cordier had come out to inspect the Mission (and I was happy when he pronounced it well back in shape again). Unofficially, however, he had come to Jerusalem to have a break from his arduous duties and to await Dag's reaction to the resignation he had felt bound to offer in order to make it easier for Dag to meet the violent Soviet attacks—one of whose main accusations was that the Secretary General had surrounded himself with an unwarranted preponderence of Western advisers.

I had many chats with Uncle Andy out on our private terrace with its beautiful view across the olive-covered hills. I know that this tranquil spot must have seemed a paradise of peace and quiet after his years of unrelenting work in the glass palace, the maelstrom of the Congo, and then the months that had led up to his fateful decision to offer his resignation.

Uncle Andy was truly a big man, a brilliant executive who had devoted the best years of his life to nursing the Secretariat from its inception into a strong and working reality. Few men fitted Dag's conception of "the international civil servant" better, and few men would have been big enough—as he was now—to sacrifice his career and life's interest for what he felt to be the good of the organization. I don't think that either of us for a moment doubted the outcome of Dag's deliberations. But it was saddening to see how infinitely expendable his own right hand could become when the international mills began to grind. Perhaps such knowledge is the one great barrier which will always inhibit the ideal of "the international civil servant"; the realization that devotion, ability, great qualities of character count little in the balance once political factors become involved.

Out on the terrace in the cool evening air, talking quietly and watching the blue and purple shadows settling gently like a cloak over the distant mountains, it was possible to feel detached, even remote. And yet one could not escape a profound sadness.

I could visualize the repercussions in the glass building once the news of Uncle Andy's resignation broke. Such visions were very far from pleasant. Although Dag would still be there, his preoccupation with affairs of state would make it impossible for him to retain the same tight rein that Cordier had held so ably and with such determination over the swarm of bureaucrats and empire builders. I could foresee Dag becoming swamped, uneasy, almost a prisoner within his own beloved Secretariat. To me, it seemed as though Cordier's going would mark a decline in those qualities of caliber, personality, standards, and behavior which alone can sustain firm leadership in an amorphous organization.

During those days while we were waiting for Dag's reaction, I had many talks with Uncle Andy. And I only wish I could reveal the gist of our conversations. Obviously there were many thoughts passing in his mind at this time, not least a concern that the original conception of the United Nations was being changed by the ever-increasing number of emergent states. He was worried, too, about the way in which the right of veto had hamstrung the Security Council so that the military staff committee had never had a chance to develop in the way it had been intended, with the result both Council and Secretary General were virtually devoid of proper technical military guidance.

I think he felt, too, that the original spirit of the charter was in danger of passing into limbo. But his views are safe in my keeping until he decides to break his silence.

I know that every word here that may give the impression that our conversations reinforced my own instinct that all was not well inside the glass building will bring down his frowning disapproval. No man could be more loyal to the United Nations. But I too have my loyalties, though they may lie along more primitive lines of contact with the men called on to be the direct instruments of policy. And who—unlike the members of the General Assembly and the Secretariat—are liable to get shot at, even killed; men liable to be called on to die are entitled to have the reason clearly explained.

I know I believed it was high time the Charter was reviewed. And never more strongly than on the day Andrew Cordier became expendable for political reasons. I have seldom seen a man's real stature more clearly revealed than was Cordier's on the day that Dag's cable finally came through. I am certain he must have guessed its contents before he opened it, but the human heart always has room for one last-minute hope. I could see immediately from his face that this had now been irrevocably extinguished. And yet there was no moment of drama, no fuss, no last-minute recriminations. Like the big man he was, Andrew Cordier knew instinctively how to behave. I shall not forget that moment; the United Nations has had few great consuls, and here was one of its best who was not afraid to face the sunset.

Chapter Twenty

RETURN TO SWEDEN

I HAVE always thought the Israeli Foreign Secretary a formidable figure. At her best, Mrs. Golda Meir is capable of radiating a certain robust charm. At her worst, however, the transformation is remarkable. Hitherto our official relationship had seemed doomed to bring out the worst—even the very worst—in her. So, shortly following my return, it came as a real surprise to find myself the unexpected recipient of one of Mrs. Meir's full-blown compliments.

The time was early July, 1961; the occasion, an official reception in Jerusalem for the visiting President of the Volta Republic. With no warning, I found myself listening flabbergasted, in front of President Yameogo and the assembled diplomatic representatives, while my bulky sparring partner expressed her own and her Government's thanks to *me* for my successful efforts in maintaining peace and tranquillity throughout the recent period of border tension.

I had never had a bouquet like this before. And behind a polite but poker-faced expression, I certainly never expected to receive one again. But the circumstances had been exceptional; during a hectic period of tension, which had lasted from June 19 to July 9 along the Israeli-Syrian borders, I had had the unusual advantage of knowing that neither side was anxious to see this flare into hostilities. The Syrians had (and were still having) their own internal troubles. The Israelis were suffering from an acute shortage of sympathy and good will abroad. Even France, usually her staunchest supporter, had reminded Israel and its itinerant Prime Minister that there *were* other areas in the world with claims to interest, aid, and support.

After a particularly militant speech by Mr. Ben Gurion at Eilat

(Israel's only outlet toward the Indian Ocean) there had, too, been very sharp reactions about the inadvisability of any "preventive" war activities. And then, in Jerusalem, the Eichmann trial with its terrible revelations was dragging on interminably, but now with the new and disturbing suspicion that its intended reaction on the outside world had somehow tragically misfired.

For once the political cards seemed stacked for peace. But the danger of an explosion had been very real, so ominous that both sides had hurriedly and clandestinely moved troops and guns up into the forbidden areas to support their first-line local defense units. I had been nearly worked into the ground, bombarded with complaints and demands from both sides as rumors mounted and a chain reaction of defensive preparations set in.

Early on, I discovered that much of the initial nervousness had developed because of the call-up of a number of field units for refresher courses. But although I had been continually requested to proceed immediately to any number of trouble spots to make clear the apprehensions felt by one government or another, the appeals I had made to the high commands for advance information about any maneuvers that were being planned had fallen on deaf ears. Even on a top-level, confidential basis, there had been a complete dearth of the sort of information that would have enabled me to take steps to cool and abate the rising tension.

But while the Israelis continued to give me little or no cooperation, I was encouraged to discover a more positive attitude on the other side. What success I had been able to achieve had come entirely through my own personal authority and standing with leading figures in the Arab States. One of the prime factors was the understanding and cooperation that arose through my personal friendship with General Amin Hilmy II, the director of Palestine Affairs in Cairo.

Oddly, though it had been Arab cooperation that had brought us through this potential crisis, the resultant calm along the frontiers (which was not destined to last long) now brought about a *rapprochement* with the Israeli High Command. In this relaxed atmosphere, I found a fresh and unfamiliar good will that soon saw the new Chief of staff, Major General Zwi Tzur, and his deputy, General Rabin, lunching with me at Government House.

I was glad to have such visible evidence that there was now, at least, a chance of our establishing a relationship that might lead to more active cooperation and lighten the Mission's task. Purely as soldiers, we all got on extremely well together and the luncheon was an unqualified success. I was interested in the contrast between the two Israeli generals: Tzur was an intellectual, quick-spoken, and with wide-ranging interest; Rabin, who had been a Palmach * commander and had commanded the Northern Area in 1958 (at the time of my first experience of border troubles) was a heavy-set, slow-speaking man in the tradition of the more orthodox field commander.

After luncheon, I presented General Tzur with one of my Congo trophies, a primitive shotgun which had been manufactured in the jungle and combined the most modern lines with the crudest workmanship. It struck me as having more lethal potential for the man who fired it than for anyone who ventured into its sights. Tzur returned the compliment by presenting me with an inscribed Uzzi submachine gun at an excellent return luncheon a week or so later.

This period was, for me, a tiny Indian Summer, but clouded by an intimation that things were far from well at home. Scarlett had been a brilliant letter writer and every Swedish post had brought me a vivid series of pen pictures, an almost day-to-day account of her life in Malmö and stories of how Johan was growing up and progressing at school; all the infinitely precious minutiae of home life. But over the last months, her letters had fallen off alarmingly; post after post would arrive with not a trace of an envelope with that familiar handwriting. She gave no indication of how she felt, nor could I get any real picture of her health from the doctors. As always, they remained hesitant and noncommittal and I felt in my own mind that it was high time I returned to discover the true situation.

For once, the situation in the Holy Land made it seem almost natural that I should ask for leave; there was no last-minute crisis,

* As long ago as 1920, during the days of the British Mandate, the Jews had set up a volunteer secret army. It was known as Haganah (a predecessor had been Hashomer, a small group of mounted watchmen). Its shock troops (not raised until 1941) were full-time units composed of young fit men and girls, known as the Palmach. On the declaration of the new State both were incorporated into the Zahal (the Israel Defense Forces) and lost their underground character.

no sudden flare-up of trouble to prevent my taking a plane to Sweden. But as I flew out of Beirut airport, there was none of that familiar elation.

In Malmö, I found that my forebodings had been well founded. For months past, my wife had been going from one specialist to another in search of relief or reassurance from the mounting attacks of acute arthritis that tortured her every day. I hate to write of these things, but they are, after all, the very stuff of human experience. Ever since we had been married, I had been proud of her appearance; indeed, I believed that I had never met a more beautiful or attractive woman. But now, under the slow destructive erosion of physical suffering, all this was gone. And I in my homecoming sensed then that all was lost.

Scarlett's eloquent need, however, and my own nature very naturally combined into a determination to fight against any tendency to recognize the inevitable. I was absolutely certain that she must come out to join me at the earliest possible moment. There was no longer any resistance. She was almost eager to come and bring Johan with her. Eagerly, we began looking up sailing dates; in no time, we had decided that they would both come out in November.

It was while I was still going from one to another of her specialists, whose grave faces and carefully guarded statements left me so little the wiser, that the news of Dag Hammarskjöld's death came through.

I can remember that moment very clearly; I could almost visualize the bush country he must have been flying over on his way to Ndola airport in Northern Rhodesia. And it had happened in the darkness. Suddenly, unexpectedly, a remarkable life snuffed out. Sleep did not come easily that night; I had too many vivid recollections. I could still hear his voice, remember so many shared moments, that the news still seemed unreal. And yet he was gone; and I doubted whether the glass building would ever be quite the same without him.

I stayed on in Sweden because I felt I ought to be there for his homecoming. At Uppsala I attended an impressive service in the ancient cathedral, conducted by the former Archbishop of Sweden.

The cathedral was thronged with those who had come to pay

their tribute. On one side of the spot where the coffin lay in state sat the royal family of Sweden, while facing them on the opposite side was the whole Hammarskjöld family.

Among the mourners were representatives from the United Nations General Assembly headed by its president, Mongi Slim of Tunisia, its Secretariat, and representatives of numerous heads of Member States. (Even on this solemn occasion there was an echo from Palestine, when a representative of one Member State complained to me about the more distinguished seat given to the representative of "the other party." Later, when we had seen him laid to rest, I felt that in this moving ceremony Dag's own country had done him the real and timeless honor he deserved. But I came away profoundly depressed because I could not escape the feeling that his death was a tragedy for the United Nations.

Dag had died at the peak of an international career, at a time when he had brought unprecedented authority to the office of Secretary General. Certainly, he had had his faults. He had been the ambiguist to end all ambiguists, a master political juggler and contortionist who had bent backward so many times in the cause of peace that it was sometimes difficult to distinguish where diplomacy ended and opportunism began. He had made his own rules, gone his own way, but somehow never strayed from the cold, clear idealism that had been his guiding light. Alone, in that political jungle of the glass building on the East River, he had been a truly dedicated man. It was sad to think that one of the legends he had left behind—as a result of a natural reticence—had been a certain cold, aloof quality of withdrawal.

This was not the way I remembered him. Within his own small, trusted circle, I had always found Dag an intensely human person. I recall an occasion when, much against his will, he had been persuaded by Ben Gurion to visit a newly established kibbutz. I had accompanied him, and we had hardly started before we became aware that the visit had been exclusively designed for propaganda purposes. Constantly ambushed by photographers, it had been a long day beneath an unrelenting sun, and Dag's temper, though still outwardly under control, had been sorely tried.

Presumably to impress us with the hard realities of the pioneer life, supper had consisted of the ordinary bread and vegetable ration served in the communal mess hall. As a special exception Dag and I were allowed an egg fried by Mrs. Ben Gurion's own hand. During this meal, Ben Gurion had made a point of introducing the secretary of the kibbutz to Dag, proudly announcing that "This is our last terrorist."

It was not until the following day, after the unsuspecting Dag had accompanied the Prime Minister on "a morning stroll" which turned out to be a sort of publicity stunt in full view of busloads of tourists and spectators (who had been promised the chance of some "unusual" snapshots), that I got the opportunity to tell him that "our last terrorist" was a former member of the Stern gang, which had assassinated Folke Bernadotte. Dag's comments on his host's peculiar behavior had rapidly convinced me (had I needed any persuasion) that there was nothing cold or aloof about him. They were very down-to-earth—in terms which I found endearing in a Secretary General.

At that time the circumstances surrounding the crash in which Dag died seemed most suspicious. But since then I have talked to so many officials who either participated in or were present at the investigations which followed that I came to abandon all suspicions.

One old friend, who attended as a technical observer, was a well-known criminologist. I have a feeling that the final word undoubtedly lay with him when he told me that in spite of much strange circumstantial evidence, raising suspicions of foul play, he was convinced that it was another tragic case of the unpredictable human factor.

After making all the necessary arrangements for Scarlett and Johan to follow me by sea in November, I flew back to Palestine on October 5, where I found that significant changes had just taken place in Syria. After less than three years the United Arab Republic had broken up, and the Syrians were now on their own again. Although I was assured, during the course of a visit to my own Syrian opposite number in Damascus, General Abdel Karem Zareddin, and his Chief of Staff (rotund young General Kemal), that I could now be certain of their full cooperation, I was inclined to be skeptical because of the very tenuous grip on power that any Syrian soldier could maintain in those troubled days. I found it wise, in the very turbulent atmosphere of Syrian politics, to observe the unwritten law of the Orient never to inquire about absent friends; any variation from this code was likely to result in distressing news of deportations, jailings, or even sudden death.

Jerusalem itself was comparatively quiet despite a minor dispute in the Scopus area over the rights of the Arab villagers to dry manure. But I soon became very worried about Lake Tiberias where Israeli patrol boats were growing more and more active against Syrian fishermen who were casting their nets to catch the Galilean haddock (or the Peter's Fish) at the height of the fishing season, roughly mid-November to the middle of April.

The Sea of Galilee (Lake Tiberias) has been a famous fishing ground since biblical days. The best fishing is at the northeast end, and a glance at the map on page 72 shows this fruitful area is close to Syrian territory as well as being uncomfortably near the headwaters of the Jordan River.

The old, prewar Palestinian boundary had followed the east shore at a distance set back ten meters parallel to the water—and as Israel based its claims on this map, its case was that the whole lake and this narrow strip of territory were an integral part of the new state. Consequently, they considered themselves justified in forbidding the Syrians to fish in its waters without a permit issued in Tiberias.

I doubt whether a single permit had ever been applied for because fishermen (like smugglers) are a remarkably independent breed. The Syrian fishermen were, moreover, supported by their Government, who claimed that under the terms of a "Good Neighborhood Convention" held in January 1926 it had been agreed that Syrian and Lebanese fishermen were to enjoy the same fishing and navigation rights on the Lake as the Palestinians. So night after night, Syrian boats ventured out to place their nets in the old, familiar fishing grounds. And night after night, Israeli patrol boats, armed officially with light machine guns, but almost certainly carrying much heavier caliber weapons that in case of need could be swiftly mounted on their reinforced decks, kept watch—observed in turn from Syrian emplacements which commanded an excellent view over the lake from their sites a little way inland on the east bank.

Inevitably, there had been endless trouble; there had been frequent shooting between the patrol boats and the emplacements, which had culminated six years earlier in a boldly executed Israeli sea and ground attack on two Syrian positions at Buteiha Farm and Koursi on the northeastern shore of the lake. Fifty-six Syrians, including three women, had been killed.

My predecessor, General Burns, suspected that the Israeli patrol boat had had deliberate orders to get involved in a fire fight the previous night in order to provide a suitable pretext for a carefully planned and mounted attack. The terms in which the Security Council condemned this action, in January 1956, had been considered "the strongest ever passed on the subject." And as a result, Hammarskjöld had requested that UNTSO be allowed to establish new observation posts in both the Israeli and Syrian sectors along the shore, and maintain a special UN patrol boat on the lake.

After tortuous evasion, the Israelis had finally agreed to the observation posts but had flatly refused to allow a UN patrol boat on the lake. Ever since—as the demand for fish rose steeply in Damascus, on one side of the frontier, and in Tiberias (where there was now a healthy tourist traffic) on the other—the fishing season had assumed the same lethal implications as the periods of ploughing and sowing.

In the Holy Land one became almost physically aware of rising tension. Inevitably, there was always a murmuring of trouble, but one grew accustomed to this in the same way that coast dwellers are hardly conscious of the sea until a certain feeling in the atmosphere rivets their attention and brings the ocean back into the forefront of their conscious thoughts. In the same way we in Jerusalem would become suddenly alert, warned by our observers, who acted like coast guards in giving us advance notice of significant signs and portents. Because trouble had a habit of coming suddenly out of an apparently clear sky, and would then build up with incredible rapidity, one developed a sort of sixth sense, a trouble sense.

I had this very acutely now. There was still no visible evidence, but we all felt instinctively the area was ripe for trouble. And there was so little action we could take to prevent it. There was no UN patrol boat on the lake; our observers were constantly refused access to the areas where troop concentrations might be taking place; all we could do was to step up their activity and bring pressure to bear in every quarter where we thought it would count.

In the midst of this uneasy period—when outwardly the situation appeared almost tranquil—I learned that after several delays, Scarlett and Johan were on their way to Alexandria by the sea route. I decided to go down there by car to meet them, and then drive them up by easy stages to Jerusalem.

I had had few letters and little real news since I had last seen Scarlett, and as I made the long trip down through Palestine and across the Egyptian frontier, I permitted myself a hope—just a hope—that the sea journey had already begun the longed-for improvement. Separation contrives to blunt reality. Yet I shall always be grateful for that short time because it granted me a few days of something approaching happiness, mercifully shielded from the realization of what lay before us.

Even when I saw the big Italian liner, the *Ausonia,* in the dock at Alexandria, I was still borne up by hope. I could not wait to see Scarlett again or tell her about the arrangements I had made. Her beloved garden at Government House was waiting to welcome her back; old Ahmed had been busy making special preparations for her homecoming amid his seed beds and glass frames. And the rooms she had so lovingly decorated and furnished to make a real home for me would be waiting too. Just as all her old friends, who remembered her so well from the last time she had been in Palestine, were eager to welcome her back again.

But once the actual moment came, I realized it would never be like this. I knew, too, with a terrible sense of finality, that we had entered a new phase. I could see immediately that the suspected but undiagnosed illness I had dreaded had come brutally to the fore. Like a shadow, it was there, a constant unwavering companion. Its presence was behind every look, every gesture, every weary though excited little sentence.

For Scarlett *was* pleased to be back, happy to be with me again in this land of brilliant sunlight. Despite the cruel evidence that told me there was little cause for hope, I was elated in a way I still cannot describe. At least, we were now all together again; Scarlett, Johan, and I, in a small, closed world which, for a tiny moment at least, thrust tragedy into the background and allowed a momentary breathing space.

We turned toward the slow journey back to Jerusalem. One after another, I telephoned to kindly friends who had arranged parties and receptions, canceling each one regretfully because, from now on, parties were unlikely to play very much of a part in our lives. All my energies had to be concentrated on preserving what little strength Scarlett had left. We halted for long periods of rest in Cairo and Gaza while I telephoned ahead to make arrangements for nurses and doctors in Jerusalem. And so, at last, we made the final journey up to Government House where she was put to bed in a room whose balcony overlooked her much loved gardens.

We were fortunate in having the devoted help of nurses and friends from both the Israeli and Arab sides during the ensuing weeks. Scarlett was desperately reluctant to enter a hospital again, and wanted to stay close to me. I knew she was happy here—as happy as continual suffering would ever allow her to be. And I used all the time I could spare from my official duties to help nurse her, sit with her, talk over old times and recall incidents from our life together; even, on occasions, daring to look into the future: a carefully simulated future.

I do not wish to dramatize those long weeks—so many other people have shared a similar experience. But it was a time that had to be lived through. A life so closely linked to my own was ebbing slowly before my eyes. And perhaps because I felt so totally helpless to halt or avert the process, I felt my spirit growing numb, imprisoned inside an ever-widening wilderness of despair.

On Christmas Day, which I had hoped to make a happy one for Scarlett, I suddenly collapsed and had to be put to bed myself. And although I was soon up and about again, I realized that her illness had reached a stage that no longer permitted the rather amateur facilities of Government House. I did not need to consult the doctors to realize that we had little choice; the effects were becoming so marked now that my heart used to sink every time I came into her room after working in my office or in the operations room below. And so, on Boxing Day, we took her to the new Hadassah hospital, where she was put under the care of the Dutch-born Professor Grohn and two charming Israeli nurses, Olga Hegyesi and Madeleine Topiol.

Strangely, this move to hospital seemed to impart a miraculous new urge to live. Within six weeks, Scarlett appeared to have made a remarkable recovery, and was fervently entreating Professor Grohn to allow her to return to Government House. I don't think that he was very happy about this idea, but at last he reluctantly agreed. And so she came back to us again, just in time to celebrate Johan's fourteenth birthday.

It was a very happy celebration, and he had much to tell her about his new friends among my staff. My trusted driver and special assistant, Max Elmvang, from Denmark, had taken him on a round trip of Israel, Jordan, Syria, and Lebanon, and he had been spending a great deal of time with another Dane, Verner Andersen, who was our staff photographer. Verner and his admirable wife, Lily, had been virtually acting as step-parents throughout this very difficult period. And Verner had not only taught Johan a great deal about photography but had also arranged for Kawade, our Japanese postmaster, to give him a sound grounding in the invaluable art of judo.

It was a very happy day, but within twenty-four hours poor Scarlett had a bad relapse. The inevitable was very near and when on a beautiful Spring morning a week later I took her back to the Hadassah hospital, her face, so much a part of my own life, was already marked by death.

I can never forget that morning. We carried her gently through the gardens she loved so much to the waiting ambulance. In that clear, brilliant sunshine, the whole world seemed to be burgeoning with new life, so vivid and fresh that it was momentarily difficult to realize that her own was coming to a close. But once back inside the hospital with those kind faces, but that terrible, familiar antiseptic smell, I felt as though the gates had closed behind us; that morning had been but one small, precious moment lost forever except in memory—which soon now would be very precious indeed.

The end came very swiftly. But first, I had the heartbreaking task of explaining the situation to Johan. We had arranged long ago that he should return to Sweden on March 13 in time for his school term in Malmö. We both felt that it was better that he should go rather than stay here with us to endure an experience which, up till this time, he had little suspected. But I could not let him go without some inkling of the truth.

I find it very difficult, even now, to write of the talk we had together; he was only just fourteen, hardly on the threshold of being able to comprehend this sort of experience. Yet he listened to all I had to tell him with an understanding and compassion far beyond his years. I admired him very much; I still do.

Less than forty-eight hours after his departure Scarlett died. During the previous weeks, I had almost welcomed the mounting crisis around Lake Tiberias because the reports that had flowed into the operations room, the visits I had had to make, the almost familiar routine, had acted as a hard but imperious diversion from my own tragedy. But, in our last few moments together, I was entirely enclosed inside our own world. When the final break came, I was grateful it was mercifully swift. But once it was over, I felt desperately alone, yet marveling because the act of her going had restored the beauty I had known so well to a face long ravaged by unrelenting suffering.

I was grateful to see so many old friends at her funeral service at the Scottish church of St. Andrews in Israeli Jerusalem. Later, we made the journey to Bethlehem in Jordan with its small Lutheran cemetery. We buried her to the full-throated roar of Israeli guns. As I stood at her graveside, I had already heard the news of the attack on Nuqeib early that morning.

Chapter Twenty-one

THE SECURITY COUNCIL

THERE had been shooting on Lake Tiberias eight days earlier. On the morning of March 8, one of our observers (who had been seven kilometers away) heard a heavy exchange of machine-gun fire and six big explosions followed by more firing.

Later, conflicting complaints had flooded into the Tiberias office of the Israel-Syrian MAC. The Israelis reported that Syrian positions at El-Koursi had opened heavy fire with machine guns, bazookas, and recoilless guns on one of their patrol boats, damaging it and wounding two of the crew. From the Syrians came a countercomplaint that an armed Israeli lighter had come within forty meters of the shore and had opened fire on their post at El-Koursi.

Our observers moved in to investigate and collected a number of conflicting statements from witnesses on both sides; the only indisputable evidence had been the damaged patrol craft: among its scars and indentations had been three large holes, the sort one would expect from 80mm-caliber armor-piercing projectiles.

Shortly after this, a fellow Swede, Commander O. W. Melin (the Chairman of the MAC) reported that the senior Israeli delegate in Tiberias had told our officers that this incident could well lead to a deterioration comparable to what had happened in 1955. I wondered at the time whether this could be a veiled warning that the Israelis were preparing another retaliatory raid. But there was no actual evidence of brewing trouble apart from the normal flow of complaints about illegal fishing and the theft of nets.

Whatever my own "sixth sense," I did not see this new incident as anything more than sudden thunder on the Sea of Galilee. But next day, March 9, I was summoned to Mrs. Meir, who requested me to go to Damascus to tell the Syrians that the Israeli Government regarded the attack on their patrol boat as an incident of the utmost gravity. In a melodramatic and thunderous voice, Mrs. Meir asked me to tell them that through such actions *they are playing with fire.*

I told her angrily that she could hardly expect the Chief of Staff of UNTSO to act as a post boy for messages that might be construed as open or implied threats—especially when, since 1951, Israel had ostentatiously boycotted the meetings of the MAC and had consistently flouted the terms of the Armistice Agreement.

Far from having the effect she anticipated, her message was much more likely to produce a hostile reaction. I was in Palestine, I told her, to keep the peace, *not* to provoke hostilities. On hearing this, her thunderous voice became muted as she assured me the Israelis had no intention of threatening the Syrians, but only wanted to make their views clear. This was more reasonable. If there was to be more shooting I did not want UNTSO reproached for failing to make the Israeli position clear. I told Mrs. Meir I would ask the Chairman of the MAC in Damascus to pass on her message. Next day Commander Melin did this when he saw the Syrian High Command in Damascus, who told him that his request to set up a new UN observation post near El-Koursi would receive favorable consideration.

From this moment on, the troubles grew worse. On March 14, Michael Comay, the Israeli Permanent Delegate to the UN in New York, called U Thant, who was Acting Secretary General, and expressed his country's deep concern over the patrol boat incident.

The following day, March 15, our observers reported another skirmish on the Lake where two Israeli patrol craft, escorting a fishing boat, had approached Moussadiye—roughly between El-Koursi and the mouth of the Jordan. It had been impossible to establish which side shot first, but during the fire fight, which lasted for twenty-five minutes, the Syrians seemed to have been using machine and antitank guns, against the machine guns and larger caliber 20mm guns of the Israeli boats. Investigations by our observer revealed that the only apparent casualty had been a young Arab girl in the village, who had died from a bullet wound.

The Syrians lodged a complaint, but the Israelis tried another method. A personal message was dispatched by Mrs. Meir to New York, asking U Thant, the Acting Secretary General, to intervene "before the matter became more serious." At that time I had never met U Thant, but his message, asking for urgent information about the incident, reached me simultaneously with reports of a new duel on Lake Tiberias between a patrol boat and a Syrian position at Kafr Aequeb (not far from El-Koursi); although our observation post at the mouth of the Jordan had not been able to see the action and it all sounded rather inconclusive, a second message from Mrs. Meir was soon on the Acting Secretary General's desk in New York demanding to know whether this new attack on a patrol boat was the Syrian answer to the representations of the United Nations.

It was quite obvious to all our observers in Tiberias, Kuneitra, Damascus, and Jerusalem that both sides were moving toward a head-on clash. On the afternoon of March 16, Commander Melin reported that although he had no concrete evidence, he could sense there had been a distinct hardening in the Syrian attitude. Local Syrian commanders around the lake had begun to refuse our observers access to places where earlier shooting had taken place, despite remonstrances from their own liaison officers who were accompanying them.

As reports started to come in of Syrian troop movements, it was plain a build-up was in process. On the Israeli side observers and civilian members of UNTSO were also reporting intense activity; field units were being called up and deployed around the border area with heavy mortars, medium guns, and armor. Our observers also reported that Israeli military police were actively preventing them from going anywhere near positions from which an offensive was likely to be launched.

On the evening before my wife's funeral in Bethlehem, I felt certain that even our last few minutes were bound to be interrupted by news from the lake. My staff loyally tried to leave me in peace, but we were all on the alert for news from our observers who, unfortunately, were not well placed to see the ensuing action.

We had two observation posts, Delta near the Jordan and Echo not far from Tawafiq. We had also sent a temporary observer to the Israeli kibbutz at Beit Katzir (because they refused to let us establish a permanent post). Toward midnight all the villages on the east shore of the lake blacked out. Obviously expecting an attack, the Syrians fired a number of flares. Within minutes our observers at the mouth of the Jordan River were reporting the sound of massive firing. It was now one o'clock in the morning and the shooting that first seemed to come from patrol boats soon spread to the land as Syrian artillery farther back opened fire.

Unfortunately our observers (on the western shore of the lake and in observation posts near the northern and southern ends of the eastern shore) were in no position to follow the development of the attack, which was now launched along the east shore from a jumping-off point at the Israeli settlement of Ein Gev. Firing lasted all night and toward dawn Israeli planes were overflying Syrian territory.

At nine o'clock next morning, the Israelis issued their first communiqué. It announced that shortly before midnight an Israeli unit had assaulted Syrian positions south of Nuqeib, had occupied their positions there, and had destroyed their fortifications.

This was the very first time we had heard a mention of that fateful name; at no time during the previous incidents had it figured in Israeli complaints. Nuqeib itself was a most difficult place to pin down; there were no less than three Nuqeibs: an old abandoned village, a former "new" village, and a new "new" village (which turned out to be the object of the Israeli attack). For us, this was to be extremely important. Until now, all Israeli complaints had centered around or about Syrian posts at El-Koursi—which was some distance away from this alleged Syrian stronghold.

According to the morning papers, it had been a formidable position, bristling with guns, which the Israeli assaulting force had been able to capture only at the cost of five killed and ten wounded. Certainly the Syrians must have been expecting them, but their own casualties, which the Israelis claimed as thirty killed and "scores wounded," seemed unusually high. Not unexpectedly, the Israelis also claimed a spectacular haul of war material and were soon arranging tours to the scene for virtually everyone down to schoolchildren—with the marked exception of UN personnel. It was not until two days later that they took the trouble to advise us officially that the position which they had attacked had been the new village of Nuqeib.

A cease fire was arranged later that day—which had seen jet planes dogfighting over Syrian territory. By this time the Israeli press was in full cry—journalists in almost company strength had been rushed out—and there was great talk of Soviet weapons captured from the Syrians in their heavily fortified positions.

Whatever the press claims on either side, it was clear that a great deal of blood had been shed, despite our having informed the Israelis shortly before the attack was launched that the Syrians were favorable to our request for a new observation post near El-Koursi (we heard through various sources that visiting newspapermen had been quietly called away the moment this news had come through).

Once the assault force with its supporting weapons had been given plently of time to withdraw, our observers were at last allowed in several days too late. By the time (March 27) that I was in a position to report to U Thant that both sides had agreed to cooperate with UNTSO there was little chance of our discovering what had actually happened on that night. As a belated sop Mrs. Meir now told me that Israel would keep her police boats out of Lake Tiberias for the next few days. But she firmly rejected my suggestion that, from now on, one of our own patrol boats should be allowed to operate there.

I informed U Thant that although we had arranged a cease fire it was likely to prove an uneasy one. At this time I did not suspect just what a serious view the outside world would take of Israel's action. But I was soon left in little doubt when the Israeli press forecast—as a result of conversations between Mr. Barbour, the American Ambassador, and Mrs. Meir—that the Americans were likely to take a highly unfavorable view in the Security Council. Even France, they predicted, was likely to take a stand against Israel because of her newfound need for understanding with the Arab world. I became aware, too, that Israeli official circles anticipated that Israel would find herself isolated on March 28 when the Security Council met to hear the Syrian complaint—a day which was fated to coincide with a new military *coup* in Syria.*

* This was but another incident in the seemingly never-ending internal struggle for power in Syria. To the best of my knowledge there have been some twenty military *coups* or counter *coups* since Syria obtained her independence.

By this time I had compiled a very full report; drafted by Henri Vigier, it was soon available to the members of the Security Council and elicited an Israeli Press comment that it was "dry" but "objective." At this time their press was in no way hostile or violent toward me. Its tone was almost favorable, because nobody could foresee the turn of events. These were startling.

On March 28 an unusual event took place in the Security Council where Adlai Stevenson—obviously representing the new American line—severely censured Israel and issued a stern warning against any further retaliatory action. Mr. Stevenson was to spring another surprise. After the Russian Permanent Delegate had demanded that the Council condemn Israel, he announced that it was now seven years since the Council had had any firsthand evidence from the Chief of Staff of UNTSO. And suggested that I should be summoned to New York for direct consultation with the members of the Council.

U Thant had never before had to grapple with the problem of the Holy Land. But now he sensibly pointed out that he would prefer to have me on the spot while the situation in the Tiberias area remained extremely tense; that I had already sent in a very full report and that it was unlikely I would be able to add much to what I had already said. Under pressure, however, he agreed that my presence in New York might give the Security Council a chance to hear fuller details about the measures I had suggested to prevent any further fighting.

I think that the Israeli press was more puzzled than apprehensive when it became known that I had been called to New York; they had already accepted the fact that Israel would be found at fault—so that it seemed the only real problem before the Council was the degree of condemnation.

The general tone of the press was not at all unfavorable. *DAVAR* commented, "Despite its cautious wording and the fact that, for formal reasons, it avoids drawing conclusions from the observer's reports, General von Horn's report confirms the Israeli version of events." *HAMODIA* said: "The von Horn report leaves no doubt where the responsibility lies." And *AL HAMISHMAR* announced: "One can only hope that von Horn's personal evidence will be in the same spirit as his written report." For the time being—although the Israelis were seriously disturbed by the new attitude of the Kennedy Administration—there was no personal hostility toward me. Personally, however, I could already see the writing on the wall. I was very alive to the complications that might arise from my visit to New York and hardly needed *HAARETZ* to tell me: "The invitation to New York puts von Horn in a difficult position. In his report he gave the maximum necessary to explain the situation and the minimum which could annoy both sides, with whom he has to continue working in the future. When he has to answer questions at the Security Council, he may be drawn into giving answers which will hamper the continuation of his work."

This was just what was worrying me and I set off with serious misgivings; service with the UN had taught me to distrust the moment when soldiering and politics merged. I could imagine the traps and pitfalls likely to encompass a soldier cross-examined by politicians more interested in exploiting answers to their own ends than establishing the truth.

I arrived in New York on April 1, a propitious date, and was relieved to find that the Acting Secretary General understood and shared my misgivings. I had never met U Thant before and was glad to find that the influence of his natural oriental composure allowed the most difficult problem to be discussed calmly without a hint of tension or irritation. Knowledgeable, serious, and dedicated, he had a surprisingly deep voice and a certain earthy robustness that I found endearing. He had not, at that time, any of Dag's intricate knowledge of the Arab-Israeli problem (a knowledge that could only really be achieved through personal experience). For this reason he leaned heavily on Ralph Bunche for advice, listening between puffs at an apparently endless succession of little black Burmese cheroots. And Ralph, despite our violent differences in the past, was very much his old, familiar self; as kind as ever and a friend in need because of his extensive experience of the maze of difficulties surrounding negotiations in the Holy Land.

Both shared my anxiety that I was likely to be pulled to pieces were I exposed to sustained cross-examination in the Council. Ralph I already knew well, but I found U Thant so friendly, simple, and full of common sense that it was easy to talk to him frankly and I was deeply relieved when he decided that I should be allowed to reply to questions in writing rather than be subjected to an oral examination.

Once U Thant made up his mind, there was a certain bluntness, a finality thoroughly refreshing after the tortuous ambiguities that had underlain most of Dag's decisions. I could sense a certain coarseness or toughness of grain, which made me feel that behind that mild, contemplative face with its almost classically rosebud mouth and donnish glasses there was a blunt, straightforward personality that one could trust.

It was strange to be sitting across the table from the two of them. I was, I suppose, still wedded to the old order; I had lived with it, worked with it, appreciated its good qualities and learned to live with its less favorable aspects. I had come to know Dag well, in the sort of intimate, personal way that made nonsense of accusations that he had been a cold mystic who had descended on the glass building from some mythical Swedish breeding-ground for Nordic St. John the Baptists.

I had only to look around the room to conjure up a dozen memories of Dag and Andy. But now those times were gone—and U Thant was here, heir to a host of problems and responsibilities and already beginning to be starved of the financial means of solving them. There was nothing very dramatic about him, no obvious sign that this was a man fitted to carry on this heavy task. He struck me as essentially conscious of the limitations that hung like a millstone around the high office he had assumed. But far from daunting him, these seemed to give him greater determination.

The next meeting of the Security Council had been fixed for April 3. I had been assigned a temporary office on the thirty-eighth floor, and here I was visited by a number of members of the permanent delegations. Most were thoroughly helpful; the American, British, and French delegates were anxious to know what sort of additional support UNTSO needed to enable it to carry out its task more effectively.

I had a visit from the Syrian delegate, which was purely a courtesy call. But, rather as I had anticipated, the visit of Michael

Comay, the South-African-born Israeli delegate, was very different. He was a well-mannered man with a pleasant, modulated voice which soon left me in no doubt that I had become an object for "well-intentioned advice." Although his conversation was larded with references to "old friendship and acquaintance," it was quite clear why he had come.

It would be best, he advised me, to forget all about that outdated United Nations idea of running a patrol boat on Lake Tiberias; the idea was stillborn and ought to be abandoned because the lake was essentially Israeli sovereign territory. He understood that this had already been made clear to me in Jerusalem. After all, why did I waste my time insisting on so many things to which I knew the Israelis were opposed? It would be wise to listen to his advice—otherwise my life was bound to become a great deal more uncomfortable.

Superficially, I liked Comay although his intentions were very clear. I told him that I had read the Israeli press for so long that I was not hard pressed for "official guidance." I appreciated his "advice," but it was really a waste of breath to attempt to influence the Chief of Staff of UNTSO—especially on United Nations territory. In fact I borrowed a phrase of Mrs. Meir's and told him that I did not want to be pushed around.

As I watched him go, it was difficult to forget Dag's warning in this same building: "Remember, whatever you do you will never have the wholehearted cooperation of the Israelis."

I had never before attended a meeting of the Security Council. And when, at half past two on April 3, I entered an almost empty council chamber, I was almost as excited as a tourist. The Secretary General is seated on the right of the Council member presiding; with Ralph Bunche, I was shown into a seat just behind him. As the chamber began to fill up, I was intrigued to see the variegated characters and personalities who made up this international body.

It was their thousandth meeting (and already the Israeli-Arab dispute had figured on no less than four hundred agendas). Listening to the initial courtesies, the flowery diplomatic phraseology, I was more glad than ever that I was not going to be called upon to speak. In this debater's paradise I was more than content to sit in the shadow of Ralph and U Thant, who rode the whirlwind with such practiced ease, where an ordinary soldier like myself would have been totally lost.

And yet there was nothing particularly alarming about the questions. I was asked for straightforward answers, elucidations, opinions, by the representatives of Syria, the United Arab Republic, Ghana, and the United States. Each question remained very clear in my own mind, even though I knew that the transcription service would soon deliver them in printed form on my desk upstairs where I would have time and thought for considered answers. Just the same, it was almost like going to the dentist to watch a dress rehearsal for your own extractions.

Soon after the Council had been adjourned, the mass of paper on my desk brought me sharply back to reality. There were two very loaded questions from the Syrian Delegate, Mr. Tazari. Had I any reason to expect another attack on Syrian territory by the Israeli armed forces? And, in my opinion, how long did it take to prepare an attack such as the one that had been launched in the early hours of March 17? Writing at leisure, I replied that, in the former case, I refused to speculate or undertake predictions; in the second, I felt it necessary to remind the Council that my job in UNTSO was limited to endeavoring to keep the peace according to the terms of the Armistice Agreement. I was therefore in no position to have the necessary information to give a satisfactory answer, but I believed that violations could be minimized, if not eliminated, *if only* we had the successful cooperation of both sides.

I do not wish to weary the reader with a documented list of all the questions and answers; I did, however, get an opportunity in my replies to state my views on what I considered the best way of increasing UNTSO's chances of effectiveness. I pointed out that freedom of movement was an essential for effective observation, but that in Syria our observers were not allowed to move more than fifty meters from their posts without escorts while on the Israeli side the situation was different but no better. I hammered home the UN's seven-year struggle to obtain permission for its own patrol boat on Lake Tiberias.

I reminded them that when, in 1956, the late Secretary General had requested a specific assurance from both sides that the principle of UN freedom of movement should be recognized, assurances to this effect had been given by all the Arab states while Israel had come up with the proviso that it would "continue to afford United Nations observers the same degree of freedom of movement inside Israel which all visitors to the country normally enjoy."

I therefore felt it necessary to point out that while Israeli-owned pleasure craft were allowed to operate freely on Lake Tiberias, the United Nations remained excluded. In the same way, while Israeli air lines brought in foreign tourists to the Roseh-Pinna-Mahanayim airfield, requests for permission for the Chief of Staff of UNTSO to land there in times of crisis were consistently refused. Our requests to use helicopters to increase the efficiency of our observer force were not even considered.

These, however, were easy, comparatively straightforward matters which were unlikely to rouse the wrath of the Israelis. The explosive question had been asked by the Syrian Delegate almost at the beginning of the session. He wanted to know whether, during the recent attack, any Syrian fortified position had been occupied or destroyed. My written answer had been quite clear. On the basis of the reports I had received from my observers, who had visited the demilitarized zone on three occasions since March 17, I was satisfied that there had been none; no fortified position —whether destroyed or still standing—had been observed at Nuqeib.

By the time that my answers had been typed and circulated to the Council, the Israeli machinery was already in action, but the full force of its venom was still masked, hidden in the eloquent confectionery of Michael Comay's speech of the April 5 when, after having considered my replies, the Council reconvened. Quite aside from the pressure Comay had tried to put on me, there had been considerable activity among Israeli supporters and sympathizers in the United States.

During the last few days a number of Congressmen had raised the issue, questioning whether Mr. Stevenson's attitude toward Israel in the Security Council represented official United States policy. In Washington, Israeli representatives had called on Dean Rusk, the American Secretary of State, while a delegation of

Zionists had been to see the Assistant Secretary of State for Middle Eastern Affairs. In New York, Michael Comay had called upon the United States Delegation to the UN (owing to Stevenson being heavily engaged, he had only been able to see Charles Yost, who was the Number Three man in the US delegation to the UN). All these meetings had proved abortive; it had been pointed out that the United States was primarily interested in strengthening the effectiveness of the United Nations.

On April 5, I was once more allowed into the Council chamber as the debate resumed. It was not long before I heard Michael Comay begin his speech for Israel. It started quietly enough, outlining the Israeli version, explaining their view of the relatonship between UNTSO and their own authorities and claiming that "any specific suggestions or requests made by the United Nations Chief of Staff were given the most careful consideration." This state of affairs, he assured the Council, would continue. But, in considering them: "My Government must have regard to questions of our national security and of our exclusive jurisdiction over our own territory."

I listened with interest; Comay's bland statement failed to disclose what we in UNTSO knew so well; in practice *none* of our suggestions or requests designed to *prevent* border incidents were, or would ever, be accepted unless on some rare occasion they could be passed off as having sprung from Israeli initiative.

Soon now Comay began to warm up. I heard the words of my own report twisted as he noted my observation that, on the Syrian side, our observers were subjected to the most stringent limitations on movements, and went on: "The General omits to state that no comparable limitations are imposed on the Israeli side." What I had actually said—and the record lay under his eye—was: "On the Israeli side the position is different but no better." As I listened, I recalled the innumerable occasions when I and my observers had been forcibly prevented from carrying out our task.

The crisis was approaching. Challenging my statement that there had been no fortified position in the demilitarized zone at Nuqeib, Comay stated: "But when a United Nations official appears to throw doubt on the factual veracity of my Government's position it is for us a very serious matter. I wish to state on the full authority of my Government that we reject any inference of doubt which may be contained in General von Horn's statement yesterday."

I knew then that the whole official machinery of the State of Israel would be swung into action against me. Doubtless I had already become a target for a sustained attack, planned just as carefully as their military operation against the Syrians. I knew, too, that—as far as my UNTSO command in Israel was concerned—I was finished. And as I listened to Comay giving a specific map reference for the position that had been attacked, offering to show UNTSO a list of the military weapons and equipment that had been captured, and announcing that a Syrian prisoner was available to testify that the post had been garrisoned by regular Syrian troops, I was recalling the conversation we had had together a few days earlier—the "advice," the hints that life could become very difficult.

Later that afternoon, when the Council had adjourned, I had a meeting with U Thant, who asked me to prepare a statement commenting on Michael Comay's claims about the existence of a fortified position at Nuqeib. Although I had the utmost confidence in the observers on whose reports my own statement had been based, I cabled UNTSO for a thorough check.

Knowing now what lay in store for me in Israel, I talked to U Thant, who was calmly puffing at one of his cheroots, and found his calm extremely reassuring. Neither of us could ignore the new situation that had arisen; it was early days yet, but the warning flares had gone up and it would not be long before organized Israeli hostility contrived to hamper my work until I became an embarrassment to the UN.

It had happened before in Jerusalem; it would happen again. Peacekeeping for a Chief of Staff of UNTSO could never be anything but a tightrope walker's nightmare. Sooner or later one end of the rope would sag. But through the cheroot smoke I did not see U Thant as a man ready to throw UN servants to the lions. Things would have to get very rough indeed before I became expendable. And I was grateful because, over Nuqeib, I knew I had been right.

While I waited for a reply from Jerusalem, I had little doubt that my observers had done their job thoroughly and efficiently. And indeed they had. When the cable arrived, I knew my confidence had been vindicated. I was able to draw up the comments U Thant had asked for, based on information hardly likely to warm the heart of Michael Comay.

Since this report was destined to unleash the full weight of Israeli fury against me, I want to set it down here for the record —just as it was circulated to the members of the Council. I reminded them that on April 5 Mr. Comay had given a specific map reference, 21090-21645, as the exact location of the "fortified" Syrian position the Israelis had attacked. My Deputy Chief of Staff, however, had reported that the two officers who had investigated the incident on March 16 and 17 had been close to this map reference.

The whole area had been covered physically or by visual observation. The actual map reference given by Comay had been observed in the course of a further visit on March 29. No fortified positions had been seen. As a result of my cable both officers had been closely interrogated. Both (and one of them was an artillery officer well versed in locating map references on the ground) had insisted that there was no fortified position in the area although they had observed several shallow slit trenches. This type of trench, better known as a foxhole, could be dug within a couple of hours; indeed the villagers frequently dug them for cooking or drainage or disposal purposes. They were essentially the sort of trenches which, in the past, had been dug by attacking units as temporary shelter for one or two soldiers. Under no circumstances could they be described as a "fortified position."

I went on to deal with Michael Comay's offer to supply us with a list of captured material (he had stressed that among the weapons there had been an 82mm recoilless gun of the D.I.O. type). I pointed out that this was the first offer to supply UNTSO with a detailed list (nineteen days after the operation). As each side was bound, under the Armistice Agreement, to show us whatever military evidence came into its hand, I could not help but feel that, at this late date, the burden of proof seemed to be on the Israelis to show that (1) they had actually captured the weapons which they claimed; (2) that they were actually captured at the position which they had indicated; and (3) that the recoilless gun had previously been used in attacks on Israeli patrol craft.

On the question of the Syrian prisoner who was prepared to substantiate Israeli claims, I was interested to know why his evidence was not made available much earlier to UNTSO in order to help us investigate the original Israeli complaints. I would be interested to know, too, whether he corroborated the map reference which Michael Comay had given—and indeed, any of the other complaints the Israelis had made.

I have no doubt that these observations bounced straight off the top of Michael Comay's head; he was, after all, a skilled diplomat fighting his country's battle. But I had the feeling that, whatever trouble might be fermenting in Israel, my evidence had made a favorable impression on the Council.

Certainly, when it met again on April 6, Sir Patrick Dean of Great Britain fully supported my proposals for improved efficiency, and went on to say: "I should like, on behalf of my Delegation, to pay a warm tribute to the work of General von Horn and the other United Nations officials for what they are doing in this area. Their task is not an easy one and is clearly beset by numerous frustrations, which make their efforts to keep the area at peace the more praiseworthy. Those of us who share the aim of keeping the peace in this highly explosive part of the world must give our unstinted support to the work of the Chief of Staff. Even more, I think we must give full weight to any recommendations he makes for increasing the effectiveness of the role he is called upon to play."

Although I knew that words alone would be little comfort in the chill wind awaiting me in the Holy Land, it was nonetheless heartwarming to hear the representatives of Chile, Ghana, Venezuela, and the United States express their appreciation of our work.

Charles Yost, speaking for the United States, strongly urged both sides to cooperate with us more fully, and told the Council: "I should like to commend General von Horn and his able colleagues on their excellent performance of duties on behalf of the United Nations under unusually difficult circumstances. General von Horn and his entire staff deserve the gratitude and the unstinting support of the Members of the United Nations, and most of all that of Israel and its Arab neighbors."

The result of the debate was now a foregone conclusion. But at Israel's request the final meeting was put back to April 9 to give her a chance to make a statement on the draft resolution that condemned her.

On the final day, I listened to this with the skepticism born of four years of hard experience. Even fighting a rearguard action, Comay was eloquent and impressive in putting forward the Israeli case in its most favorable light. But it was with a wry smile that I heard him say; "Our security situation might have suggested to us that rigid restrictions should be imposed on the movements of nationals of a score of different countries who pass freely back and forth across the border, some of whom live on the Arab side. The fact that they temporarily wear a United Nations armband does not automatically make them good security risks. In the past I cannot say that every single member of the UNTSO staff has proved worthy of the trust required by his assignment."

I heard this with a certain sadness. And although I knew only too well what a wealth of truth it concealed, it struck me as strange that the Israelis, who had spent so much money, trouble, and time on subverting our people, should now be highlighting a lamentable weakness I had fought so hard to correct. Our dossiers and security files in Jerusalem would not have made pleasant reading for the Israelis here in the Council Chamber. But Comay made no mention of this and concluded by stating:

"We welcome any suggestions by the Chief of Staff. We will give them our earnest consideration and if they appear useful and acceptable, we will assist the Chief of Staff in their early implementation."

When—on April 9—the Council condemned Israel, endorsed my recommendations for strengthening UNTSO, and urged both sides to reactivate the MAC's and make full use of the machinery designed for the observation of the Armistice Agreement, I had no illusions about the future. Comay's "advice" was still clear in my mind. I knew it was only a matter of time.

Chapter Twenty-two

FALSE ACCUSATIONS

BENEATH the ginger crewcut Albert Grand's normally mischievous face was somber.

"I'm afraid, General, that we are in for an exceptionally difficult time." His voice could not disguise a note of sympathy despite his long training as a press officer.

This was no understatement. He placed a fresh sheaf of press summaries on my desk and stood back as though expecting a sudden outburst of irritation. But (besides grunting in a gruff, appreciative sort of way) I had no comment to make; things were working out exactly as I had anticipated.

Over the years I had come to think of Government House as home. But driving up the valley from Jordan two days before, I had felt no resurgence of spirits, only the certainty that I was on my way back to face a prolonged and infinitely bitter experience.

If anything, I had underestimated Israel's talent for denigration and vilification. But a brief talk with the Old Fox had brought me up sharply. Had I heeded the "advice" of Michael Comay in the glass building, had I knuckled under and decided that discretion was the better part of valor, no doubt things would have been very different. But I had decided to stand by the truth, knowing this was bound to make me *persona non grata*. And this, Vigier told me, was exactly what had happened. Nor was this to stop at a mere expression of official displeasure.

I gathered that my old sparring partner, Mrs. Meir, had initiated the battle—and this time with a new weight of lead in her gloves. "You see, General," Vigier told me gently, "the point she has been exploiting—if that's the right word for it—is the possibility that had you not been at Mrs. von Horn's funeral things might have gone differently at Nuqeib."

"My God," I said.

Vigier, who is very French, shrugged his shoulders. "Take it easy, my dear General. Don't distress yourself. You know the sort of people we have to deal with."

I knew them only too well. But the false accusation hurt none the less. I thought of the Israelis planning their attack while poor Scarlett was dying, deliberately preventing our observers going near the scene of their nefarious operations, and then launching their night attack secure in the knowledge that the UN Chief of Staff was safely out of the way burying his wife in Bethlehem. And now, when world opinion had gone against them, using this pretext to accuse me of neglecting my duties and hinting that had I been doing my job properly the Israeli army might have acted very differently and thought twice about attacking the wicked Syrians.

Mrs. Meir's unscrupulous tactics were only a foretaste of the shape of things to come. Even before she entered the lists, bitter attacks had been launched on me in the Knesset where I was held up as an example of the worst and most prejudiced of Israel's enemies. Government policy was henceforth based on this same outlook. An official boycott was proclaimed with the express purpose of making it impossible for me to carry out my work. By hook or by crook, they were determined to make me an embarrassment to the United Nations.

"Look at this," said Albert Grand, showing me a copy of *Lamerhav* (the Government newspaper) for April 10, 1961. I read:

> von Horn's hostile and biased appearance in the Security Council created the definite impression that he had decided in his heart not to continue his high and responsible post. There seems to be no other explanation for his support of Syria without any reservations. Von Horn deliberately misled the Council and endeavoured to obtain Israel's condemnation. In doing so he undercut the moral and practical basis which the U.N.T.S.O. Chief needs in order to function. Perhaps he will now enjoy more prestige in Syrian eyes but he will no longer enjoy Israel's confidence. He now has no choice but to give way for another and better U.N.T.S.O. Chief.

These attacks, the decision to declare me *persona non grata,* were only a prelude to a sustained attempt to get me out of the Holy Land and, if possible, right out of United Nations service. Had I been a less determined and more easily influenced character, I might have assumed—as the British have it—that I had had my chips. I did not, however, subscribe to the implication that doing one's duty and telling the truth were an automatic passport to premature retirement. Nor did I take kindly to the arrogant Israeli assumption that a servant of the United Nations could be treated with blatant impunity, denigrated and "pushed around" (as Mrs. Meir would have put it) until life had become so impossible that the only alternative became discreet surrender. So long as I enjoyed U Thant's backing, so long as the organization I had the honor of serving relied on my probity and integrity, I had no intention of allowing myself to be browbeaten or overawed.

Oddly enough, there were chinks in the Israeli armor. Albert Grand and I studied them carefully. *Kol Ham,* the Communist paper, wrote: "The Security Council resolution showed once more that Ben Gurion's adventurous policies have brought Israel a political defeat. In the long run Ben Gurion has injured Israel's national interests. The Nuqeib action was a black mark against Israel in the eyes of the world. It isolated Israel and increased Israeli-Arab tension."

It was an unusual quarter from which to receive support, but it did show there were divergences of opinion in the Israeli front. More welcome was an article, "Crisis of Confidence," that appeared in *Ner,* the monthly journal of the Ihud Association for Jewish-Arab Rapprochement. This association, which had been founded by the first dean of the Hebrew University (the late Dr. J. L. Magnus), included many well-known cultural personalities. Perhaps one of the foremost figures in the Society was the wise old philosopher, Professor Martin Buber,* whom Dag always managed to visit whenever he was in the area. It was a long article, written by Dr. S. Shereshevsky. Not only does it give a remarkably true and objective view of what actually *did* happen (the only one I came across in Israel), but it shows that wise counsel and generosity of spirit where not entirely missing in Israel.

* He died only a short time ago.

Dr. Shereshevsky stated that the Israeli raid on Syrian positions on the Kinneret had created a serious crisis of confidence at home, in the United Nations, and in the world at large. He pointed out that many of the people were beginning to doubt the wisdom of the sudden escalation of the earlier shooting incidents along the border.

He went on to say that "the questioning and the discussions were heard in all walks of life, among workers and government officials. They found it hard to understand why these shooting incidents—even if they did involve the wounding of two policemen and damage to a patrol boat—had merited a retaliatory operation of such scope, involving tens of casualties and widespread destruction."

Meanwhile, Dr. Shereshevsky explained, the situation along the border remained tense, and the general air of confusion was heightened by the fact that the raid had taken place at the very time the United Nations Truce Supervisory Organization in Jerusalem was attempting to mediate the dispute. The Israeli government had, in fact, proposed the establishment of a UN observation post in the vicinity of El-Kursi in Syria, and I had been asked to go to Damascus to negotiate with the Syrians. Only the fatal illness of Mrs. von Horn, culminating in her death the day before the Israeli raid, prevented my making the trip.

After quoting from my report to the Secretary General, Dr. Shereshevsky's article continued: "According to *DAVAR* (a daily newspaper) Israel maintained constant contact not only with the Armistice Commission but also with the UN Headquarters in Jerusalem. It was in the midst of this attempt at mediation by General von Horn that the raid on Nuqeib and the neighboring Syrian outpost was carried out. . . . These facts which add to the crisis of confidence should raise the questions: Why did the Israeli Government not give the TSO a few days in which to act? Why did it not stop sending out patrol boats? Why did the Foreign Minister wait until four days after the raid to tell General von Horn that Israel would stop sending patrol boats onto the lake for a few days until the UN observation post at El-Kursi was organized 'in order to facilitate his efforts'?"

The article then shifted its attention to the debates over the conflict that took place in the Security Council of the United Nations in New York. Dr. Shereshevsky revealed how Michael Comay accused me of giving misleading answers to questions and insisted that no Syrian fortifications were found in the demilitarized zone and that the Israeli operation had been launched in the demilitarized zone on the eastern shore of the lake and not actually into Syrian territory—whereas a sketch in the Army magazine, *Bamahaneh,* of March 20 clearly showed that military penetration had been made into Syria.

Dr. Shereshevsky further stated that those who read the facts in the Israeli press would not be surprised by the Security Council's resolution to condemn Israel, and would necessarily come to the regretful conclusion that "the Government did *not* 'consider the issue carefully' and did make a 'rush decision.' They will deplore a warlike act that took heavy toll of human life without achieving anything except to earn us another political defeat and to increase our isolation on the international arena."

The article also suggested that the Israeli people would come to regret the deterioration of their relations with the United Nations and ought to consider adopting a more positive attitude toward that international body, even to the point of being willing to make concessions as other sovereign nations had done in similar situations. Dr. Shereshevsky concluded that those who read the facts in the press would "denounce those Israeli circles which are trying to cover up their mistakes by assuming an arrogant attitude and by insulting personal attacks on General von Horn. . . . And they will warn against a policy that can only win us enemies and in the end turn those who sympathize with us into opponents."

This was a remarkable exception to the weight of calumny against me. But its sober tone and sound common sense found no echo in the Israeli press. A few days later Albert Grand was showing me files of press cuttings.

"What's this?" I asked, looking up at his mischievously smiling face.

"You may well ask, General. You'll see," Albert said wryly, "that they now claim you won the German Iron Cross in the war while everyone's relatives here were dying in concentration camps."

And there it was! A full and ingenious article on my shady past, which was to appear in newspapers whose readership spread halfway across Europe. We had not got the American press cuttings yet, but no doubt it would be there too, disseminated through a supremely efficient information service which had doubtless had its orders to "turn the heat on von Horn."

As I read on, I was interested to learn that I had acquired the Iron Cross from the Nazis for handling German transit traffic through Sweden during the war. I had never disguised my feelings toward the Nazis, but in this hot, vindictive state, who was to know or care about the truth of what had happened in a distant country like Sweden? People would believe what they *wanted* to believe; now the Chief of Staff of UNTSO had been officially pronounced one of Israel's public enemies. I was not quite in the same heavyweight class as President Nasser and the Arabs. But whereas no flight of imagination could envisage them as anything other than a permanency, *I* was expendable and with ingenuity could be got rid of.

"I'm sorry to disappoint them, Albert," I said when I had finished reading the cuttings, "but I don't number this particular decoration among my medals. I *do* have a few from Norway and Denmark as mementos of the time when I was supposed to be helping the Germans. As a matter of fact, the English also gave me their Order of the British Empire. And in those days they were remarkably shrewd judges of where a neutral's wartime sympathies lay."

Albert nodded sympathetically and collected the cuttings. There was little point in wasting breath. Before long he would be back with new and even fatter files.

A month before, I had heard Michael Comay assure the Security Council that the Israeli Governmeent had every intention of continuing to cooperate with the Chief of Staff of UNTSO. Now thousands of miles from the Council chamber, I was to get a taste of the Israeli idea of "cooperation."

Some time before I had been summoned to New York I had had a series of complaints from the Israelis (and from Jordan too) about traffic violations ranging from parking offenses to speeding and dangerous driving by members of the United Nations staff.

I had been asked to take action. Otherwise, I was told, the Government would have no alternative but to try the offenders in the Israeli courts.

I appreciated their position, and I immediately set up a special UN traffic patrol consisting of jeeps manned by personnel who had had experience in police work and traffic control in their own countries. I had discussed the way in which we would use them with our liaison officers in Israel and the Arab States. My impression was that the new patrols would be welcome everywhere, and we were looking forward to a marked improvement in UN standards of driving and traffic discipline.

As soon as I returned from New York, I told Victor Mills, my conscientious American Chief Administration Officer, to get the patrols started. The vehicles were ready and the men were standing by. Before we started it was only necessary to inform both the Israeli and Arab authorities that our jeeps would begin operating on a certain date.

This was done in the course of a meeting with Colonel Yacov Monbaz, the Senior Delegate and Chief Liaison Officer at the Israeli Foreign Office. But to Victor's surprise the earlier mood of cooperation had vanished. In a gruff and not exceptionally amiable voice. Monbaz told him that his Government considered a UN Traffic Patrol incompatible with Israel's sovereign rights. It must therefore be canceled and any attempt to put it into operation would only lead to the arrest of the Traffic Patrol by the Israeli police.

I had no alternative but to accept, although I was determined not to let those of our personnel who violated traffic regulations be dealt with by the Israeli courts. Next morning, I began to doubt whether representations of any sort would have much effect. When Albert brought in the press summaries, I read that we had already started our traffic patrols! The article went on to warn us that the next one found operating would be arrested by the Israeli police. I went at once to see Moshe Erell, who had succeeded Avraham Biran as Director of Armistice Affairs. It was plain that this article could only have been officially inspired and could be taken as an indication that any further chance of negotiation was doomed.

Erell proved totally uncooperative. It was a waste of breath to remind him that the whole conception of the patrols had arisen from direct Israeli requests that we take action to prevent traffic offenses. When I cited the well-established custom whereby foreign countries maintained shore patrols in the ports their naval units visited and suggested that our traffic patrols ought to be regarded in the same light, Erell took refuge in a long and sanctimonious statement about Israel's "sovereign rights."

It was so parrotlike that I found it impossible to refrain from observing that since Israel appeared to be so preoccupied with sovereign rights, it was strange she apparently neglected to observe them where other countries were concerned. I was thinking, I said, of Argentina whose rights had been violated by a famous abduction, which had been carried out not so very long before. Our conversation came to a predictable and chilly end.

It was quite plain that this decision had been taken in order to embarrass me, and I knew that every attempt would be made to make it crystal-clear in New York that the Chief of Staff in Jerusalem was washed up, incapable, and long overdue for replacement. Had I still harbored any illusions, these would have been soon dissipated by private information about the clandestine approaches being made to U Thant. He had already been informed "unofficially" by the Israeli Permanent Delegate to the United Nations (my old friend Michael Comay) that I had outlived my usefulness to the Israeli Government. And these "unofficial" moves were very shortly followed by a series of official *démarches* requesting my removal.

At times like these—and even more so during the more unorthodox and unscrupulous activities that were to follow—I was very grateful to the Acting Secretary General for his unswerving sympathy and support. It was comforting to imagine him, wreathed in familiar cigar smoke, firmly but courteously informing the persuasive Israelis that the burden of proof of their complaints must rest fairly and squarely on *their* Government and that such proof must be both crystal-clear and entirely authenticated. Until such time as such proof *was* available, the Acting Secretary General had every confidence in the Chief of Staff.

One had to hand it to the Israelis for dogged persistence. One evening in New York, about half past eight, Ralph Bunche was working in his office when he received a telephone call from one of the chief members of the Israel Delegation. He had, he told Ralph, just received a "most immediate" message from Jerusalem containing highly important information and it was vital he come to discuss it at once. Late already, Ralph told him that he was not available that night and that the matter would have to wait until the next day. But this rebuff raised such a torrent of entreaties that Ralph finally changed his mind and agreed to let him meet at his own home later that evening.

Once back at his house in Forest Hills, Ralph had hardly had time to take off his hat before there was an urgent buzzing at the doorbell. And shortly after that his visitor was pacing up and down Ralph's carpet, explaining that he could hardly bring himself to break such news to his reluctant host. A trifle nettled, Ralph told him to get on with it, and the dreadful secret was revealed—General von Horn had been discovered to be regularly transmitting military, political, and economic intelligence to the Arabs during recent visits to Gaza and Cairo.

This was not the sort of accusation Ralph had been expecting; indeed it was almost "old hat" and was easily recognizable as a distorted interpretation of my excellent relations with General Amin Hilmy II (the director of Nasser's Palestine Department) through whom I had often been able to achieve a relaxation of tension on the Israeli frontier. There had been a time when Mrs. Meir had actually thanked me for my efforts, but that had been before the Security Council meeting on April 4. Now here was this excellent personal relationship twisted and served up as slander brought personally by a high Israeli official to one of the Secretary General's chief executives.

Ralph, despite the fierce disagreements we had had, was a man of caliber with considerable experience of the Middle East. No wonder he looked at his visitor coldly, asked him to produce his proof in writing, and then showed him to the door. Unhappily, however, mud sticks if you throw it long and assiduously enough, and while, when I heard this story, my heart warmed toward Ralph, I had little doubt that here and there in the Secretariat this sordid campaign was bound to find a credulous or sympathetic listener.

I knew, too, that it would be pressed with unflagging energy, lie after ingenious lie manufactured and propagated down the countless channels the Israelis maintained into every circle that promised exploitable value.

I had plenty of opportunity to observe their new tactics in Jerusalem. Whereas a month or so ago the Israeli authorities had dealt directly with me on all important matters, I now noted a marked eagerness to bypass me in favor of my senior assistants.

Henri Vigier and Colonel Churley, my new American Assistant COS, discovered that overnight their offices had become the mecca for all problems unless a direct confrontation with me was utterly unavoidable. I had been sent to Coventry. But I had an exceptionally loyal staff. The Old Fox was a tower of strength and his advice, based on an intuitive understanding of the Israeli mind, was to stand me in incomparable stead. Because it now become virtually ridiculous for me to attend any Israeli official social functions (where I should simply have stood talking to foreign diplomats since no Israeli was willing to speak to me), he took over part of the burden. And very well he managed, too, in the role of guest and as the host at our own functions, where Madame Vigier made a delightful hostess while I remained in the untroubled quiet of my own quarters at Government House.

It turned out, however, that there were other Israelis who were only too anxious to meet me! One Sunday afternoon in May, I was on the point of setting off by car on a bathing party when a letter addressed to me was delivered at our main gate on the Israeli side of the compound. Victor Mills was Duty Officer when it arrived. Expecting an official message (which the Israelis were often in the habit of delivering on Sundays) he opened it, only to discover a typewritten document which, after listing my "crimes" for a paragraph or two, advised me to leave the country at the earliest possible date. Were I not gone by May 20, the only way I was likely to leave was in a coffin. It was signed melodramatically "The Avenging Hand," which we took to represent some anonymous Action Group.

Poor Victor, who had come hurrying over to show me this document, looked extremely upset. I cannot say that I was exactly surprised myself, but I told him to hand it over to the Israeli police. Needless to say this was the last time we ever saw it.

Although I had very clear memories of what had happened to Folke Bernadotte and Hansen, I lost little sleep over it that night. What annoyed me a great deal was when several people came to me next morning to express their indignation and concern. As I had told Victor to keep the whole matter quiet, I asked them how they had heard about it. At this they looked amazed.

"We heard it was in the newspapers last night."

"In the newspapers!"

"That's what we gather, General."

"I see," I said. I knew none of them could read Hebrew, but the news must have rapidly spread over the grapevine.

I thanked them and got down to a long chat with Albert. Sure enough, copies of the letter must have been handed in to the newspaper editors long before the message had reached me. It had even been mentioned in a news broadcast from Vienna the previous evening.

I felt that I ought to cable U Thant. In a remarkably short time a heartening message came back. U Thant told me that he had hastened to remind the Israeli Government of its responsibilities for the safety of the members of the UNTSO staff. I was further instructed to make my own representations. Nothing could have pleased me more for, despite the boycott, I was anxious to have a personal talk with Mrs. Meir.

Our meeting took place two days later; elusive as ever, the Foreign Secretary had shown no great eagerness to see me despite the unusual circumstances. Our conversation was not exactly warm.

"General," she said, "I can assure you that our police are going into the matter thoroughly. Nonetheless, I think I ought to make it plain that they discount this letter as the result of some deranged mind."

"That may be, Madame. Nor do I intend to lose any sleep over the matter because I feel *sure* appropriate steps are being taken by the responsible authorities. As the same time, I can't help feeling that there are some very odd circumstances about the whole business."

I gave her details of the timing and delivery of the message and explained that the press had been given previous notice of its contents.

When I had finished, I added, "I'm sure you will agree that any further losses among UNTSO staff members would be very harmful to Israel's reputation. Especially if they happen to be Swedish casualties."

Mrs. Meir became indignant.

"Listen, Madame," I said. "I am making myself plain because a few days ago, I read a most interesting account in your newspapers of a reunion at Abu-Gosh, held for some Arabs who collaborated with your people in mandate days. But there seems to have been a happy little gathering of the Stern gang there too. Among them"—and I caught her eye, "I note the presence of two gentlemen who were involved in Folke Bernadotte's murder. If I remember rightly, your Government pardoned them after a token sentence and sent them into a rather comfortable exile. Now they are back to such a warm welcome, I trust they won't be resuming their previous activities?"

Mrs. Meir took my point.

From this moment we had little more to say to each other.

As a precaution I now had to travel everywhere in Israel with a police escort; every journey had to be notified in advance to the Jerusalem police commander. Jim Gander, my British Chief Security Officer, and I were both convinced (and I told the Israelis so) that it was virtually impossible to prevent a carefully planned assassination. For this reason, I was reluctant to have an escort. Politically, however, there was no choice. The Israeli Government was taking U Thant's reminder to heart; doubtless, too, it was also a convenient method of checking on all my movements.

My first trial run with an Israeli escort proved to be such a slow and cumbersome business that I insisted on taking the lead and navigating myself. Diplomatically it was also important that I should have a UN escort with me as well. And from that time on one or both of my bodyguards, Max Elmvang from Denmark and Giuseppi Ravalico from Italy, were always in attendance when our little column set forth on its journeys. I soon discovered (like all people who are forced to travel with an escort) the perverse joy of suddenly putting on speed and losing it from time to time; partly because of the sense of freedom it gave me, partly because of the desperate "General hunt" which then ensued.

The short time the "terrorists" had given me to get out of the country was now rapidly expiring. On May 20—the day after which I had been warned my only hopes of exit from Israel would now be by coffin—I was interested to read in the newspapers that I had received further and more bloodcurdling warnings. When in due course these *did* arrive, I never had a chance to get my own typewriter identification experts to work because the Israeli police were literally waiting to collect them.

It was not a very free existence but at least it had the merit of seldom being boring. One morning we discovered that a hut had been mysteriously erected overnight in the no man's land between Government House and the Israeli checkpoint that led into the New City. We were at a loss to understand how this had suddenly sprung up in territory supposed to be entirely neutral but in fact had been a cause for friction between the two sides. Indeed, much to our distaste a bullet-scarred old building (only ten yards from the fence surrounding UNTSO headquarters) had for years been occupied every night as a listening post by three Israeli soldiers disguised not very convincingly in battered old police hats.

Naturally, I was interested to learn what this fresh nocturnal creative activity portended. But inquiries produced nothing but evasions. It was not until some days later that the big secret was revealed: the hut was intended as a police shelter for my personal protection.

Gradually the excitement the anonymous threats had stirred up began to subside. But police precautions remained very much in evidence. After a polite request from the Jerusalem police commander, I was reluctantly forced to abandon the pleasurable game of slipping my escort. But before long I started to venture out on foot through the streets of Jerusalem. This nearly gave Jim Gander heart failure, but I had taken this course quite deliberately, not just to "show the flag" but to make it plain that the Chief of Staff of UNTSO did not personally believe in being "pushed around."

Eventually, I agreed to let Jim accompany me, and from then on we took the opportunity of dropping in on many friendly people who were surprised but gratifyingly glad to see us. We also took to giving other less friendly souls a nasty little shock when we arrived unexpectedly at places known to be used as contact points for shady transactions.

On the official level, however, the boycott was relentlessly maintained. I could see the time approaching when I was likely to share the dilemma that had encompassed Andrew Cordier. I had always recognized the hazards of a job in which observers and Chiefs of Staff alike were likely to become expendable. Our *raison d'être* as peacekeepers was objectivity and impartiality. Yet these very qualities were exactly those which led to hostility.

It was understandable; time and time again in the course of frank discussions with Israeli officers and officials, I had heard them openly repudiate the idea of objectivity. Their flat statement, "You are either for or against us," explained why—having dared to *be* entirely objective—I had now been branded as irrevocably "against." I had seen it happen many times before—from my predecessors down to the ordinary observer on the frontiers who, in the course of his duty, had incurred Arab or Israeli hostility simply because his *impartial* version had been *very* different from theirs. Even nastier was an Israeli tendency to immediately brand objectivity as anti-Semitic: a convenient label that could be smeared onto any UN soldier whose impartial report did not weigh down in favor of the Israelis.

We had from time to time incurred a certain degree of animosity in our dealings with the Arabs, but never in the same implacable and frenetic way. The Arabs could be difficult, intolerant, indeed often impossible, but their code of behavior was on an infinitely higher and more civilized level. I think we all came to this conclusion in UNTSO—which was strange because there was hardly a man among us who had not originally arrived in the Holy Land with the most positive and sympathetic attitude toward the Israelis and their ambitions for their country.

Never in my life have I encountered a nation with such an infinite talent for turning good will into disillusion and often into disgust. It seemed as though the State were possessed of some daemon with a capacity to turn potential friends into enemies. I am certain that I shall be bitterly attacked for setting down my impressions so frankly, but unfortunately they are the truth.

All of us who went to Israel knew very little about the Arabs but a great deal about the Jews and their appalling sufferings in the Second World War. I have never been and I am not anti-Semitic; I have always numbered Jews among some of my closest friends since boyhood. I have good friends in Israel, wonderful families who stood by me and welcomed me into their homes during the height of the boycott. Many of our personnel, too, had close friends in the new State long before they came out to Jerusalem, and I would think that seldom before have the members of any organization—and this was a truly international one—started off with such a fund of good will toward a State which had emerged at the cost of such dreadful suffering.

What went wrong? I always had a talk with staff members who were leaving the Mission. Invariably it was the same story. Nearly all of them had arrived with the honest intention to help *both* parties to the Armistice Agreement, but with a conscious sympathy for the people of "poor little Israel." Yet, after two or three years in daily contact with officials, soldiers, and private individuals on both sides, there had been a remarkable change in their attitude. I found it sad but very significant that when I asked them what their most negative experiences had been during their service with UNTSO the reply was almost invariably: "The consistent cheating and deception of the Israelis."

Chapter Twenty-three

NUMBERED DAYS

It was early February 1963.

"Henri," I said, "I'm afraid it looks as though my days here are numbered."

"No. General. You must not get such ideas into your head . . ." But the Old Fox's voice lacked its normal ring of conviction and I sensed the signs, the way the weather cock was veering. The boycott had succeeded in isolating me and neutralizing my usefulness so that now although I continued to deal with the Arabs successfully, I might not, as far as the Israelis were concerned, even have existed.

Officially, that was, because the campaign against me remained in full swing. And although I had anticipated this moment, it was still bitter. But there it was. I was an international soldier who by experience had every reason to know the odds. It was no use complaining.

I was fond of Henri Vigier. No one in the world could have sustained me with more devoted help and support. Over the years I had come to look on him as an elder statesman. And in his eyes now I saw that look one associates with men who have the political balance of affairs eternally at their fingertips. It was plain that circumstances had forced a parting of the ways.

I had advised U Thant that I thought my usefulness in Jerusalem was drawing to a close. Fortunately there was to be little time for brooding or regrets. The cable that summoned me to the glass building next day came almost as an order of release.

Outwardly, the glass building looked exactly the same. But inside the whole atmosphere had undergone a sea change. Since I had been away some thirty new African states had sent their delegates here and now the visitors' lounges and, above all, the delegates' dining room and lounge reflected the arrival of the emergent nations. The old ambience was gone. The new states were reveling in the politically inspired largesse of the great powers, and had discovered how well it paid to shout and snarl and be abusive.

Here in the UN—which served as a godsent platform for their views—their political importance had become grotesquely exaggerated. Their voices were heard everywhere—and listened to—despite the fact that their delgates represented small ruling cliques in backward countries whose populations seldom approached the numbers of American Negroes in Harlem. Few, if any, had paid (or intended to pay) their United Nations dues, let alone their contributions to the Congo operation. But in the happy position of enjoying influence without responsibility, they were using their inflated importance to band together to become a pressure group that was slowly but surely transforming the United Nations into a forum for racial hatred.

It struck me that the Americans and Russians must be regretting their rivalry in bringing these new states into their respective spheres of influence. All that their massive financial and technological handouts had achieved had been a playing off of benefactor against benefactor, the strengthening of nationalistic and all too often corrupt ruling cliques, and great embarrassment to themselves in the United Nations where the balance of power had been seriously upset. It had, too, contributed to the organization's eventual decline. No great power and few smaller powers would risk their policies or aspirations being upset in the UN by these vociferous little countries.

From now on I was sure power would inevitably escape the United Nations; the real world crises would be solved by direct negotiation. I found this sad but understandable as I observed the change since I had been away. Everywhere there were eager little groups of Africans in animated discussion, whose rather conspiratorial look would suddenly evaporate when a white girl joined their small, enclosed ring.

I saw this happen on so many occasions—the lone white girl surrounded by a circle of beaming black faces—that I was hard put not to recall the rumors about enterprising states enlisting appreciative sympathy among these delegates by politically sponsored call girl operations. I had heard too of three hard-working but well remunerated ladies who had surfaced in Warsaw after being hustled out of New York by the police, who had been observing their activities on glass building premises. It was plain that for some nations who wanted to make friends and influence people, white girls were a useful adjunct to financial and technological aid to underdeveloped countries.

Altogether, it was rather a gloomy homecoming. There were also many new faces in the Secretariat, but up on the thirty-eighth floor the top brass was functioning in much the same way and the door handles still had to be used gingerly to avoid an electric shock. In the Secretary General's office, I found U Thant still wreathed in cigar smoke and as understanding and sympathetic as ever.

He had the files of our correspondence in front of him. Greatly to my surprise, his first question was:

"General. Are you prepared to stay on in Jerusalem?"

"Yes, Sir," I said. "Providing you feel confident I've not outlived my usefulness."

U Thant regarded me inscrutably.

"I should have thought," I added, "that that point had been reached and passed."

"That may be, General. But we are very conscious of the way in which you have carried out your task under extreme difficulties. I see that your term of service with the United Nations is very nearly up."

"Yes," I said, "it has only another couple of weeks to run."

"And after that? Would you consider staying on? Say—in some new role if a suitable opportunity should arise."

I looked at him closely.

"I think it will, General. There are many troubled spots in the world besides Jerusalem. If you are agreeable, I'd like you to stay on there until we can find a suitable successor."

"Mr. Secretary General," I said, "when you talk about a new mission, I presume you mean the Yemen?"

Wreathed in cigar smoke, U Thant neither confirmed nor denied this question.

"If it is," I told him, "I shall be glad to accept. But it will have to be on certain conditions."

U Thant looked at me quizzically.

"You must remember that I've served the United Nations for five years. I've been through some hard times and learned some fundamental lessons. I'm not so much worried about myself as the people whom I have to command. I have a duty to them. And in my experience this has been very difficult to carry out."

"You had better speak entirely frankly, General."

"I appreciate that, Sir. The terms on which I'm prepared to serve on, wherever the United Nations chooses to send me, are these. First, I have *got* to have clear—and I mean *clear*—terms of reference. Second, when I advise you of the physical, material, and financial supports I consider vital I shall expect to get them and to be backed up to the hilt. Lastly—I insist on being consulted over the appointment of senior staff."

U Thant removed the cheroot from his mouth. "Well, General, that sounds perfectly reasonable. I assure you that we can and will meet your requests and that you will have my full support."

A cynic might have had the temerity to request that those promises were put in writing. I did not bother.

Even then, however, as I settled down with U Thant to give him a comprehensive briefing on the security problems in UNTSO, I could not escape a niggling sensation of doubt. It had nothing to do with him. I had then and still have implicit trust in U Thant's genuine and honest nature. But at the back of my mind was the administration and the positive genius of its field operations service for maladministration. I recalled the resentment on the occasions when the sufferings and shortages my troops had undergone had compelled me to go over the administration's head to get things put right.

I was, I knew, rated by many on the twenty-first floor as a difficult, intractable, and domineering figure whose habit of calling a spade a spade had caused tremors of indignation up and down the corridors. Whatever measure of good will might exist on the thirty-eighth floor, there was bound to be a residue of hostility among certain people lower down which, if I knew anything about it, was certain to short-circuit the promise U Thant had made in such good faith.

These thoughts were troubling my mind as I showed U Thant a file on an Israeli girl who had come to the new state from Europe. I produced her picture and we looked at it together. This was typical of the sort of thing we were up against. Her national service—once she had emigrated to Israel—had been done in the Jerusalem "Commando" where Hansen had discovered her "working" intimately on our staff. Even U Thant's inscrutable poker face betrayed itself by a lifted eyebrow when I told him that her next move had been to apply to *us* to help her obtain a US visa. She was anxious to marry an American officer who had just been posted back from Europe. Failing this happy event coming off, she would like to get a job with the *United Nations!*

I stayed on in New York a few days longer, where the mills ground on in the Secretariat as though there had never been a Congo. Nothing had dented its conception of self-sufficiency; the "21 Club" continued to flourish. The old atmosphere of unreality prevailed.

I returned to Jerusalem to await my successor and began to study the situation in the Yemen. It was not an inviting prospect. This small, wild Republic about two hundred miles wide and three hundred long is situated in the southwestern part of the Arabian peninsula. It is a barren country of desert and rock with a population of between four and five million; its mountainous frontier runs with Saudi Arabia to the north, while to the west its long coastline is lapped by the Red Sea until the border moves inland to encounter a southern and eastern inland frontier along the British Colony of Aden and its Protectorates. From its coastline the plain stretches between thirty to fifty miles inland. Where it ends the mountains begin, running more or less down the middle of the country both in the north and south. Away to the east they taper gradually away into desert.

It is a poor country with a highly developed tribal society. Until very recently the Yemen had been ruled by Imam (King) Ahmed Ibn Jahja, whose death in September 1962 had ended a remarkably despotic regime. By any standards Imam Ahmed had been a Middle Eastern despot on the grand scale. Two of his brothers, Ahmed and Abbas, attracted by the prospects of power, had fallen victim to his executioner together with innumerable politicians and soldiers with similar ambitions.

The Imam had ruled his medieval state with an admixture of wisdom, intuition, and terror. Constantly on the worst of terms with the British in Southern Arabia, he had, in more recent years, graciously allowed a wealth of Russian material aid and technical help to be showered upon him. His attitude toward his benefactors, however, had not been compliant. While they were toiling to build him a modern port on the Red Sea at Hodeida and an extensive airfield outside his capital at Sanaa (where he already had another two to accommodate his three aircraft), he had been craftily playing them off against the Chinese who were soon constructing a hundred-and-fifty-mile stretch of road from the port to his capital. The Chinese, too, must have come to harbor a degree of hard feeling toward the Imam. For when, having completed the road, they courteously asked for payment, he refused. "I am not going to pay because I do not like the road. You can take it away."

This Communist beneficence, however, eventually brought a rather backhanded reward. With the old-fashioned despot's death on September 19, 1962, the regime crumbled fast. Unrest, which had long been seething in the country, had been carefully fostered by the Egyptians, backed by the Chinese and Russians, who both wished to see a weakening of relationships between the Arabs and the West. President Nasser's Voice of Cairo was soon pouring out propaganda to any Yemenis who could afford the luxury of a radio set, while Nasser himself ordered the new Imam Al Badar to announce his sympathy with the "anti-imperialist" powers. The new Imam, who wanted to see reforms carried out in the country but was fiercely independent, refused and announced:

"The Yemen is an independent country. I wish it to be neutral like Switzerland and I want to have good relations with my neighbors in Aden and with the Saudis in the north. I do not intend to subject my country to you Egyptians."

This was a rebuff for Nasser, who was worried about Syria's breakaway from the UAR, and saw an adventure in the Yemen as an easy way of restoring his prestige among the Arabs and at the same time opening the way toward a domination of the Arabian peninsula.

Within a week revolution had broken out. An attempt was made to shoot the Imam, and while the Guards were questioning the unsuccessful assassin, an attack was opened on the Palace by troops led by the Commander of the Royal Guard, Abdullah Sallal. The top stories were blown off the Palace, and Sallal claimed the Imam was dead. While he and his men were busy murdering a number of the ministers and royal princes, however, the Imam was making his way to safety through the City. Under cover of darkness, he fled north to loyal tribes among the mountains close to the Saudi Arabian border. Here among men who had always been staunch for his father, he raised his standard, set up a government, organized an army, and was soon receiving supplies of guns, ammunition, and gold from the Saudi Arabians.

In Sanaa, Brigadier (he had just promoted himself from Colonel) Sallal hastily formed a revolutionary government, but its support was limited to the towns and certain tribal areas in the western part of the country and it would have had little chance of lasting success had not military support been made rapidly available from outside. This was not slow in arriving in the shape of two Egyptian parachute battalions, which had the misfortune to be dropped in mountainous country in the midst of a savagely hostile population. They suffered disastrous casualties.

To redeem this inauspicious start a massive invasion of Egyptian troops was soon streaming in through the port of Hodeida where their tank, artillery, and supply officers must have blessed the Russians for their hard work on the port installations and the Chinese for their labors on the road along which their columns rolled smoothly into Sanaa.

What had started as a limited degree of military assistance soon escalated until the best part of a third of the Egyptian army found itself drawn into the struggle. Under the cover of their guns, tanks and, above all, their bomber squadrons, Sallal was able to establish his government and start his new regime of democratic freedom and progress by taking a bloody revenge on the supporters of the old regime unlucky enough to fall into his hands. His grip on the country, however, remained tenuous. While

Egyptian troops garrisoned the larger towns and controlled the roads, the Imam—whose position is something approaching a combination of temporal King and spiritual Pope—built up his forces in the mountains until soon they were strong enough to occupy most of the north and central mountains and the eastern plateau and deserts, occupying a third of the country, pinning the Egyptian garrisons inside the towns and ambushing the convoys that kept them supplied.

It was difficult to imagine a harder, more primitive campaign in which modern Soviet weapons were pitted against tribesmen often armed with nothing more than outdated rifles. But the will to fight was fierce, the Imam and his tribesmen proclaimed a Jehad or Holy War, and equipped themselves with large quantities of captured weapons in addition to the supplies the Saudi Arabian Government was sending them. Their growing numbers and ferocious fighting spirit proved in such marked contrast to the timidity and lack of enthusiasm of the Egyptian troops that Nasser's expeditionary force and the Sallal regime might have collapsed together had it not been for their total air superiority.

Day after day, Egyptian bombers (based on a hurriedly constructed new airfield at Hodeida) unloaded tons of Soviet-made missiles on the Royalist mountain villages until the tall, gaunt houses built on precipitous slopes subsided into rubble. Fighters and fighter bombers strafed suspected Royalist concentration areas while reconnaissance planes flew mission after mission. Gradually a stalemate ensued, with the Royalists in control of large sectors of the country while Sallal, bolstered up by the Egyptian Expeditionary Force, maintained his regime in Sanaa, the coastal plain, most of the larger towns, and the Shafei areas in the south where the tribesmen (whose allegiances fluctuated in a frightening manner) were favorably disposed toward the new Government.

Early on, while fighting was still raging and the eventual outcome remained unknown, the United States Government (after some feverish consultations with Cairo whose nature still remains cloaked in secrecy) had recognized the Sallal regime. And a sorry story it was for, although the State Department believed that Nasser as a Nationalist was a sound barrier against communism, it was also felt that the Middle East provided an excellent field for American business interests.

The real position was that Nasser's intervention was being armed by Russia and financed (whether they liked it or not) by America. Perhaps this situation worried them, because after a deal whereby the Egyptians were to pull their troops out in exchange for recognition, the USA recognized the new Republic on December 19, 1962 and doubtless must have brought great pressure to bear in New York because the following day came further recognition from the General Assembly of the United Nations.*

This precipitate American recognition of the Republic (where Sallal had now elevated himself to General and was about to appoint himself President and Field Marshal) was officially explained by a desire to end hostilities and the rather naïve hope that President Nasser really would withdraw his troops. No doubt the State Department had still not awakened to the reality that there was nothing Nasser enjoyed more than taking them for a ride, and now that Sallal's Republic had been recognized, felt free to do what he liked in the Yemen. Doubtless, too, they still imagined benevolent recognition would help to weaken Russian influence in a part of the world so close to Africa and the Arabian oilfields. I have always thought, and I still do, that beneath this apparently logical decision by the Americans lay a baser policy aimed at embarrassing the British in Southern Arabia, linked with a desire to further their own oil interests in the Arabian peninsula.

Britain, which had not recognized the new regime, was possibly less surprised than the Americans when the State Department's hopes were not fulfilled. Far from withdrawing any troops, Nasser continued to pour in more; he had little alternative because otherwise the new Republic would have collapsed. The Yemen had become the stage for a full-scale civil war in which one side was supported by Egypt and the other by Saudi Arabia and (to an extent which was more or less confined to good will) Jordan and Iran, and this situation soon brought about the realization that the new

* Despite the fact that the Yemen had a delegate to the United Nations, Crown Prince Al Hassan, who returned from New York to become Prime Minister of the Royalist Government in the mountains.

regime in the Yemen was likely to become an embarrassment to its instigators, supporters, and "benevolent recognizers" alike.

Intensive activity ensued in New York and Washington, with the result that in March 1963 two missions were dispatched to the Middle East, to investigate the possibilities of bringing about some form of disengagement. Each was a one-man mission. First came Ellsworth Bunker, a former American Ambassador, followed closely by my old friend Dr. Ralph Bunche, representing the United Nations.

Exactly what conversations took place in Cairo, Jeddah, and Sanaa I do not know, but pressure must have been applied most persuasively. Bunker, in fact, made two separate journeys (no doubt observed with considerable interest and distrust by the British from the Aden Protectorate, who rightly equated this American zeal with the consolidation of the new Yemen Republic). On the face of it, however, it seemed that the negotiations in all three capitals were designed to limit the spread of hostilities and prepare the way for a United Nations peace-observing group.

Since America and the United Nations had recognized the Sallal regime, it was hardly surprising that the Imam and his Royalist Government in their mountainous retreat were rigorously excluded from these talks. Encouraging progress, however, was made with the United Arab Republic, Saudi Arabia, and the new Yemeni Republic, who all agreed to accept two major terms of disengagement.

The first was the establishment of a demilitarized zone extending twenty kilometers back on either side of the demarcated Saudi Arabian—Yemen border from which all military and paramilitary forces and military equipment were to be excluded. The second was agreement over the stationing of UN observers within this zone on both sides of the border to observe, report on, and prevent any continued attempt by the Saudi Arabians to supply the Royalist forces with arms and supplies.

The Egyptians gave reluctant lip service to an arrangement that they were to stop fighting and bombing the Royalists as soon as the disengagement agreement came into force. They also agreed that observers should be stationed inside the territory they controlled to insure their troops kept out of the buffer zone and supervise the withdrawal of their units (when and if that took place) from the whole country.

On the face of it this sounded a praiseworthy step toward the eventual cessation of hostilities. To anyone who knew the Middle East and in particular the nature of the terrain over which observers would have to operate, it gave considerable food for thought. I had seen those daunting mountains from the air, shimmering in the distance. And although I had never flown over them, their rugged, inhospitable appearance had left such a lasting impression that I doubted an observer force could operate in such country. Almost, perhaps, more pertinent, I doubted whether the Egyptians or the Saudis had any intention of seriously observing these terms of disengagement.

I was confined to bed with a severe attack of gastric flu when I received a long dispatch from U Thant, ordering me to proceed at once on an exploratory expedition to discover what sort of an observer force the United Nations would need in order to fulfil "its new responsibilities."

The dispatch arrived on April 27, 1963, and although I was in no shape to get airborne until three days later, I was given time to meditate on my instructions. I had been told to get together a staff, travel by plane to Cairo, on to Jeddah, and finally to Sanaa, at each of which capitals I was to discuss the function and scope of the observation operation with the responsible authorities. I had, too, to get an impression of what was happening in the projected buffer zone. I was to select a suitable place as Headquarters, suggest convenient control points for the observer teams, and report on the supply lines, communications, quarters, facilities, and living conditions that were either available or could be established. On the basis of the knowledge I gained, I was then to make recommendations about the Mission's size.

For my guidance, U Thant told me that he had been thinking along the lines of a total staff of about fifty, but in taking this view he accepted the fact that this would only permit a degree of nominal observation. He suggested that in view of the large areas involved and the very difficult nature of the country the United Nations should not commit itself to do more.

At this stage my journey must be exploratory. I was to make

no commitment. Not only had I strict instructions not to go further than *discussing* the possibilities of an effective observer setup, but I was entrusted with the ticklish job of sounding out each Government's reaction to helping to bear the costs of the operation.

There was a pressing reason for this. More than sixty Member States (about half of the total membership of the United Nations) were in default or arrears on their subscriptions and their contributions to the expenses of the Congo operations. But although U Thant was reduced to operating on a shoestring, mainly by courtesy of America and the British Commonwealth, I was instructed not to press this point unduly. I was, however, to remind them that both Indonesia and the Netherlands had shared the total costs of the United Nations forces in West Iran.

Although my visit was primarily concerned with the military factors, it was bound to have strong political and even diplomatic undertones. So I picked my staff extremely carefully, selecting as my Operations Officer Major Larry David, an able American who was an accomplished Arab linguist and had had long experience of the Middle East.

It was a first-rate and experienced team that climbed on board our UNTSO Dakota with me on April 30. We took off from Jerusalem airport and arrived in Cairo the same evening. From that moment onward there must have seemed hardly a moment when my Swedish, Irish, American, Guatemalan, British, and Canadian staff was not in the air or locked in one long and detailed discussion after another.

In Cairo next morning, I went to the Palestine department of the Foreign Ministry for discussions with the Egyptian authorities. Here I was received by my old friend General Amin Hilmy II * who took me to see Sayed Omar Sabry, the Deputy Minister for Foreign Affairs. Almost at once, I became aware that U Thant's

* Major General Amin Hilmy II el Thaly, Egyptian officer and diplomat. Commissioned as a gunner, he has held various appointments, even in the Egyptian Air Force, and while Chief of Staff Canal Zone District in 1956 he was appointed Senior Liaison Officer to General Burns and UNEF, where he began a close relationship with the UN in the Middle East. Highly intelligent, efficient, and an extrovert character with a marked sense of humor, he has been instrumental in ironing out problems for the UN, more so since he became head of the Palestine Department in Cairo; he was at least slated to join the Egyptian delegation to the United Nations.

strictures on the exploratory nature of my mission were reciprocated here.

Mr. Sabry, an ex-officer like so many of Colonel Nasser's ministers, struck me as a man with a diplomatic veneer of marked affability. He immediately pointed out that any discussions we held must necessarily be inconclusive because the gist of our talks would have to be referred to his Foreign Secretary. The atmosphere, however, was realistic and friendly and became increasingly helpful as the discussion continued well into the afternoon when I met Field-Marshal Amer,* the Commander in Chief of the Armed Forces, who made no bones about the Egyptian attitude. Amer's rather sleepy-looking face hardly moved a muscle as he imparted the rather surprising news that the Egyptians were *not* willing to withdraw their troops from any buffer zone at the moment—although they might be willing to do so later. *That,* however, must depend entirely on events.

Moreover, he wanted to make it clear that the Egyptians had no intention of withdrawing *all* their troops from the Yemen. Whatever international agreements might be reached, a security force would always have to be left to insure the continuation of Sallal's regime. He stressed, however (and I found it difficult not to speculate what part the performance of his troops against the Royalists played in his outwardly confident statement) that Egypt was anxious to get as many of her troops home as soon as possible, that one thousand men had been withdrawn from Hodeida only two days before, but that further withdrawals would be governed entirely by whether or not the Saudis stopped supplying the Royalists with arms and supplies.

He was, he said, quite certain that any major retirement by Egyptian troops from the buffer zone would merely reopen the door for Saudi-trained and Saudi-equipped tribal forces into the Yemen. Indeed, the situation on the Yemen-Saudi Arabian border had recently deteriorated sharply because of a last-minute rush to pour in men and supplies before a United Nations Observer Mission could arrive. He was obviously well informed about activi-

* Abd El Hakim (or Amer), Field-Marshal and Vice President. One of the original group which formed first around Naguib and then Nasser. Commander in Chief Egyptian Forces during Sinai campaign and ever since.

ties in the suggested buffer zone and he produced a map on which he showed me the routes through it by which the Saudis were sending the Royalists supplies and reinforcements. He pointed to the towns of Najran and Jizan and claimed that they were the two bases where the Saudis trained the Imam's forces.

When I asked whether fresh assurances of the Saudi willingness to allow our Mission to operate on their side of the buffer zone would make any change in the Egyptian attitude, Amer smiled and cynically remarked that such assurances would have little more worth than the paper on which they were written. Were they actually forthcoming, however, he would appreciate being kept informed.

As the conversation went on, I had the growing impression that despite their rigid front, the Egyptians were almost eager to see a Mission established. Their views on its strength, though, were on a scale which, although militarily sound, were quite beyond the financial resources of the United Nations. I had the feeling that both Amer and General Hilmy would have liked to see a really strong force take over the buffer zone so that they could withdraw as it gained control over the frontiers.

Hilmy spared no pains to make it clear that if we really wanted to be realistic about sealing off the supply of arms, ammunition, and gold entering the Yemen, we ought to think in terms of divisions and give up any thought of posting a few military observers at odd intervals. They were both anxious, too, that we should extend our observations down to Yemen's border with the Beihan State in the Western Aden Protectorate across which supplies were reaching the Royalists. As this area,* however, was not included in the projected buffer zone that had been drawn up on the map in New York (and its inclusion would undoubtedly have raised thunderous political repercussions from the British) I told them that I would refer this to the Secretary General.

Despite an uneasy start, we had made satisfactory progress. I was assured that I should have every chance when I visited their

* This area where the mountains tail off into desert along the border of the Western Protectorate of the South Arabian Federation was never to be included in the sphere of the United Nations operations.

Army headquarters at Sanaa for further discussions on the actual help they would be prepared to give us.

I came away without unduly pressing the question of a contribution toward the mission's finances. My tentative suggestion had not met with a flat refusal but there had been a certain inconclusiveness that doubtless reflected a combination of the serious drain the Yemen was already exerting on the Egyptian treasury and a naïve astonishment that (after years of milking America and the Soviet Union for vast financial support) they were actually being asked to *pay* for international good offices!

I flew on to Jeddah the following day. As we left the fertile green of the Nile Delta behind, passed over the familiar camel-colored desert, and flew on across the Red Sea until the heat-misted shores of Saudi Arabia came hazily into view, I recalled Hilmy's suggestion that *divisions* would be more appropriate for the job in hand than a few isolated observer posts scattered across the desert and mountains. I could see those mountains in the distance: cruel, jagged peaks with a desolation about them that contrasted jarringly with the spring sunshine in Cairo and the sophisticated atmosphere of a large city. We were, as the British say, "approaching the sharp end."

But whatever might be happening in those mountains, there was nothing warlike about the small seaport of Jeddah with its white walls and minarets interspersed with more modern buildings. Jeddah in Saudi Arabia was no longer merely a seaport for the pilgrim traffic. Great quantities of building and earth-moving equipment, heavy vehicles, and roadmaking material were pouring in every month. The result could be observed in the huge size of the airport where we landed. Although all airfields in Saudi Arabia are oversize for civilian traffic (being specifically designed by their American architects for military purposes), this was a monster. Close by was a vast concrete transit block for pilgrims landing by air, and a little way away across a square our own destination, the Kandara Palace Hotel.

I did not see a great deal of the city, but I was soon aware that the Haj (the Pilgrimage) was still very much a reality. The Holy City of Mecca (out of bounds to infidels) is situated some fifty miles east of Jeddah, and on the morning of my arrival its affairs were occupying Prince Feisal's time to such an extent that I was unable to see him, being received instead by Omar Saqqaff, his Deputy Minister for Foreign Affairs. As the Prince was to do later, Saqqaff made an extraordinarily good impression. An attractive man, whose heavy eyelids heightened a natural Eastern inscrutability, he immediately gave me the feeling that in him ambition took second place to vision and integrity. He was most pleasant to deal with but shrewd and to the point, and started by telling me that any agreement reached over the formation of a buffer zone must lie exclusively with Egypt because Saudi Arabia did not recognize the Yemeni Republic.

He gave me an unqualified assurance, however, that as from April 29 his Government had ceased to send any arms, ammunition, money, or men to the Royalists. Remembering Amer's claim of a last-minute rush before the United Nations appeared on the scene, I introduced this matter tactfully—only to be assured that all support had ceased and that Prince Feisal had given his word of honor that this was indeed the truth.

It soon became clear that whatever success a United Nations Mission might achieve in the buffer zone, any long-term prospects of a lasting peace were extremely dubious. Saqqaff told me categorically that his country was simply not prepared to accept any attempt by the Egyptians to leave security forces in the country when, eventually, their Army withdrew. Saudi Arabia was going to insist on complete withdrawal; she would take the same attitude toward any Egyptian military personnel left behind in mufti.

Although Saqqaff was insistent that all military supplies had ceased, he told me his Government had every intention of continuing to send the Royalists food and medical stores until such time as the Republic might have gained control over the whole country, and offered to allow the United Nations complete freedom to inspect them—providing we gave them notice in advance. His Government would, he assured me, be willing to bear a proportion of the costs of an observer force, would support it in every way they could, and accord us full freedom of movement in and out of the buffer zone north of the border.

He had no suggestions to make about the size of the force: "For that is something you can best judge yourself when you have seen something of our country. The terrain there is not easy. For you, it may pose certain problems. But go and look at it, General. We will give you every assistance we can."

Chapter Twenty-four

YEMEN OBSERVER MISSION

OUR faithful Dakota *Scarlett,* piloted by Bob Denson, was awaiting us at the airport next morning with an extra crew member, Olimac, a pilot of the Saudi Arabian Airlines who had been detailed as flight-deck guide to look after us and presumably insure that we completed our reconnaissance without crashing into one of those razor-edged peaks. It was a comparatively short flight down the Red Sea coast to the small seaport of Jizan in Saudi Arabia (which Hilmy had claimed was in use as a Royalist training base), but we were soon given a vivid impression of the country.

Here was a dry and broken land which almost seemed to have been pressed down like a sheet of corrugated cardboard by some great hand, from the motionless blue water to the distant mountains. Sitting up above in comfort, picking out the recognizable configurations from the map on one's knee, it was possible to feel comfortably isolated from the heat simmering down in that waterless wilderness. But when we landed on the concrete airstrip and saw the white walls of the port, the huddled houses and the old fort glinting in the sunlight, the oppressive warmth seemed to enfold us.

We were received with great courtesy by the Emir, Prince Turki-al-Sadiri, and several officers of the Royal Saudi Arabian army who, far from appearing to have any wish to conceal anything, took me on a conducted tour around the seaport and their hospital and barracks. I noticed no sign of training activities, but

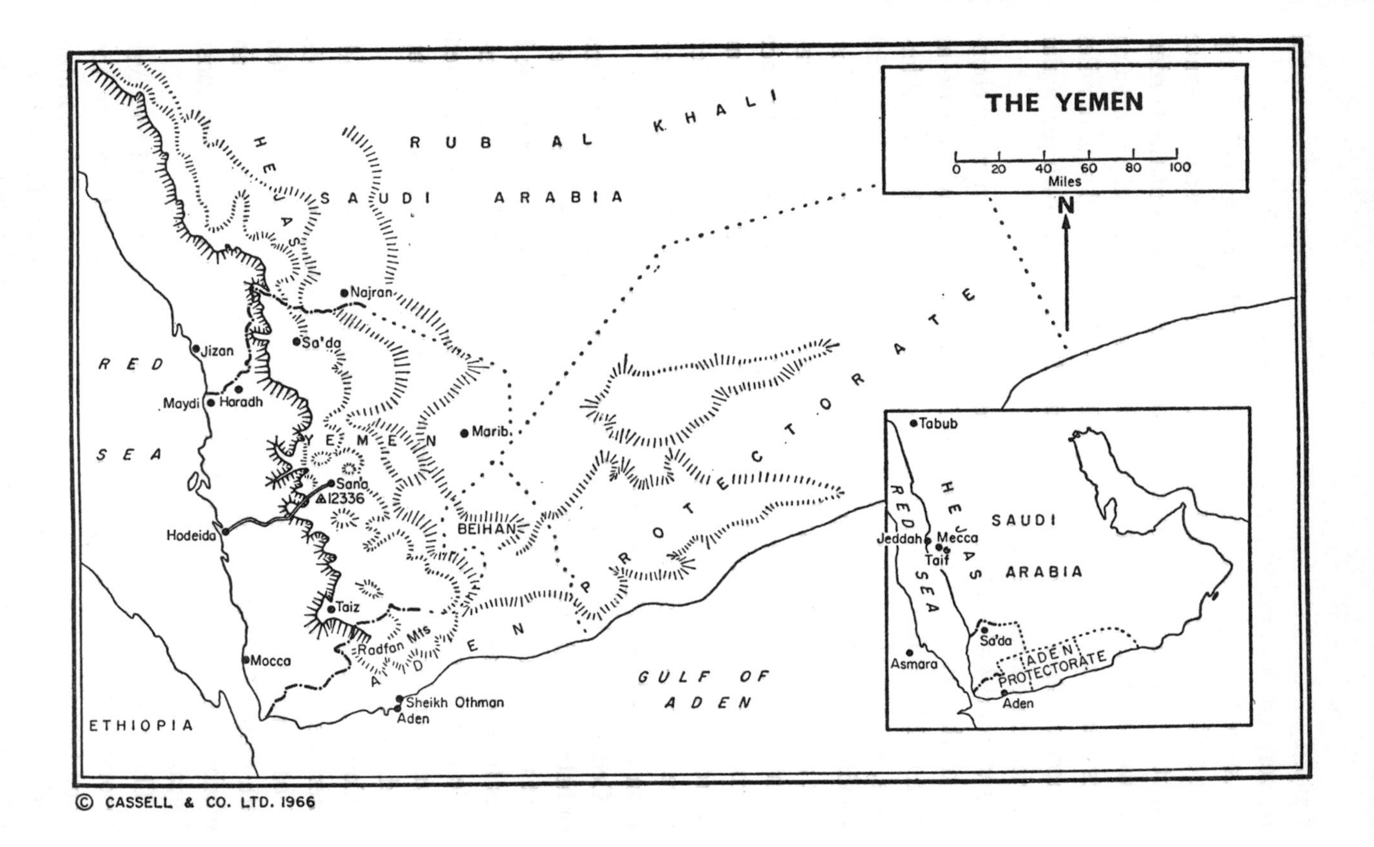
THE YEMEN
0 20 40 60 80 100
Miles
N
RUB AL KHALI
SAUDI ARABIA
HEJAS
ADEN PROTECTORATE
YEMEN
BEIHAN
Marib
Najran
Sa'da
Jizan
Haradh
Maydi
Hodeida
Sana
▲12336
Taiz
Radfan Mts
Mocca
Sheikh Othman
Aden
RED SEA
GULF OF ADEN
ETHIOPIA
Tabub
HEJAS
SAUDI ARABIA
Jeddah
Mecca
Taif
RED SEA
Asmara
Sa'da
ADEN PROTECTORATE
Aden

I rapidly formed the impression that living conditions here would be very uncomfortable for our observers.

Assured by my hosts that our people could rely on all the help that could be given them, I took off again on a long reconnaissance flight to trace a pattern along the buffer zone north of the border. As we flew on, the country beneath us became almost frightening in its starkness. This was our "parish"—six thousand square miles of heat-crushed desert and mountain. Each had its own particular unyielding characteristics.

I wondered which was worse: the desert and broken rocky country or the savage, jagged peaks of the mountains, which rose as high as 12,300 feet. The former appeared a hot and humid wilderness, devoid of water save in the rainy season when torrential floods poured down the gullies and canyons from the mountains. But at least this wasteland was comparatively flat so that cross-country navigation would be fairly easy despite the virtual absence of roads or tracks. Looking down, however, I could see that our patrols would have to be very skilled to enter certain areas, which were so broken and scarred that it looked as though the earth had been hacked up with some titanic prehistoric rake.

Occasionally, isolated in this barren desolation, one saw signs of habitation; tiny clusters of stone houses huddled near some well that must mean life to those few dwellers in a barren land. But I was told by Larry David, who was with me, that despite the terrible climate during the summer months, when the sun burned down relentlessly and windstorms raised great clouds of choking sand, there was considerable animal life.

Cobras, sand vipers, scorpions, and black vipers abounded. There were wolves too, gepards (resembling a leopard), and bands of baboons, which roamed the wilderness in military formation with scouts and pickets out in front. As for the scattered human inhabitants, I gathered that all were hostile to visitors and most Royalist sympathizers.

This was the least inviting terrain for observer teams I had ever encountered; even air patrols would be hampered because the cloud formations that commenced building up early each morning during the summer were going to make flying very difficult. As our plane droned on and the flat lands gave way to precipitous mountains torn with deep chasms and canyons, I began to feel that this part of the world truly merited its title as "The country God forgot."

It was obvious that no manmade vehicle would be capable of functioning successfully in these tortuous, razor-edged mountains. As far as the eye could see, range after range twisted first one way and then the other in a conglomeration of sheer fierce gray peaks: a giant stone barrier cast scross the face of the earth.

Yet compared with the coastal flatlands, this mountainous country was comparatively densely populated. From our plane, we could see village after village of tall, mud-colored houses perched precariously on the slopes. Some were so massive that they reminded me of the old Crusader castles in Palestine; others looked like crumbling mud skyscrapers. Doubtless ancient tracks linked these villages together through the maze of canyons and rocky valleys; track mules or donkeys could negotiate them led by hardy bowlegged mountaineers who had never seen (or wanted to see) foreign intruders.

This was territory no UN jeep would be capable of penetrating. Even were our observers to abandon their vehicles and make the weary trek up and down those mountainsides, they would be entering a world where the mountain villages recognized no authority, Saudi Arabian, Yemeni Royalist, or Republican. This was territory we could only hope to cover by air observation. And since most convoys already moved at night to escape the heat of the day and the possible attention of Egyptian planes, it seemed unrealistic to anticipate that there would be very much to observe.

Toward the east the mountains stretched away until gradually and reluctantly they conceded the terrain to the great sand desert of the Rub al Khali (the Empty Quarter). Though the climate here was more bearable, the same hostility was known to prevail. Outsiders—and what could seem more "foreign" than an invasion of observers drawn from many unknown lands—were bound to be bitterly resented.

After tracing our pattern, we came in to land at the airstrip at Najran. This village, at the eastern end of the buffer zone and well inside Saudi Arabia, was close to an oasis surrounded by mountains rising to nearly four thousand feet. As I got off the plane, I noticed radar-controlled antiaircraft guns between the airstrip and the village, while craters gave clear evidence that Egyptian bombers must have visited Najran comparatively recently. But no signs of strife marred the traditional Arab hospitality of the Emir (Prince) Khalid-al-Sadiri and his military commander Colonel Mahmoud Abdul Hadj. We were conducted to a tent close to the airstrip, where we drank cups of coffee and glasses of tea and enjoyed a polite discussion before driving to the village in the Emir's Land Rover.

There was not a great deal to see. But my eye fell on personnel in flowing robes engaged in some sort of military drill. I estimated there must be the best part of two battalions * in the area. And after spotting several gun positions in the surrounding mountains, I came to the conclusion that here, at least, Hilmy had probably been right. Small and insignificant as it was, Najran had the atmosphere of a village on a battle footing although its meager facilities, its primitive hospital, and almost medieval living conditions held out little hope of comfort or amenities for our observers.

The Emir, however, assured me that whatever facilities he possessed would be put entirely at our disposal. I found him a charming man, courteous, hawknosed, and proud, whose impeccable manners concealed a hint of amusement at our arrival. I had the impression he was summing up our potential and would be in no hurry to remove his men and guns from this part of the buffer zone. Those bomb craters spoke for him. He would want to see what we could do to insure the safety of his people before he took us seriously.

We said good-bye and with Olimac as copilot flew back over the godforsaken mountains, hedgehopping over nasty ranges and winding our way through gorges with such sharp bends that it often looked as though one of our wingtips must strike the projecting rock. Back at Jeddah we were soon ensconced in the Kandarah Palace Hotel with a cooling and well-earned drink of nonalcoholic Tuborg (a horrible concoction).

Olimac, a tall, well-built, and good-looking White Russian, but a naturalized Saudi Arabian with a French wife and an extensive

* Though whether these were Saudis or Royalists undergoing training, it was impossible to tell.

knowledge of the country and its customs, had proved the greatest help. We regretted that as a Saudi Arabian citizen he was not allowed to accompany us into the Yemen.

Next morning we took off on a flight to Hodeida where General Hilmy would be awaiting us. We crossed the coast and flew for hours across the deep blue waters of the shark-infested Red Sea with its multitude of coral reefs (whose jagged crests were mercifully covered in opalescent foam from the surf) until eventually we came into sight of the port, situated on a barren strip of coastline, where we landed on a huge new concrete runway that the Egyptians had constructed on the site of the Russian-built airfield. It was now in full use as an Egyptian Air Force base and resounded with the high-pitched whine of jet fighters and bombers; the air had the tang of paraffin.

General Hilmy took me into the town, a dejected old oriental seaport which boasted a few modern buildings (I gathered they were nearly all inhabited by Russian technicians) looking strangely out of character alongside the crumbling mud and stone houses and a large area entirely covered with Somali-type reed huts. The port and its installations, however, were brand new and clearly functioning efficiently.

General Hilmy was accompanied by Brigadier Solh, Lieutenant Colonel Hammay, and Lieutenant Colonel Zayyat of the United Arab Republican Forces. During my tour I gathered from Hilmy and his officers that the main drawback to the port of Hodeida was its appalling humid climate, usually closer to 100 per cent humidity than 90 per cent.

None of the officers appeared overenthusiastic about this out-of-the-way part of the world (although in Hilmy's presence they were careful not to go into details). I could hardly blame them. I had, however, the strongest feeling that I was destined to see a great deal more of Hodeida, because here was the obvious and only viable place to establish a supply base for the Mission.

The tour of inspection over, we took off inland for Sanaa, the capital of Yemen. For a start we had to climb from sea level to pass through a mountain range some nine thousand feet high, with peaks projected yet another three thousand feet above our flying height into a cloud-burdened sky. The air was extremely turbulent, our plane was unpressurized, and there were no navigational aids. At times this had its exciting moments but we were all grateful to come into sight of Sanaa airfield. Circling around it, we had plenty of time to observe the capital, a really medieval city, a congestion of antique and decaying buildings, tortuous streets, and mosques all surrounded by a high but crumbling city wall.

While the airfield at Hodeida had been a base for modern jet aircraft, that at Sanaa looked like a junk heap for worn-out transport planes. Dejectedly scattered around a haphazard perimeter were also numbers of obsolete Czech YAK fighters, which had stood inviolate since the day some years back when they had been flown in as a present to the late Imam (who had never paid for them). Only one ever took to the air; unfortunately it crashed on its maiden flight.

On landing, we were escorted to the base commander's office, where General Hilmy valiantly protected me from a mob of photographers and reporters from the Public Relations section of the Egyptian Army. Amid the shouting, I gradually realized that the very small young man who insisted on speaking to me was actually the Chief of Protocol of the Yemeni Republic (who had been appointed to the post on the strength of his having learned English at the Italian school in Khartoum). He proved most helpful, told me that quarters had been prepared for us in the capital, and suggested that we might like to proceed to our car. This—following the direction of his apologetic glance—was situated on the other side of a vast mud pool which, as a result of torrential rains, was temporarily blocking the normal route to the city.

I learned (while we scrounged a lift around the mud pool in a jeep) that it invariably rained in Sanaa at three o'clock each afternoon. But my forebodings were diverted by the sight of the enormous vehicle awaiting us on the other side of the pool. On coming closer, I was informed by the Chief of Protocol that this magnificent machine had been a present to the late Imam from the King of Saudi Arabia.

It had certainly been a gift on the royal scale—a vast Daimler chassis on which a famous Paris coach builder had erected (built could never describe such a labor of love) a magnificent body complete with sumptuous (but now somewhat faded) upholstery, armored windows and windshield, and a wealth of opulent fittings, which included a huge mahogany cabinet with a positive plethora of drawers.

The crew of this impressive road cruiser was made up of a wrinkled old driver clad in picturesque garb with an enormous curved knife slung through his waistband, and a very small but alert boy who was now salaaming low and holding open the door. Later I discovered this munificent gift had included a beautiful slave girl. Alas, times had changed, and under the new democratic Republic, her services were no longer available!

Our progress toward the city was slow and dignified, but at last we entered its gates and arrived at The Guest House (which in the good old days had been the Number One harem), but for our purposes was uncomfortably cramped. As my party numbered twelve (including the air crew and our secretary, Miss Dorothy Stevens, a remarkable Scottish lady who was efficiency and dignity itself but could drink and swear like a trooper when the necessity arose), we found ourselves facing an unusual situation that was to tax UN diplomacy to the full.

Although we managed to sort ourselves out in the available bedrooms, we soon discovered to our dismay that there was only one bathroom and that this boasted the house's sole "throne," strategically placed alongside a bathtub that lacked a plug. The latter was no disaster because the supply of water proved remarkably erratic, but the former posed a real problem. The "throne," we discovered, faced the door, which although it had a lock possessed no key or bolt. After a high-level discussion we solved this problem by arranging to post sentries whenever Miss Stevens chose a moment to retire into our remarkable *salle de bain.*

Had I known that six weeks later our numbers would have soared to twenty-five (still including the indomitable Miss Stevens) I might not have settled down so lightheartedly in the room which in happier days had housed the Favorite. Installing myself in a huge canopied four-poster bed, I offered the couch to General Hilmy. It must have been the first time this room had seen an all-male occupation in the shape of two major generals.

After dusk had fallen, we set out into the city in the road cruiser to visit President Sallal. His residence was imposing but our outsize vehicle barely succeeded in squeezing through its gates. Hilmy (who had come as my sponsor), Larry David, and I were led into the heart of this medieval building through one narrow, ill-lit corridor after another manned by lines of picturesque guards armed with modern submachine guns. Repeated security checks followed, and at last we emerged into a small reception room furnished with sumptuous golden chairs and beautiful carpets. We waited until suddenly the President of the Yemeni Republic appeared.

Sallal turned out to be a small man whose swarthy features and suspicious eyes showed unmistakable strain. Nor did he appear very pleased to see us. His attitude was almost hostile, and as Hilmy opened the conversation in Arabic, explaining the nature of my visit, Sallal continued to scowl, watching us intently and occasionally making monosyllabic comments. There was no change even when Hilmy was translating the speech of greeting that Larry had prepared for me, and it was only when I concluded by asking Sallal to confirm that he intended to honor his earlier agreement to cooperate in helping us with our task that he suddenly came to life and began to describe the background to the revolution, its aims, and the immediate situation the new Republic was facing.

As he talked now, his whole attitude changed, he grew animated, and it was not long before I became convinced that Sallal was patently sincere and genuinely devoted to what he believed the best interests of his people. As he talked on, telling us that our mission would be a "nice present" from the Secretary General and launching into a bitter tirade against the Saudi Arabians, I had the feeling that however convinced he was of the rightness of his cause, he remained dubious about its chances of success.

His speech was a strange mixture of fear and hatred for the Saudis (who, he claimed, had already provided the Royalists with sufficient arms for a year's fighting whether or not the United Nations could seal the borders) and a passionate exposition of the poverty and lack of resources of the new Republic, combined with equally eloquent pleas for technical help.

He ended with a strong appeal for United Nations assistance, assured me that his Government would give the Mission what aid it could, and stressed that the Yemen was a poor country and was in no position to be able to contribute toward the costs of the Mission. On this familiar note he bade us goodnight, and we were escorted back to our road cruiser.

The day after this interview we carried out another aerial reconnaissance, flying first to Hodeida and then up to Saada, an Egyptian-garrisoned town some forty-five miles south of the Saudi-Yemen border. I had already gathered that although Egyptian patros occasionally penetrated north of the town, Saada marked the northern limit of their tenuous hold in the Yemen. It was a completely walled little town with very poor amenities and medical facilities and was virtually maintained by airlift because of the success of the Royalists in ambushing road convoys despite their strong tank escorts.

A brief talk with the military authorities convinced me that the majority of the Egyptians were not only unhappy, walled up in this desolate town, but were only too well aware that their original plans had miscarried. The original force of three thousand men had arrived in the Yemen under the impression that they had come to help a popular revolution and that their own part in the business would be finished within the best part of a few weeks. To their dismay they had been plunged into the midst of heavy fighting, in the course of which they had discovered that there was nothing "popular" about the revolution, Nasser's ambitions, and brand of Arab socialism—least of all themselves. Now there were some twenty to thirty thousand Egyptian troops in the Yemen who, during the past seven months, had done nothing better than to lose half the territory they had taken over in October.

We took to the air again and flew a pattern along the southern buffer zone. Once again the same desolate, broken country revealed itself, the same enormous barrier of fissured and scarred mountains. As we stared down on the villages, the desolate nature of the country was borne in even more strongly. It seemed almost a miracle that human beings could exist amid such a wilderness of rock and stone.

The following day (May 6) I had a meeting with General Hilmy and General Qadi at the headquarters of the Egyptian Expeditionary Force in Sanaa. They were old acquaintances, so that the atmosphere was friendly and helpful.

General Anwar el Qadi, a gray-haired, portly man with a friendly smile on his face, was the field commander in charge of the whole expeditionary force. I had known him when he had been Chief of Staff in Syria during the period when that country had been merged with Egypt into the United Arab Republic. He had a Hungarian-born wife, was an able, thoroughly decent type of officer, and I was glad to see him again—because I had heard it rumored that he had been killed during the muddled period when the alliance had broken up. (Much later: When I had left the United Nations and was staying in Beirut, I heard that he had been ambushed and killed on the road from Hodeida. Greatly to my relief, however, the report turned out to be false; the victim had been another Egyptian general.)

Our subsequent talk reinforced the impression I had obtained when General Sallal had told me the Royalists had enough Saudi Arabian arms and ammunition to continue fighting for the best part of another year. Despite this gloomy picture, both Egyptians assured me that three of their battalions had been withdrawn to Egypt within the last few days.

It was quite clear, however, that the bulk of the expeditionary force was due to remain in the Yemen for a long time. On this basis we got down to a practical discussion on the sort of help they would be willing to give us. Once the Mission *was* here, they told me, they would be prepared to give us detailed information about the military districts they controlled and would provide us with accurate maps showing the infiltration routes used by the Royalist tribesmen after their training period in Saudi Arabia. They were prepared, too, to keep us abreast of all information received on the activities and whereabouts of the Royalist forces.

On the matter of accommodations for the Mission they thought there should be sufficient for our needs among the many large houses in Sanaa, standing empty since the Government had acquired them. They promised to do everything they could to help us find suitable accommodations, and were very cooperative when I told them that we planned to use Hodeida as a supply base with facilities at Egyptian-controlled airfields for flying supplies to our various control centers. We would, they assured me, also be able to make use of their own hospital facilities.

Hilmy then told me that he would need to know the estimated size of our Mission as soon as possible in order to set up a liaison unit, and provide us with guides and interpreters. But I was in no position to make forecasts, at this stage, and merely said that I thought any Mission would have to be made up of a combination of military units and observers.

Egyptian intelligence (in an Arab country) is usually extremely reliable. In the discussion that followed, I gained a very clear idea of the main trouble spots in the Yemen, the infiltration routes the Saudis and the Royalist tribesmen were or had till now been using, and an interesting picture of the amounts of arms, ammunition, and money the Egyptians had succeeded in capturing. I learned for the first time that Nasser's machinations had produced trouble in the Saudi Air Force, where some of the pilots had gone on strike; others had recently defected and flown their cargoes of arms straight to Cairo. Qadi gave me a formidable list of war material infiltrated into the country, which in due course I passed on to the Secretary General.

Within the next forty-eight hours a banquet was arranged for us by General Sallal. In the full glory of my road cruiser, I drove to the "Revolutionary Palace," which was a large, square building several stories high that had been used for the reception of guests in the days of the old Imam. It turned out to be a strange setting, both picturesque and pathetic, with many signs of the glorious past. But even stranger—and much more alarming—were the dozens of guards on every floor and in every nook and cranny. Some were security men, others ordinary Yemeni soldiers detailed to form a guard of honor. All turned out to be small men armed to the teeth with an assortment of almost every make of submachine gun. Uniforms were a rarity; the only item of attire they all shared was sandals, and these were of various shapes and colors. Their arms drill was enough to send a shiver down one's spine, especially when they grounded arms with a terrific banging of butt ends almost guaranteed to discharge a loaded weapon.

Sallal, who presided over a banquet of lamb and chicken interspersed with cups of fruit juice, was a pleasant if preoccupied host. He told us that once free from autocratic oppression the Yemen would bloom like a long-neglected flower. And on this note we bade him farewell to the accompaniment of a renewed crashing of submachine gun butts on the stone floor. I kept my fingers crossed in the hope that the guard had heard of safety catches.

The following morning (May 7) we abandoned the Guest House and flew back to Jerusalem, where I set to work to draw up a full report for U Thant. Most of my party were suffering from an exhausting week in a climate alternating between humid heat and a rarefied atmosphere. A couple of them had already fallen victims to the gastric hazards concomitant with medieval society. It was a pointer to the physical ailments a full-strength Mission was bound to experience.

But at this stage—besides making a mental note that medical officers would be priority Number One—I was more preoccupied with the forbidding nature of the terrain, which made it absolutely inevitable that the sort of token force of fifty observers the Secretary General had in mind would be totally incapable of carrying out the task with which it was likely to be entrusted.

There were six thousand five hundred square miles of barren waste and mountains through which thousands of trails, tracks, defiles, passes, riverbeds, and canyons known to the mountain people would have to be observed to seal the routes along which men and arms could make their way (mainly in darkness) from Saudi Arabia into the Yemen. It was an impossible task; as Hilmy had rightly pointed out, this was an operation that could be successfully undertaken only by divisions. Yet this, too, was an impossibility; even had the troops been available, the finances were lacking.

On the other hand, provided we concentrated on the traditional routes that led down into the flatter country and established control centers within the Yemen and at selected centers in Saudi Arabia, there might be some reasonable chance of maintaining a limited degree of control. We would, of course, be mainly dependent on air reconnaissance to locate movement through the mountains. But the immediate business of supervising the removal of units from the buffer zones could be carried out by ground forces in such places as Jizan, Najran, and Saada, where our units could operate without difficulty.

Writing to U Thant, I described my journey and discussions and gave a clear description of the physical difficulties that would face a mission. Although I was well aware that he was contemplating nominal observation only at this stage, I felt it essential to point out that any attempt to station a few military observers in the buffer zones would not only be unrealistic but extremely dangerous. A policy based on these lines might invite casualties in hostile country and could only lead to the discredit of the United Nations.

I suggested that first of all the exact demarcation of the buffer zone ought to be decided on since neither the Egyptian or Saudi Arabia maps agreed on the length of the border. Secondly, I was of the opinion that any Mission with the misfortune to be sent to this desolate spot must think in terms of operational activities lasting over a period of between ninety and one hundred and twenty days; any lesser time was bound to invite failure. Finally, I set out my recommendations for a medium-sized Mission.

Its absolute minimum over-all strength would need to be some two hundred and thirty-four and should be based on an operational headquarters of military and civilian personnel. For operations in the field, I suggested six military observers backed by an armored car reconnaissance squadron with an integral air reconnaissance unit (based on the Canadian War Establishment). Aerial observation could probably be maintained by patrols of six Otters. For supply, I estimated our basic needs at not less than three two-engined transport aircraft.

Even while I was drafting this report, I had the suspicion that these recommendations, moderate though they were, would disturb U Thant. I was worried, too, about the reaction on the twenty-first floor. But these requests were essentially reasonable unless the Yemen Mission was to turn into a farce; the transport aircraft were vital: there was no other way of supply in this area; the reconnaissance squadron too was essential in a country where force alone was understood and the defenceless went to the wall. Its psychological effect alone would be invaluable in dealing with the tribesmen—among whom it would have to carry out missions which bore no relation to the sort of observer duties we had hitherto been called on to carry out in the Middle East.

I must confess, I had the gravest misgivings. Perhaps, I should have resigned then. It would have saved a lot of money and even greater costs in broken hearts and promises. But I trusted U Thant, I believed in the assurances he had given me in New York that "we can and will meet your requests and that you will have my full support." And yet, I sometimes wonder. Otherwise why should I have offered to bet Larry David and the other members of my fledgling Mission that my minimum requirements, for they were assuredly that, would be the object of frantic cheese-paring in New York?

Perhaps the clearest omen was: no one would take the bet.

Chapter Twenty-five

THE EGYPTIANS AND THE SAUDI ARABIANS

LIEUTENANT GENERAL ODD BULL * is a redoubtable, likable man. I had known this stalwart Norwegian over many years and was delighted when U Thant appointed him as my successor in Jerusalem, from June 1. Although by that time I would be busy elsewhere, setting up my new Mission, which in typical UN style had already been christened UNYOM (United Nations Yemen Observer Mission), I had no doubt that UNTSO would take warmly to its new chief. Not only did we share the same basic ideas on military ethics, but I had seen and admired his energy and determination in the near-impossible task of bringing order out of chaos in the UNOGIL operation.

I would have liked to have stayed to see him in, but there was all too little time in which to get the new Mission started. Besides, being a stickler for old-fashioned military tradition, I was anxious to strike my own flag and leave my command before General Bull

* General Odd Bull. Served with the RAF in Canada during World War II and also with Coastal Command. Military Executive of UNOGIL during the Lebanon crisis. Then became Chief of the Royal Norwegian Air Force until appointed Chief of Staff UNTSO.

came to Jerusalem. During those last weeks, I was busy packing up and assembling a nucleus for my new headquarters staff from the officers who wanted to come with me from UNTSO. I was borrowing people, too, from General Gyani, an old and trusted friend from India who was commanding UNEF in Gaza. Gradually our numbers built up, but it was not until the end of May that I was able to take leave of the Holy Land.

In the normal way striking one's flag in an overseas station is not a terribly dramatic moment; a small parade, a bugle call, and then the flag under which one has had the honor of serving comes slowly down the flagstaff in the still, hot sunshine. It is essentially a simple military tradition, nothing very grand, but for most outgoing commanders it has a significance seldom reflected in their expression or bearing.

For me there was to be no such actual ceremony; the UN flag on Government House was flown right around the clock (as the British colors had done on the Residency at Lucknow until 1947); possibly as a legacy from the troubled days when this area between the lines was a beacon of refuge, possibly through sheer laziness, which had become a custom down the years. I do not know which, but as a result my own flag-striking was purely symbolic, a sentence in a report to New York, a long moment of reflective silence in my own mind.

It is a moment few commanders are likely to forget. For them it marks the closing of a chapter, an experience that may have enriched or marred their lives. It may signal a step forward in advancement; in contrast, it could herald the evening of a military career. I know there were many memories that kept me company. UNTSO had been my first UN command, the nursery steps in the business of international soldiering. In the five and a half years I had been here, I had given of my best, had endeavored to remain scrupulously impartial, and had worked always on basic ethics that forty years of soldiering had taught me were vital to instil trust, order, and efficiency into any national or international force.

I knew I had kept those standards, had never allowed myself to be deflected. I had worked, fought, and struggled to maintain order, probity, and to build within my force an *esprit de corps* that would be supranational. I had attained a measure of success possibly rare in United Nations missions. But inevitably I had found myself fighting on two fronts. First, against the Alice-in-Wonderland mentality of the United Nations, which made nonsense of the concept of an integrated force, and then against implacable Israeli hostility, which for good or evil would always stand in the way of the UN ideal in the Holy Land. I had fought it hard but in the tangle of Zionist fanaticism and Arab nationalism I had come to grief.

Perhaps the Holy Land is naturally a path of thorns and pitfalls. Maybe the task had been impossible from the start, as I had suspected back in those early days when I had first met Dag and read the reports of my predecessors. But whatever the rights or wrongs, the curtain was coming down.

Oddly enough, the very fact that I had mentioned flags in my report attracted considerable attention in New York. Although it had been merely a figure of speech, certain hypersensitive souls must have envisaged a full-scale parade whose repetition in other theaters (where the ubiquitous von Horn might now be expected to start *hoisting* flags) might cause serious political repercussions. Needless to say, few people in the Secretariat knew anything about flag drill—let alone military customs. And so no doubt their fears multiplied, although they had only to ask Rikhye who had been with an Indian Cavalry Regiment in Italy and knew the form. In any event, the repercussions of this one phrase in a cable were to follow me into the dusty heat of the Yemen.

The day before I was due to leave Government House, I drove out to the little Lutheran cemetery in Bethlehem. It was an early summer day and the hard, clear sunshine blazed down on the rows of headstones. Scarlett's grave was beneath a mimosa tree whose powdery yellow branches hung gently over the slab of Swedish granite.

I had come to say good-bye. But as I stood there very quietly the realization came that this was almost a superfluous gesture, because a part of my own heart was somehow buried here too. The Holy Land had been an exacting taskmaster. It had taken the best that I could give for five long, hard, frustrating years. Yet now, when my work was ended, its claims upon me had grown even stronger than before. Time after time the silent mimosa tree would see me here again, humble and deep in thoughts and memories. The little cemetery was quiet and very peaceful; no echoes of war or strife disturbed the surrounding hills. After a time, I went slowly back to my car.

On May 30 I said good-bye to Government House. For good or bad, it had been my home for a long time and my departure was very much a family parting. All my staff accompanied me to the Kalandia airport and as I shook hands with them, all sorts of pictures were vividly etched in my mind. Henri Vigier and his colleagues of the Fifth Republic, Bob Churley, Victor Mills, Jim Gander, and all the others who had stood by me. And behind them, the whole of the kitchen, garden, and garage staff—row after row of friendly Jordanian faces with old Ahmed the gardener in their midst, all eager to shake me by the hand and insist on my posing with them for a commemorative photograph ranged before the gleaming fuselage of our Dakota, *Scarlett*. From Ahmed downward every one of them had volunteered to accompany me to the Yemen. Later, I was able to bring several of them out, and even today, I get letters from them offering to serve me.

Our destination was Beirut, the capital of Lebanon. I had chosen to establish an advanced headquarters for UNYOM here because the city was conveniently situated at a busy center of air traffic and communications, and had a joint office which served several United Nations agencies and units in the Middle East. I felt, too, that the officers who would be coming to join the Mission from Jerusalem, Damascus, Tiberias, and Gaza had done me such a compliment in volunteering that they deserved the chance of decent food, adequate plumbing, and hot and cold water for a brief spell before the hardships of the Yemen closed in around us.

Inevitably, I had to organize everything myself. Arriving in Beirut, I discovered that the UN office had no space available to house us and that the Beirut hotels were full to overflowing. I had, however, been a faithful customer of the Phoenicia Hotel over the past five years and now that manager put three rooms at our disposal. Larry David, Harold McLennan, a Canadian Horse Gunner, and Charles Akrell, a rare specimen of Swedish officer with a knowledge both of Arabic and the Yemen, having first been the old Imam's private air pilot and later liaison officer in Gaza for many years, whom I had brought with me, set about with a will organizing a makeshift office. Before long, we had hoisted a UN flag on the corner of the building and UNYOM was in business!

The first two days, however, had to be devoted to briefing Odd Bull, who had flown in on his way to Jerusalem. But once we had seen him off, we got down to compiling lists of our requirements. General Gyani kindly sent me up a couple of staff officers on loan from Gaza while the UNTSO signals unit in Jerusalem was soon engaged in getting together the essential W/T sets and communications equipment we would need immediately on our arrival in the Yemen.

Although I had expected U Thant to balk at my recommendations, there had so far been no reaction. The Secretary General was probably too preoccupied, coping with a Soviet demand that were a Mission to be dispatched at all the decision should be taken by the Security Council—despite the fact that while I had been in Jerusalem both Egypt and Saudi Arabia had made it clear through their permanent delegates in New York that they would be willing to contribute one half each of the costs of a Mission, which was to operate for an initial period of two months.

On this basis and using the strength figures I had suggested in my report as a yardstick, the Secretariat accountants had gone to work on cost estimates that were rushed to the Secretary General without ever being shown to me for comments. The accountants (who had no conception of the country and the difficulties under which a Mission would have to operate) arrived at their own arbitrary figure of $400,000, to be shared jointly between Egypt and Saudi Arabia.

These figures were rushed to Cairo and Jeddah, where they were accepted with so little fuss that it was obvious that more realistic (but necessarily higher) contributions would have been accepted without quibbling. In this way the seeds of disaster were sown by the panic rush of the Secretariat: for, once agreed by the two parties, the figures became sacrosanct and gave no room for leeway. To add insult to injury, I was sharply told during subsequent arguments that these estimates had been based on the recommendations in my survey.

Had I been consulted we would never have found ourselves starved of men and supplies because I was well aware how high the initial costs of establishing a Mission in a completely undeveloped country were likely to be. I would also have taken care to insure that there could be no danger of the Mission degenerating into a mere token force through lack of support from New York.

Long before we started, I was aware that were we to make any real impression on the Egyptians and the Saudi Arabians, the Mission would have to be capable of carrying out its role *efficiently and with the minimum delay.* Strength—or a show of strength—is the one factor that invariably produces results in the Middle East; any hesitation, any delay in coming into action, would inevitably lead to skepticism and fast degenerate into contempt. Neither side would believe that we were capable of fulfilling our promises.

As soon as I heard that the estimates had gone in without being referred to me, I brought this omission to U Thant's notice and requested that I should have a chance to go over them in detail so that I could make all the recommendations which I was certain were bound to be necessary. As head of the mission, *I should have seen them.* But the reply from the "mountain dwellers" in the Secretariat was both unconvincing and infuriating; there had been an administrative oversight, it was too late, the estimates had already been completed, the urgent need for getting the Mission to the Yemen made any further delay impossible.

This "administrative oversight" was to haunt our operations. Time and again my complaints of lack of proper support were to be countered with the same blatant untruth that the estimates had been drawn up on the basis of my recommendations. But even *had* I been consulted, would it *really* have made a vast difference in the long run? I wanted the Mission launched with the minimum delay and the maximum chance of operational success. U Thant, on the other hand, as head of the Secretariat, possibly still nurtured different hopes, hamstrung as he was with financial troubles. Was he still secretly thinking in terms of a mere political "presence"? I do not know, but already the split had occurred that was to divorce command from administrative authority.

I became even more certain of this after a meeting in Cairo. I had been asked to fly there to meet José Rolz Bennet, a charming Guatemalan Under Secretary in the Secretariat and one of U Thant's closest advisers, who was flying there to attend the funeral of Omar Loutfi (whom I remembered well as the Egyptian Permanent Delegate to the United Nations).

I liked Rolz Bennet and when I lunched with him at the Gezira Club, I found him thoroughly receptive when I told him that the Mission must be both strong and effective enough to impress both sides that we were capable of insuring that the disengagement terms were carried out. I told him about my Congo experiences and explained why I considered the forces I had asked for an absolute minimum. Our talk was frank and open—at least I thought so, and left under the impression that I could count on his support. He was very close to U Thant and I knew how much weight his advice would carry.

It certainly did! Although at no time had Rolz Bennet questioned the validity of what I told him, I chanced later to see the report he must have sent to U Thant almost immediately after our meeting. Its recommendations were shaking: U Thant was advised to cut down my requirements until all that would be left would be a UN presence in the Yemen. This, it was pointed out, would save considerable expense.

True enough. But why in that case was I left to lead a Mission into one of the wildest countries in the world in the belief I was to be fully supported? The Yemen was a hard and dangerous country in which to serve—and I felt very strongly that the officers and men for whom I was going to be responsible should have known the truth. I realize now that I should have resigned then; the news would probably have aborted the whole operation and saved the United Nations a great deal of expense and ignominy.

Every Commander makes mistakes. I made one when I did not resign. And this was for two reasons. First, I believed that even if I did, the Mission would still go to the Yemen so that the officers who had volunteered to come with me were bound to suffer even more frustration and hardship under a new Commander appointed at the last minute. Secondly, I honestly felt myself committed to a point where it would be dishonorable to draw back. From then on, however, I served with a heavy heart because I knew that unless a complete process of rethinking revitalized the military arm of the United Nations, international soldiering was a dead duck for any Commander worth his salt. The burden of responsibility was too great, the moral dilemma of endangering the health and lives of one's officers and men too heavy for any honest man truly aware of the state of affairs within the Secretariat.

I doubt whether I was very popular in New York in those days. A disapproving silence greeted my requests for information about the medical, communication, and air transport facilities I could expect. Above all, I wanted assurance that I could expect the Canadian air-ground reconnaissance squadron, which was vital for patrols in the buffer zones. Perhaps some of the annoyance stemmed from my insistence on the hazards of operations in the Yemen. I had stressed them in a note which I had attached to my original report. In this I had informed U Thant that on my return to Jerusalem, I heard that the Royalists had staged a special attack while I was in the Yemen. Its object had been to demonstrate what limited control the Egyptians exercised over the areas they claimed to hold.

A silent night attack had been launched in the heart of Egyptian-held country and a fifty-man-strong Egyptian platoon had been wiped out in typical Yemen style. The bodies had been decapitated, the stomachs slit, and the wretched victims' heads stuffed into them. I can imagine the fastidious reaction in the Secretariat at the advice I appended to this news: "I have no, repeat no reason to expect more considerate treatment for wearers of blue hats or UN brassards." This was no overstatement, but I knew it was bound to be another black mark chalked up against the outspoken and "irresponsible" von Horn.

Although there was no confirmation that the Mission would be allotted the transport planes it needed, nor even a mention that a plane was likely to be available to lift in the first party, I was suddenly ordered to stand by to fly in an advanced Mission headquarters and establish a base at Sanaa. I cabled back that it would be quite useless for a Mission Commander to establish himself until some sort of W/T communications had been set up, and I suggested that I should send down a small advance party to hoist my flag and set up a suitable headquarters in preparation for my arrival.

I worded this message strongly, reminding U Thant of the mistakes that had marred the early stages of the Congo operation. In reply, I was told that *this* operation would be *completely different.* I was also instructed to obey orders and get on with establishing my HQ but *at all costs* to eschew any spectacular flag-hoisting ceremony lest its significance be misinterpreted; the simple message from Jerusalem had come home to roost.

I was far more preoccupied trying to raise a doctor to accompany us. Despite the nature of the country we were going into, I was told that there were absolutely *no* doctors to spare in the Middle East. The fly in the ointment turned out to be the Swedes who were running the base hospital for UNEF at Gaza. Perfectionists to a man, they had long ago put in such massive requests for more doctors that they simply did not dare loan me one lest New York notice the gesture and clamp down on their future demands.

New York, however, was clearly under the impression that Gaza was my *only* possible source and even when the Swedes were not forthcoming, made no attempt to draw on their massive resources elsewhere. Between them, it seemed I was to be consigned to the Yemen without even so much as a medical orderly. Although I knew that several of the doctors at Gaza had volunteered to join the Mission, neither smell, hair, nor hide of a medical officer was forthcoming.

I had no alternative but to become an amateur "medicine man" and equip myself, at my own expense, with a private medicine chest and do-it-yourself surgical kit. But maybe my burning resentment was tempered by a healing touch, for in all those early scorching days the von Horn private medical service never lost a patient!

Soon after I received my movement order the Security Council authorized the dispatch of the full Mission. This news came through on June 11 when our small advance party with no adequate W/T communications was still waiting to take off, for the simple reason that New York had omitted to provide us with a plane. None of my signals had been answered, and remembering the Congo fiasco, I had already been searching round for some form of private transport. Although our old UNTSO Dakota (now at the disposal of General Bull) was hopelessly inadequate to carry our full weight load, I had nevertheless staked a claim on it as the best practical means of getting to our destination.

It was just as well. No suitable plane was made available when, on June 12, I received final orders to set out for Sanaa. Thanks to General Bull, "Scarlett" appeared on time at Beirut airport and we loaded all the radio equipment we dared and took off on the first stage of our Mission.

I had a small but intrepid party with me. But all of us, cramped in the familiar interior of that devoted old plane, soon found ourselves wondering whether she was going to be able to lift herself over the Hejaz hump, a great chain of mountains barring our way across the Southern Arabian peninsula.

But the old Dakota responded nobly. After a long flight over barren Jordanian hills and desert, we progressed along the eastern shore of the Red Sea where we looked down on innumerable jagged coral reefs that struck up from the bluest of blue water. Finally, the testing moment came, and *Scarlett* rose heroically above the peaks and ranges of the formidable Hejaz hump, until soon we were flying over the familiar desolate country and circling Sanaa airfield.

Remarkable changes seemed to have taken place during the weeks we had been away. The vast mud pool on the airfield had dried up so that the VIP road cruiser—alerted for our arrival—was able to drive right up to the imaginary apron of the gravel runway and in no time we were on our way back to the Guest House.

There, a remarkable transformation had taken place. As a first step toward cooperation, the Egyptians must have been busily at work. The bathtub boasted a plug and the plumbing appeared to be in excellent working condition. Even more: the door to this *salle de bain,* which still alas boasted the only "throne" in the house, had been provided with a lock that *worked,* while the air bore witness to energetic Egyptian attempts to deodorize the insalubrious atmosphere.

Cheered by these signs of progress, I gave orders that the UN flag be hoisted over the Guest House. And, once it had been run up, our radio technicians got busy, trying to set up a workable communications center. Unfortunately, we had only been able to bring the lightest of equipment with us, and now found ourselves —in a theater where "face" was naturally equated with power and authority—somewhat out of touch with the seat of power in New York.

None of our sets had a long enough range to contact our masters whose radio antennae sprouted on the roof of the glass building on the East River. Instead, we were forced to use the United Nations office in Addis Ababa as a relay station. But once we had announced our arrival through this channel, a snag arose. No one in New York had taken the trouble to insure that Addis Ababa was capable of a round-the-clock communications service. The one and *only* operator there turned out to be available solely during *his* office hours. For the time being the advance element of the Mission was entirely dependent on his good will.

We were not entirely forgotten. Almost the first communication I received through the obliging operator in Addis Ababa bore the news that—despite the fact that U Thant had agreed that I should be consulted on all senior civilian appointments—I could shortly expect the arrival of a Haitian Chief Administrative Officer, an Iranian Political Adviser, and a Colombian Finance Officer.

The next few days proved busy ones. Somehow or other we set up a skeleton framework for a Mission with Headquarters at Sanaa and outlying control points at Saada in the Egyptian-held part of the Yemen and at Jizan and Najran in Saudi Arabian territory. But before the groundwork could be laid for the arrival of troops and observers, our most immediate task was to establish a supply base at Hodeida with its port and airfields facilities and organize a logistic setup capable of servicing the forward units.

Although the Egyptians were extremely helpful in putting airfield facilities at our disposal, there was no immediate sign of the transport planes on which the whole success of our operation would depend. Fortunately, as soon as our temporary communications were working satisfactorily (the operator in Addis Ababa was bearing up bravely) I heard that the Canadian Air Force was coming to our help. A special transport unit, No. 134, had been formed at El Arish and we had been allotted two Caribou transport planes, three Otters, and three helicopters. Before long the first of the Caribous made its welcome appearance with a new load of signals equipment and personnel on board.

I have always found the Canadians resourceful and enterprising, with a talent for improvisation and common sense, which is fortunate because this marked ingenuity was due for some cramping of style. As the ground staff, communications personnel, and crews of ATU 134 began to reach Sanaa in increasing numbers, we realized that there was nowhere for them to lay their heads other than alongside ours in the cramped confines of our overcrowded Guest House.

Amid this general confusion, I went out to welcome my new chief administrative and political officers as they descended into the burning sun from their aircraft. Ali Nekunam, my new Iranian Political Officer, is a man of sterling character who was to serve us loyally once he had grasped the implications of our situation. The other fellow was a rather different kettle of fish: charming and well-meaning, his stiff leg and the emotional strain of a wife expecting a baby hardly suited him for service in the rugged Yemen. No one could have been more willing, but the impact of brutal soldiers working under heavy and continuous strain proved too much for his sensitive nature. Time and again when I castigated him for some administrative failing, I was to be embarrassed (and often touched) by his capacity for bursting into tears. Although this hardly helped to solve our problems, it was a novel experience. I sometimes wondered whether I might not have achieved more success with my own political masters had I adopted lachrymal tactics.

After questioning them carefully (because I was anxious to know whether the attitude I suspected in New York was reflected in any orders they might have received before setting out), I felt quite satisfied that they had arrived with no cheese-paring intentions. I set them to work immediately, Ali Nekunam to liaise with the Egyptian army authorities and the Administrative officer to see what he could do to discover quarters for the unfortunate Canadians.

I told him that my eye had already fallen on the battle-scarred palace of the late Imam. Its two top floors were missing as a result of the activities of the Russian tanks he had unwisely allowed into his country, but having housed the Royal harem during more opulent days, it was equipped with *several* bathrooms, which reconnaissance revealed were in tolerable working order.

The Palace had been taken over by an enterprising Ethiopian, who had had it patched up in a fashion to function as a rather unusual hotel. In addition, he ran a thriving restaurant in the former reception wing and was understandably not anxious to see his premises overrun by an influx of UN personnel. However, we persuaded him to accommodate our Headquarters and give us a number of oddly shaped rooms, which we converted into sleeping quarters. We even managed to get sufficient space for an operations room and a dining room, which was favored with a makeshift kitchen.

Exerting my prerogative, I once more took possession of the Favorite's room, whose bed had been tactically situated in the middle of the floor space where it seemed more or less immune from the rain that seeped in through ceiling and walls from the shot-away top stories. Its bathroom looked immaculate beneath a new coat of paint, but it was not long before I discovered that an essential S-bend pipe was lacking from the throne.

There were other minor inconveniences. The four priceless bathrooms stood in a row, and appeared to share the same bath water. As soon as I had had a bath in Number One and the water had gurgled down the plughole, it somehow mysteriously contrived to reappear to fill the bathtub in Number Two. This spontaneous process then duplicated itself down the line until in desperation the user of Number Four had to sit on the bath plug to prevent a flow of excessively soapy water welling up into his tub.

We soon discovered that the Palace must have been built exclusively for dwarfs. Loud cries and floods of curses invariably heralded movement from one room to another. The lintels were so low that one might have imagined that a tribe of Swedish trolls had inhabited the dark winding stairways of the old Palace, whose every corner had niches that must have once concealed a crouching Yemeni guard. The steps were built high so that one progressed only at the cost of steeply lifted knees. The window sills were even higher—as though specially built to prevent the inhabitants from looking out. In contrast the headway from one room to another was so low that a European inevitably bumped his head against the unyielding Yemeni stone. Only gradually one acquired the essential "Yemen stoop"; a sort of shuffling, defensive crouch particularly repulsive to an old guardsman like myself.

While we were settling down in these new quarters there arrived our long-awaited and almost despaired-of medical officer. Dr. Gerhard Lechner, a charming young Austrian, had been wrenched away at short notice from the Congo and confided to me that he had accepted this post only because of the promise that it was one step closer toward a longed-for reunion with his fiancée in Vienna. He was to prove a great acquisition, a keen horseman who combined wit and an indomitable sense of humor with a pioneer medical spirit.

The day after his arrival we discovered neat but sternly worded notices posted above every tap with the information (which we had long suspected) that the water supply was unsuitable—even dangerous—for washing, let alone drinking. No sooner had we got our local Yemeni staff (now reinforced by a few stalwarts I had brought down from Jerusalem) busy on the laborious task of boiling water in an array of kettles and pans than we discovered our doctor making forays into our kitchen. Before long, he was observed ruminating with a pained expression over a heap of Yemeni vegetables. Next he produced a hypodermic syringe and proceeded to inject each individual potato with a strong shot of chlorine.

From that moment onward everything in the mess—tea, coffee, fruit, and vegetables—began to suffer from this familiar but unpalatable flavor. Only our bottles of gin and whisky (which were fortunately heavily sealed) escaped his zealous attention. Before long mutiny was simmering in the mess. A tactful talk with Dr. Lechner became inevitable. I lauded his professional efforts, but pointed out that life was hard enough without a perpetual flavor of chlorine at every meal. A realist, Dr. Lechner took my point with a smile and the potatoes at least were spared inoculation. Somehow we contrived to live as happily as Spartan conditions allowed.

Chapter Twenty-six

A CLOSED WORLD

ABBIE was a beauty—a spick-and-span white jeep with blue markings. A red identity plate bore my two General's stars and when we traveled at speed her small United Nations flag fluttered bravely in the hot air.

Setting out in her in the early mornings, I experienced an odd sensation of elation—despite the circumstances that made it essential for a General in a jeep to embark on a tour of "showing the flag" in order to demonstrate the existence of a Mission that had failed to materialize.

This was what our enterprise came down to. After several weeks, the total operational strength of the Mission in Sanaa still amounted to five officers, two jeeps. and one Caribou aircraft. Every day I inquired for news of my other planes, my missing personnel, above all my reconnaissance squadron.

The longer this went on, the more I became certain that unless the Mission grew overnight both Egyptians and Saudi Arabians would interpret our total failure to establish a strong presence as a sign of weakness. Already heavy Egyptian bombing and continual Royalist activity indicated that both sides were resuming their former activities secure in the knowledge that the United Nations could neither see nor stop them.

My most urgent needs were transport planes and the reconnaissance squadron. With these, I could have set up control points in the buffer zone. But although I was impotent to make a start without men or materials there was, ironically enough, no shortage of messages from New York urging me to establish a United Nations "presence" at the earliest moment possible.

I took it that New York's real desire was that somehow or other the United Nations flag should actually be seen in the buffer zone, which although they insisted on calling it the "demilitarized" zone was probably more bristling with arms and hostile intruders than most corners of the World. Since I had no intention of asking the few officers I had with me to go up into these inhospitable regions alone and risk their lives just to keep New York happy, I decided that if anyone were to be exposed to the hazards this ridiculous farce entailed, it ought to be me.

It was thus I came to be setting out on my "flag-showing" tours, bumping along the road from Sanaa to the airfield where the mud pool had now made an unwelcome reappearance. Frequently the whole field was busy with Egyptian transport squadrons, loading supplies for their beleaguered garrisons up country. But when the coast was clear, we would drive right onto the gravel runway where our faithful Caribou 522 would be awaiting us with her stalwart Canadian crew. The ramps would be already down and I had only to jump out of "Abbie" while Larry, my chief staff officer, or Major "Gunner" McLennan of the Royal Canadian Horse Artillery, drove her straight on board. If we were lucky, we could taxi straight out for takeoff on one of our lone border patrols.

I don't think any Commander could have asked for two better or more long-suffering staff officers than Larry and Mac. Efficient, able, and cheerful, they contrived to do a fine job and keep my spirits up into the bargain. I had long ago discussed the details of my plans with them—the plans we hoped to put into operation once our missing men, jeeps, and planes arrived.

Once we had the reconnaissance squadron, I planned to post one troop to Egyptian-held Saada, forty-five miles south of the border. The rest of the squadron would operate north of the border between Jizan and Najran in Saudi Arabia, patroling and observing the tracks inside the buffer zone. I wanted the Otters and helicopters stationed there, too. There would be observers at all these places and a liaison office in Jeddah. Although main headquarters was in Sanaa and our supply base at Hodeida, it was from these border towns that the real work would be done.

Our own "flag-showing" patrols were accordingly based on alternate visits to the border towns. Sometimes we would fly clockwise to Jizan, Najran, Saada and then back to Sanaa; sometimes anticlockwise in order to vary the procedure and enliven our hosts with a little surprise.

We had to start off very early because it was essential to get back to Sanaa by three o'clock in the afternoon before the rain started and the clouds closed over the airfield. On most days, it was already warm when we started and the cloud layers could be seen building up in a hard blue sky long before we were on our way toward the buffer zone. Starting at six hundred feet, they rose in dense white formation to a height of sixteen thousand feet so that flying through them was often an eerie sensation—especially when a sudden break in the drifting mist revealed a jagged peak uncomfortably close beneath our Caribou.

On the clockwise run, we invariably passed the highest peak in the Yemen, which rose to something over twelve thousand feet, before descending toward the coastal plain where we could see the old fort of Jizan on its dominating hill. Since my first visit, the bombers had been busy again and craters were clearly evident around the airstrip and close to the hospital and district headquarters where the Egyptian pilots had scored some very near misses.

Although we always notified the authorities of our arrival (at Najran the antiaircraft guns made this a wise precaution) we were often able, as we came in to land, to see the reception committee setting out from the fort to greet us.

Our landings followed a set pattern. As soon as we were on the ground, the ramps came down and "Abbie" roared out to the perpetual astonishment of the white-robed locals, busy filling in craters or leveling the ground. Our escort officer and guides would be waiting and, stopping only to greet them, we set off toward the border.

After ten bumpy miles of tarred road, we would find ourselves on dust tracks that wound through bush country and dry wadis. There was little to see; no men, guns, or convoys, nothing except the same wilderness we had observed from the air. Had there been any convoys moving in this area over the past twenty-four hours, they would now be safely on their way across the border or lying low in some dry river bed where they had gone to ground immediately the sound of a plane had been heard.

It was not, however, my impression that there was anything going on; the country was silent, barren, and desolate beneath a scorching sun and had the Saudis been passing convoys through, they would have done it by night when the air was cooler and the going unobserved. Other than "showing the flag," I was wasting my time driving to the frontier (which took the best part of three hours there and back), only to find it looking less like a frontier than a mere continuation of broken rock-strewn country.

Back at the airstrip, we would be revived by the reception committee with fruit juice, coffee, and tea, and sit grimy and grateful for a brief space, trying to convince our hospitable hosts that the long day's journey ahead simply did not permit the time to accompany them to their Headquarters for a long lunch.

We took off again, circling the airstrip with its ugly craters and little groups of picturesquely clad guards and officials. Soon we were over the mountains, sometimes almost seeming to hang suspended in the hot air above the jagged peaks. At Harradh we spotted forward Egyptian gun positions, camps, and armored and soft-skinned vehicle parks. They appeared to be in strength and permanent, and I remembered Hilmy's suggestion that any withdrawal would have to be linked with our own buildup in strength. At the rate we were going—one general and a couple of staff officers in a Caribou—it was difficult not to believe that this moment was likely to be long delayed.

On we flew over the familiar mountains, trying from our maps to trace the border among that waste of chaotic rock whose seams and gullies ran like giant scars through the heat-shrouded wilderness. As we approached Najran, it became necessary to search for the airstrip from valley to valley, because we had long ago discovered how intensely similar each one looked.

At last, we sighted the old Turkish fort and the peculiar Hadramuth mud-built skyscrapers, the tall, gaunt houses clinging to the precipitous slopes of the Najran Valley, and came down lower until the 3.7 antiaircraft guns dug in around the town became visible. Here too there were many more craters than since our last visit; a sure sign the war had taken an unpleasant turn for the worse.

I had always known that the only hope of making the disengagement terms work here had lain in the swift and impressive assembly of an international force whose appearance would have made an impact. But the chance had been missed. Both sides had had time for second thoughts. Quite apart from an assurance that bombing of Saudi Territory would cease, the Egyptians had originally agreed to stop operations against the Royalists. There was no sign of it now and Najran, as a Number One trouble spot on their list, had caught it with a vengeance.

But it seemed peaceful enough on the ground. I was greeted by my cheerful Saudi Arabian friend "Hawknose Haji," the Saudi Arabian Colonel, a remarkable soldier hailing from Palestine who had attended the School of Artillery at Larkhill and whose appearance reminded me of Anthony Quinn in the Lawrence film.

Since we had both become accustomed to "the drill" over the last few days, "Hawknose" wasted little time in pleasantries but set off flat out in his Land Rover, piloting "Abbie" through a swirling mass of dust toward the nearest border pass. It was impossible country, but as on the flatter territory at Jizan, I was determined to show the Saudis that the United Nations "presence" was actually *here*—even though I knew it was not capable of doing much more than looking at the mountains. Pulling his Land Rover up sharp amid a cloud of gritty dust, "Hawknose" would gesture benignly toward a steep track where three camels could be seen laboriously plodding uphill.

"You see, General. No arms, no ammunition, and no gold today. Insh'allah."

I was forced to agree with this cheerful rascal—although I wondered whether he would look quite so pleased with himself had circumstances made it possible for me to turn up unexpectedly in the middle of the night!

I bade him farewell and we took off again south across a succession of high plateaus. Before long, it was possible to make out the Saada Valley and follow its course until it debouched into the flatter, rocky country where a number of dust roads could be seen converging on the ancient mud-walled city. Saada was an important communications' center and, as we came closer, we could see from the clearly defined gun positions around airfield and town that the Egyptians had every intention of holding onto it, even though the road leading south to Sanaa was frequently under attack by Royalists, and so many convoys had been ambushed and cut up that the garrison now relied almost entirely on air supply.

It was plain that Saada was the center of a shooting war. No sooner had we landed and been welcomed by the commanding officer, Lieutenant Colonel Hilmy (a Gunner like General Hilmy, but no relation) than I was asked whether I would take a wounded officer back to Sanaa in the Caribou. Colonel Hilmy also begged a lift and I was glad to give it to him. While he was busy collecting his kit, we had a long chat with his officers whose morale struck me as reasonably good.

Their main complaint, they told me, was the insecurity of all roads, which confirmed my impression that the Egyptian control of so-called Republican territory was precarious. I had the feeling that after the treatment their patrols had received and the rough handling their convoys encountered on their attempts to get through to the town, they were now loath to take any initiative or venture far afield without the cover of strong tank, artillery, and air support.

Altogether it was a sad and lonely little group, patently disillusioned and homesick for the gentler atmosphere of the Nile Delta where soldiering must have been a less dangerous and altogether more gratifying profession. One of them had a tame monkey called Alice, a charming little creature, too fragile to be marooned out here in the unrelenting desert. I felt that were the UN ever able to establish themselves strongly in this part of the southern buffer zone, no one in the world would have been more thankful than the garrison of Saada.

When Lieutenant Colonel Hilmy reappeared, we loaded the wounded officer on board our Caribou and took off for Sanaa where we arrived at five minutes past three. Dead on time, the rain had started at 3 p.m. and we now had considerable difficulty, circling through thick cloud and hoping a sudden loud and splintering crash was not about to herald our scraping the top of a mist-shrouded peak. Luckily, a sudden gap in the rain clouds enabled us to get down safely on the airfield—dog-tired at the end of a long and exacting day.

Day after day wore on like this while my increasingly irascible signals to New York failed to elicit news about the arrival of the remainder of the Mission. A trickle of men and supplies came through now and again, but I still had no alternative but to fly more and more dreary "flag-showing" missions to convince both sides that our presence was not just a political smoke-screen.

Few situations could have been more infuriating. I knew and had reported exactly what had to be done, and how, but neither the men nor machines were available to make our operational blueprint a working reality. Of the Otters I had been promised the first ran out of petrol on its delivery flight, made a forced landing, and was grounded. The helicopters transported at great cost from the Congo had arrived at Aden for reassembly, where it was discovered that climatic conditions rendered them operationally unsuitable because the rotors could not safely achieve enough lift in that clear and rarified air.

As for the vital reconnaissance squadron, there was still no news, there was not a smell of them. They should have been patrolling the western and eastern sectors while the inaccessible central area ought to have been covered by air patrols. Everything was laid on.

In my original report to New York, I had estimated that it should take a week to establish Mission Headquarters and a further week to get the Mission fully operational . . . *provided there was clear thinking and efficient staff work in New York and I was fully and promptly backed up with the men and supplies which I had recommended as an essential minimum.* Not one of these conditions had been fulfilled. The result was that I was hamstrung, the officers and men who were with me were suffering unnecessary hardships (which an adequate supply system could have put right in a matter of days), and the United Nations was falling into disrepute with both sides as the delay dragged on.

Another problem was giving me increasing concern. My instructions had been that under no circumstances was I to enter into contact with the Royalist authorities. I could understand the reasons behind these orders, but I wondered whether their political motivation was not somewhat out of context in the reality of the situation.

It was already clear to me that the Imam controlled large sectors of the southern buffer zone where we were proposing to operate. The Zaidi tribes there were loyal to him and were likely to be hostile to our people were they to enter this territory without the Imam's blessing. Moreover, the Royalists were a force to be reckoned with and the Egyptian armor and planes had been able to achieve little result. Territory had been occupied in this area for short periods only and then at the cost of heavy casualties. On the face of it our political veto looked stupid. Sooner or later some sort of contact would *have* to be made for our patrols to operate in what was de facto Royalist territory.

A short time before, a letter had arrived mysteriously in our liaison office at Jeddah. Its tone was friendly if antique.

TRANSLATION

KINGDOM OF YEMEN
MINISTRY OF DEFENSE
FOURTH COMMAND

UNDATED. Given to
Commander UNYOM on
29 July 1963

HONORABLE MR CHAIRMAN

You arrived in Yemen with members of your mission to observe on the one hand the rudeness of the Egyptian forces in our country and, on the other hand, the rudeness of untrue propaganda which is provoked and led by the Egyptians. The falsehood in the Egyptian propaganda is: that in Yemen, English, Jordanian, Israeli and Saudi forces are fighting.

Now you have already arrived and have seen who is, in fact, fighting in this country. The proposal was that after the arrival of the UN forces the Egyptians should start with neutrality, but they pay no heed to the presence of the UN mission. Most of the evidence in our hands shows that the Egyptian forces are continuously strafing and killing the Yemeni people in their country and far up to the border. You are requested to send a mission from one of your centres situated nearest the border to come to Zagraf and to observe who is fighting against the Yemenis in their country. Are they Englishmen, Jordanians or Egyptians only? You are kindly requested to send this mission as soon as possible so as to see and certify the war which is on between sons of the homeland and armed Egyptians and the air activity of the Egyptians in Yemen territory. We expect your early reply to our request.

(signed) One of the grateful sons of Yemen,
Commander of Hasheva and Ha'ga
area Prince Ahmed son of Hassan
(or Hussein)

PRINCE AHMED BEN AL HUSSEIN.

From this it was plain that the Royalists were anxious to contact us. Only direct orders stopped my taking this logical, sensible step. I was anxious to make our troop's task as straightforward and successful as possible once they did arrive. It was no use blinking the truth. The Imam's forces controlled great sectors of the country and could not be ignored. Being in Sanaa made one acutely aware just how tenuous a hold the Egyptians and Republicans had on the country. Even close to the capital it was the same story.

On June 16, General Qadi invited us to a reception at Command Headquarters' mess. During an enjoyable evening, I spoke with Major General Abbas whose face, as he gave me a clear assessment of the neighboring tribal situation, was eloquent of the dangers of the bloody clashes that were a feature of almost daily travel on the road between Hodeida and Sanaa. I gathered from him—and from General Qadi the following day—that there were two main tribal factions in the Yemen. Each represented a different sect within the Muslim faith.

The Shaafis, in the south of the country, the coastal plain, and the twin capitals of Sanaa and Taiz were mostly Sunni Muslims and had had a hard time under the old Imam; as a result the Republic could rely on them for a considerable degree of support. The reason for their unpopularity with the old Imam was explained by the fact that he had been the head (as his son, the present Imam, was now) of the fierce Zaidi tribal confederations which lived mainly in the populous mountain areas of north, central, and east Yemen. Distinctions, however, were not fine-drawn. Although the Zaidis were strong supporters of the Royalists; almost all the members of the new Republic government were adherents of this faith.

But whatever their sect, few had any love for the Egyptians and the situation around Sanaa reflected the attitude of the tribes. The Beni Mutter had been involved in a clash with the Egyptians as recently as June 9, but were since said to have pledged loyalty to Sallal. North of Sanaa were the Beni Hamdan—a far from peaceful tribe—whom the Egyptians and Republicans had recently endeavored to disarm without conspicuous success.

Indeed, the Beni Hamdan had joined forces with the neighboring Beni Khaimah and had showed great enterprise in sallying out from their villages in the northwest to attack Egyptian convoys on the Hodeida-Sanaa road. On more than one occasion they had cut this motorway completely, forcing the Egyptians to send up tanks to reopen it and making it necessary for them to keep their armor permanently deployed along the two principal ridges overlooking this vital supply route from Hodeida.

I told Qadi that our Headquarters was now firmly established in the capital and that we were anxious to set up a control point in Hodeida whence we could certify the withdrawal of Egyptian troops. In the last few days I had noticed two troopships in the port, and since I guessed these had arrived to evacuate certain units, I suggested that we ought to begin our work right away. News like this would be most welcome in Jeddah where I was flying on June 18 for a meeting with Prince Feisal.

General Qadi courteously sidestepped this request, telling me that although certain units had returned to Egypt, they had been replaced. He told me, too, and stressed, that although he had plans for relieving and withdrawing some of his more severely tried units in the interior, there was no over-all plan for a phased withdrawal. This would be entirely dependent on proof that the Saudis had stopped assisting the Royalists. According to his intelligence reports this was highly unlikely; he had every reason to believe that convoys of men and arms had been restarted within the last few days.

This forthright approach did not inhibit his assuring me that he would give us all the help he could and that, as a first step, he had appointed Lieutenant Colonel Hilmy as my senior liaison officer. He introduced me to my late passenger and then to his assistant, Major Khandil, whom I recognized as an officer who had served on General Hilmy's liaison staff with UNEF in Gaza; I recalled that he had had legal training and was reputed to be a pleasant if difficult customer. Having shaken hands all round with my new guides and helpmeets, I took the opportunity during all this good will of asking Qadi to help us to purchase or borrow two Yemeni Aero-Commando planes, which I had noticed roosting on the Sanaa airfield; once overhauled, we could put them to invaluable use. Qadi smiled again and promised to do what he could. When I left the Yemen, however, the Aero-Commandos were still deteriorating quietly in the blazing sun, drenched regularly at three o'clock each afternoon by torrential rain.

On June 18, I flew up to Jeddah to see Prince Feisal, pondering on the presence of a familiar face at General Qadi's party. As—true to UN style—I had no sources of information available other than what I could glean from the Saudi and Egyptian authorities, I thought it rather overestimating my importance to bring in an extremely able counterintelligence officer (whom I remembered from Palestine days) to keep an eye on me. More restful had been the sight of the frustrated Egyptian diplomat, saddled with the hair-raising task of training the Sanaa Yemenis as civil servants. Although the Yemen had the highest literacy rate in Arabia his resigned shrug expressed his despair as he observed: "What a job! What a job! All they really need is a senior clerk who will knock some idea of office work and administrative organization into their heads. One can't hope to teach them more."

On arrival at Jeddah, I was driven to the Palace where I was to have an audience with Prince Feisal. This remarkable man, later to become king, was a wise, dignified but warm figure. Our meeting took place in the audience room of his old private palace against a background of lofty arches, venetian blinds, sumptuous carpets, and ceremonial coffee. And in this oriental atmosphere I had the immediate feeling that I was dealing with a man of honor who (unlike the normal run of Arab rulers) had the interests of his people very much at heart.

Despite an aquiline, almost sharp cast of features, Prince Feisal radiated a charm that concealed a strong though flexible personality. According to protocol, I waited for him to speak first. When his speech was over, my interpreter conveyed my own salutations and greetings. I told him that while my mission once it arrived, had been alerted for movement into the northern buffer zone, and once there would carry out its task most efficiently, I felt certain that its best hope of success rested primarily on Saudi Arabian good will.

I was, I said, aware that the situation was complicated and difficult. I knew, too, that the Egyptians had started to bomb Saudi Arabian territory, but I hoped that despite this violation of the disengagement terms, Saudi Arabia was not contemplating reactivating supply convoys to the Royalist forces. Undoubtedly, delay in the arrival of the Mission had contributed to a deterioration in the situation, and I regretted so much time had elapsed since my exploratory visit. I was sure that His Highness would realize that it was only in the nature of governments and international organizations to move slowly.

All this was translated into the most beautiful and flowery phrases and it was only when at long last the interpreter had finished that Prince Feisal showed signs of animation. For just as I was about to beg permission to take my leave, his face crinkled into an infectious smile and to my astonishment, I found myself being addressed in fluent English. It proved a short but very pleasant speech in the course of which he told me that I could count on his full cooperation but that he expected the UN to insure an equal cooperation from the Egyptians. When we parted, I felt that I had his personal good will whatever his unspoken impression of the United Nations.

I returned to Sanaa convinced that a mere "presence" would never be enough, a mere drop in the ocean whose impotence would exacerbate rather than dispel mutual suspicion. On the face of it, it began to look as though even were my minimum requirements to be belatedly met, our full strength would be little more than window-dressing. I knew now that I had made the gravest mistake in taking over the Mission. There was still a hope, a very frail one, but with every day the sands were running out.

I suffered from many gloomy thoughts that night in my four-poster in the erstwhile Favorite's bedroom. The next morning, I went gloomily out once more to "show the flag." It was literally the only thing I *could* do. Sensing how fast the situation was deteriorating, it was at least a sop to one's doubts to do something active. Once more "Abbie" roared down to the airfield, once again she was driven on board the faithful Caribou, and we took off on one more flight in our rather pathetic attempt to insure the "presence" of the United Nations.

It was on this trip that we had considerable difficulty locating Saada. The mountains must have seemed all very alike to our Canadian pilot, who was being assisted by Larry David leaning forward into the cabin from the steps of the flight deck. As I knew we were running low on fuel I had been keeping a careful eye on the terrain myself, and now, thoughtfully prodding him in the rump with my swagger stick, I tactfully inquired the object of their concern.

"We can't find Saada, sir," he replied without so much as turning round.

"It's over there," I told him, putting down the book I had been reading and pointing through the window at a spot at least 45 degrees east of our course.

And sure enough, it was. Smugly, I picked up my book to disclaim all praise. One of the invaluable advantages that years of soldiering gives one (and which no quirk of politics or governmental policy can ever take away) is an eye for country.

We were late that afternoon returning from Saada. The sky was already very dark as we took off and after a few minutes' flying, we found ourselves in the middle of a first-class thunderstorm. Electric flashes seemed to be lancing all around us to the accompaniment of exploding thunder claps. By now we were fairly hardened to these conditions, so that an especially violent bang and crack failed to disturb us unduly. The plane rocked a little but continued on a steady keel and before long, were were back over Sanaa again, searching for a hole in the rain clouds.

I never gave this incident much thought. And once I was back at the Palace other things cropped up to occupy my mind. Dog-tired, I was met by "Mac" with the news that my Chief Administrative Officer had ordered our Canadian airmen to evacuate the

Guest House. Menaced with eviction from their comparatively comfortable quarters in the harem, the inmates were showing understandable signs of indignation.

There was nothing for it. Before I even had a chance to get so much as a cup of tea, I had to summon my well-meaning but highly emotional administrative "wizard." In a little while he stood before me, dragging his stiff leg and already looking agitated. When I asked him why he had taken it upon himself to issue orders to military personnel, he indignantly denied having done anything of the kind. All he had done had been to "ask them" to leave.

"And why did you do that?" I inquired.

"Because the authorities want the Guest House, General."

"What authorities?"

"The Yemenis, General. They tell me they want the harem for visiting Egyptian officials."

Perhaps it was because I was tired, dirty, and avid for a cup of tea. I let fly. And the gist of the ticking off I now administered was that no blank, blank Egyptian tourists were going to enjoy priority over my hard-working Canadians.

The poor fellow dissolved into tears. He was not, he informed me between sobs, used to "this sort of thing." Beginning to feel sorry for him, I reminded him more gently that I was not used to "*that* sort of thing" either. Finally, I was reduced to patting the unfortunate Haitian on the shoulder until his tears ceased. And in the end all was well; the Canadians remained undisturbed in the Guest House. I did not inquire about the fate of the visiting Egyptians.

Next morning I discovered great excitement around the Caribou. "Just look at that, General," the pilot called out as soon as I arrived on the scene—not without a trace of pride in his voice. I looked. The violent bang on our way back to Sanaa the night before was now explained. A neat pattern of holes through the fuselage recorded the enterprise of some heavily armed private citizen (I doubt whether a soldier on either side in the area would have been able to hit a slow-flying plane at 1,600 feet) who had bagged us fair and square.

We admired his enterprise. Not so my "masters" in New York, who had been urging me in cable after cable to estabish a "UN presence." I doubt whether the routine report of the incident, which I did not stress, having far more important things to think about, had even arrived before I received a message from them that forcibly reported the concern of the Canadian Government about the damage to the plane they had so kindly loaned us. I could understand this, but not the signal that went on to instruct me *on no account* to take any further risks involving life, equipment, or property. This was too much!

I replied bluntly that the UN should never have sent us out if the possibility of bullet holes in aircraft, equipment, and UN personnel had not occurred to them. And now it had, why did they leave us here so wretchedly under strength and ill equipped? Life in the Yemen was not like a picnic in Connecticut. Unless this was clearly understood, it would be best to call off the Mission immediately.

I was very, very angry. And with good reason. Even our civilian staff members (whose loyalties normally lay with the Administration) had for some time been echoing my views. I did not blame them.

There had been an almost callous disregard for our health and welfare. No doctor had been available during the first days of our arrival in a notoriously unhealthy spot. Our food was a constant diet of corned beef hash and hardtack. Our living conditions and facilities were close to rock bottom. When we protested our demands were castigated as "excessive," while at the same time we were forbidden to risk damage to life, limb, and property, in a country where the former was held the cheapest commodity.

These were the sort of frustrations with which we were beset at Headquarters. And although we were a happy enough family, well coped with by the indomitable Dorothy Stevens, I always felt that our little world was like a stifling vacuum from which we could see little more than our own immediate surroundings. Apart from Egyptian intelligence, we had no true picture of the bitter fighting raging in the Yemen, no awareness of the shifts of power on the international stage or the maneuvering affecting the picture from above. We lived in a small closed world dominated by the magic word supply. And unfortunately there was no magic, nothing but a continual dusty struggle against creeping frustration.

There were lighter moments that enlivened these frustrating days while the Mission built up at tortoise-like speed. A story Colonel Hilmy told us illustrated the necessarily stark sense of humor the Yemen imposes on its visitors, whether armed with guns or brassards.

Some weeks before, it had seemed as though peace was about to descend on a tribal area not far from Saada. The Egyptian colonel in command of the sector thought it a distinct step in the right direction when he received an invitation to take coffee with the local Sheikh. Their meeting proved most amicable and it was only after the traditional hospitality of three cups of coffee that the Sheikh and his elders cut the unfortunate colonel's throat.

One could hardly blame the Egyptian army for taking offense. A punitive operation was launched, an impressive joint ground and air strike pulverized the area—watched with professional appreciation by the Sheikh and the tribal elders from the relative comfort and security of a safe, deep cave on the rocky slopes of a mountain.

A tremendous weight of bombs and shells must have devastated the villages of their unfortunate tribe. But hardly had the last mud wall toppled and the dust settled than a visitor was announced at the command post of the punitive expedition. It proved to be the old Mukthar of one of the devastated villages, craving audience. And when he was ushered into the presence of the new Egyptian colonel, the old man salaamed and proceeded to express deep respect and profound gratitude.

A trifle taken aback, the Colonel inquired the reason. Not at all abashed, the Mukhtar replied in flowery Arabic.

"You see, your eminence, it is like this. My wife had died in the bombing of our village. She was old and ugly and has been a sore pain in my neck for many years. But of course it has never been possible for me to get rid of her. Now—suddenly—you have solved my dilemma and are thus my benefactor. I have already installed a young and shapely new wife and two more are on the way to comfort my few remaining years. Abu [which means father and is an extremely complimentary term in the Yemen], I owe you a debt of eternal gratitude and affection. What remains of my poor village is yours."

Although I had this story from Hilmy himself, I did not report it to New York.

Chapter Twenty-seven

KING FEISAL

On a memorable morning toward the end of June, Larry David came bustling into our makeshift Operations Room.

"At last, General." For once he was actually smiling. "We've been assigned a light reconnaissance squadron."

"A Canadian one?" I was already visualizing the excellent work an integrated air-ground reconnaissance squadron could achieve in mountainous country.

"No such luck, sir. We've been given a Yugoslav outfit. I've no idea of their state of training or operational efficiency, but I'm told they are wonderful soldiers."

I did not doubt it, and my immediate concern was to get them out here as rapidly as possible. Whatever their standard of training, whatever the state and quality of their equipment, we needed men on the ground—and needed them urgently.

But Yugoslavia was a very long way from the Yemen. If I knew anything about the Field Operations Service in New York, it was inevitable they would have already planned to send the unit by sea, on the slowest possible route, and taking the maximum amount of time.

I told Larry to send a cable requesting they be flown out on a high priority basis. I might, however, just as well have saved the expense; an incoming cable informed us that this was an impossibility, that the squadron would travel by sea to Hodeida and that it would then become my responsibility to move its men and vehicles by road to the stations in the mountainous buffer zone.

These instructions were little short of insane, and I immediately requested that if the Yugoslavs *had* to come by sea, they should be disembarked at Jeddah. From there the detachments I had earmarked for the northern buffer zone could move by road and track to Jizan and Najran in Saudi Arabia while the remainder could make their way by air or along the coastal road to arrive in Egyptian-held territory and take up position at Saada.

I had excellent reasons. Were the whole unit to arrive at Hodeida, I would find myself faced with the impossible prospect of moving them on vehicles (which the UN apparently expected the Egyptians to provide) across territory either held or constantly threatened by Royalist forces—with whom I was forbidden to establish any sort of contact.

I little suspected then that the Yugoslavs had already set sail under orders not to enter Royalist-held territory in any circumstances. But even had I known, this would only have reinforced the arguments I was putting up to New York; arguments which, as one angry cable succeeded another, were continually castigated as being too expensive and out of line with the cost estimates which, I was constantly and quite wrongly reminded, had been based on my original recommendations.

It soon became obvious that whether I liked it or not, the Yugoslavs would be sailing into Hodeida. Nothing I could do or say could reverse this penny-pinching decision and in due course an advance party flew in to join us on June 27. It was headed by Colonel Branco Pavlovic (who was eventually to become my deputy commander).

I liked rugged, square-shouldered Pavlovic, who seemed to be a good soldier, but it was plain that he and his eight-man advance party had come to the Yemen with preconceived ideas and very definite orders, which were quietly kept in abeyance until the full squadron arrived. His little party consisted of Major Popovic, the equally broad Squadron commander, several interpreters, and the guiding star of the unit, who was promptly assigned as my personal liaison officer. As I came to like Captain Kraejger, I hesitate to depict him as a full-blown commissar, but that was what he was, and his long training and natural secretiveness enabled him to exercise political control over his men and obey orders from Belgrade under our unsuspecting noses, which added no luster to the history of United Nations military operations—coming on top of the activities of the Guinea and UAR battalions in the Congo.

I was told to expect the arrival of the rest of the squadron on July 4. It would be one hundred fourteen men strong and was equipped with jeeps and light trucks, which were not unsuitable for operating in trackless country. There would, however, be no integrated air unit to operate with them, and there were bound to be language difficulties once they began patrolling in company with the Canadian Otter aircraft, which had now arrived at Aden and were due to join us within the next few days. But over and above these drawbacks there remained the supreme problem of actually *getting* them to their patrol areas.

Movement overland was quite out of the question. Air was equally hopeless without the necessary aircraft, even with the aid of Wing Commander Olsen (who had just joined the Mission as my air staff officer) and Squadron Leader Ian Umbach, who was due to arrive any minute with the only extra Caribou the Canadian government could spare. Our airlift capacity was virtually nonexistent and until New York woke up and read my cables the Yugoslavs would remain at Hodeida while we tried to lift them in miserable penny packets. If there was anything that years of soldiering had taught me it was how to move and deploy troops in an efficient and economic way. But since I was not going to be given the chance I had no immediate intention of torturing myself with this insuperable problem. I had made my essential requirements crystal-clear and sooner or later sheer necessity would force New York to face up to the airlift problem.

As far back as February, I had told U Thant that one of my conditions for accepting the Mission would be a period of leave at the beginning of July. And to do him justice, when I cabled him a reminder of this there was no recrimination. I had every confidence in leaving Larry David in charge at Sanaa where the mission had reached a stalemate and there was little more I could do.

Before I took off for the relative sanity of Sweden, however, I drew up a report on our lack of progress. Drafting this on July 3 (the day on which the Mission *should* have been fully operational), I listed the pathetic figures of the build-up achieved so far. Contrasted with the minimum strength I had recommended, these made poor showing. Our military element was still 77 per cent below strength. On the civilian side, the paper figures looked a little more encouraging; only 51 per cent under strength; 89 per cent of our aircraft was still due to make an appearance. On the ground, however, our air staff had reached the heartening total of 86 per cent of the total need to keep the planes operational when they *did* arrive.

My report was passed back to a fellow countryman of Rikhye's: C. V. Narasimhan, an Indian whom Dag had appointed as his Chef de Cabinet. Presumably this had been done to adjust the balance of Western dominance inside the Secretariat.

On my return from Sweden three weeks later, I discovered that things had worked out very much along the lines I had anticipated. I had been away twenty-one days. In that time New York had been forced to the conclusion that the reconnaissance squadron that had arrived at Hodeida on July 4 was likely to remain there indefinitely unless something drastic was done.

For a time it seemed as though the chairborne wizards might be content to leave the Yugoslavs immobilized, tied up to the dock, vaguely hoping that the problem would solve itself. But then it was discovered the ship was costing $1,000 a day so long as it remained in port and at long last, emergency measures were put in hand and two American C.130s were dispatched to airlift the Yugoslavs to my selected control points at Jizan, Najran, and Saada.

The supply position, however, remained as unsatisfactory as ever and rations, petrol, and spare parts were desperately short. There was a frightening dearth of all the supplies we needed to keep operational. Our airlift capacity was virtually nonexistent and our external supply flights hopelessly out of tune with our minimum requirements.

Briefing me on my return, Larry David told me that although an attempt had been made to extend the regular Canadian supply flight (which brought stores and equipment from Canada and Europe to the UNEF force at Gaza) on down to us, it had not been anything like sufficient; the backlog of Sanaa-bound freight was building up alarmingly at the UNEF air base at Gaza.

I discovered that although the Otters had now arrived and had begun limited operations, I had lost my Air Staff Officer, Wing

Commander Olsen, who had been returned to Canada. No replacement appeared to be available.

Although the Yugoslavs were now operational, it was difficult to escape the feeling that they had come too late to achieve much more than I could have accomplished with my single jeep. Too much time had slipped away. As Larry outlined the situation to me, it was obvious that certain elements in Saudi Arabia had lost patience with our inability to make the Egyptians observe the disengagement terms. Supply convoys across the mountains had been restarted, with or without official blessing, and the Imam's forces had become increasingly active. Every day there was news of raids, ambushes, and small-scale attacks on Egyptian and Republican garrisons. Countermeasures were constantly in progress, but despite the Egyptian planes and armor the Republican Government had failed to increase its control over another inch of territory.

On the face of it, it seemed to me that we now had little hope of expecting cooperation from the Saudis. At the beginning, they had complied with the disengagement terms, but before long they had been driven to the conclusion that this was a very one-sided agreement, because the Egyptians had little or no intention of keeping their side of the bargain. And the complete lack of interest by the United Nations toward any Royalist complaints about the bombing and massacres in Royalist-held territory by the Egyptians had obviously convinced the Saudis that the high-minded conception of human rights and justice that prevailed on the East River had nothing in common with the basic truths in the Yemen.

I found it difficult not to sympathize because the tribal loyalties and customs that lay at the heart of the Imam's very real and formidable support were based on values that could not be denied, since the customs of the tribes went back to the old Sabean and Himyerite Kingdoms long before Islam was known. It was a highly developed system of tribal society and the Imamate, freely accepted, had existed for well over a thousand years. Its very existence was an expression of the deep-rooted feelings of the people of the Yemen, but this was a reality that would never be understood or evaluated in the rarefied atmosphere of the Secretariat.

Yet if there ever was to be any lasting chance of peace in this country, these values were something with which terms *had* to be made. It was no use blinding oneself to the truth. The Royalists controlled the best part of half the Yemen, were gaining ground and support despite the terror bombing devastating their villages and were, in their own view, fighting against an illegal Republic recognized by many of the countries which paid lip service to the United Nations.

I was really worried about New York's attitude to the Royalists. Time and again I had asked permission to be allowed to make contact with them, and time and again this had been flatly turned down. The only result had been to seal off vital channels of information that would have been invaluable. Without contact with them I was virtually operating blind, dependent only on the information I could obtain from the Egyptians and Republicans, and consequently hamstrung in making practical recommendations for the Mission's operational role.

There were some vital priorities. First, I ought to obtain another audience with Prince Feisal of Saudi Arabia in order to try to persuade him to halt the supplies of arms which we knew had started coming over the border again. Because we suspected that this help was the result of private enterprise rather than official Saudi policy, there was still a chance of achieving a degree of success. Second, I had to visit the Yugoslavs at their control stations on either side of the border to discover what degree of success, if any, their patrols were achieving. Thirdly, I must again take up the cudgels with New York to try to persuade them to let me make contact with the Royalists.

We had already had a number of approaches—usually by letters which mysteriously found their way into our Headquarters in the Old Palace—but unless I was soon in a position to reply affirmatively the feelers would be withdrawn and the opportunity lost. Finally, I must resume the interminable battle with New York to build up our supply base, reinforce our airlift capacity, and evolve some sort of logistic order into the chaos of our present supply system.

Unfortunately, a whole month was to elapse before Prince Feisal expressed himself ready to grant me audience. Although this was not entirely a surprise, it came nonetheless with a sense of shock because I had pinned great hopes on an early meeting and the delay was an unhappy indication of the value the Saudis now attached to our Mission. In essence, it all boiled down to the neglect of one simple, vital military principle. Command and administrative authority had been separated with disastrous results. I do not know of an occasion in the history of military operations when this mistake has not had disastrous repercussions.

Although I could see the writing clearly on the wall, I had no intention of abdicating just yet. I had soldiers who trusted me and looked to me for guidance and whatever my private thoughts, I had a duty to them as well as to the organization. Whether or not this was to prove the swan song of my international soldiering, I was determined to carry on to the best of my ability until the moment arrived when even the most long-suffering soldier had no alternative but to lay aside the blue beret.

Since I could not see Prince Feisal, I did the next best thing, starting with an inspection of the Yugoslavs at Jizan and Najran, where I had heard that although they had proved smart and efficient soldiers, there had been a marked reluctance to commit themselves to patrolling what had come to be considered "dangerous" territory.

I found this was certainly inclined to be the case. There was a strange hesitation about their ponderous operations, and whenever I was with them I found myself heading their patrols, which consisted of two heavily armed jeeps under the substantial air cover of an Otter patrol.

The Yugoslavs seemed to have an obsession about moving cautiously in territory where one hardly ever saw a soul. They seemed, too, to have an inbuilt suspicion that their path was likely to be strewn with mines, though doubtless had any passed through this vicinity they had long ago been laid along the roads that bore Egyptian traffic into the Yemen. Altogether, the situation was unsatisfactory. There was a marked lack of dash, and the tight and inflexible Yugoslav command system inhibited troop commanders from exercising any degree of initiative.

They were never allowed to remain long on their own and were always subject to constant supervision by their squadron commander. Consequently, Major Popovic became a very busy man, hopping across the mountains to visit his units on either side of the border. This demanded the services of a plane and one of our precious Otters was almost constantly at his disposal. I had enough trouble explaining our aircraft requirements to New York for me not to take a jaundiced view of this.

It was not that the Yugoslavs were timorous or reluctant soldiers. Some of the finest fighting troops in the world, they were confident of themselves and handled their weapons with the ease of familiarity.

Only much later did the true reason for their failure to match up to their reputation become apparent, and by that time they were leaving for home and the Mission was being broken up. A request for a suspiciously generous allowance of air freight led to the discovery that they had been concealing a powerful radio transmitter in their Sanaa embassy. Beamed on Belgrade, it had kept their masters fully informed of their activities. And doubtless over the same channels had come the instructions that had contributed to the foot-dragging which had puzzled and distressed me so much at the time. Unknown to me—and equally unsuspected by New York—the Yugoslavs had arrived with specific instructions not to enter Royalist territory. And as the hot and dusty country in which they were operating now had no carefully delineated borders, they were interpreting their orders in the most empirical way.

Shortly after I returned to Sanaa from visiting the Yugoslavs there was a distinct shift in the UN attitude toward the Royalists. Their outraged but somehow still polite complaints that the Egyptians had bombed villages in their territory with poison gas had been given world-wide publicity (publicity which I suspect had been most skilfully, and rightly, disseminated by a well-known English public relations firm retained by the Saudi Arabian Government) and it certainly worked wonders in New York. There was a remarkable *volte face*. Where before my request to be allowed to contact the Royalists had been flatly rejected, I now began to receive pressing instructions to take every step possible to establish the truth "however ill-founded the allegations may be."

Before long I began to receive fresh cables reproaching me for my failure to stop the arms traffic across the border. I soon discovered that this was the result of Prince Feisal's expressed dissatisfaction with the UN, which had been made plain to the Secretariat in a letter couched in no uncertain terms. The main attack was on the Yugoslavs for inefficiency and for their alleged exaggerated sighting reports of arms convoys—convoys which Feisal said had never been inspected or at worst simply invented.

As a result New York panicked and I was shortly showered with draft instructions for my observers. Since these were put forward for my comments, I replied in reasonably polite terms, pointing out that they were totally unrealistic. In fact, they were infantile and so revealing of the total lack of knowledge about the circumstances under which we were operating that the only conclusion I could reach was that my reports had either been ignored or simply dumped unread into a filing tray.

Toward the end of that hectic July two interviews brought a gleam of hope. On August 3, I had a long talk with General Qadi, at the end of which I almost began to believe I had been able to convince him that it was in the Egyptians' best interests to pull out of the buffer zone and stage a token withdrawal from the country, if only to prevent the war from escalating as the Saudi Arabians resumed full-scale support for the Royalists.

Qadi was remarkably forthcoming on this occasion. Not only did he assure me that he had every intention of pulling his troops out of the buffer zone, but he told me that he had prepared a plan for a phased withdrawal of Egyptian forces from the country at the rate of a thousand men every ten days. Although this would have meant the whole force would still not have evacuated the country until the beginning of next year and although I frankly doubted whether what he said was much more than a verbal smoke screen, it nonetheless proved invaluable to take north with me to Jeddah. Even more surprising, Qadi informed me that he had no objection to our observers entering Royalist-controlled territory to investigate alleged violations of the disengagement terms.

I was glad to have this news when I flew to Jeddah. From my talks with Mr. Saqqaff, the Deputy Foreign Minister, and Prince Sultan, Prince Feisal's brother and his Minister of Defense, there the next day, I gained the impression that all hope was not yet lost. I listened with interest to Prince Sultan, a volatile and emotional young man. From the conversation, I gained the impression that the Government was divided into two factions.

On the one hand there was Sultan who, as Minister of Defense, had undoubtedly allied himself with a number of other princely figures who occupied an influential position outside the Government. This group was not at all interested whether the disengagement terms succeeded or failed; its only interest was to see the Royalists win. I had no doubt that it was this unofficial group which was responsible for the resumption of the supply of arms over the frontier. The other faction, smaller and less powerful, was still highly influential and far more farsighted, seeing clearly that sooner or later Saudi Arabia and Egypt must come to some understanding in the interests of Arab unity. I felt certain that Saqqaff was a member of this faction and thought it probable that Prince Feisal was strongly inclined to favor the same policy.

Although Sultan and Saqqaff both assured me that the official ban on arms traffic was still in force, I thought that the course of the war and in consequence all worthwhile cooperation with my mission depended entirely on which faction managed to get the upper hand. The news I had brought from Qadi proved very helpful. I only hoped that his actions were likely to speak louder than words. Were the Egyptians to show real signs of observing the disengagement terms, then Prince Feisal would side with Saqqaff. On the other hand, any indication that they had no intention of withdrawing would mean that Prince Sultan and his militant supporters would gain the upper hand. Once this happened hostilities were bound to escalate and Arab unity would be set back a decade.

I stayed on in Jeddah for a few days and then flew before dawn up to Taif to visit Prince Feisal in his favorite summer resort. Although it was still very hot, the climate was a wonderful change from the Yemen. I was first brought to a large palace, one half of which consisted of a VIP guest house, while the other was part of the Ministry of Defense.

Here in sumptuously furnished quarters, where broad balconies protected one from the glaring sun, I was given a meal and a rest before proceeding to my audience at Feisal's own palace, where I could hardly have had a kinder or more courteous reception. When, however, we began our talk the atmosphere was more reserved. Through my interpreter I told the Prince that the initial two-month period of the Mission was now drawing toward a close and expressed the hope that, whatever policy the Egyptians might follow, the Saudi Arabian Government would continue to honor the terms of the disengagement.

Prince Feisal told me that he could not conceal his disappointment over the lack of Egyptian implementation of the disengagement agreement. Infinitely polite, he never mentioned the impotence of the UN but this was hardly necessary because I was so acutely aware of it myself. Altogether it was not an easy interview. I said what I had come to say but some of the Prince's observations on the reports of my Yugoslav patrols struck home. Arms convoys had been reported where patently no arms convoys existed. Food trucks had been identified as lorries loaded with munitions because no one had considered it his duty to go close enough to observe their contents.

From time to time, I found myself at a loss—just as when, having reproached the Prince for continuing to maintain antiaircraft guns at Najran, he asked whether I believed they were there for aggressive reasons. Feisal had a great deal to say and much of it did not make comfortable listening, if only for the reason I frequently found myself in agreement with him. Nor was I able to come up with a satisfactory answer when he asked why it was the United Nations continued to ignore the existence of the Royalists although they were in control of nearly half the country.

Knowing him far too astute and wise a man to listen to trumped-up excuses, I explained the position as best I could and told him that I hoped to be able to spare observers from our scanty force to conduct investigations into the use of poison gas bombs. I had, however, no success in persuading him (or indeed myself) that New York's attitude toward the Imam was likely to undergo any transformation. The Prince listened calmly. He then told me that he had full confidence in me as the leader of the Mission and explained that his recent letter to the Secretary General expressing his Government's lack of confidence in the Mission had been due to a slight misunderstanding. Translated into flowery complimentary phrases, this diplomatic gesture induced a temporary sensation of euphoria.

I returned to Sanaa with Ali Nekunam, my charming Iranian political adviser, whom I had brought along to Jeddah with me because I knew that one of his greatest ambitions was to visit Mecca.

During the days following my return I managed to get an occasional break by early morning rides on a beautiful white stallion that had belonged to the late Imam. At that early hour there were no papers to read and the intelligence summaries had not yet arrived on my desk. I found my rides an excellent way of keeping up with local and regional news.

I had a simple method. After circling round the mud walls of the city at a canter, I used to slow down to a walk in order to inspect the main gate. I would count the fresh heads that had been stuck up on spikes in niches easily reached by milling crowds of vociferous urchins. Reining in, I had a good look. If the number of heads was the same as on the previous day, I knew that local politics were reasonably stable. A fresh batch indicated that (making allowances for the normal quota of petty criminals) a number of backsliding Republicans or unfortunate Royalist supporters had been taken to task. On the basis of my observations, I would then start discreet inquiries through the limited means which were at my disposal.

Nothing could have demonstrated the medieval temper of the country so vividly. The main gate was a horrible sight, rendered more macabre by the hordes of children who delighted in climbing up to the niches and adorning the mouths, ears, and nostrils of the unfortunate victims with cigarette ends. Before long the presence of the Mission achieved a visible improvement.

So many UN personnel were taking color films of this evidence of progress and democracy that the Government took fright. The heads were removed and all public executions ceased. This drastic step curtailed the city's inhabitants' main source of amusement and recreation and did not enhance our popularity in Sanaa. Executions were conducted behind stone walls and my morning rides abruptly ceased to be a useful source of intelligence.

I kept them up, however. And one morning, having returned to the old palace, I dismounted, patted the neck of my magnificent mount (whose headstall and saddlecloth still sported the royal crown of the deposed Imam) and handed the reins to the syce, who had survived from the royal regime in the palace stables. Starting to walk up the stair steps, I didn't see him handing over the reins to a member of the kitchen staff who (presumably in exchange for some services rendered) promptly led the stallion out of sight, mounted, and set off on a jaunt through the city.

Later we learned the full story. Not being an accomplished horseman, the kitchen hand grew bewildered amid the heavy flow of Egyptian staff cars and trucks that hooted and blared their way through the medieval streets. He ran down an unfortunate pedestrian, a misfortune that rapidly brought a squad of Republican police onto the scene. Their police work proved highly original. First, they arrested the stallion, next the kitchen hand, and finally the unlucky victim was picked up and brought along for good measure.

As soon as we heard this I sent Jim Gander, my Scots Chief Security Officer, to the central police station. Jim, who had had plenty of experience in the Middle East and had begun his career as a mounted policeman in Palestine, reported later that it had been much more difficult to secure the release of the stallion than his unlucky rider. The latter was swiftly released once Jim, to the amazement of the police, assured them that we did not desire to have him decapitated or even jailed for a decade or so. Jim told me the culprit seemed more flabbergasted at this magnanimity than the police. Nevertheless, when last seen, he was energetically trekking out of the city to rejoin his tribe in the hills.

The stallion proved a much more complicated matter. After long and involved argument, Jim fortunately remembered that the Republic's first anniversary was only a month away. The snow-white steed would, he pointed out, be urgently needed for the rehearsals of the march past to acclaim President Sallal's *coup d'état*. After considerable head scratching, the police agreed; that night the stallion was back in its stable in the old royal mews.

There still remained the victim. Jim finally ran him to ground in the central hospital where his captors had transported him. Amid the stench and filth of this insalubrious haven, the unfortunate man's identity was finally revealed. He proved to be a junior clerk in the Foreign Ministry who, once he had been told that he would not be prosecuted, climbed weakly from his reeking pallet; but when Jim explained that there was no chance of his putting in a claim for compensation he strode indignantly out into the sunlight.

These were only incidents that temporarily lightened the gloom. But by now I was becoming so worried over our shortage of transport planes that I asked my old friend, General Gyani at UNEF in Gaza, for the temporary loan of an experienced Air Staff Officer. Gyani, blissfully unaware of the fate in store for him, sent me a stout-hearted Canadian, Wing Commander Hlady, the very same man who had helped us out of a tight spot at N'Djili airport in the Congo. I set him to work to make a survey of the situation and report on the minimum number of planes essential to keep the Mission from collapsing.

The situation was now ludicrous; we had only two transport planes, which were frequently grounded for overhaul and maintenance, and our supply situation was in a desperate state. It was now so bad that it became necessary to send staff officers across to Asmara, in Eritrea, to discover what local produce we could buy in the markets there. We were so short of food, let alone petrol, spare parts, and the basic necessities that I foresaw a major supply crisis looming up toward the end of August. Despite the massive stockpile at Gaza, lack of transport to bring it down would insure our being virtually out of rations within a few more weeks.

Asmara turned out to be a fruitful market and source of stores, and the supplies my foragers brought back resulted in a visible increase in morale. Although we had been a happy enough family, shortage of food, continual frustration, and the trying climate had set tempers on edge. Now there was a distinct improvement although living conditions remained primitive in the extreme. What hit us hardest was the knowledge that unless we had taken the initiative of buying food, we would have found ourselves left in a state of near-starvation.

I was fully aware of the Organization's financial troubles and could appreciate their apprehension lest the Yemen might become another running sore on the last vestiges of a dwindling treasury. But these fears could have been taken into account *before* a decision had been taken to send a Mission at all.

The story of the Mission was a sorry one. I, its Commanding Officer, had been misled, the general public had been deluded, and the Egyptians and Saudi Arabians had been taken straight up the garden path. Worst of all, New York had shown a total inability to learn from past mistakes and seemed incapable of grasping the fact that their failings were jeopardizing the Mission's future.

Recriminations can be boring. But not when men's health and lives are at stake. I was well aware of the truth; I was equally aware that the necessity to "save face" in New York would keep their abject failure shrouded in face-saving maneuvers. I had not, however, realized to quite what lengths they would go nor how bitterly they would resent my efforts to make the truth known. I was to learn the hard way.

Obviously the realization that I had been forced to take matters into my own hands and make direct purchases from Asmara nettled them. I had been forced to do this because the transport planes needed to fly supplies from the base at Gaza simply did not exist. Any Commander worth his salt would have done the same. After my resignation, I was to learn the "true" reason for my initiative. This came from an official UN spokesman who claimed that my request for air lift space to and from Asmara had been "for my own weekend trips there."

Chapter Twenty-eight

LOOKING AHEAD

HALFWAY through August, while Hlady labored on his survey, I was forced to do a great deal of hard and clear thinking in the solitary splendor of the Favorite's room. One could hardly have picked a stranger place in which to reach a crucial decision; my ancient wooden four-poster stood isolated in the middle of the room that eleven months ago must have rocked to the explosions of high-velocity Russian tank shells. Water still seeped through the ceiling from the shattered stories above. But immediately the rains ceased, it became hot and stifling, resonant to the droning of marauding insects whose song was loud through the cramped and crumbling mud-walled medieval city.

It was not a propitious setting for a decision that must influence my whole future. But other commanders had had to take more crucial ones in far odder and more out-of-the-way places. Perhaps because a soldier is conditioned to the servitudes and grandeurs of the military role, perhaps because he rates service and devotion to duty in a different way from his civilian counterparts (who do not bear responsibility in the same hard ratio of lives and trust and faith), there is a terrible finality about a decision to resign on active service. I do not know how other men feel. I can only relate the motives and reasons that stirred me. It was not a dramatic occasion, but it was very personal.

Few major decisions are easy. And one which means writing "finis" to a lifetime of soldiering can be a hard and cruel one to make. But, in my own heart, the turning point had already been reached and passed. I had no alternative, were I to retain the trust and confidence of the Mission. And if a sacrifice had to be made, then who could be better spared than the man whose resignation might force a new sense of reality into an enterprise otherwise doomed?

Many thoughts were passing through my mind at this time: all the frustrations I have already described and other wider implications too. What part had America played in all this? Had she wanted to see the new Republic consolidated as a potential embarrassment to the British federation of Southern Arabian States? Had she exerted pressure behind the scenes to bring about the disengagement agreement from which she hoped for a new *status quo*, giving her oil interests a stronger and preferential position? Had she been up to her old game of playing politics in order to appear a champion of the Afro-Asian bloc? I had the strongest suspicion that this was the case. But basically I had the impression that, under the cloak of a benefactor and supporter of national aspirations in the Middle East, there was the desire to cut the throat of British influence in the Persian Gulf.

There was no doubt that American policy had been in a tearing hurry to see the new Republic firmly established in the Yemen.

Nothing else could explain the sudden recognition of a *coup d'état,* nothing make plain the motives behind the precipitate hurry to acknowledge a regime which had not succeeded in establishing itself in control of half the country, nor to try to present the struggle as the forces of progress against a backward tribal despot whose resources would soon evaporate once the Saudi supply line dried up. As I knew very well, it was nothing of the kind, and I had the uncomfortable feeling that the Americans had an almost vested interest in seeing the Imam go down. All my earlier fears were to be reinforced when, after my resignation from the UN, a well-informed American friend told me: "I hope you will not be too harsh in your judgment on us if you ever write your memoirs."

At that time, I was still inclined to be charitable despite my belief that the State Department had backed Nasser for a mixture of ill-judged reasons. It was only later, when I read the reply of Dean Rusk's Under Secretary of State, Phillip Talbot, to accusations by Senator Bourke Hickenlooper (a Republican member of the Senate Foreign Relations Committee) that I was able to understand Talbot's earlier comment that "von Horn had not been the right man in the Yemen." Doubtless this was a reflection on my insistence that the Egyptians *should* be made to withdraw, and my constant demands to be allowed to make contact with the Royalists.

Talbot's reply was revealing. He disclosed that the US Government had never insisted on the withdrawal of Egyptian troops after Saudi Arabia had honored its truce obligations but had merely *expected* them to withdraw in a phased and expeditious fashion. In the official view, "The Imam's cause is no more than tribal guerrilla warfare and peace has been established in the country." It went on to say, "The restoration of the notoriously despotic Imamate would not be supported by the Yemeni people at large and is generally acknowledged to be out of the question."

So here was the United States, apparently acquiescing in steamrollering flat a small heroic people. And why? Because of business interests in the Middle East, a political "hunch" that Nasser was the next best thing to Communism? Or was it through a desire to strike at the British oil interests in Southern Arabia, allowing

Nasser enough rein in his drive toward the Gulf seriously to upset the State of Saudi Arabia, bring down King Saud, and insure his replacement with the more sympathetic Prince Feisal?

I had my doubts. And they were heavy on me now.

The crisis began to move toward its climax. Within a few days, I received the astonishing information from New York that in future all supplies would be shipped in by sea. This near-lunatic news created a minor tornado inside Headquarters. I was deluged with wrathful protests. My staff complained. The Canadians complained. The Yugoslavs complained. But when I forwarded their protests, New York took not the slightest notice.

On August 14, Hlady submitted his report, set out our air supply position very clearly, and painted an unnerving picture—supplies for the Mission were running out fast. It was clear, Hlady stated, that two Caribou aircraft were totally inadequate to cope with UNYOM's needs. The whole future of the Mission would be in jeopardy unless its airlift capacity was increased. He recommended that our transport strength be immediately built up with a third Caribou and that our supply base should be transferred from Gaza to Hodeida at the earliest opportunity.

Here was clear, independent opinion, highly professional and emanating from a source not directly involved in the day-to-day affairs of the Mission. I was delighted to have it to reinforce my own requests. I forwarded it to New York with a covering letter detailing the Mission's present strength. After all these months, it remained hopelessly inadequate. Our military personnel were still 20 per cent under strength, our civilian element had achieved 54 per cent of the minimum I considered necessary, but the administrative officer had just received a direct order to reduce his staff. Most depressing of all, and reinforcing Hlady's survey, was the staggering (but consistently reported) gap of 63 per cent in our airlift capacity.

As a rider, I reiterated that this paucity of transport planes made it totally impossible for us to accumulate reserve supplies. Far from having a supply base, we were living from hand to mouth, dependent on each new planeload and such food buying as we could afford for our daily needs and requirements. Unless another Caribou was received within the next few days, I must advise that the reconnaissance squadron be withdrawn because the supplies to keep it operating were simply not available.

I had not long to wait for a reply. Its tone was dictatorial. I was told that everything was being done which could be done, and I was advised, in so many words, to stop bellyaching and get on with my job. This gratuitous advice was totally unacceptable; it was so unrealistic that it put me in mind of irresponsible little boys playing with soldiers on a comfortable nursery floor. I knew that the moment of no return had arrived. I did not even trouble to take the matter up personally with Rikhye. Instead, I sent a priority personal message to U Thant, telling him exactly what I thought about the administrative failure that was strangling the Mission. I also made it very clear that I doubted whether his advisers had ever given him a true picture of what was happening.

The reaction, for once, was volcanic. No doubt copies of my message were circulated throughout many of the offices in the glass building. Like a swarm of angry bees who sense their comfortable hive in danger, the occupants of these offices must have rushed to the thirty-eighth floor to denounce me to U Thant. For many in the building, a great deal was at stake; their "face," their jobs.

I do not know who drafted his reply. Whoever it was doubtless went home to an excellent dinner while thousands of miles away we munched our tinned sardines and slices of sweating corned beef. But its tone was magisterially severe. It informed me that there was no question whatsoever of the Field Service having failed to carry out its functions. Nor, it stated, had there been any question of its members advising me on how to handle my resources. After further acidic observations, I was advised to take a tighter hold on administrative procedures and insure that *reasonable* economy was observed. The Secretary General felt sure that I would agree that the somewhat offensive remarks in my message were entirely unwarranted.

I did not agree. I was fighting for the Mission's life and every word in my signal was well warranted. After all the enormities that had been perpetrated against us, U Thant's admonitory message was the final straw. I sent for Colonel Branco Pavlovic.

Although this stalwart Yugoslav was officially my deputy commander, he showed a remarkable lack of enthusiasm for taking over temporary command of the Mission. His face fell when I told him that I was resigning and he flatly refused to take the helm even on an acting basis. I watched him hurry away into the sunlight, little suspecting that he must have been on his way to seek "official guidance" over his secret radio link.

I had no option but to transmit this news to U Thant as I drafted a cable, informing him of my decision. I told him that I could not, repeat not, agree that my remarks had been unwarranted, reminded him of the promises and assurance he had given me before I had set out, and told him that since he evidently considered that the representations which it was my duty to make were unwarranted, I felt that I had lost his confidence. I therefore had no choice but to offer my resignation.

There is a certain finality about such a moment. But once the cable had gone to our signal office, I knew that I had done the right thing. A Commander can only do his very best and keep on doing it. If I had to come to the end of the road, then I had been motivated by the belief that resignation was the only way in which I could still help the Mission. I don't think I was mistaken, and I was deeply touched when one of my aides, who had been a tower of strength through these weeks of frustration, came to me and told me that I had the full support of all hands in the Mission. He too, he told me, had decided on a similar course. He would request to be posted back to UNTSO at the earliest opportunity.

There was not long to wait. Next day (August 21) U Thant cabled that he was reluctantly accepting my resignation. Although he told me: "I would like to repeat how much I regret this situation that has arisen and to tell you personally, in spite of the present conflict of views, how much I have appreciated your work in setting up and conducting the Mission in the initial period," his next words indicated that he was more preoccupied with the effect the news of my resignation might have on the outside world:

"It is extremely important for the Yemen Operation, for the United Nations and, I think you will agree, for yourself, that your departure from the Service of the United Nations in the Yemen should be arranged with propriety and without causing either disruption in the Operation itself or undesirable publicity. I propose therefore, to send General Rikhye to meet you in Cairo to work out the details of the handover of responsibility and the necessary public statements that have to be made."

I had no great desire to meet with Rikhye, but I entirely agreed with U Thant that in the best interests of the United Nations and the Mission (which was the most important consideration to me even at that point), the thing must be done with diplomatic propriety.

I started packing at once for the trip to Cairo, taking only what I needed and leaving my heavy kit to be packed up by my trusted assistants. With our transport facilities at such a low ebb, I wondered whether I should ever see it again.

Before I left, I became aware that my resignation had brought about a flurry of activity in New York; discreet pressures were already being applied to insure that my staff did not rise up and try to follow me in a body. Colonel Pavlovic, too, must have received orders from his masters in Belgrade; rather woefully, he told me that he *would* be taking over from me in an acting capacity after all. Meanwhile, the aide who had told me he would ask to be posted back to UNTSO, had received a personal appeal from his government superiors, urging him to reconsider his request for a transfer. His reply—which he only showed me on the day I said good-bye to him—is, I think, worth quoting in full if only because this independent source goes far to vindicate the authenticity of my "unwarranted" reports which New York consistently disregarded:

> There has been a constant struggle with the administrative staff in New York because of the budgetary limitations (which the UN in New York imposed) to curtail and limit the operation. They have chosen to dictate or "suggest" without basic knowledge how we should run certain aspects of the mission. Footdragging has been their watchword. *We are literally scrounging rations at the outposts;* morale, with the exception of loyalty to the General, is low; living conditions are very poor . . . with Sanaa only a trifle better. Surprisingly enough inconsistencies in top direction have also appeared. For instance: on the one hand the U.N. directed "not under any circumstances to expose personnel to unnecessary risks" whilst on the other it queries why alleged illicit Saudi traffic has not been stopped.

U.N.Y.O.M. has reduced its staff wherever possible, communications have been pared, Caribou aircraft have been grossly overweighted in order to subsist, personnel have worked 10 to 14 hours a day without time off and are continually losing leave. We have sincerely tried to live with what the U.N. has allotted, well below the General's minimum, but find we cannot. He feels strongly that the administrative, political and military advisers have led the Secretary General to believe the minimum requirements of the mission, as outlined by the General, could be reduced for the sake of budgetary considerations (at the expense of the operational and personal considerations in the field) without consulting the General as to its effects on the mission. U.N.Y.O.M. is operating from 35% to 80% below minimum force in most cases.

The General did not, repeat not wish to add to the burdens of the Secretary General by resigning. But his loyalty to U.N.Y.O.M. troops and personnel, plus his professional and personal pride (augmented by his U.N. experience in the Congo and the Middle East) have forced him to do so.

General von Horn will reconsider his resignation (and I wish to add that the high regard which the Arabs have for him be considered) if he can be assured of the following:

1. Adequate and timely logistic support, without questioning requirements.
2. Freedom to run his mission administratively as he sees fit.
3. A minimum of three Caribou aircraft and six Otters.
4. An increase in administrative personnel, communicators, security officers, finance personnel etc.
5. An equity pay for military personnel, e.g. officers attached from U.N.T.S.O. receive $11.30 per day, officers from U.N.E.F. $1.30 per day. Officers seconded from the Royal Canadian Air Force have nothing except for a recently granted Canadian allowance. The Yugoslavs, I believe, receive 50 cents a day. The General has several times suggested a reasonable pay scale.
6. Travel and time off to reasonably civilized areas outside the mission for U.N.Y.O.M. personnel.

Operationally, with refinements, I feel we are fulfilling our mission. However, to have to beg and bark for bread as we have been doing will mean that the mission cannot continue to function.

I could not help wishing that this first-rate officer, whose report assessed my own inner thoughts so clearly, was going to be with me at my forthcoming talk with General Rikhye. But he had been persuaded to stay, at least for a time, and as I shook him warmly by the hand, I knew that whoever was unlucky enough to inherit my job would be very fortunate indeed in having him.

I left Sanaa on August 24 and it proved a wrench to say good-bye to the team who had stood by me so loyally. I was rather moved to see them all there, a determined and long-suffering little band gathered together in a spirit of solidarity whose patent sincerity was very much in evidence. For me, it was no ordinary parting: it was the end of my active career.

I could have wished for better places. But if it had to be on this gravel runway, hot and dusty and encircled by a ring of sullen mountains, then I was fortunate in the loyalty of the men who had come to say good-bye. Among them were "Mac," and my ADC "Charles." Next to him stood Jim Gander, a sterling friend and a first-rate policeman. I was happy to have them around me and hear their farewells echoed by a group of Canadian pilots and ground crew. Then the civilians: Ali Nekunam—whose visit to Mecca had, I trusted, restored him to the maternal bosom. And my poor Chief Administration Officer, whose tears had flowed so freely when confronted with a brutal soldier like myself. There was Dorothy, my secretary, who had braved the hazards of a pre-medieval land. All the people who had served, and perhaps suffered a little, beneath the paternal but sometimes short-tempered von Horn rule. All had stood by me. And now as though to commemorate the hardships and frustrations we had endured together, they had come to wish me well. That moment still stays vividly in my mind; the handclasps, the familiar faces, the mundane phrases which cloaked a wealth of feeling. And all beneath that burning sun, amid the drone of Egyptian planes that grew rarefied and diffused in that burning air beneath the sullen gaze of the heat-shrouded mountains.

I said my good-byes and climbed into the Caribou. Soon we were circling until Sanaa's mud walls lay beneath us. Then we turned for the last time and flew over the mountains until we crossed the littoral and came over the Red Sea, heading toward Asmara, where I had decided to transfer to an Ethiopian plane to take me on to Cairo. The Caribou I planned to send back to

Sanaa loaded with fresh foodstuffs that would bring a touch of color into the Mission's diet. It was my first and only visit to this Eritrean town: and as I changed planes on its airfield, I had no suspicion that it was shortly to be designated as the mecca for which I had used the Caribou for "weekend trips."

In Cairo I stayed as usual at Shepheards Hotel, where I met Rikhye. Greatly to my disgust, one of his first suggestions was that I should agree to a communique announcing that reasons of health were responsible for my resignation.

"On the contrary, Rikhye," I told him, "I'm in excellent health."

General Rikhye favored me with something that might be described as an old-fashioned look. He began to tell me it was my duty to U Thant, but I lost my patience and told him exactly what I thought of the whole sorry affair. By the time I had finished, I had made my position quite clear, and there could be little doubt that he knew exactly where I stood.

This was the first of several meetings. As their atmosphere grew a little more relaxed, and Rikhye accepted that I had no intention of collaborating in fabricating the sort of outworn explanation that looks so suspicious on an official communique, it became plain that like Colonel Pavlovic before him he would have to consult his masters.

While cables were passing between Cairo and New York, I received an unexpected visit from my old friend General Hilmy II, who wanted to persuade me to withdraw my resignation and go back to the Yemen. When I explained that this was out of the question, Hilmy argued that I ought to think again because there was no other UN Commander who enjoyed such high standing among Egyptians and Saudis alike. Their leaders, he explained, knew and trusted me and he was sure it would be disastrous were a new unknown Commander to appear on the scene at this late stage. I told him that I was proud to have their trust but I doubted whether this feeling was reciprocated in New York. Hilmy refused to take "no" for an answer and eventually persuaded me to think it over before coming to an irrevocable decision.

I did. I brooded over his suggestions for many hours. The more I reflected on their implications, the more I feared that the logic of his arguments combined with my wish that the Yemen Mission should be a success was going to be strong enough to override my disinclination to swallow my professional pride. Even now, I doubt whether I did not make a mistake. But one does not always see the picture clearly at such times. And eventually, I decided to send a personal message to U Thant.

It was our last official exchange of cables. I told him that I was sure that even Rikhye had become aware that the logistic troubles I had all along complained about had strong foundations. I realized that I had presented these complaints in a blunt fashion and regretted any misinterpretation that may have arisen through my habit of calling a spade a spade. But the responsibility for the security and welfare of the officers and men under my command had been mine, and because I had felt the situation was deteriorating rapidly and was harming the reputation of the United Nations, I had had no alternative but to resign in the hope that my protest would save UNYOM. However, because I felt that the Mission's future was likely to be decided during the coming month and a change of command at this juncture might jeopardize operations, I would withdraw my resignation if the Secretary General felt that my services and experience were still desired.

I was relieved to learn next day that they were not! I could have done without the flowery assurances of appreciation for past services, but I have a high personal regard for U Thant and I feel that they were worth something more than mere politeness. U Thant's words were something I liked to remember later on when the explanations for my resignation were being fabricated in New York.

I never did reach any agreement with Rikhye over the official statement, but I had no doubt that he would be capable of arriving at some formula "suitable" in consultation with New York. On my final evening in Cairo, he was kind enough to ask me to dinner. I sent him a note expressing my thanks but begging to decline. I felt certain, I said, that he would understand the reasons why I preferred to spend my last evening surrounded by my own companions.

On August 28 I left for Beirut. Everything had happened so suddenly that I had no immediate plans other than a long rest in the Lebanon. Six days later, I received a message via the Israeli-Lebanon MAC telling me that New York had forbidden the distribution of my farewell message to the men of my former Mission. I had drafted it in Cairo and given it to my temporary Yugoslav ADC for distribution on his return. It had been simple enough:

> In my report to the Secretary General on the estimated needs for the Yemen Observation Mission my recommendations were presented as an "absolute minimum." My firm conviction was that anything less would only "invite failure" and be detrimental to the UN reputation. I did my utmost to provide you with the bare minimum to which I felt my soldiers' arduous duties in forbidden areas automatically entitled you. But I was repeatedly told that "for budgetary reasons" the Secretary General was unable to meet these minimum requirements.
>
> My failure to achieve such administrative support as did not jeopardize your lives and health unnecessarily has compelled me to tender my resignation in a last-minute attempt to give you and what you represent a square deal. The Secretary General has graciously approved my resignation.
>
> Before leaving the mission area, I want to thank you all for the devotion to duty which you have shown in the performance of your daily tasks under conditions of extreme hardship. The unswerving loyalty you have shown me, in spite of my regrettable failure to give you your dues, has been a great asset to me which I shall never forget. In bidding you farewell, I want all junior leaders "present or prospective" never to forget that it is every commander's basic duty to look after his troops and never let them down.
>
> I can only wish you from my heart the best of luck now and always. Rest assured that what you have achieved over the past two months has gone far beyond the normal call of duty.

I can only presume that the ADC must have shown it to Colonel Pavlovic or to Rikhye (who had now flown down to the Yemen). As a result it was declared "political" and returned to me with a note advising me that should I wish to present a "nonpolitical" message, the United Nations would gladly have it issued.

I doubted whether it was worthwhile. Too much water had flowed under the bridge and Rikhye was now in Sanaa, discovering the truth of all I had told New York over the past two months. The fact that he had been forced to leave his comfortable office in New York and plunge into the heat and dust of the Yemen to view the situation firsthand was an indication that steps might at last be taken to build up the nonexistent supply system. Directly or indirectly, I had achieved my purpose. At last the Mission would have a reasonable chance; but in terms of personal values, it had been a costly operation.

Being still in United Nations employment until August 31, I refused to talk to the newspapermen who besieged my hotel in Beirut. I had no intention of saying anything at all *unless* the statements issued in New York gave a deliberately fabricated version. I had a gloomy feeling that this was more than likely; already the Swedish Permanent Delegate to the United Nations had advised me that it would be in my own best interests to let it be known that my resignation had come about through health reasons.

On September 4 New York had issued a report on the UNYOM Mission; in it, there were references to "some rather irresponsible and reckless accounts relating to the mission" which had appeared in the press. Although these were the work of newspapermen to whom I had been meticulously careful *not* to air my views, I had little doubt that New York would suspect me as the source of these criticisms. It was time to set the record straight. I felt absolutely convinced, too, that unless I spoke clearly other Commanders who came after me would discover themselves in a similar situation. Above all, I believed in one of the last sentences of my farewell message which had never reached my soldiers: "It is every Commander's basic duty to look after his troops and never let them down." I had devoted myself to trying to live up to this advice, and if my efforts were now to be castigated as "irresponsible and reckless," I owed my comrades one last duty. I had hung up my blue beret now and was free. So I made my statement, citing many of the reasons which I have tried to surround with flesh and blood and bring alive in this book. Repetition would be wearisome. But the point I stressed—because I knew that unless it was put right, the same situation would occur again and again—was my belief that the reports I had sent from the field had never been presented to the Secretary General in their true light.

I wonder sometimes whether, when he read what I had said (or saw it in one of those carefully prepared news summaries at which the Secretariat excels) U Thant may not have been inclined to agree with me. But being a very wise man, he discreetly refused to comment on a statement by a former United Nations employee.

My last command was over. But on this occasion—despite six years with the United Nations in a lifetime of soldiering—there was no ceremony of striking my flag. On the contrary, I have kept my colors flying. I think, too, I have kept faith with my conscience and my duty. But as I took my holiday in the Lebanon, my own master at last, sitting beneath the great cedar trees and looking toward the snow-topped mountains, my heart was somehow always close to the men who had served me in the Yemen and in Palestine and the Congo, until there were moments when I longed for that heat and choking dust.

Soldiers will understand.

I wonder sometimes whether, when he read what I had said [illegible] in one of those [illegible] in which the [illegible] they may have been [illegible] to [illegible] with [illegible] to [illegible] I [illegible]

My [illegible] on the [illegible] years with the United Nations in a lifetime of [illegible] was [illegible]. On the contrary, I have kept my [illegible] I [illegible] with my con[illegible] my [illegible] my own place [illegible] and looking toward [illegible] my heart was con[illegible] who had [illegible] in the [illegible] and in [illegible] when I [illegible]

[illegible]

INDEX